AI and Emotions in Digital Society

Adrian Scribano
CONICET, University of Buenos Aires, Argentina

Maximiliano E. Korstanje
University of Palermo, Argentina

A volume in the Advances in Human and Social Aspects of Technology (AHSAT) Book Series

IGI Global
PUBLISHER of TIMELY KNOWLEDGE

Published in the United States of America by
IGI Global
Information Science Reference (an imprint of IGI Global)
701 E. Chocolate Avenue
Hershey PA, USA 17033
Tel: 717-533-8845
Fax: 717-533-8661
E-mail: cust@igi-global.com
Web site: http://www.igi-global.com

Library of Congress Cataloging-in-Publication Data

Names: Scribano, Adrián, editor. | Korstanje, Maximiliano E., editor.
Title: AI and emotions in digital society / edited by Adrian Scribano, Maximiliano E. Korstanje.
Description: Hershey PA : Information Science Reference, 2024. | Includes bibliographical references and index. | Summary: "The book is aimed at bringing critical discussion in scholarship on the consequences of adopting Artificial Intelligence in the different levels and facets of societal structures; a point which remains undiscussed in the academic circles"-- Provided by publisher.
Identifiers: LCCN 2023038688 (print) | LCCN 2023038689 (ebook) | ISBN 9798369308028 (hardcover) | ISBN 9798369308035 (ebook)
Subjects: LCSH: Artificial intelligence--Social aspects. | Human-computer interaction. | Computers and civilization.
Classification: LCC Q334.7 .A425 2024 (print) | LCC Q334.7 (ebook) | DDC 303.48/34--dc23/eng/20231102
LC record available at https://lccn.loc.gov/2023038688
LC ebook record available at https://lccn.loc.gov/2023038689

This book is published in the IGI Global book series Advances in Human and Social Aspects of Technology (AHSAT) (ISSN: 2328-1316; eISSN: 2328-1324)

British Cataloguing in Publication Data
A Cataloguing in Publication record for this book is available from the British Library.

For electronic access to this publication, please contact: eresources@igi-global.com.

Advances in Human and Social Aspects of Technology (AHSAT) Book Series

ISSN:2328-1316
EISSN:2328-1324

Editor-in-Chief: Mehdi Khosrow-Pour, D.B.A., Information Resources Management Association, USA

MISSION

In recent years, the societal impact of technology has been noted as we become increasingly more connected and are presented with more digital tools and devices. With the popularity of digital devices such as cell phones and tablets, it is crucial to consider the implications of our digital dependence and the presence of technology in our everyday lives.

The **Advances in Human and Social Aspects of Technology (AHSAT) Book Series** seeks to explore the ways in which society and human beings have been affected by technology and how the technological revolution has changed the way we conduct our lives as well as our behavior. The AHSAT book series aims to publish the most cutting-edge research on human behavior and interaction with technology and the ways in which the digital age is changing society.

COVERAGE

- ICTs and social change
- Technology Adoption
- Human Rights and Digitization
- Activism and ICTs
- Technology Dependence
- Philosophy of technology
- Technoself
- Human-Computer Interaction
- Gender and Technology
- Cyber Bullying

IGI Global is currently accepting manuscripts for publication within this series. To submit a proposal for a volume in this series, please contact our Acquisition Editors at Acquisitions@igi-global.com or visit: http://www.igi-global.com/publish/.

The Advances in Human and Social Aspects of Technology (AHSAT) Book Series (ISSN 2328-1316) is published by IGI Global, 701 E. Chocolate Avenue, Hershey, PA 17033-1240, USA, www.igi-global.com. This series is composed of titles available for purchase individually; each title is edited to be contextually exclusive from any other title within the series. For pricing and ordering information please visit http://www.igi-global.com/book-series/advances-human-social-aspects-technology/37145. Postmaster: Send all address changes to above address.

Titles in this Series

For a list of additional titles in this series, please visit:
www.igi-global.com/book-series/advances-human-social-aspects-technology/37145

Considerations on Cyber Behavior and Mass Technology in Modern Society
Paolo Beneventi (Independent Researcher, Italy)
Engineering Science Reference • copyright 2024 • 300pp • H/C (ISBN: 9781668482285) • US $240.00 (our price)

Adoption and Use of Technology Tools and Services by Economically Disadvantaged Communities Implications for Growth and Sustainability
Alice S. Etim (Winston-Salem State University, USA)
Information Science Reference • copyright 2024 • 383pp • H/C (ISBN: 9781668453476) • US $225.00 (our price)

Philosophy of Artificial Intelligence and Its Place in Society
Luiz Moutinho (University of Suffolk, UK) Luís Cavique (Universidade Aberta, Portugal) and Enrique Bigné (Universitat de València, Spain)
Engineering Science Reference • copyright 2023 • 439pp • H/C (ISBN: 9781668495919) • US $215.00 (our price)

Cyberfeminism and Gender Violence in Social Media
Deepanjali Mishra (KIIT University, India)
Information Science Reference • copyright 2023 • 442pp • H/C (ISBN: 9781668488935) • US $215.00 (our price)

Investigating the Impact of AI on Ethics and Spirituality
Swati Chakraborty (GLA University, India & Concordia University, Canada)
Information Science Reference • copyright 2023 • 230pp • H/C (ISBN: 9781668491966) • US $225.00 (our price)

Applied Research Approaches to Technology, Healthcare, and Business
Darrell Norman Burrell (Marymount University, USA)

For an entire list of titles in this series, please visit:
www.igi-global.com/book-series/advances-human-social-aspects-technology/37145

IGI Global
PUBLISHER of TIMELY KNOWLEDGE

701 East Chocolate Avenue, Hershey, PA 17033, USA
Tel: 717-533-8845 x100 • Fax: 717-533-8661
E-Mail: cust@igi-global.com • www.igi-global.com

Editorial Advisory Board

Table of Contents

Detailed Table of Contents

Artificial intelligence is one of the most widespread and discussed mechanisms of the current post-globalization situation. AI has impacted medicine, sports, education, and more. With the proposal to discuss what it means to feel in the era of digital experiences managed through AI, this chapter intends to briefly analyze three practices of feeling that find in artificial intelligence a mechanism that generates "mirror experiences." Firstly, the chapter reviews different approaches to the connection between AI and emotions, and secondly, what we will call experiences of sexualization will be examined through an exploratory observation of The Rrrealist on Instagram and Twitter. This experience implies a set of emotional ecologies that make up a geometry of enjoyment, pleasure, and jouissance in terms of a sociology of the virtual/mobile/digital world with important consequences for the structuring of society and its politics of sensibilities.

This chapter presents a systematic review on the relationship between artificial intelligence and emotions in education in Latin America and the Caribbean. The PRISMA systematic review methodology was used to describe the state of the situation of research on this topic, taking into account theories, methodologies, countries, and educational levels. Fifteen published articles were finally selected, focusing on Brazil

The authors intend to reflect on the "metamorphosis of work" in the dairy farms of the Villa María Basin (Córdoba, Argentina) as a consequence of the robotization and automation of production. In this sense, they emphasize the changes in the "politics of the senses" that update the ways of touching and looking at the dairy farms, simultaneously updating the demands of capital for the use of labor force and introducing new mechanisms of control and surveillance. The proposed approach recovers testimonies from the protagonists of the "metamorphosis" indicated to reflect on the policy of changes in capitalism.

In recent decades, the use of robotic tools has expanded in various areas of work and daily life, therefore also in school at different levels, particularly at the initial level. Reviewing the use of robotics tools implies turning our gaze towards teachers. This chapter aims to understand the meaning of the use, along with the emotions and experiences by teachers, of the Blue-Bot Programmable Children's Robot, as a digital education tool at the initial level. To do this, it analyzes the particular case of kindergartens in Vicente Lopez, Buenos Aires, Argentina, based on a qualitative methodology, with the use of ethnography and Expressive Creative Encounters device (ECE). This allows understanding of the elements that operate in the robot's experience, on the one hand, tied to local contexts and, on the other, to the robot device between the analog and the virtual which combines fear, uncertainty, and anxiety.

Artificial intelligence has revolved around the ideological core of social sciences as never before. Public opinion shows exegetes of AI and detractors who feared the advance of robots and AI in human life. Although AI makes life for humans faster and easier, no less true is that it reduces human autonomy, probably threatening future jobs. Quite aside from this, this chapter interrogates the impacts of AI and technology in science fiction movies. The authors analyze the critical position of different scholars regarding movies or Sagas such as The Terminator, Matrix, and HBO Saga Westworld. From a sociological perspective, they approach the problem of technology while placing it under the critical lens of scrutiny. In so doing, seminal voices like Paul Virilio, Jean Baudrillard, and Jacques Ellul are put in the foreground. Plausibly discussing the advance of AI in daily life is interrogating the future of digital society.

This chapter delves into the emergence of sensibilities surrounding death, driven by recent technological advancements in the field of artificial intelligence. The primary focus lies in the realm of emotions and bodies connected to the digital recreation of the deceased. To accomplish this, it employs virtual ethnography principles to scrutinize visual components within both fictional contexts, such as series and films addressing this phenomenon, and non-fictional domains, including emerging interactive devices and platforms related to 'death'. Drawing from the foundations of sociology of emotions and bodies, the analysis centers on a collection of 'contemporary postcards'. These postcards serve as condensed depictions, offering valuable insights into the evolving sensibilities associated with death, a crucial element for comprehending ongoing processes of social structuration.

Science fiction (SF) is pivotal in shaping the readers' attitudes towards the future. Still, the main objective of a science fiction novel or film is not to predict the future or to assess any technological advancement. SF, mainly, teaches us what it means to be humane in a changing world of citizenship cum globalization. To convey this message, novelists and movie makers portray artificial intelligence (AI) as an autonomous or human-like character to ponder the condition of humans in flux and the social, economic, and political issues regarding technological advancement. Through the perspective of Klara, the robot protagonist, we explore artificial intelligence and consciousness, the posthuman situation of humanity, the future of utopia, humanity's changing ideologies, and the human-machine relationship or human-nonhuman relationship. The way AI enacts humans is debatable as AI introspection reflects new capacities for human potential and mirrors the limits of humanity (i.e., the creature is defined and associated with its creator).

The text explores the transformative impact of virtual reality, augmented reality, and the metaverse on human experiences. These technologies offer new ways of interaction and learning, revolutionizing sectors such as education, mental health, and entertainment. Immersion and controlled manipulation of the virtual environment are crucial in creating engaging experiences, supporting personal transformation. Presence in virtual environments plays a key role, inducing a feeling of being physically immersed. The therapeutic use of virtual reality shows promise for mental and neurological disorders, providing a safe space to confront fears and anxieties.

However, constant development of standardized protocols is necessary to ensure personalized and effective therapies. Responsible use of immersive technologies is essential to avoid issues of excessive virtual identity and addiction. Interdisciplinary research and ethics will guide the future application of these technologies, opening new perspectives in understanding the human mind and enhancing overall well-being.

Preface: Artificial Intelligence and Society 4.0 in a New Millennium

The capitalist expansion has successfully materialized according not only to the technological breakthrough but also to the wealth concentration. In fact, both issues are inextricably intertwined. Today some voices have alerted on the technological revolution and the given global paradox prompted by high technologies (Naisbitt, 1994). As Jacques Ellul puts it, technology has paved the way for the rise of an automatic mind which is finely regulated by a much deeper bureaucratic logic that ultimately transcends the control of nation-states. He argues convincingly that technology works jointly with the technique, which should be understood as a process designed to domesticate human minds (Ellul 1962; 1984; 2018; 2021). Other works have focused on the positive effects of technology on health, services and life. Doubtless, technology has impacted the fields of economy, power and experience in which case, it molds our perception and being in this world. Having said this, there is a radical dissociation between the self and the environment provoked by high tech; while the information age liberated people it paradoxically created standardized forms of relationships (Castells, 2010; 2020). At a closer look, Artificial Intelligence (AI) occupied an important position in social science in recent decades as well as relationships, emotions and sensibilities (Rafele, Scribano & Korstanje, 2022; Dettano, 2023; Scribano 2020). Adrian Scribano scrutinizes the changes predicted by McLuhan in the mid of the 60s decade. Per his viewpoint, the digital world has being created significant asymmetries in social behavior. What is more important, sociology should rethink the possibilities to create new digital research to understand human behavior. In the first 20 years, digital technology has successfully structured solidarity as well as emotions according to the politics of sensibilities. In perspective, this politics of sensibilities is associated with a specific labor rule while legitimating the predatory nature of global capitalism (Scribano 2022). To wit, and of course, this is one of the goals of this book, technology leads us to reconsider the nature of emotions as something that can be politically and externally created and manipulated (even confronting our sense of reality). Technology moves around a climate of *creative destruction* in a world that sooner or later should be purged. The notion of terror needs a human sacrifice to legitimate the logic of scarcity. In this vein, the notion of scarcity which is culturally enrooted in global capitalism, speaks to us of a state of knowledge where self-consciousness is familiarized with its finitude. This invariably creates a stage of perversion where the spectacle of death is a commodity mainly exchanged. To put the same in other terms, in a world where our certainties are constantly destroyed and the end seems to be imminent, the power of prophecy elevates humankind over nature (Korstanje, 2019). In consonance with this, there is a dearth of mythical narratives revolving around what ethnographers dubbed as "scatological myths or bottom day theory" that explains –if not describes- the difficult position of technology in culture. As Korstanje (2019) noted, the figure of sin is vital to understanding the complexity of culture and its ambiguous engagement -which combines aversion-attraction- with technology. We certainly love technology because it gives us more power to meet our goals but at the same time, it opens the doors to unseen risks which should be monitored. The human mind, controlling the machine, is the quintessential feature of mythological narratives. One day, because of human greed or lack of control, the machines subvert the logic and ultimately oppress or destroy humanity. Having said this, this is the main point in the discussion put in modern movies like *The Terminator, The Matrix, Minority Report and Westworld HBO Saga* (only to name a few). Over the recent years, AI and the dominance of technology in various fields of human fields which include global trade, tourism, services, emotions, sexuality, bodies, safety-security and health, have made our lives easier but more fragmented. To some extent, the efficacy has subverted the human autonomy to regulate a new division of labor. Of course, this new division of labor has winners and losers, asymmetries and points of convergences if not, social conflict and stability. The present book, which is formed by 11 chapters authored by well-reputed experts, inscribes the constellations of society 4.0, emotions, sensibilities and AI (so to speak digital technologies). This chapter looks to give fresh answers to social sciences respecting three clear-cut axes: the real effects of AI in society, the formation of a new digital consciousness articulated in a disciplined body, and the articulation of liberal policies drawn by a new division of labor convened by the hegemony of a rising techno-world. The future of humanity, the environment, the planet as well and human relationships are placed in the foreground in the present project. We, the editors, like to thank all authors, reviewers, and IGI Global staff members (a well-renowned publisher) who had made this project.

Adrian Scribano
CONICET, University of Buenos Aires, Argentina

Maximiliano E. Korstanje
University of Palermo, Argentina

REFERENCES

Castells, M. (2010). The information age. *Media Studies: A Reader, 2*(7), 152-158

Castells, M. (2020). Space of flows, space of places: Materials for a theory of urbanism in the information age. In *The city reader* (pp. 240–251). Routledge. doi:10.4324/9780429261732-30

Dettano, A. (2023). Sociology of the Digital Space, Social Research and Emotions. *The American Sociologist, 54*(3), 389–398. doi:10.100712108-023-09593-0

Ellul, J. (1962). The technological order. *Technology and Culture, 3*(4), 394–421. doi:10.2307/3100993

Ellul, J. (1984). *Technique and the opening chapters of Genesis. Theology and Technology*. Wipf & Stock Publishers.

Ellul, J. (2018). *The technological system*. Wipf and Stock Publishers.

Ellul, J. (2021). *The technological society*. Vintage.

Korstanje, M. E. (2019). *Terrorism, technology and apocalyptic futures*. Springer. doi:10.1007/978-3-030-13385-6

Naisbitt, J. (1994). Global paradox: The bigger the world economy, the more powerful its smallest players. *Journal of Leisure Research, 26*(4), 406–420. doi:10.1080/00222216.1994.11969972

Rafele, A., Scribano, A., & Korstanje, M. (2022). *Global Emotion Communications: Narratives, Technology and Power*. Nova Science.

Scribano, A. (2020). Life as Tangram: Towards multiplicities of emotional ecologies. *Revista Latinoamericana de Estudios sobre Cuerpos. Emociones y Sociedad*, (33), 8–11.

Scribano, A. (2022). *Emotions in a Digital World: Social Research 4.0*. Taylor & Francis.

Acknowledgment

We, the editors, wish to thank to IGI global staff, as well as authors and reviewers who generously have donated their time for this book project to be feasible. This high quality product would be impossible without the emotional support of our families and loved ones. At the same time, we appreciate the place given by IGI global, which is a leading global publisher, for the space as well as the opportunity to express our ideas and arguments. We do believe AI and Robotics will occupy a central position in the academic debate within and beyond social sciences in the years to come.

Chapter 1
Artificial Intelligence – A Way to Feel?
Politics of Sensibilities

Adrian Scribano
https://orcid.org/0000-0002-0523-8056
CONICET, University of Buenos Aires, Argentina

ABSTRACT

Artificial intelligence is one of the most widespread and discussed mechanisms of the current post-globalization situation. AI has impacted medicine, sports, education, and more. With the proposal to discuss what it means to feel in the era of digital experiences managed through AI, this chapter intends to briefly analyze three practices of feeling that find in artificial intelligence a mechanism that generates "mirror experiences." Firstly, the chapter reviews different approaches to the connection between AI and emotions, and secondly, what we will call experiences of sexualization will be examined through an exploratory observation of The Rrrealist on Instagram and Twitter. This experience implies a set of emotional ecologies that make up a geometry of enjoyment, pleasure, and jouissance in terms of a sociology of the virtual/mobile/digital world with important consequences for the structuring of society and its politics of sensibilities.

INTRODUCTION

Artificial intelligence is one of the most widespread and discussed mechanisms of the current trans-globalization situation. AI has impacted education, medicine and sports. In this direction, the OECD in its report on AI affirms:

DOI: 10.4018/979-8-3693-0802-8.ch001

As artificial intelligence (AI) integrates all sectors at a rapid pace, different AI systems bring different benefits and risks. In comparing virtual assistants, self-driving vehicles, and video recommendations for children, it is easy to see that the benefits and risks of each are very different. Their specificities will require different approaches to policy-making and governance. (OECD, 2022: 3)

The idea of a mechanism that reproduces ideas, sensations, or works of human beings is very old. In 1842, mathematician and computer pioneer Ada Lovelace programmed the first algorithm intended to be processed by a machine. Ada speculated that the machine "could act on other things besides more than the numbers... the motor (the machine) could compose elaborate and scientific musical pieces of any degree of complexity or length". Decades later, Ada's vision is a reality thanks to Artificial Intelligence (AI) (Abeliuk, 2021: 26).

Moreover, today AI is a reality with global scope and whose geopolitics exceeds institutional limits. In this direction, the AI Index maintains: "Despite rising geopolitical tensions, the United States and China had the greatest number of cross-country collaborations in AI publications from 2010 to 2021, increasing five times since 2010. The collaboration between the two countries produced 2.7 times more publications than between the United Kingdom and China—the second highest on the list". (Zhang et al, 2022: 10)

This chapter seeks to discuss what it means to feel in the era of digital experiences managed through AI. It is intended to briefly analyze three practices of feeling that find in artificial intelligence a mechanism that generates "mirror experiences".

Firstly, the chapter reviews different approaches to the connection between AI and emotions, and secondly, what we will call experiences of sexualization will be examined through an exploratory observation of The Rrrealist on Instagram and Twitter. This experience implies a set of emotional ecologies that make up a geometry of enjoyment, pleasure, and jouissance in terms of a sociology of the virtual/mobile/digital world with important consequences for the structuring of society and its politics of sensibilities.

The chapter aims to draw attention to three aspects of the impacts of AI on society: the limits and possibilities of AI to produce sensations, the emotional content made from inputs managed by AI, and the meaning of learning processes generated by the interaction between human beings and learning machines.

The chapter is divided into five parts) Feel, make feel and AI; 2) Some academic clues about AI and emotions; 3) Sex and AI, a theoretical approach; 4) Photos, women's digital world and AI; and 5) Sexualization and algorithms consequences for a sociology of digital emotions. The text seeks to systematize a reflection on digital emotions from a particular experience but that allows us to think about the sociology of emotions in a general way.

Feel, Make Feel and IA

Is it possible to feel in a digital interaction? Can it be felt across and in the virtual/mobile/digital world? Artificial intelligence is an instrument that can make people feel. These and many other questions emerge in a world that expands through algorithms and multiplies using sensations. In fact, an algorithm is:

1690s, "Arabic system of computation," from French algorithms, refashioned (under mistaken connection with Greek arithmos "number") from Old French algorisme "the Arabic numeral system" (13c.), from Medieval Latin algorismus, a mangled transliteration of Arabic al-Khwarizmi "native of Khwarazm" (modern Khiva in Uzbekistan), surname of the mathematician whose works introduced sophisticated mathematics to the West (see algebra). The earlier form in Middle English was algorism (early 13c.), from Old French. The meaning broadened to any method of computation; from mid-20c. especially concerning computing.[1]

It is a set of mathematical procedures that, when articulated, produce a result automatically. Each component is the result of previous processes whose results are known (and trusted) and whose purpose is to solve a problem. To advance the connections between algorithms, artificial intelligence and emotions, this section is dedicated to exploring some possible answers to what this means.

To begin an exploration of the AI notion, we found it interesting to appeal to two undeniable ways, firstly, ask an AI and reproduce the definitions of a company that sells AI services.

According to "Chat AI"

Chat AI app, in their "Terms of Use", states that: "The App is created for entertainment purposes and provides tools based on Artificial Intelligence models and technologies to chat with Artificial Intelligence and receive answers to your questions. The complete list of features is available on the App's page on play.google.com. The App is meant for your personal, non-commercial use, and you must use it only for the purposes mentioned above".[2]

In connection with this chapter's objectives, it is exciting to note how, in the same legal terms of the application, the entertainment and the question/answer connection are appealed to, two interactions that are undoubtedly based on practices of feeling. The applications seek to entertain as a form of spectacular personal experience and with a sense of private participation, which becomes crucial to one of the most critical aspects of the production of emotions in the virtual/mobile/digital world.

When we asked about AI, the app responded:

There are several types of artificial intelligence, some of them are:

1. Rule-based artificial intelligence: It is based on a set of predefined rules that the AI follows to make decisions.
2. Artificial neural networks: they are designed to imitate the functioning of the human brain's neural networks. They are used to classify data and recognize patterns.
3. Natural language processing: used to understand and process human language.
4. Machine Learning: Uses algorithms to let AI learn from data and improve its performance over time.
5. Computer vision: used to analyze images and videos.
6. Robotics: used to control robots and automate processes.
7. Expert systems: are designed to simulate the knowledge and skills of a human expert in a specific area.

This first approximation of the AI concept gives us some trace of a connection between "feeling practices" and digital experiences. Rules, imitation, performance, and skills talk about how senses, perceptions, and sensibilities are included in the different types of AI models.

From another point of view, several types of artificial intelligence can be classified in different ways, depending on the criteria used. Some of the most common classifications include:

1. According to your learning capacity:
   - Supervised learning: AI is trained with a set of data labelled by humans.
   - Unsupervised learning: AI is trained with a set of unlabeled data and must find patterns on its own.
   - Reinforcement learning: AI learns through the feedback it receives when interacting with the environment.
2. According to your reasoning ability:
   - Logic: AI uses rules and axioms to deduce new conclusions.
   - Probabilistics: AI uses probability theory to make decisions and estimates.
   - Case-based: AI learns and makes decisions from specific cases it has seen before.
3. According to your objective:
   - Expert systems: AI is used to solve problems in specific areas of human knowledge, such as medicine or law.
   - Neural networks: AI is used to simulate the way the human brain works, to make predictions or recognize patterns.

- Robotics: AI is used to control robots and allow them to interact with the world autonomously.

It should be noted that these classifications are not mutually exclusive and that many AI systems may use different techniques or combinations of them. In this context, three factors emerge that influence the relationship between the possibilities of AI and its goals: the delicate task of being a mirror of human practices, the complexity that it implies for human beings to distinguish the actions of humans from those produced by A", and the necessary appeal to emotions to seek the greatest possible analogy between AI and human beings.

According the Quinyx

The first of our sources to know what AI implies, is Quinyx, an important company that, according to the website, helps millions of people achieve a better working life and manage their companies. Founded in Sweden, Erik Fjellborg proposed an alternative after acknowledging the numerous challenges managers face in organizing work at McDonald's. The solution was adopted by the global chain as the first customer, and since then, Quinyx has completely changed the world of workforce management. Today, Quinyx helps more than 1000 companies around the world leverage AI forecasting to streamline and write scheduling, streamline time reporting, and ensure workers have the flexibility they need for a balanced work life. Quinyx's site[3] argues that the words artificial intelligence (AI), machine learning (ML), and algorithm are too often used and misunderstood. They are used interchangeably when they shouldn't be, giving the following definitions:

What is an Algorithm? An algorithm is any form of automated instruction. The majority of algorithms are simpler than most people think. Sometimes, they can be a single if → then statement. If this button is pressed, execute that action. An algorithm can either be a sequence of simple if → then statements or a sequence of more complex mathematical equations. The complexity of an algorithm will depend on the complexity of each step it needs to execute, and on the sheer number of steps the algorithm needs to execute.

Automated, sequential, and executing are the words of a practice of feeling that reproduces the necessary skills to perform a basic activity. Without any reflexivity, one action is repeated like a reproduction of a kind of skill necessary to make something. It's doing something (…)

What is Machine Learning?

Whereas algorithms are the building blocks that makeup machine learning and artificial intelligence, there is a distinct difference between ML and AI, and it has to do with the data that serves as the input. Machine learning is a set of algorithms that are fed with structured data to complete a task without being programmed to do so.

The data that this particular algorithm receives is structured. Banks store data in a fixed format, where each transaction has a date, location, amount, etc. If the value for the location variable suddenly deviates from what the algorithm usually receives, it will alert you and stop the transaction from happening. It's this type of structured data that we define as machine learning.

What is Artificial Intelligence?

Before we jump into what AI is, we have to mark that there is no clear separation between AI and ML. Machine learning is, in fact, a part of AI. However, we define Artificial intelligence as a set of algorithms that can cope with unforeseen circumstances. It differs from machine learning in that it can be fed unstructured data and still function.

One of the reasons why AI is often used interchangeably with ML is because it's not always straightforward to know whether the underlying data is structured or unstructured. This is not so much about supervised and unsupervised learning (which is another article on its own), but about the way it's formatted and presented to the AI algorithm.

The different ways of classifying and understanding AI leave us at the gates of various practices of feeling that are altering human interactions. In the first place, the idea of the automatic as a mirror but at the same time overcoming the capacity to respond to a problem. Secondly, the modification of the sensation of the artificial in terms of what is far from the natural, but also of not having been created based on any previous component. Thirdly, the appeal of programming tricks as a source of the answer to a specific problem.

AI, in this way, is a procedure to assemble specular situations that allow the results of human practices to be produced, but especially perceptions and sensations as sources of knowledge and interpretation of reality.

Some Academic Clues About AI and Emotions

This section aims to provide a brief introduction to the theoretical conversations about emotions and AI. In 2005, in his work on emotions and artificial intelligence, he gave an account of affective computing Matínez-Miranda and Aldea (2005) sustained:

According to Picard (1995), the term affective computing encapsulates a new approach in Artificial Intelligence, to build computers that show human affections. Preliminary results in affective computing can be found in facial expression, and voice recognition and synthesis. However, this area requires further investigation, as a wide variety of psychological aspects need to be analysed. Picard (1997) in her investigations in affective computing, considers Damasios (1994) research on the importance of emotions in the human decision-making process (see Section 2.2). Picard claimed that if the most suitable computing tool for decision-making is required, this tool should include emotional mechanisms as well as a knowledge base. Based on Damasios experiments on neurological dysfunction, the goal of Picard's approach is to create a computer which can recognise and show affections. (Martínez-Miranda and Aldea, 2005: 330)

In this statement, we find a clear connection between affectivity and computing for more than two decades, since facial expression and voice recognition have already appeared as ways to evoke, represent and reproduce human emotions. Computers sought to recognize and show conditions. It can also be seen how neurology and its procedures began to gain space in collaboration with computing to create sentient machines, as Asiri and his colleagues maintain:

In recent decades, human emotions-related research studies have given more attention to neuroscience and affective Computing [1]. In our daily life emotions plays a crucial role, we as a human can comprehend the emotions of different people yet it is truly inconceivable for computers to do likewise. In earlier decades researchers have investigated emotion detection through text [2], speech [3], facial expressions and gestures [4–7]. However, the disadvantage of using these techniques is that if someone conceals their feelings [8], the results are vague and this turns out to be a question mark on their reliability. Currently, electroencephalography (EEG) signals are a promising way to implement communication between a person and a machine. Different studies have been conducted in the literature, so far, on emotion classification based on EEG signals, which yields significant growth in terms of accuracy. (Asiri et al, 2022: 5076)

The body/emotion is clearly described as the source and result of AI: gestures, facial expressions, speech, and texts are an emotional scenario that is articulated in and through the construction of a new sensation regulation device now in its digital version. The application of the electroencephalogram and its results obtained have also been associated with the advent of whole-body positron emission tomography (PET) systems, which allow the simultaneous measurement of the central and peripheral axis of the emotional response. It is in this sense that more and more information is available about what happens and where it happens when a human being has an emotion.

According to the global consulting firm McKinsey, Industry 4.0 must be understood as a new step in the digitization of the manufacturing sector, driven by four clusters: more data managed by industrial companies; powerful and cheaper computers; analytical capacity; and improvements in the interactions between people and machines, robots and 3D printers. Reduce costs, improve production lines and use new databases.

It would not be an exaggeration if we say that the area of emotions, experience and consciousness (all interconnected) is the holy grail of AI and AGI research. It is the main obstacle to the realization of true artificial intelligence and artificial general intelligence. Without this, any claims and achievements of AI and AGI research will remain hollow and impalpable. Since the accent of mainstream AI research has been on cognition, perception, reasoning and logic this area was largely sidelined and got a kind of stepmotherly treatment for a long time. (Tariq, 2022: 56)

Sociology, since its inception, has had the paradoxical task of observing the action as it is being done; the research on how to reproduce (and create?) emotions in and through the digital underscores the importance of the epistemic, theoretical, and methodological content of studying digital emotions today (Scribano, 2023).

The beginning of the 'AI of emotions', as a proper field of AI research, came in 1995. It was conceived and created as a tool to measure, understand, simulate, and react to human emotions to enable more natural interaction between humans and machines (Somers, 2019). Many algorithms and tools are used for this. They have been developed for the automated recognition of emotions through facial expressions, postural movements, physiology, and even dialogue (Picard, 2002). Deep learning methods are being employed to "develop emotion classifiers... models of dialogue and dialogue services". (Huang et al., 2020: 1). These are trained to track human emotions and intentions and respond accordingly during interaction with humans. (Tariq and Alt, 2022: 65)

In this developmental context, AI seeks to identify, describe, classify, systematize, understand, and learn human emotions and use them in interaction with humans and other forms of intelligent individuals. The entire human body, together with its creative/expressive capacities, are sources of information to elaborate "mirrors" of two processes characteristic of human beings: knowing that something is being done (the proxy of consciousness) and the knowledge that an emotion is being emulated (the proxy of feeling).

Another way to track the sequence of learning, AI, and interaction with humans is to trace the multiple connections between android, robotics, and emotions. The most common way to achieve human-robot interaction based on natural language is to build a dialogue system that is an interactive vocal interface. Fundamentally, the dialogue system encloses a knowledge base (i.e., a dataset) with organized domain questions and their corresponding answers, and the dialogue service must design an accurate mapping mechanism that can correctly retrieve responses to user questions. The system is run on a question-and-answer basis, and most traditional approaches rely on hand-crafted rules or templates. Beyond the content of the dialogue, emotion plays an important role in determining the relevance of the answer to a specific question. By incorporating emotional information into applications, a service system can allow its services to automatically adapt to changes in the operating environment, leading to a better user experience (Huang et al, 2020).

As Sylvain Lavelle (2020) developed, the cognitive map given by emotions leads to the elaboration of a sentient process as a producer/emulator of emotions and practices of feeling:

The problem is even more acute when it comes to substituting the machine for the human as regards other functions, sometimes called "inferior" when compared to those of intelligence. More precisely, these are abilities that can be broadly described as empirical and aesthetical (from the Greek empiria, experience, and aisthesis, sensation). These multiple aptitudes of experience, namely, sensation, perception, emotion and sentiment, to which consciousness can be added, turn attention to the sentience. In this other dimension, perhaps even more complex, of human life lies the origin of a research program which supplements that of artificial intelligence. One could name it, with all the precautions of use, the Artificial Sentience (AS), that is to say, the exploration and the transfer of the functions and abilities of human experience and senses to a machine. (Lavelle, 2020: 64)

We have here a machine, according to the Oxford Advanced Learner's Dictionary a machine is "a piece of equipment with many parts that work together to do a particular task. The power used to work a machine may be electricity, steam, gas, etc. or human power".[4]

We have a process that, as composed of different parts and using human emotions as energy, creates a machine that emulates/creates/displays practices of feeling that can be identified as human.

However, it would be legitimate to ask, critically, if it goes for artificial sentience as for artificial intelligence, so that one could state as well that "Artificial sentience doesn't exist". Sentience is a challenge for artificial intelligence, but it can also be presented as its new frontier, and some, like Husain, speak without hesitation of the "sentient machine". The difficulty of a shift from AI to AS comes from the fact that all human functions and abilities, from the most intellectual to the most sensory, can be transferred to machines. The idea of a total substitution, which concerns both the mind and the body, corresponds to an ancient myth of technology, of the art of production of artefacts and possibly, of artificial creatures. I propose to call it the Myth of the Humanities, that is, the fictitious or imaginary idea of a humanoid artificial creature which allows a total and perfect substitution between human and machine. (Lavelle, 2020: 64)

Beyond many advances, one of the areas that is abundantly researched and still poses a challenge for AI is emotion detection. Emotion detection can be done on texts as well as facial expressions. Detecting emotions from facial expressions is more challenging because expressions can vary on many billions of human faces around the world. Anyway, the development is undeniable AI: it can detect humour, identify feelings, generate poetry, automate complex processes, and beat humans in games. The list goes on, making it even harder to find techniques that can demarcate human and machine intelligence. Not only this, but machines are also constantly trying to improvise and become superior in areas that are yet to be perfected. (Priyadarshini and Cotton, 2022.)

It is in this context that in the next section, we take an example of a proposal for AI-based pornography to show how emotions are generated in this context.

Sex and AI: A Theoretical Approach

There are various ways to connect the expansion of the virtual/mobile/digital world and sexualities, for example, the creation of Queering Artificial Intelligence (Bragazzi et al, 2023), sex and gender discrimination in AI (Buslón et al, 2023) and oriented to computer-generated pornography, animation and algorithms as new digital desire (Saunders, 2019).

AI applied to the production of eroticism, seduction, and digital pornography "dispensing" with physical bodies is a new stage in the commodification of the sexual life of human beings.

According to Nash and Gorman-Murray (2019), new technologies are increasingly ubiquitous in everyday life, and they maintain that their central approach has as its starting point the acceptance of the transformations that we are experiencing that impact the spheres of intimacy, romance and life. sexual and gender. Thus, they observe that the massive use of the digital is remodelling bodies and bodily practices, domestic intimacies, habits, and routines, what is understood as erotic and what we know can be the object of our desire and perhaps even the meaning of "desire" itself. For Nash and Gorman-Murray, new technologies are shaping "a new sexual revolution', one that is rewriting the way we understand what our bodies can 'do' and how we understand ourselves as sexual beings and reach to argue that we are experiencing a technologically mediated reorganization of the social relations of sexuality (Nash and Gorman-Murray, 2019).

In 2016, Burgess, Cassidy, Duguay, and Light, argued that digital sociocultural research has investigated gender and sexuality for most of its history. These authors perceived that at first much research in the area pointed optimistically toward the possibilities of gender fluidity, but also criticized the problems of gender tourism and the potential for the reinforcement of biologically deterministic conceptions of gender roles in what regards technology. Burgess and his colleagues also described how sexualities and sexual cultures have also been digitally mediated and remediated in various ways; arguing that people with diverse sexual identities have found support and sociability through networked media, experienced the intertwining of physically and digitally mediated embodiments of sexuality, and confronted the role of digital media in challenging and preservation of heteronormativity (Burgess et al, 2016).

Within the framework of the development of robotics and AI, the emergence of "demisexuality", Aoky and Kimura (2021) say:

In a chapter entitled "Sexuality" in The Oxford Handbook of Ethics of AI (Danaher 2020), Danaher refers to two examples of human–artificial partner marriage from East Asia. One is the case of Mr. Kondo who married Hatsune Miku, a virtual singer, from which the author analyzes ethical implications and challenges that may emerge from the use of AI in human sexual experiences. Mr. Kondo's case is also referred to in Bendel's article "Hologram Girl" (Bendel 2020). Danaher questions the meaning of sexual identity and the use of new sexual labels such as demisexuality. The term was coined by McArthur and Twist (2017), referring to sexual experiences that depend on advanced technology, as further explained in this article. Danaher also considers the role of AI in facilitating and assisting sexual practices and the possibility of seeing a highly developed robot as an object of human love (Danaher 2020). (Aoki and Kimura, 2021: 6)

Kennet Hanson (2022) elaborates on the concept of the silicone self by seeking to analyze how stigma shapes the self of doll owners and investigate how broader social trends of individualism, liberalism, and sex-positive feminism were causing the emergence of individuality, and sexuality projected in online spaces. Hanson in his digital ethnographic study of the sex and love doll community, showed how this subculture frames the transgressive desire for inanimate dolls as a builder of a new normativity emphasizing sexual individualism and highlighting the emotional and sexual deficiencies of human relationships.

For their part, Dubé and Anctil (2021) have pointed out the construction of an erotic robot, generating the term ero-robots:

> *Technology interacts and co-evolves with human eroticism. Advancements in artificial intelligence (AI), robotics, virtual, augmented, and mixed reality (VR, AR, MR), as well as the Internet of Things/Senses (IoT/IoS), are transforming how, and with whom, we can intimately connect. Amidst what some consider a new (sexual) revolution, we are witnessing the rise of artificial agents capable of erotically engaging with humans, which we call erobots. The term erobots includes but is not limited to virtual or augmented partners, erotic chatbots, and sex robots. Unlike previous technology, erobots do not simply mediate erotic experiences, but can also increasingly be perceived as subjects, rather than objects of desire, in part due to their growing agency (i.e., the capability to act in/on the world to achieve goals. This exposes humanity to the possibility of intimacy and sexuality with machines. (Dubé and Anctil, 2021: 1205)*

For Ley and Rambukkana (2021), digital intimacy studies explore the various modalities in which human beings have intimacy in the virtual/mobile/digital world, often, and increasingly, through platforms. In this direction, according to these authors, "digital intimacies" allow connecting two fields of research. While digital culture studies frequently explore the interconnections, interactivity, and proximities offered by such technologies, this work has rarely been considered about the study of "intimacies" specifically. Likewise, while critical intimacy studies address the impact of media on the intimate public sphere in general, critical intimacy studies explore digital platforms remain scarce. The critical conjunction of "digital intimacies" connects these fields, making them complementary. Critical intimacy studies provide an important framework for the growing sociocultural phenomenon of digital intimacy, which research has shown drives transformative change in how people develop and express intimate relationships using technology.

Digitisexuality, erobots, silicon self and digital intimacy, are only some of the plural ways to connect the virtual/mobile/digital experience with erotic, pornography, and monetization of sexuality.

Photos, Women, Digital World, and AI

The digital phenomenon of pornography is analyzed here with images generated through AI, a convergence of multiple factors that combines the technologies, cultures, and aesthetics of digital animation, video games, and pornographic films and photos.

In the paradoxical context of globalization of women's rights from Me Too to young Iranian women fighting for their education in the virtual/mobile/digital world, "pornographic" monetization of images of women under patriarchal norms expands.

There are several examples of the "sexualization" of the virtual/mobile/digital world and its rapid expansion in terms of character anthropomorphization and humanization of digital creations. Two paradigmatic examples are Shudu Gram and Lili Miquela and the creation of human bodies to embody the fighters of Street Fighter: Chun-Li, Cammy and Rainbow Mika.

Shudu Gram is a computer-generated social media personality and model, a "virtual influencer". The character is considered the world's first digital supermodel. She was created in April 2017 by the fashion photographer Cameron-James Wilson. Her appearance draws largely from the "Princess of South Africa" Barbie doll. The character has generated controversy as Shudu, depicted as a black woman, was created by a white man.[5]

Lil Miquela is a character that was created by Trevor McFedries and Sara DeCou. The project started in 2016 as an Instagram profile. The account tells a fictional narrative in which Miquela, a computer animation character and a model, who sells several brands, mainly fashion, are presented. As a marketing tool, Lil Miquela has been presented as a character in favor of streetwear products and luxury brands such as Calvin Klein and Prada; even so, the character conflicts with other digital projects.[6]

Chun-Li, Cammy and Rainbow Mika are the central characters, now with a "real" body from the Street Fighter video game with millions of followers. Chun-Li was the first female wrestler to appear in a fighting game. She made her debut in "Street Fighter II" in 1991 and quickly became a fan favourite. Chun-Li is a martial arts expert and is a member of Interpol. His main motivation for fighting is to avenge his father, who was killed by crime boss M. Bison. Cammy debuted in "Super Street Fighter II: The New Challengers" in 1993. She is an agent of the British special operations group known as Delta Red. Originally, Cammy had a green hat as part of her costume, but it was later replaced with a red cap due to animation issues. Rainbow Mika is a professional wrestler who made her debut in "Street Fighter Alpha 3" in 1998; she has a strong admiration for Zangief, another wrestler in the game, and considers him his mentor and role model.[7]

It is in this context and the emergence of Only Fans that the X and Instagram accounts of The Rrrealist have been created, whose intention is to produce a digital body that is perceived as physical and that produces empathy and seduction. The account has free photos and photo shoots for which you must pay.

The media has echoed this successful beginning of a clear commodification of the body of "women" narrating almost in the same way its meaning, Univision is a case: "The project called "TheRRRealist" is responsible for creating the first images of hyperrealistic models and monetizes their content on a large scale thanks to its growing popularity. The "young women" who are shown despite not being real looks like flesh and blood people, interact with their followers through messages and pose in lingerie, giving the illusion that there is someone behind the screen".[8]

In X (Twitter) The Realist presents himself as creating artificial hotties NSFW AI / AI Erotica 100% artificially manufactured, AI girls, AI erotica with a link to deviantart.com. Account created in January 2023 and has 64,339 followers and follows 19.

The proposal is to create artificial beauties using AI with two features: erotic on the verge of pornographic and ready for commercialization.

In this account, there is an attempt to give a realistic effect not only to the body shapes but also to the character, the "ethnicity", the age, and the type of nudity. There are photos of singers, astronauts, lingerie models, etc. where the type of clothing, bodies and setting are "intended to be eroticized." There are also models of different skin colors "representing" the stigmatized body of different ethnicities. There are very young and not so young, there are thin and others very thin, responding to the most widespread pornography stereotypes.

DeviantArt, Bleed and Breed Art, the creator of The Realist defines herself as "We are where art starts, but that's only the beginning. We are the movement for the liberation of creative expression. We believe that art is for everyone, and we're creating the cultural context for how it is created, discovered, and shared".[9]

The Instagram account identified as AI Models Agency has likes, comments and the indication of whether it is a photo or a short video; with 10.800 followers and 0 followers.

Figure 1. The Rrrealist account

The comments range from amazement to praise, through fear and lasciviousness; short sentences with a very macho accent. The approval instances cover the adjectives of similarity to the real, the perfection of the image, and the "realistic" of the creation, accompanied by modelling of taste and with parameters of the delicious and the stickers of the fruity. It is an image that provokes being on the internet, that is, it precisely seduces and mobilizes. One aspect to highlight is that stickers are more frequent than narratives in terms of comments.

More of her, please...

I like

I like the background and the clothes

I like

The picture is incredible

I like

Amazing girrrl 🔥 ❤️

Hello pretty thing, you look beautiful, my pretty princess. 🖤🖤🖤🖤🖤🖤

So cute. 😍 👏

🥰😍🥰🥰😍🥰😍😍

There is no such thing as perfection

It impresses me and scares me

😂😂 *they will never replace a real one*

I get inspired by those dolls

😲

Hello pretty thing, you look beautiful my pretty princess ❤️ ❤️ ❤️ ❤️ ❤️

🔥🔥🔥🔥🔥🔥

👏👏👏👏👏👏

Stunning beauty 😍

Incredible ❤️

is it possible to create a girl?

🔥🔥🔥🔥🔥🔥🔥

Better than the real ones ❤️

these have become so good 😜

🔥🔥🔥🔥🔥🔥🔥

🔥🔥🔥🔥😍😍

💕🤩💕💕🤩💕🤩🤩😘🤩😘🤩😘🤩

Omg I love the thigh highs

🔥

Godsss, I want to be in the virtual world... 😍

Delicious

🍑🔥🔥🔥

👏👏👏👏😲😲😲

Impressive model 🔥🍑👀😳💯

This experience implies a set of emotional ecologies that make up a geometry of enjoyment, pleasure, and jouissance in terms of a sociology of the virtual/mobile/digital world with important consequences for the structuring of society and its politics of sensibilities.

This emotional ecology implies that AI can move from the level of the individual impacted by the senses to that of the actor as a reproducer of a macho "script", to that of the agent who wishes to make his digital girlfriend. These simple images allow us to reflect on the complexity of our digital lives.

The sexualization and commodification of the female body through AI bring about some phenomena that are the nodes of this chapter: algorithms are human beings because they are born from them, artificial intelligence learns because it captures the schematics of our practices of feeling and these "digital women" are objects just as women in the world of immediate enjoyment are.

Sexualization and Algorithms, Consequences for Sociology of Digital Emotions

This section is an outline of the consequences of the previous analysis and the outline of some axes for a sociology of digital emotions.

Objectification of Body Parts

The bodies of sexy women are made with and in parts, which implies a set of algorithms that are fed by a large number of photos from which the most appropriate parts are selected based on predetermined models to build a sexy image with sexist patterns and masculinist. Arms, legs, breasts, and hands from different humans or artificial sources make up the eroticizing body. They are members of other bodies at the service of the production of an experience anchored in looking.

Commodification and Attractive Suggestion

On the other hand, the offering of groups of bodies that attract, bodies that suggest and eroticize monetizes suggestion as much as what those bodies suggest and as an attraction to the observer's gaze. They are bodies to be touched by the gaze, they are bodies to experience a presence of attractiveness, to suggest, to produce a social magic of digitalized sexual enjoyment. Real experiences of perfectly organized bodies are offered through digital media. The observer feels the impossible attraction inhabited in another time/space, in the digitalization of seduction as an experience.

Reification of the Gaze

They are bodies that look and provoke the look, an attitude of proximity and "personalization", almost an exclusive look for those who accept to be looked at. A look that transforms the observer into the object looked at. They are "photos" that look at you, they are scenes where the actor is the one looking, and the naked women are the spectators. The look is a thing that is sold and an attribute of those who look: they who look offering and provoking and they who experience the sought-after seduction.

Creation of Habitus, Standards, and Sensations

Rrrealist is a device that creates feelings, sets evaluation patterns and reproduces habitus regarding sexual relations and their content in the virtual world. Structures of experiences that are created in applications with the "participation" of users through emojis, likes, comments and subscriptions. It is a shared feeling that becomes standard for "everyone." The modelling of AI impacts the modelling of sexualization, it shapes it.

Returning to the central question of this chapter, it is possible to maintain, at least provisionally, that AI can detect, systematize and create processes of commercialized sexualization where some challenges appear for the sociology of digital emotions.

Firstly, the tension between artificiality, fictionality and practices of feeling is presented in terms of the volume of information about our desires, enjoyments and joys with which human beings have populated the virtual/mobile/digital world. The sentient machine is both the seductive mirror of our politics of sensibilities and at the same time the commodifying apparatus of our desiring energies.

Secondly, since there is a structural discontinuity between the material conditions of digital existence, the offline positions/conditions, and virtual/mobile/digital life are not an alternate space but rather a contiguous space of possibilities and inequalities that, by evoking sentient life, matter its powers and negativities.

Thirdly, the digital world with its immense possibilities of creativity/expressiveness is at the same time a path of autonomy or dependence, of configuration of a person in terms of exercising the condition of author or the coloniality of the fictitious that nests in AI as a mechanism of power.

Beyond repeating a sterile discussion between apocalyptic and integrated, we should think that the sociology of digital emotions has the challenge of reversing the trend of the last century, where the colonization of the world of life by systems was verified, and creating the listening conditions to transfer intelligent systems with the utopias of new worlds of life. But none of this could be carried out without assuming that AI is part of the ways of constructing sensations, emotions, and the politics of sensibilities of the 21st century.

REFERENCES

Abeliuk, A. (2021). History and evolution of artificial intelligence. Revista Bits de Ciencia, (21), *25–21.*

Aoki, B. Y., & Kimura, T. (2021). Sexuality and Affection in the Time of Technological Innovation: Artificial Partners in the Japanese Context. Religions, 12(5), 296. doi:10.*3390/rel*12050296

Asiri, A., Badshah, F., Muhammad, H. A., & Alshamrani, K. (2022). Human emotions classification using eeg via audiovisual stimuli and ai. Computers, Materials & Con*tinua, 73(3), 5075–5089. doi:10.*32604/cmc.2022.031156

BragazziN. L.CrapanzanoA.ConvertiM.ZerbettoR.Khamisy-FarahR. (2023). Queering Artificial Intelligence: The Impact of Generative Conversational AI on the 2SLGBTQIAP Community. A Scoping Review. Available at SSRN: ht*t*ps://ssrn.com/abstract=4548411 doi:10.2139/ssrn.4548411

Burgess, J., Cassidy, E., Duguay, S., & Light, B. (2016). Making Digital Cultures of Gender and Sexuality With Social Media. Social Media + Socie*ty, 2(4). Advance onli*ne publication. doi:10.1177/2056305116672487

Buslón, N., Cortés, A., Catuara-Solarz, S., Cirillo, D., & Rementeria, M. J. (2023). Raising awareness of sex and gender bias in artificial intelligence and health. Frontiers in Glob*al Women's Health, 4, 1–8. doi:10.*3389/fgwh.2023.970312 PMID:37746321

Dubé, S., & Anctil, D. (2021). Foundations of Erobotics. International *Journal of Social Robotics, 13(6), 1205–*12*33.* doi:10.100712369-020-00706-0 PMID:33133302

Hanson, K. R. (2022). The Silicone Self: Examining Sexual Selfhood and Stigma within the Love and Sex Doll Community. Symbolic In*teraction, 45(2), 189–21*0. doi:10.1002ymb.575

Huang, J.-Y., Lee, W.-P., Chen, C.-C., & Dong, B.-W. (2020). Developing Emotion-Aware Human–Robot Dialogues for Domain-Specific and Goal-Oriented Tasks. Robotics *(Basel, Switzerland), 9(2),* 31. doi:10.3390/robotics9020031

Lavelle, S. (2020). The Machine with a Human Face:From Artificial Intelligence to Artificial Sentience. In S. Dupuy-Chessa & H. Proper (Eds.), Advan*ced Information Systems Engineering Workshops. CAiSE 2020. Lecture Notes in Business Information Processing (Vol.* 382). Springer.

Ley, M., & Rambukkana, N. (2021). Touching at a Distance: Digital Intimacies, Haptic Platforms, and the Ethics of Consent. Sc*ience and Engineering Ethics,* 27(*6*3), 1–17. doi:10.100711948-021-00338-1 PMID:34546467

Martínez-Miranda, J., & Aldea, A. (2005). Emotions in human and artificial intelligence. *Computers in Human Behavior*, *21*(2), 323–341. doi:10.1016/j.chb.2004.02.010

Nash, C., & Gorman-Murray, A. (Eds.). (2019). *The Geographies of Digital Sexuality*. Palgrave Macmillan Singapore., doi:10.1007/978-981-13-6876-9

OECD. (2022). *Framework for the classification of AI systems. OECD Digital economy papers, number 323*. OECD Publishing.

Priyadarshini, I., & Cotton, C. (2022). Ai cannot understand memes: Experiments with ocr and facial emotions. *Computers, Materials & Continua*, *70*(1), 781–800. doi:10.32604/cmc.2022.019284

Saunders, R. (2019). Computer-generated pornography and convergence: Animation and algorithms as new digital desire. *Convergence (London)*, *25*(2), 241–259. doi:10.1177/1354856519833591

Scribano, A. (2023). *Emotions in a digital world: social research 4.0*. Routledge.

Tariq, S., Iftikhar, A., Chaudhary, P., & Khurshid, K. (2022). Examining Some Serious Challenges and Possibility of AI Emulating Human Emotions, Consciousness, Understanding and 'Self'. *Journal of NeuroPhilosophy*, *1*(1), 55–75.

Zhang, D., Maslej, N., Brynjolfsson, E., & Etchemendy, J. (2022. The AI Index 2022 Annual Report. AI Index Steering Committee, Stanford Institute for Human-Centered AI. Stanford University.

ADDITIONAL READING

Ferrante, E. (2021). Inteligencia artificial y sesgos algorítmicos ¿Por qué deberían importarnos? *Nueva Sociedad*, *27*(294), 37.

Franzen, A. (2023). Big data, big problems: Why scientists should refrain from using Google Trends. *Acta Sociologica*, *66*(3), 1–5. doi:10.1177/00016993221151118

Ghosh, S., Ekbal, A., & Bhattacharyya, P. A. (2021). A multitask framework to detect depression, sentiment and multi-label emotion from suicide notes. *Cognitive Computation*, *14*(1), 110–129. doi:10.100712559-021-09828-7

Hamrick, L. (2023). Artificial intimacy: Virtual friends, digital lovers, algorithmic matchmakers. *AI & Society*, *1-2*. Advance online publication. doi:10.100700146-022-01624-7

Scribano, A. (2020). La vida como Tangram: Hacia multiplicidades de ecologías emocionales. *Revista Latinoamericana de Estudios sobre Cuerpos, Emociones y Sociedad*, *33*(12), 4-7.

Scribano, A., & Mairano, M. V. (2023). Narratives, emotions and artificial intelligence: A reading of artificial intelligence from emotions. *SN Social Sciences*, *1*(9), 229. doi:10.100743545-021-00237-z

Vargas, E. P., García Delgado, A., Torres, S. C., Carrasco-Ribelles, L. A., Marín-Morales, J., & Alcañiz Raya, M. (2022). Virtual reality stimulation and organizational neuroscience for the assessment of empathy. *Frontiers in Psychology*, *13*, 993162. doi:10.3389/fpsyg.2022.993162 PMID:36420385

KEY TERMS AND DEFINITIONS

Emotional Ecology: "An emotional ecology can be characterized by three factors: first, in each policy of sensibilities a set of emotions connected by family lines, kinships of practice, proximities and emotional amplitudes are constituted. Secondly, this set of emotions constitutes a reference system for each of these emotions in a particular geopolitical and geocultural context that gives them a specific valence. Thirdly, they are groups of feeling practices whose particular experience regarding an element of life can only be understood in its collective context" (Scribano, 2020: 4).

Emotions: "Sensations as a result and as an antecedent of perceptions give rise to emotions as an effect of the processes of adjudication and correspondence between perceptions and sensations. Emotions understood as consequences of sensations can be seen as the puzzle that comes as an action and effect of feeling. Emotions are rooted in the states of feeling the world that allow us to hold perceptions associated with them. socially constructed forms of sensations" (Scribano, 2013: 102).

Politics of Sensibilities: "A set of cognitive-affective social practices aimed at the production, management and reproduction of horizons of action, disposition and cognition. These horizons refer to: 1) the organization of daily life (day to day, wakefulness/sleep, eating/abstinence, etc.); 2) information to classify preferences and values (adequate/inappropriate, acceptable/unacceptable, bearable/unbearable) and 3) parameters for time/space management (displacement/location, walls/bridges; enjoyment)" (Scribano, 2018, p. 10).

ENDNOTES

1 https://www.etymonline.com/word/algorithm?utm_source=extension_searchhint
2 https://aichatassistant.app/terms.html
3 https://www.quinyx.com/producthub?utm_campaign=new_login_page&utm_source=login_page&utm_medium=product_hub
4 https://www.oxfordlearnersdictionaries.com/definition/english/machine_1?q=machine
5 https://en.m.wikipedia.org/wiki/Shudu_Gram
6 https://es.m.wikipedia.org/wiki/Lil_Miquela#
7 https://depor.com/depor-play/videojuegos/street-fighter-chun-li-cammy-y-rainbow-mika-en-version-hiperrealista-sorprenden-a-los-fans-mexico-espana-mx-noticia/
8 https://www.univision.com/entretenimiento/cultura-pop/modelos-only-fans-inteligencia-artificial-fotos
9 https://www.deviantart.com/about

Chapter 2
Relationships Between Artificial Intelligence and Emotions in Education:
A Literature Review From Latin America

Gabriela Vergara
https://orcid.org/0000-0001-8078-1270
National University of Rafaela, Argentina

Solana Salessi
National University of Rafaela, Argentina

ABSTRACT

This chapter presents a systematic review on the relationship between artificial intelligence and emotions in education in Latin America and the Caribbean. The PRISMA systematic review methodology was used to describe the state of the situation of research on this topic, taking into account theories, methodologies, countries, and educational levels. Fifteen published articles were finally selected, focusing on Brazil and Colombia, university level, students as unit of analysis, methodologies based on facial recognition, psychology and software combined. It is hoped to deepen the research in other disciplines, with other theories and methodologies.

INTRODUCTION

The 21st century is a challenging landscape for the social sciences, due to structural inequalities in the conditions of many people living with breakneck technological

DOI: 10.4018/979-8-3693-0802-8.ch002

advances that humanity has never seen before. From the point of view of a sociology of bodies/emotions (Scribano, 2012), this chapter is raised to identify, through a literature review, how the relationship between Artificial Intelligence (AI) in formal education and emotions is analysed. The relevance of this is based on three assumptions/claims described below: 1) Society 4.0 has modified all aspects of life, including formal education on the one hand, and ways of sensibility on the other; 2) in recent years, AI has become either a phantom or a fantasy for education, and in the Latin American context this is complex due to technological gaps in socioeconomic and gender terms; 3) in the crossover/intersection of these issues, emotions are being reconfigured by Society 4.0 and have a relevant place in discussions about teaching/learning processes, in terms of managing emotions and emotions that people (teachers and students) have experienced in school or university.

Regarding the first topic, it is assumed that from the changes caused by the "Fourth Industrial Revolution", the concept "Society 4.0" proposed by Scribano and Lisdero (2019) describes how information and communication technologies have penetrated all areas of life, rebuilding them. Communication, entertainment, work, public policies, marketing, social interactions, in other words, social and public activities down to intimate expressions or effects, breaking down barriers between public and private, work and home. This type of society has even changed the ways of capturing and interpreting the world through the amount of images, audio and video that are constantly sent through mobile devices (Scribano & Lisdero, 2019).

From the second topic, it is assumed that education has not been an exception. Academics have proposed the term "Education 4.0" to describe in a general sense the impact of ICT and changes in pedagogical methods and roles of educators/students based on a pedagogical philosophy more centred in the latter (Ramírez-Montoya, Castillo-Martínez, Sanabria, & Miranda, 2022). A more specific concept is defined as a model to learn competencies and skills adapted to the needs of Industry 4.0. Some competencies are collaboration, creativity, networking, self-management, and critical thinking (Fidalgo-Blanco, Sein-Echaluce & García-Peñalvo, 2022).

From Turing's question in the 50s about whether machines can think, expert systems can think and act like humans or artificially, so today it is understood that AI can be defined as "computing systems that can engage in human-like processes such as learning, adapting, synthesising, self-correcting, and using data for complex processing tasks" (Popenici et al., 2017, p. 2 cited in Salas Pilco & Yang, 2022). UNESCO (2019) has made 44 recommendations to include AI in educational policies, for the management of education, to accompany teachers, and to provide lifelong learning opportunities in terms of inclusion and equity. It also includes references to aspects such as the ethical and reliable use of educational data and algorithms (García Peñalvo, Llorens-Largo & Vidal 2024).

In light of this, how can these recommendations be applied in a region of inequality such as Latin America, considering that a little more than 15 years ago, four aspects were raised about ICT in education: on the one hand, its character of exteriority and the question of temporality in its incorporation, in terms of being able to learn "from" and "with" technology. On the other hand, ICT appeared as facilitators and positive to equalise opportunities, but at the same time they were considered as tools whose final effect does not depend on themselves, but on the social and educational context in which they are registered, this requires educational policies and relevant pedagogies. In this line, a "social" vision of ICT was advocated, whose main objective was human development, with a global consensus maintained since the World Summits on the Information Society in Geneva in 2003 and Tunis in 2005.

But in 2004, Internet access in Latin America and the Caribbean (11 per cent) was below the average for the United States (63 per cent) and European countries (44 per cent). This external gap coexisted with an internal one, due to large differences in income quintiles (Sunkel, 2006). In 2019, 67% of the population of this region had access to the Internet, and one year later, in 2020, 44% of countries did not have sufficient download speed to perform many activities online at the same time (CEPAL, 2020). In line with "learning from technology", a survey of training programs in digital technologies in higher education (university, tertiary and non-university) in 7 countries of the region found that the majority are oriented towards robotics, big data and AI; the main country is Brazil and the higher education system shows fragmentation and diversification, with private education dominating over public (Katz, 2018).

The third issue mentioned above relates to emotions. For example, in a heterogeneous region such as Latin America and the Caribbean, during the COVID-19 pandemic, digital access was a topic for many researchers who analysed the relationship between teachers' work and emotions. Measuring stress levels according to gender (Oducado et al., 2021), registering tension and emotional exhaustion, anxiety, worries about the future, and pressure to meet deadlines set by schools (Gómez Dávalos & Rodríguez Fernández, 2020). In a previous study, it was found that the component motivational/emotional decreases according to different levels, from primary to secondary school (Vergara, Fraire, Manavella, Salessi, 2021), but emotions are a component through the system because there is a management process of emotions. A point of view that justifies this phenomenon states that an integral development in children and adolescents includes emotional and social needs and that it is necessary to promote a greater self-awareness of emotions. This allows for a satisfactory climate in the classroom (Bernal Guerrero & Cárdenas Gutiérrez, 2009; Cabello et al., 2010; Hernández Barraza, 2017).

A sociology of bodies/emotions assumes that bodies allow social agents to know the world. In different ways, bodies connect perceptions, sensations and emotions from the set of impressions that affect when subjects act in the socio-environmental context.

Emotions, understood as the consequences of sensations, can be seen as a puzzle that becomes the action and effect of feeling something or feeling oneself. Emotions are rooted in the "state of feeling" in the world that allows sustaining perceptions. These are associated with socially constructed forms of sensations (Scribano & Lisdero, 2019, p. 13).

In this context, the teacher emerges as a paradigmatic figure to cross these processes mentioned before: they are workers of Society 4.0 (which includes the metamorphosis of the world of labour); they are moved to an unlimited process of lifelong learning (including ICT and AI); their emotions and sensibilities are changing, so what is the experience of them? As a first step, we have proposed this systematic literature review that will provide us with an overview of research in the region that frames these questions.

According to what has been said so far, this chapter asks: how many studies on AI and emotions in formal education have been carried out in Latin America? What are the Latin American countries in which such studies have been developed? What are the levels of formal education in Latin America at which such studies have focused? What are the predominant units of analysis in published Latin American research? Are teacher or student samples predominant? What are the designs used in such studies? Are quantitative or qualitative methods most often used to approach this object of study? What is the place of emotions in the research corpus generated so far? How are emotions defined in such studies? And Which emotion theory do they use?

To answer these questions, a systematic review is appropriate to gather information about the impact of AI applications on teaching and learning activities in formal educational institutions and their relationship with emotions and effects in Latin American countries.

METHOD

A systematic review examines previous studies to answer specific research questions based on an explicit, systematic, and replicable search strategy with inclusion and exclusion criteria (Xiao & Watson, 2019). It is useful for understanding the work that has been done in a particular area by analysing and synthesising empirical evidence from previous studies to answer general research questions. This systematic review approach supports an unbiased synthesis of the data in an unbiased manner (Salas-Pilco & Yang, 2022).

Specifically, a PRISMA systematic review methodology was used to answer the questions that guided this study. The PRISMA extension Preferred Reporting Items for Systematic Reviews and Meta-Analysis (PRISMA principles; Page et al., 20-21) was used to search, identify, and select articles for inclusion in the review. The research begins with the search for research articles to be included in the study. Based on the research question, the study parameters are defined, including the search years, quality, and types of publications to be included. Next, databases and journals are selected. A Boolean search is created and used to search these databases and journals.

Once a set of publications is found from these searches, they are screened against inclusion and exclusion criteria to determine which studies will be included in the final study. Data relevant to the research questions are then extracted and coded from the final set of studies. This methods section is organised to describe each of these methods in full detail to ensure transparency.

Search Strategy and Article Selection

Latin American scientific articles are usually published in Spanish or Portuguese. The largest repository in the region is Scielo, which indexes national and regional Latin American journals. Another important source is the CAPES portal, which indexes high-quality Brazilian journals. A third relevant Latin American scientific information system is Redalyc. In total, three databases were searched: Scielo, CAPES Portal and Redalyc. These repositories were chosen as primary databases because of their comprehensiveness and ease of use.

A typical search string was "artificial intelligence" AND "education" AND "emotions" OR "affect" OR "feelings", plus the name of each Latin American country, with the search performed in English, Spanish, and Portuguese. The following inclusion criteria were used to select articles from the databases:

- Published from January 2018 to August 2023.
- Published in English, Spanish, or Portuguese.
- Published in a peer-reviewed journal or conference proceedings.
- Present empirical primary research, systematic literature review, or reflective essay on the topic.
- Include data relevant to AI applications in Latin American educational institutions and their relationships with affective or emotional states.

An initial search was conducted in the databases using titles, abstracts and keywords, which resulted in 65 articles. The search was then refined based on the inclusion and exclusion criteria to ensure that the selected articles were able to answer the research questions. This reduced the number of potential articles to 48. After removing duplicates, 29 articles remained. We screened the abstracts of these papers and removed 6 articles that were deemed not relevant. The remaining 23 articles were then screened for full content and a further 8 articles that did not meet the inclusion criteria were removed. Finally, 15 published articles were selected for analysis. Figure 1 shows the flowchart of the article selection process.

Figure 1. Flow diagram of the article selection process
Source: Adapted from Page et al. (2021) and Salas-Pilco & Yang (2022)

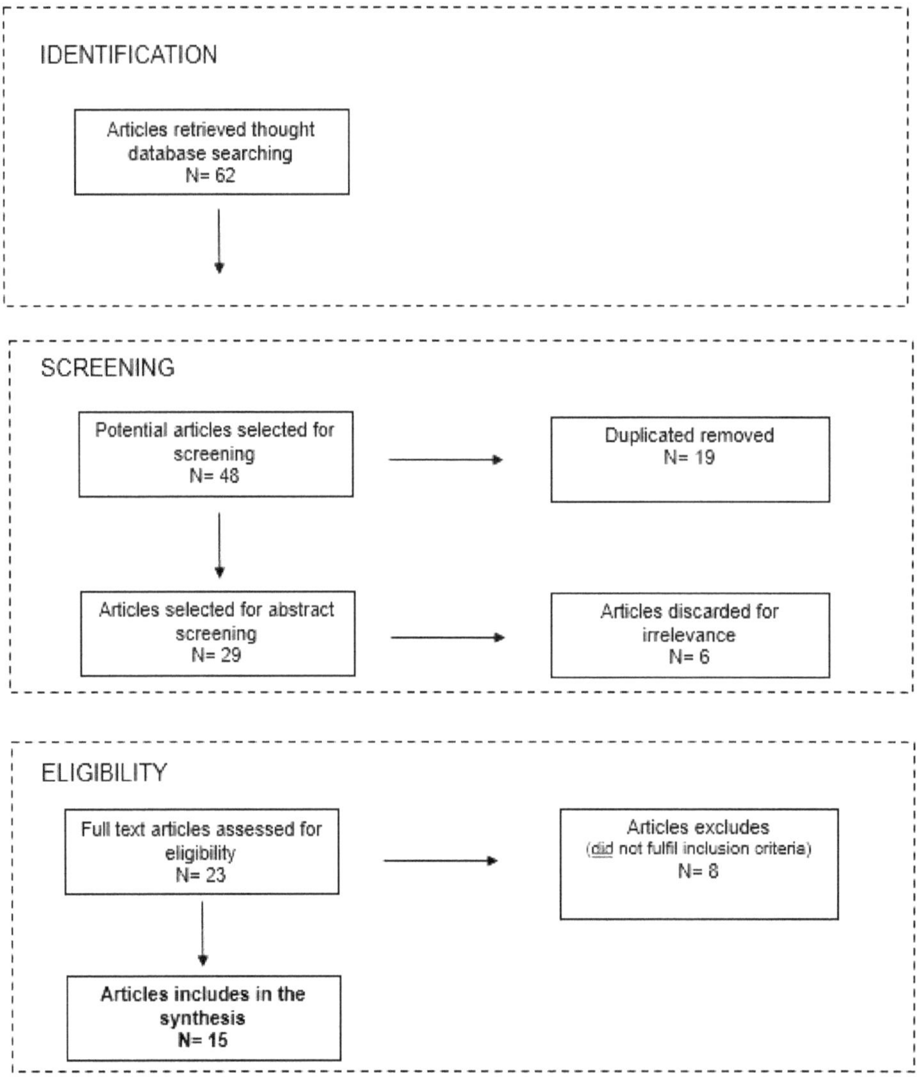

Data extraction involved collecting and coding information for each of the 17 studies, with the following information identified to help organise the data for analysis:

- Title, author(s), year of publication, source
- Country where the study took place or nationality of the authors.
- Education level of the Latin American education system on which the study focuses
- Unit of analysis of the study
- Methodological design and type of study
- Emotion theory, conceptual model or operationalization

RESULTS AND DISCUSSION

The findings and discussion section is organised according to the six questions that guided this study. The first two questions provide information that allows contextualising the existing Latin American literature on the topic of this review, focusing on the number of studies and the countries in which they have been developed. The next three questions allow us to know the levels of education and units of analysis that have been analysed, as well as the main methodological designs used. The last question provides a qualitative analysis of the place of emotions in these studies, allowing the discovery of trends and gaps in knowledge.

RQ1: How many studies on AI and emotions in formal education have been conducted in Latin America?

Although there is a body of research on artificial intelligence and education in Latin America, as shown in a recent systematic review (Salas-Pilco & Yang, 2022), there is less development of the topic from the perspective of emotions and affect. As can be seen in Figure 1, only 15 valid results were obtained in this review. However, not all the included studies are empirical reports. In this sense, 8 research reports, 4 essays, 2 systematic reviews and 1 editorial were found. The information on article title, author(s), year of publication and source is systematised in Table 1.

RQ2: Which are the Latin American countries where such studies have been developed? And what kind of studies have they been, in terms of empirical or theoretical research?

Taking into account the geographical location where the study was carried out, or the nationality of the authors in the case of essays, editorials and systematic reviews, it can be observed that Brazil and Colombia lead the research on this topic in the region, followed by Argentina and Perú.

Specifically, in the case of Brazil, 3 of the 5 published scientific productions correspond to empirical research. The remaining papers are reviews or essays. In

Table 1. Description information about the articles included in the revision

Title	Year	Authors	Journal	Type of study
The search for the Holy Grail... in the teaching of law [La búsqueda del Santo Grial... en la enseñanza del Derecho]	2018	Galarza, M.	Revista Anales de la Facultad de Ciencias Jurídicas y Sociales. Universidad Nacional de La Plata, 15(48) ttp://sedici.unlp.edu.ar/handle/10915/73886	Essay
Flow Theory to Promote Learning in Educational Systems: Is it Really Relevant? [Teoría del flow para promover el aprendizaje en los sistemas educativos: ¿es realmente relevante?]	2018	Oliveira dos Santos, W., Bittencourt, I., Isotani, S., Dermeval, D., Brandão Marques, L., & Frango Silveira, I.	Revista Brasileira de Informática na Educação, 26(02). https://doi.org 10.5753/rbie.2018.26.02.29	Systematic Literature Review
The arrival of artificial intelligence to education [La llegada de la inteligencia artificial a la educación]	2019	Moreno Padilla, R.	Revista de Investigación en Tecnologías de la Información, 7(14), 260–270.	Essay
Artificial Intelligence and its Implications in Higher Education [Inteligencia artificial y sus implicaciones en la educación superior]	2019	Ocaña-Fernández, Y., Valenzuela-Fernández, L., & Garro-Aburto, L.	Propósitos y Representaciones 7(2), 536 - 568	Essay
Education, Big Data and Artificial Intelligence: Mixed methods in digital platforms. [Educación, Big Data e Inteligencia Artificial: Metodologías mixtas en plataformas digitales]	2020	Bonami, B., Piazentini, L., & Dala-Possa, A.	Comunicar 65(28) https://doi. org 10.3916/C65-2020-04	Essay
Artificial Intelligence-Based Chatbot for Anxiety and Depression in University Students: Pilot Randomized Controlled Trial [Chatbot basado en inteligencia artificial para la ansiedad y la depresión en estudiantes universitarios]	2021	Klos M., Escoredo M., Joerin A., Lemos V, Rauws M., & Bunge E.	JMIR Form Res, 12;5(8): e20678. https://doi. org/10.2196/20678	Research report
Web application for the analysis of emotions and attention of students [Aplicación web para el análisis de emociones y atención de estudiantes]	2021	Piedrahíta-Carvajal, A., Rodríguez-Marín, A., Terraza-Arciniegas. D., Amaya-Gómez, M. Duque-Muñoz, L. & Martínez-Vargas, J.	TecnoLógicas, 24 (51), e1821. https:// doi.org/10.22430/ 22565337.1821.	Research report
Fuzzy Artificial Intelligence—Based Model Proposal to Forecast Student Performance and Retention Risk in Engineering Education: An Alternative for Handling with Small Data [Propuesta de modelo basado en inteligencia artificial difusa para pronosticar el rendimiento de los estudiantes y el riesgo de retención en la educación de ingeniería: una alternativa para el manejo de datos pequeños]	2022	Bressane, A., Spalding, M., Zwirn, D., Loureiro, A.I.S., Bankole, A.O., Negri, R.G., de Brito Junior, I., Formiga, J.K. et al.	Sustainability 14, 14071. https://doi.org/10.3390/ su142114071	Research report
Emotion identification system through facial recognition using artificial intelligence [Sistema de identificación de emociones a través de reconocimiento facial utilizando inteligencia artificial]	2022	Paricela Canazas, A., Ramos Blaz, J., Torres Martínez, P. & Jaquehua Mamani, X.	Innovación y Software, 3(2), 140-150	Research report

continued on following page

Table 1. Continued

Title	Year	Authors	Journal	Type of study
Sentiment analysis with artificial intelligence to improve the teaching-learning process in the virtual classroom [Análisis de sentimientos con inteligencia artificial para mejorar el proceso enseñanza-aprendizaje en el aula virtual]	2023	Flores Masias, E. J., Livia Segovia, J. H., García Casique, A., & Dávila Díaz, M. E.	Publicaciones 53(2), 185-200. https://doi.org/10.30827/publicaciones.v53i2.26825	Research report
Artificial intelligence in the analysis of emotions of nursing students undergoing clinical simulation [Inteligencia artificial en el análisis de emociones de estudiantes de enfermería sometidos a simulación clínica]	2023	Leon, C., Mano, L., Fernandes, D., Parente, P., da Costa Brasil, G. & Medeiros Ribeiro, L.	Revista brasileira de enfermagem, 76(4), e20210909.	Research report
Facial and emotion recognition system applied to basic and secondary education. An educational institution in Colombia with 4IR tools [Sistema de reconocimiento facial y de emociones aplicado en institución educativa en Colombia con herramientas de la 4RI]	2023	Campaña Bastidas, S., Méndez Porras, A., Santacruz Madroñero, A. A. Díaz Toro & Cervelión Bastidas, A.	Conference paper EIEI ACOFI 2023	Research report
Teachers motivation regarding the development of artificial intelligence [La motivación de los docentes con respecto al desarrollo de la inteligencia artificial]	2023	Franco López, J.	Revista Virtual Universidad Católica Del Norte, (70), 1–3. https://doi.org/10.35575/rvucn.n70a1	Editorial
Research trends regarding the use of Artificial Intelligence in university context [Tendencias investigativas frente al uso de Inteligencia Artificial en contextos universitarios]	2023	Patiño-Vanegas, J., Mardones-Espinosa, R., Garcés-Giraldo, L., Valencia-Arias, A., Arango-Botero, D. et al.	Revista Ibérica de Sistemas e Tecnologias de Informação, 59.	Systematic Literature Review
The dynamics of Brazilian students' emotions in digital learning systems [La dinámica de las emociones de los estudiantes brasileños en los sistemas digitales de aprendizaje]	2023	Morais, F. & Jaques, P.	International Journal of Artificial Intelligence in Education (July 2023) https://doi.org/10.1007/s40593-023-00339-0	Research report

Source: self-elaboration from studies collected.

this sense, the review by Oliveira dos Santos et al. (2018) aims to identify how students' flow state is measured during learning activities, how such activities are designed, what are the flow models used in computing and education, and what are the main benefits of being in the flow state for students. On the other hand, the study by Bonami et al. (2020) combines a systematic review of case studies to create a position paper that sheds light on how AI and big data work and at what level they can be applied in the field of education. They aim to offer a triangular analysis within a multimodal approach to better understand the interface between education and new technological perspectives, taking into account qualitative and quantitative procedures.

In the case of Colombian scientific production, it can be observed that 2 of their publications are empirical research and 3 are reviews or essays. On the one hand,

Figure 2. Geographical distribution of Latin America studies

there is the editorial by Franco Lopez (2020), in which the author reflects on the attitude that teachers should adopt in the face of this new technological incursion in the field of education. "Could it be that teaching is threatened by this technological incursion? Do teachers see artificial intelligence as an aid to their students' learning?" the author asks (Franco López, 2020, p. 2). In the same way, Moreno Padilla's (2019) essay intended to reflect on the importance and true usefulness of the implementation and support of AI in our teaching work, which also allows us to see clear examples worldwide of digital literacy, which aims to understand more in-depth about the true usefulness and practicality of AI, to focus and build true pedagogical skills aimed at building a scientific thought and technological. On the other hand, it stands out the bibliometric analysis carried out by Patiño-Venegas et al. (2023), whose main objective was to know the research trends regarding the use of AI in university contexts.

Peru emerges as the country most dedicated to empirical research on the subject, with 3 studies published to date. In the case of Argentina, there is 1 empirical research and 1 essay. In the last one, Galarza (2018) proposes to reflect on the new demands of the operators of education in all areas and levels, the new ways of learning outside the classroom interaction that affect the students' motivation to learn, promoting the redesign of new strategies and methods of teaching that include emotions and empathy.

RQ3: At which levels of the formal education system in Latin America have such studies focused?

The analysis of the selected literature shows that interest in the university level is more predominant than elementary or secondary level. Two remarkable exceptions are Flores Masias et al. (2023) study and Morais and Jaques (2023) study. The first one integrates some students from the initial level and basic education into its sampling strategy. The last one was randomly selected students from two classes in the seventh grade at a private elementary school. In 35% of the studies analysed, the education level object of the reviews or reflections is not specified, talking about education in general.

This high percentage of studies focusing on the undergraduate population may be because university students are more easily accessible to researchers, who in some cases may be studying their students. On the other hand, the ethical review process is also typically much shorter at the university level than at the primary or secondary level. Either way, this disparity between educational levels is a concern because AI has the potential to be valuable in all academic settings.

Figure 3. Education level in which analysis of IA-Emotion is focused

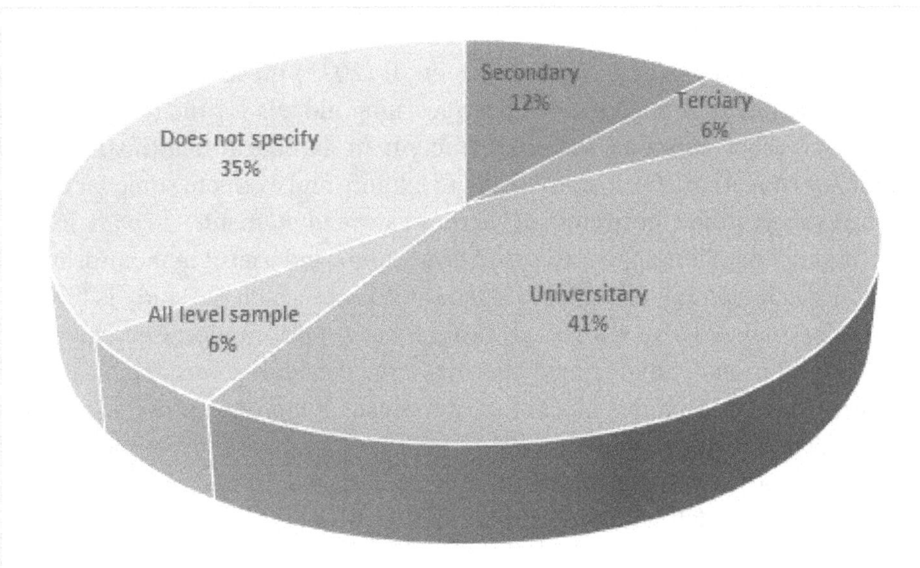

RQ4: What units of analysis predominate in published Latin American research?

The data revealed a strong emphasis on students, especially university students, over teachers. Especially in the empirical or applied research analysed. This high percentage of studies focused on the student population was consistent with other systematic reviews (Crompton & Burke, 2023; Zawacki-Richter et al., 2019). However, another recent systematic review focused on K-12 education and found that AI studies in these settings prioritised teachers (Crompton & Burke, 2022).

RQ5: Which are the designs used in such studies?

Regarding the study designs, the majority of systematic reviews were according to the PRISMA statements (PRISMA, 2021). Only the study of Oliveira dos Santos et al. (2018) was developed following the review protocol suggested by Kitchenham (2004). An important aspect to highlight in the reviews analysed is that, in all cases, the search strategy was not limited to Latin America, as in the current study. On the contrary, the selected digital libraries include American, European and Asian publications. Some of the databases used were, for example, PsycNet, Engineering Village, IEEE Xplore, PubMed Central, Science Direct, Scopus and Web of Science.

In the case of empirical studies, except the study by Ponce de León et al. (2022), which was an observational qualitative study, in the remaining research, the methodological approach was focused on the development of a system to identify emotions using face recognition through AI. This line includes, for example, the research of Flores Macías et al. (2023) was oriented to develop an application with neural networks to capture the emotional state of students in the virtual classroom to show the teacher the perception of their students during the virtual class session, as an efficient form of continuous improvement for active learning processes within the classroom in real-time.

In the same way, Campaña Bastidas et al. (2023) presented an advance of their development of machine and deep learning models for the recognition of people and their emotions, aimed at students of an educational institution of secondary education. Their study seeks to explore and evaluate some facial and emotion recognition algorithms so that they can be implemented to work in real-time, hoping that their application will be accurate and useful in monitoring the behaviour and learning of students at the same time. which the study is directed at. Finally, the study by Klos et al. (2021) was a pilot randomised controlled parallel group study that aimed to assess the feasibility, acceptability, and potential impact of using a chatbot to investigate symptoms of depression and anxiety in university students.

RQ6: What is the place of emotions in the research corpus generated so far? How are emotions defined in these studies? Which emotion theory do they use?

In general, emotions have been understood as a signal that something is wrong, as a warning to teachers to act: change the learning strategy, increase motivation, and so on. From this point of view, research has been thought with a practical or useful orientation, in the sense of making a diagnosis about students' learning conditions to intervene to improve the situation.

The Main Interest in Emotions

The majority of studies have a focus on emotions. Emotions (including symptoms of anxiety or depression) are central because they have been defined as a main, important and relevant factor for the learning process. This assumption is relevant whether it's for the teachers who accompany the learning process or as a self-knowledge for the students. In general, it is assumed that the focus on identifying emotions is the key to improving learning, especially in virtual conditions. In the cases of literature reviews, the interest has been oriented to specific theories in psychology with emphasis on emotions, such as Positive Psychology or Flow Theory. In the following, in Table 2, the articles with a brief mention of the relevance of emotions are presented.

Table 2. Articles according to the centrality of emotions

Authors	Study Aim
Flores Masias, et al (2023)	To identify the emotional state of the students in the virtual classroom, to allow the teacher to evaluate their perception during their class session and thus improve their teaching-learning strategies in real-time.
Klos MC, et al.(2021)	To evaluate the use of chatbots to identify emotions or symptoms linked to anxiety and depression.
Ponce de Leon, C. G et al (2023).	To identify emotions in nursing students when experiencing the maternal-child clinical simulation and what is the relationship between these emotions and learning
Parcel Canazas et. Al (2022)	To acquire algorithms to identify emotions by facial recognition from AI
S. Campaña Bastidas et al (2023)	This paper, which presents a research advance, seeks to explore and evaluate some facial recognition and emotion algorithms, to be implemented in real-time in the monitoring of student behaviour and learning.
Morais & Jaques (2023).	To identify emotions like confusion, frustration, boredom, and engagement with an affect dynamics model for Brazilian students using a Maths DLS in a school setting.
Oliveira dos Santos (2018)	To identify flow theory-based research
Bittencourt, (2023)	To identify and understand how the intersection of Positive Psychology and AI in Education can support the promotion of learning and well-being of students, teachers, and other educational stakeholders

Source: self-elaboration from studies collected.

Emotions With Other Categories Involved in the Learning Process

In these cases, the concept of emotion has been accompanied by other categories relevant to the learning and teaching process, maintaining the same interest as in the previous paragraph, in that this research could contribute to improving the environment of education.

In one case, emotions have been analysed with the attention level of students (Piedrahíta et al, 2021), and in the other "emotion control" concept has been defined together with other variables in the framework of "learning strategies" (Bressane, et al. 2022).

In a literature review, there is no specific search for emotions, but in many cases, authors find secondary references in their results, for example about satisfaction, mathematics anxiety and motivation. (Patiño-Vanegas et al, 2023).

Other systematic reviews identify that XXI century skills achieved socio-emotionality, in the sense of the model proposed by OECD (Organization for Economic Cooperation and Development), close to digital literacy, and mental and physical health (Bonami et al., 2020).

HOW ARE EMOTIONS DEFINED IN SUCH STUDIES? AND IS THERE A THEORETICAL FRAMEWORK? WHAT IS IT?

Research or reviews have used different definitions and theories about them. Not in all cases are these definitions completely clear or specific. In some studies, there is an ambiguous or fuzzy meaning. In this section, studies with a clear and rigorous theory and definition are presented first:

Studies With Clear Definitions of Emotions and/or Theory

- Emotions as part of learning strategies: Learning strategies must be considered not only as a set of cognitive skills but also as behavioural skills and self-regulatory (emotional) control used by learners to control their psychological learning processes. It is considered that emotional control and motivation are soft skills needed in companies to work under pressure and to keep calm, which is important in students. Emotional control is defined within learning strategies. There is no explicit theory of emotions (Bressane et al., 2022).
- Emotions in terms of pathologies: definitions have been established from DMS (Diagnostic and Statistical Manual) and their measurement is standardised, so the researchers have applied specific surveys such as The Patient Health

Questionnaire-9 (PHQ-9) for depression and the Generalised Anxiety Disorder Scale (GAD-7). The chatbot that has been implemented (Tess) brings assistance through an integrative approach using words and emoticons in the messages. Authors have mentioned a combination of perspectives between a cognitive-behavioural model, emotion-focused therapy, solution-focused brief therapy and motivational interviewing (Klos MC, et al., 2021).

- Emotions from Scherer's Circumplex Model: In this article, emotions are defined as a complex response that includes needs, goals, values, and well-being. It mentions continuous and categorical models of emotions, highlighting Ekman's perspective on positive and negative emotions. This definition makes it possible to measure emotions all over the world by defining patterns of basic emotions (happiness, disgust, fear, anger, surprise and sadness) with the addition of the expression "neutral" (as ground zero for emotions). It allows the underlying facial recognition. It is also based on Scherer's Circumplex model, which represents basic emotions in a continuous two-dimensional space. (Leon, C. G et al, 2023).
- Flow theory-oriented literature review: The term "flow state" was introduced by Csikszentmihalyi (1975) to describe a good feeling or experience that people have as a motivating factor in their daily activities. As an emotional state opposite to apathy, flow is located between arousal/anxiety/worry control/ relaxation/boredom (Oliveira dos Santos et al., 2018).
- Academic emotions: Ekman's theory does not fit the context of digital learning systems (DLS), so researchers have considered other specific points of view: affective states, learning-centred emotions or academic emotions. From this framework, four emotions have been identified: confusion, boredom, frustration and engagement (Morais & Jaques, 2023).
- Positive Psychology: This systematic review follows this particular theory. The findings included positive emotion and engagement from constructs Seligman and Csikszentmihalyi suggested that psychology needs to focus on the strengths and positive aspects of individuals (Bittencourt et al. 2023).

Studies With an Approximate or Unclear Definition and Non-Explicit Theory

This section presents two axes that bundle research and reviews around body parts as indicators of emotions and software/algorithms on the one hand and the mention of technophobia on the other:

- Emotions, feelings or emotional states and programming libraries of emotions are addressed as an essential communication way between people to convey their feelings and currently, people apply social networks for this. It is combined with other categories such as feelings or emotional states (angry, fear, neutral, sad, excited, happy, surprised). In theoretical terms, this study has proposed relativism because each individual has a particular perception through constructions. There is no explicit theory of emotions, but it is mentioned that they are available in programming libraries of Python based on face recognition such as ArcFace, Google Facenet, DeepID, OpenFace, Dlib, VGG-Face y Facebook Deepface, with high precision and validity (Flores Masias, et al.,2023).

Emotions are thought to modify the learning process. Basic prototypical facial expressions are universally recognized, such as anger, disgust, fear, happiness, sadness, and surprise. Each type of emotion with its intensity can be captured by a face recognition system. In this case, the Eigenfaces algorithm, one of the most widely used face recognition models, was selected. This model is based on the mathematical properties of the digitised image, which captures invariant features of faces (Paricela Canazas et. Al, 2022).

The recognition of basic emotions can be established in three categories (neutral, happiness, anger). It is assumed that the emotional disposition of the learner facilitates learning. Since the development of software such as Turk and Pentland or Sirovich and Kirby, emotions have gained an important role in vision and artificial intelligence studies (Piedrahíta et al., 2021).

Machine and deep learning are needed for the recognition of people and their emotions, aimed at students of an institution. The first face and emotion recognition algorithms have been taken from software tools (Campaña Bastidas et. Al, 2023).

- Emotions mentioned but not defined in depth: no theory or definition of explicit emotions. The only mention of technophobia or emotions as part of other skills (Patiño-Vanegas et al, 2023; Moreno Padilla, 2019; Bonami, et al., 2020; Ocaña-Fernandez et. al, 2019; Franco López, 2023).

CONCLUSION

Along the systematic review, we have found various studies dealing with PAIED or AIED. The integration of these fields has a positive impact by acknowledging clear connections.

The COVID-19 pandemic was a unique period of intensified online education and the explicit adoption of emotion management as a strategy, affecting educational systems. This explains why several articles analysed in this chapter focus on it.

However, since the pandemic stopped, AI research has expanded significantly, and it is expected to continue to do so because it is a key component of Society 4.0.

Limited and fragmented research is evident in the intersection of the three dimensions of interest in this review at both national and methodological levels. This appears to align with the overall structural conditions of Latin America and the specific usage of technology and digital tools.

In general, we have identified three main features of current research in Latin America:

a) In theoretical and disciplinary terms, there is an overrepresentation of psychology and computer science. This presents an opportunity for generating interdisciplinary studies. Alternatively, research from other social disciplines, such as anthropology, political science, and sociology, can be promoted.
b) Methodologically, the application of algorithms and software for facial recognition of emotions, that is, visual registration of a portion of people's bodies, is a notable development. Other online social research methods, such as interviews conducted through platforms or applications, or the creation of digital experiences, may complement these strategies (Salmons, 2016; Scribano, 2013, 2022).
c) AI appears as a research instrument and methodological tool, rather than a component of a teaching-learning process, or as a part of social interactions between institutions, parents, students, and teachers. Thus, Education 4.0 seems unclear in its structure as a research object with little consideration for teachers' experiences, similar to other regions of the world (Chounta, Bardone & Pedaste, 2021).

We do not want to close this review without a final reflection based on two articles that are not included, but which implicitly motivate us to consider that a line of studies on teachers, emotions and AI may be relevant to deepen in the future.

While we were developing the "eligibility" phase, we found two opposite articles that didn't qualify for this literature review but conveyed a particular emotional state of teachers towards AIED. So we decided not to include them in the review, but to consider them for a brief reflection according to our future research interests.

In one case, an English teacher shared a classroom experience with CHAT GPT. Her students wrote a text and then, using a chat to check for completion, corrected errors or broad vocabulary. She then ran the texts through plagiarism detection software to show them the importance of doing something on their own, with their authorship. At the end of the lesson, a student told her that he had used chat with other software that the plagiarism detector did not detect. The teacher concludes that we are in a complex time, and sometimes they don't have the material and emotional resources to afford it. (Galarza, 2018).

In the other case, teachers of a university in Argentina analysed the working of Chat GPT for solving exams about programming. Chat GPT could solve exercises with higher efficiency so that a student can pass an exam without having the necessary knowledge. They refer to the expression "Currently evaluation methods are in danger" (Ambrosini et. al, 2023).

How do teachers deal with IA and their challenges? What emotions of what bodies are living together in the classrooms in Latin America? Who or how will be responsible for "managing" emotions in teachers to promote learning? In the teaching-learning process, how will it configure emotions?

After what has been outlined, we argue that a sociology of bodies and emotions can contribute to understanding how the experiences (practices in a cognitive-affective sense) of teachers are being transformed in the context of Society 4.0 and Education 4.0. This also suggests that they can be identified as (¿digital?) workers within a specific Latin American context, amidst its heterogeneity.

REFERENCES

Ambrosini, A., Bottini, F., Robledo, V., Lavezzari, F., & Lencina, A. (2023). Estudio del impacto de ChatGPT en la enseñanza de materias introductorias a la programación. Paper presentation at the 21 LACCEI International Multi-Conference for Engineering, Education, and Technology: Leadership in Education and Innovation in Engineering in the Framework of Global Transformations: Integration and Alliances for Integral Development, Buenos Aires, Argentina.

Bernal Guerrero, A., & Cárdenas Gutiérrez, A. R. (2009). Influence of teacher emotional competence in the formation of motivational and identity processes in secondary education students. An approach from the autobiographical memory of students. *Revista de investigación educativa, 27*(1), 203-222. https://revistas.um.es/rie/article/view/94371

Bonami, B., Piazentini, L., & Dala-Possa, A. (2020). Education, Big Data and Artificial Intelligence: Mixed methods in digital platforms. *Comunicar, 65*(65), 43–52. doi:10.3916/C65-2020-04

Bressane, A., Spalding, M., Zwirn, D., Loureiro, A., Bankole, A., Negri, R., de Brito Junior, I., Formiga, J. K. S., Medeiros, L. C. C., Pampuch Bortolozo, L. A., & Moruzzi, R. (2022). Fuzzy artificial intelligence-based model proposal to forecast student performance and retention risk in engineering education: An alternative for handling with small data. *Sustainability (Basel), 214*(21), 14071. doi:10.3390u142114071

Cabello, R., Ruiz-Aranda, D., & Fernández-Berrocal, P. (2010). Docentes emocionalmente inteligentes [Emotionally intelligent teachers]. *Revista Electrónica Interuniversitaria de Formación del Profesorado, 13*(1), 41-49. https://www.redalyc.org/pdf/2170/217014922005.pdf

Campaña Bastidas, S., Méndez Porras, A., Santacruz Madroñero, A. M., Díaz Toro, A. A., & Cervelión Bastidas, Á. J. (2023). Sistema de reconocimiento facial y de emociones aplicado a la educación básica y media de una institución educativa en Colombia con herramientas de la 4RI [Facial and emotion recognition system applied to elementary and secondary education in an educational institution in Colombia with 4RI tools]. *Encuentro Internacional De Educación En Ingeniería.* doi:10.26507/paper.3342

CEPAL. (2020). *Economic Survey of Latin America and the Caribbean 2020: Main determinants of fiscal and monetary policies in the post-COVID-19 pandemic era.* ECLAC. https://hdl.handle.net/11362/46071

Crompton, H., & Burke, D. (2022). Artificial intelligence in K-12 education. *SN Social Sciences, 2*(113), 113. Advance online publication. doi:10.100743545-022-00425-5

Crompton, H., & Burke, D. (2023). Artificial intelligence in higher education: The state of the field. *International Journal of Educational Technology in Higher Education, 20*(1), 22. Advance online publication. doi:10.118641239-023-00392-8

Fidalgo-Blanco, Á., Sein-Echaluce, M., García-Peñalvo, F., & Balbín Bastidas, A. (2021). A critical review of the flipped classroom method from an experience-based perspective. In M. L. Sein-Echaluce Lacleta, Á. Fidalgo-Blanco, & F. J. García-Peñalvo (Eds.), *Innovaciones docentes en tiempos de pandemia* (pp. 659–664). Servicio de Publicaciones Universidad de Zaragoza. doi:10.26754/CINAIC.2021.0127

Flores Masias, E., Livia Segovia, J., García Casique, A., & Dávila Díaz, M. (2023). Análisis de sentimientos con inteligencia artificial para mejorar el proceso enseñanza-aprendizaje en el aula virtual [Sentiment analysis with artificial intelligence to improve the teaching-learning process in the virtual classroom]. *Publicaciones, 53*(2), 185–200. doi:10.30827/publicaciones.v53i2.26825

Franco López, J. A. (2023). La motivación de los docentes con respecto al desarrollo de la inteligencia artificial [Motivation of teachers regarding the development of artificial intelligence]. *Revista Virtual Universidad Católica del Norte, 70*, 1-3. https://www.doi.org/10.35575/rvucn.n70a1

Galarza, M. L. (2018). In search of the Holly Grail. *Anales de la Facultad de Ciencias Jurídicas y Sociales de la Universidad de La Plata, 48*, 1055–1174. https://revistas.unlp.edu.ar/RevistaAnalesJursoc/issue/view/379

García-Peñalvo, F. J., Llorens-Largo, F., & Vidal, J. (2024). The new reality of education in the face of advances in generative artificial intelligence. *RIED: Revista Iberoamericana de Educación a Distancia*, *27*(1). Advance online publication. doi:10.5944/ried.27.1

Gómez Dávalos, N., & Rodríguez Fernández, P. (2020). Stress in teachers in the context of the COVID-19 pandemic and education. *Academic Disclosure, 1*, 216-234. https://revistascientificas.una.py/ojs/index.php/rfenob/article/view/150/124

Hernández Barraza, V. (2017). The emotional competencies of the teacher and their professional performance. *Alternativas en Psicología*, *37*, 79–92. https://www.alternativas.me/attachments/article/147/06%20-%20Las%20competencias%20emocionales%20del%20docente.pdf

Katz, R. (2018). *Capital humano para la transformación digital en América Latina* [Human capital for digital transformation in Latin America]. CEPAL. https://www.cepal.org/es/publicaciones/43529-capital-humano-la-transformacion-digital-america-latina

Kitchenham, B. (2004). *Procedures for performing systematic reviews.* Keele University Technical Report 33.

Klos, M., Escoredo, M., Joerin, A., Lemos, V., Rauws, M., & Bunge, E. (2021). Artificial intelligence-based chatbot for anxiety and depression in university students: Pilot randomised controlled trial. *JMIR Formative Research, 12*(8). doi:10.2196/20678

Morais, F., & Jaques, P. A. (2023). The dynamics of Brazilian students' emotions in digital learning systems. *International Journal of Artificial Intelligence in Education*. Advance online publication. doi:10.100740593-023-00339-0

Moreno Padilla, R. (2019). La llegada de la inteligencia artificial a la educación [The arrival of artificial intelligence in education]. *Revista de Investigación en Tecnologías de la información*, *7*(14), 260–270. doi:10.36825/RITI.07.14.022

Ocaña-Fernández, Y., Valenzuela-Fernández, L., & Garro-Aburto, L. (2019). Inteligencia artificial y sus implicaciones en la educación superior [Artificial intelligence and its implications in higher education]. *Propósitos y Representaciones*, *7*(2), 536–568. doi:10.20511/pyr2019.v7n2.274

Oducado, R., Parreño-Lachica, G. & Rabacal, J. (2021). Estrés percibido debido a la pandemia de COVID-19 entre los profesores profesionales empleados [Perceived stress due to the COVID-19 pandemic among employed professional teachers]. *IJERI: Revista internacional de investigación e innovación educativas, 15*, 305-316. doi:10.46661/ijeri.5284

Page, M. J., McKenzie, J. E., Bossuyt, P. M., Boutron, I., Hoffmann, T., & Mulrow, C. (2021). The PRISMA 2020 statement: An updated guideline for reporting systematic reviews. *British Medical Journal*, *372*(71). https://doi.org/. n71 doi:10.1136/bmj

Patiño-Vanegas, J., Mardones-Espinosa, R., Garcés-Giraldo, L., Valencia-Arias, A., & Rango-Botero, D. (2023). Tendencias investigativas frente al uso de Inteligencia Artificial en contextos universitarios [Research trends regarding the use of Artificial Intelligence in university context]. *Revista Ibérica de Sistemas e Tecnologias de Informação*, *59*, 245–260.

Piedrahíta-Carvajal, P., Rodríguez-Marín, D., Terraza-Arciniegas, M., Amaya-Gómez, L., Duque-Muñoz, J., & Martínez-Vargas, D. (2021). Aplicación web para el análisis de emociones y atención de estudiantes. *TecnoLógicas*, *24*(51), e1821. doi:10.22430/22565337.1821

Ponce de Leon, C., Mano, L., Fernandes, D., Paula, R., & Ribeiro, L. (2023). Artificial intelligence in the analysis of emotions of nursing students undergoing clinical simulation. *Revista Brasileira de Enfermagem*, *76*(4, suppl 4), e20210909. doi:10.1590/0034-7167-2021-0909 PMID:37075358

Ramírez-Montoya, M., Castillo-Martínez, I., Sanabria-Zepeda, J., & Miranda, J. (2022). Complex thinking in the framework of education 4.0 and open innovation. A systematic literature review. *Journal of Open Innovation*, *8*(4), 4. Advance online publication. doi:10.3390/joitmc8010004

Salas-Pilco, S., & Yang, Y. (2022). Artificial intelligence applications in Latin American higher education: A systematic review. *International Journal of Educational Technology in Higher Education*, *19*(21), 21. Advance online publication. doi:10.118641239-022-00326-w

Salmons, J. (2016). *Choosing methodologies and methods for online studies*. SAGE Publications. doi:10.4135/9781473921955.n2

Scribano, A. (2012). Sociología de los cuerpos/emociones [Sociology of bodies/emotions]. *RELACES, 10*, 93-113. https://dialnet.unirioja.es/servlet/articulo?codigo=6981013

Scribano, A. (2013). Expressive creative encounters: A strategy for sociological research of expressiveness. *Global Journal of Human Social Science*, *13*(5), 33–38. doi:10.4324/9781003319771-7

Scribano, A. (2022). *Emotions in a digital world. Social Research 4.0*. Routledge. doi:10.4324/9781003319771

Scribano, A., & Lisdero, P. (2019). *Digital Labour, society and the politics of sensibilities*. Palgrave Macmillan. doi:10.1007/978-3-030-12306-2

Statement, P. R. I. S. M. A. (2021). *PRISMA endorsers*. http://www.prisma-statement.org/?AspxAutoDetectCookieSupport=1

Sunkel, G. (2006). Las tecnologías de la información y de la comunicación (TIC) en la educación en América Latina. Una exploración de indicadores [Information and communication technologies (ICT) in education in Latin America. An exploration of indicators]. CEPAL.

UNESCO. (2019). *El aporte de la inteligencia artificial y las TIC avanzadas a las sociedades del conocimiento: una perspectiva de derechos, apertura, acceso y múltiples actores* [Contribution of artificial intelligence and advanced ICT to knowledge societies: a perspective of rights, openness, access and multiple actors]. UNESCO.

Vergara, G., Fraire, V., Manavella, A., & Salessi, S. (2021). Prácticas, percepciones y emociones de docentes de Argentina en tiempos de pandemia Covid-19 [Practices, perceptions and emotions of teachers in Argentina in times of the Covid-19 pandemic]. *International Journal of Educational Research and Innovation*, *15*(15), 568–584. doi:10.46661/ijeri.5903

Xiao, Y., & Watson, M. (2019). Guidance on conducting a systematic literature review. *Journal of Planning Education and Research*, *39*(1), 93–112. doi:10.1177/0739456X17723971

Zawacki-Richter, O., Marín, V. I., Bond, M., & Gouverneur, F. (2019). Systematic review of research on artificial intelligence applications in higher education. Where are the educators? *International Journal of Educational Technology in Higher Education*, *16*(1), 1–27. doi:10.118641239-019-0171-0

ADDITIONAL READING

Blanchard, E., Volfson, B., & Lajoie, S. (2009). Affective artificial intelligence in education: from detection to adaptation. In V. Dimitrova, R. Mizoguchi, B, Boulay, & A. Graesser (Eds.), Artificial Intelligence in Education: Building Learning (pp. 81–88). IOS Press BV.

Chounta, I.-A., Bardone, E., Raudsep, A., & Pedaste, M. (2021). Exploring teachers' perceptions of artificial intelligence as a tool to support their practice in Estonian K-12 education. *International Journal of Artificial Intelligence in Education*, *32*(3), 725–755. Advance online publication. doi:10.100740593-021-00243-5

Dai, C., & Ke, F. (2022). Educational applications of artificial intelligence in simulation-based learning: A systematic mapping review. *Computers and Education: Artificial Intelligence, 3*, 100087. Advance online publication. doi:10.1016/j.caeai.2022.100087

Lai, T., Zeng, X., Xu, B., Xie, C., Liu, Y., Wang, Z., Lu, H., & Fu, S. (2023). The application of artificial intelligence technology in education influences Chinese adolescent's emotional perception. *Current Psychology (New Brunswick, N.J.)*. Advance online publication. doi:10.100712144-023-04727-6 PMID:37359676

Su, J., & Yang, W. (2022). Artificial intelligence in early childhood education: A scoping review. *Computers and Education: Artificial Intelligence, 3*(100049). Advance online publication. doi:10.1016/j.caeai.2022.100049

Tang, S., Yen Lee, A., & Lee, M. (2022). A systematic review of artificial intelligence techniques for collaborative learning over the past two decades. *Computers and Education Artificial Intelligence, 3*(10009710). Advance online publication. 1016/j.caeai.2022.100097

KEY TERMS AND DEFINITIONS

Artificial Intelligence (AI): Computing systems that are able to engage in human-like processes such as learning, adapting, synthesising, self-correction and the use of data for complex processing tasks.

Education 4.0: To describe in a general sense the impact of ICT, changes in pedagogical methods and roles of educators/students based on a pedagogical philosophy more centred in the latter.

Emotions: The consequences of sensations, as a puzzle that becomes action and effect of feeling something or feeling oneself. Emotions are rooted in the "state of feeling" the world that allows sustaining perceptions. These are associated with socially constructed forms of sensations.

Information and Communication Technologies: This term includes technological tools and resources that allow us to transmit, store, create, share, or exchange information, such as computers, telephony devices, internet, live and recorded broadcasting technologies.

Lifelong Learning: It is a process of acquiring knowledge and improving skills that can occur at any time in a person's life, outside the formal educational system. It allows you to strengthen your chances of acquiring or maintaining a job.

Society 4.0: Information and communication technologies have penetrated all areas of life, rebuilding them. Communication, entertainment, work, public policies, marketing, social interactions, in other words, social and public activities down to intimate expressions or affects, breaking down barriers between public and private, work and home.

Sociology of Bodies and Emotions: Sociological theoretical perspective that assumes the intrinsic relationship between bodies and emotions, and recognising that social agents know the world from their body.

Chapter 3
AI, Mindfulness, and Emotional Well-Being:
Nurturing Awareness and Compassionate Balance

Ranjit Singha
https://orcid.org/0000-0002-3541-8752
Christ University, India

ABSTRACT

This chapter examines the intricate relationship between artificial intelligence (AI), mindfulness, and emotional health. It explored the synergistic potential of AI and mindfulness in enhancing emotional awareness and the function of AI in promoting emotional well-being in educational, occupational, and mental health settings. The discussion addressed emerging trends and ethical considerations. It emphasized the transformative potential of AI and mindfulness in promoting emotional well-being, focusing on maintaining a compassionate balance in the AI-driven world.

INTRODUCTION

The symbiotic relationship between technology and human emotions has never been more profound in our swiftly evolving digital society. As artificial Intelligence (AI) continues to permeate every facet of our lives, from virtual assistants and social media algorithms to healthcare diagnostics and autonomous vehicles, it is increasingly apparent that the boundaries between humans and machines are becoming less distinct. The convergence of AI, mindfulness, and emotional well-being emerges

DOI: 10.4018/979-8-3693-0802-8.ch003

as a pivotal and thought-provoking node in this transforming landscape, offering promise and danger. This chapter explores the fascinating intersection between AI and human emotions, with an emphasis on the role of mindfulness and compassionate balance. It investigates this intersection's far-reaching implications for individuals and society (LaGrandeur, 2015). This chapter's central objective is to explore how we can utilize the potential of artificial Intelligence to enhance emotional awareness and nurture compassionate equilibrium while remaining vigilant about the ethical and psychological considerations that arise along this complex path. The digital age has introduced unprecedented connectivity and convenience but has also presented new emotional health challenges. The continuous bombardment of notifications, the allure of social media, and the pressure to keep up with the unrelenting flow of information can leave us feeling disconnected from our own and others' emotions. Nurturing emotional awareness and cultivating compassionate balance has never been more critical in this context. Emotional Intelligence, the capacity to recognize, comprehend, and control one's emotions and those of others, is a defining characteristic of human cognition. Developing healthy relationships, making sensible decisions, and cultivating empathy are essential in an increasingly interconnected world. However, as we navigate this digital landscape, it is not only our emotional Intelligence that is at risk; the algorithms and AI systems that influence our behaviours, attitudes, and beliefs are shaping the very fabric of our society (Audrin & Audrin, 2023).

This chapter investigated how AI can foster mindfulness, emotive self-awareness, and compassionate balance in individuals and society. We examined the novel applications of artificial Intelligence for mental health support, tension reduction, and emotional well-being enhancement. In addition, we explored the ethical concerns surrounding the use of AI to influence emotions, the possibility of algorithmic biases, and the significance of preserving our inherent humanity in the face of technological advancements. Understanding the relationship between AI, mindfulness, and emotional well-being is intellectually stimulating and crucial when technology is both the problem and the solution. The subsequent chapters will examine these themes in depth, revealing the opportunities and challenges that await us as we navigate the complex landscape of AI and emotions in our digital society.

The rapid integration of artificial Intelligence (AI) into various aspects of our lives has transformed the landscape of human-machine interactions. This integration has led to a profound connection between technology and human emotions, blurring the lines that traditionally separated the two. The growing prevalence of AI, from virtual assistants to complex algorithms, raises intriguing questions about its impact on emotional well-being. This chapter explores the intersection of AI, mindfulness, and emotional well-being, recognizing the symbiotic relationship that has developed between technology and human emotions. Mindfulness, rooted in ancient contemplative practices, involves a heightened awareness of the present. In the context of AI and emotions, mindfulness becomes a crucial tool for individuals to navigate the complexities of the digital age. This chapter aims to delve into the multifaceted relationship between AI and human emotions, emphasizing the role of mindfulness and compassionate balance. It seeks to understand how AI can contribute to emotional awareness and foster a sense of equilibrium in a world increasingly influenced by technology (Mantello & Ho, 2023; Jiménez-Picón et al., 2021).

This chapter's central objective is to explore AI's potential for enhancing emotional awareness and nurturing compassionate balance. It aims to investigate the implications of the intersection between AI and human emotions for individuals and society. By focusing on the role of mindfulness, the chapter seeks to unravel how technology can be leveraged to promote emotional self-awareness and contribute positively to emotional well-being. The scope of this exploration encompasses various dimensions. First, the chapter will investigate the challenges posed to emotional health by the digital age, including issues related to constant connectivity, information overload, and the impact of social media. Next, the chapter will explore how AI can address these challenges by examining novel applications in mental health support, tension reduction, and emotional well-being enhancement.

Furthermore, ethical considerations form a critical aspect of this exploration. The chapter will scrutinize the ethical implications of using AI to influence emotions, addressing concerns about privacy, consent, and the potential for algorithmic biases. Preserving humanity in the face of technological advancements will be a recurrent theme, emphasizing the need for a balanced approach to integrating AI into emotions. In summary, this chapter seeks to provide a comprehensive understanding of the symbiotic relationship between AI, mindfulness, and emotional well-being. It aims to uncover opportunities for utilizing AI to positively impact mental health while navigating the challenges of an evolving digital society. By carefully examining ethical considerations, the chapter aims to contribute a nuanced perspective on the intersection of AI and emotions (Katirai, 2023; Andreotta et al., 2021). Subsequent chapters will further explore these themes, offering a deeper insight into the opportunities and challenges that lie ahead in our technologically-infused emotional landscape.

UNDERSTANDING MINDFULNESS

Mindfulness has become immensely relevant in our modern, fast-paced society, rooted in ancient wisdom. Mindfulness is a mental state characterized by focused attention on the present moment without judgment or attachment to the arising thoughts and emotions. This practice cultivates awareness, clarity, and compassion in daily interactions. In this section, we will examine the fundamental principles of mindfulness, its historical origins, its contemporary applications, and the numerous mental and emotional health benefits it offers. Mindfulness encourages individuals to concentrate on the present instant. It involves observing thoughts, emotions, bodily sensations, and the encompassing environment without judgment. Pauly et al. (2023) found a strong connection between a heightened trait of present-moment awareness and reduced overall experiences of pain. The findings of this research, conducted in two distinct studies with different groups of adults, highlight that individuals who demonstrate greater mindfulness and a heightened focus on the present moment tend to report lower pain levels.

Furthermore, the first study reveals that participants experienced lower pain levels on days when they said they were more attuned to the present moment. Interestingly, this correlation was particularly pronounced in the second study among individuals who did not possess post-secondary education. These findings significantly enhance our comprehension of the intricate interplay between mindfulness and pain, emphasizing that being in the moment may indeed contribute to alleviating pain experiences, remarkably, when evaluated near their occurrence. Witnessing thoughts and emotions without judgment is central to mindfulness. Instead of classifying experiences as ‘excellent’ or ‘poor,’ mindfulness fosters acceptance and inquiry.

This non-reactive stance enables individuals to acquire self-understanding without self-criticism. The study by De Souza Miller (2023) emphasizes non-judgmental awareness’s key role in mindfulness, linking it to distinct mental health and well-being outcomes. On the other hand, individuals in profiles like “judgmental observing,” characterized by self-criticism and heightened judgment, may experience less favourable outcomes in these areas. This study highlights the pivotal role of non-judgmental awareness within the mindfulness framework. It demonstrates how different levels of non-judging can differentiate individuals into various mindfulness profiles, each associated with its own mental and emotional consequences, emphasizing the potential benefits of cultivating non-judgmental awareness in mindfulness practice. Mindfulness promotes tranquillity, which is a state of consciousness that is unaffected by external circumstances. This equilibrium enables individuals to respond with greater resilience and composure to life’s challenges. Equanimity, in the context of mindfulness and resilience, typically refers to maintaining emotional balance and equilibrium in the face of adversity or stress. According to Fulambarkar et al. (2023), mindfulness-based interventions (MBIs) have effectively mitigated adolescent stress in school environments. According to Broderick & Jennings (2012), mindfulness, which has a well-established reputation for reducing stress and improving emotional balance in adults, is also promising as a practical approach for adolescents.

Ancient contemplative traditions, notably Buddhism, cultivated mindfulness to attain insight and spiritual awakening. In recent decades, however, mindfulness has transcended its religious and cultural roots to become a widely adopted secular practice in psychology, medicine, education, and corporate contexts. Jon Kabat-Zinn created Mindfulness-Based Stress Reduction (MBSR) in the 1970s, a secular program that introduced mindfulness practices to the medical community. Mindfulness-Based Cognitive Therapy (MBCT) and Mindfulness-Based Relapse Prevention (MBRP) have effectively treated anxiety, depression, and addiction. Mindfulness offers a spectrum of uses for mental and emotional well-being. Mindfulness has gained wide recognition for its ability to relieve stress. Encouraging relaxation and teaching individuals to respond with equanimity to stressors can reduce cortisol levels and alleviate the physical and psychological symptoms of stress.

Mindfulness cultivates emotional Intelligence by encouraging individuals to observe and understand their emotions. This heightened awareness enables people to respond to dynamic challenges with greater self-control and compassion (Bharti et al., 2023). Mindfulness practice enhances attention span, cognitive flexibility, and problem-solving skills (Bharti et al., 2023). It improves the capacity to maintain engagement and concentration on duties. Guillaume et al. (2020) emphasize the stark contrast between how mindfulness meditation is often portrayed in Western psychology and traditional Buddhist meditation practices, including the Buddhist definition of mindfulness. They underscore the ambiguity and lack of rigour in the contemporary concept of mindfulness, both from a Buddhist and cognitive-neuropsychological standpoint. The discussion draws attention to the confusion surrounding shamata and vipassana, frequently mistaken as meditation techniques. It proposes that classical Buddhist practices like tranquil abiding offer greater coherence, logicality, and functionality, especially in cultivating concentration, compared to mindfulness meditation today. Mindfulness-Based Interventions (MBIs) by Im et al. (2021) show a small positive impact on executive function, with variable effects on attention.

Mindfulness enhances stability by enabling individuals to adapt to adversity and recover from setbacks. It facilitates a more balanced outlook on life's ups and downs. Cepeda-Lopez et al. (2023) found that their 12-week online mind-body intervention significantly reduced stress, anxiety, and negative emotions among nurses during the pandemic. Mindfulness fosters a non-judgmental, empathetic perspective that can improve communication, deepen connections, and strengthen relationships. The primary finding of the study conducted by Carson et al. (2004) is the notable and long-lasting effects of the mindfulness-based relationship improvement intervention on couples' relationships and well-being. This intervention improved various aspects of relationships, such as satisfaction, autonomy, relatedness, closeness, and mutual acceptance, while reducing relationship distress. Mindfulness positively impacts optimism, spirituality, relaxation, and psychological distress. Active engagement enhances relationship happiness, stress coping, and anxiety reduction (Bharti et al., 2023; Baroni et al., 2016). As we continue to investigate the intersection of AI, mindfulness, and emotional well-being, understanding the principles and benefits of mindfulness is essential to cultivating awareness and compassionate balance in our daily lives.

THE ROLE OF AI IN EMOTIONAL WELL-BEING

Artificial Intelligence (AI) has emerged as a transformative force in the domain of emotional well-being, offering a variety of innovative applications designed to support, manage, and regulate emotions. This section will explore the utilization of AI in expressive well-being applications, examine AI-powered tools for stress management, anxiety reduction, and mood modulation, and analyze the potential benefits and drawbacks of AI's involvement in this vital domain. Zhou et al. (2023) have made a significant breakthrough in emotion recognition from EEG signals. Their core finding is developing an advanced method that surpasses traditional approaches. By combining data pre-processing, feature extraction through the discrete wave transform, and a k-nearest neighbour machine learning model, they achieved an impressive recognition precision of 86.4%. This innovative approach maintains simplicity and operational efficiency, making it suitable for real-time applications. This research holds promise for improving emotion recognition in human-computer interaction and intelligent healthcare, providing a solution to challenges faced by conventional methods.

Chatbots and virtual assistants powered by AI are increasingly adept at recognizing and responding to human emotions. These digital companions can offer emotional support, engage in empathic conversations, and provide stress and anxiety management resources. Dhimolea et al. (2022) underscore the pivotal role of AI-based technologies, including chatbots, virtual assistants, and socially assistive robots, in addressing challenges to social and emotional well-being. The chapter accentuates the influence of two critical factors on human emotional and mental states: mental conditions (e.g., depression or anxiety) and social interactions (e.g., loneliness or social isolation). It highlights the potential advantages of AI technologies in aiding individuals dealing with these issues while acknowledging the hurdles and intricacies associated with implementing and utilizing AI-driven solutions for supporting mental health and social well-being.

Apps and wearables enabled by AI can track and analyze users' sentiments and emotional patterns over time. By identifying triggers and trends, these instruments provide insights into emotional health and can provide individualized recommendations for improvement. According to Caldeira et al. (2017), the central finding of this study is a comprehensive analysis of commercially available mood-tracking apps and their users' experiences. The research reveals that these apps offer robust features for collecting and reflecting on mood data but need adequate support for the preparation and action stages of self-tracking. Users primarily utilize these apps to understand their mood patterns, enhance their emotional well-being, and self-manage their mental health conditions. These insights provide valuable information for improving the design of mobile apps aimed at promoting emotional wellness.

AI improves meditation and mindfulness practices. These applications may offer guided meditation sessions, biofeedback, and personalized meditation suggestions based on the user's emotional state. Flett et al. (2019) conducted a pre-registered randomized controlled trial (RCT). They found that using smartphone-based mindfulness meditation apps for short daily sessions led to significant short-term improvements in mental health among university students. Those who practised mindfulness for 10 minutes daily over ten days experienced reduced depressive symptoms, better college adjustment, enhanced resilience (with the Smiling Mind app), and improved mindfulness (with the Headspace app) compared to a control group. Furthermore, participants who continued regular app use during a 30-day extended access period were likelier to maintain these mental health improvements. It highlights the potential of mindfulness meditation apps to strengthen positive mental well-being, but the long-term effects require further investigation.

AI-driven therapeutic interventions, such as cognitive-behavioural therapy (CBT) administered via digital platforms, can assist people in managing conditions such as depression and anxiety. These interventions offer users seeking mental health support convenience and accessibility. Slutsker et al. (2010) reported a core finding demonstrating the successful treatment of medication-unresponsive cyclic vomiting syndrome (CVS) in a 13-year-old patient. This treatment utilized cognitive-behavioural therapy (CBT) and heart rate variability (HRV) biofeedback training. Addressing autonomic dysregulation and anticipatory anxiety effectively managed CVS, which is characterized by recurring vomiting episodes triggered by various stressors. The results indicate that helping the patient identify and manage stressors, regulate HRV patterns, and enhance their sense of bodily control and self-efficacy can prevent vomiting episodes. The study shows cognitive behavioural therapy (CBT) and biofeedback training might help manage CVS. It also calls for more research that compares these methods with drug therapy and a placebo in controlled studies.

AI can analyze user data, such as behaviour, preferences, and emotional states, to provide individualized suggestions for tension-reduction techniques, relaxation exercises, and mood-boosting activities. AI systems with emotion recognition technology can detect alterations in users' emotional states based on facial expressions, vocal tone, and text analysis. AI systems with emotion recognition technology can utilize this data to provide timely interventions and propose coping strategies. Some AI applications provide real-time encouragement and feedback to assist users in regulating their emotions. For example, a wearable device could provide vibration feedback when it detects rising tension levels, prompting the user to perform relaxation exercises (Brelet & Gaffary, 2022).

Powered by artificial Intelligence, crisis intervention systems can recognize signs of severe emotional distress and connect individuals to the appropriate mental health resources, such as crisis hotlines and emergency services. AI-driven emotional support tools can reach a broad audience, providing accessible assistance to individuals who may not have access to traditional mental health services. AI can give individualized interventions and suggestions, considering individual differences in emotional responses and coping mechanisms. AI systems can provide round-the-clock surveillance and assistance, particularly useful in crises. Collecting and analyzing emotionally sensitive data raises privacy and security concerns. Users must trust that their sensitive data will be handled ethically and responsibly. Even for positive outcomes, using AI to influence or manipulate emotions raises ethical concerns about autonomy and consent (Cao, 2023). AI systems may inadvertently perpetuate biases in emotional support and mental health care, resulting in treatment and outcome disparities. AI can provide helpful assistance but cannot supplant the human connection, and empathy is often essential to emotional well-being. AI offers a variety of tools and interventions for stress management, anxiety reduction, and mood modulation, thus playing a significant role in emotional well-being (Xu et al., 2023). These applications have the potential to provide invaluable assistance to those in need. Still, they also raise significant ethical and privacy concerns that must be carefully addressed as we navigate the evolving landscape of artificial Intelligence and emotional support in the digital age.

MINDFULNESS AND AI: COMPLEMENTARY ASPECTS

Mindfulness and artificial Intelligence (AI) represent a compelling synthesis of ancient wisdom and cutting-edge technology. There is a growing recognition that mindfulness and artificial intelligence can work together synergistically to enhance the practice of mindfulness, increase its accessibility, and guide individuals towards greater emotional well-being. Rawtaer et al. (2015) The primary finding of this study underscores the positive impact of community-based psychosocial interventions on the mental well-being of elderly Singaporeans experiencing subsyndromal depression (SSD) and subsyndromal anxiety (SSA). The interventions, encompassing Tai Chi exercise, art therapy, mindfulness-awareness practice, and music reminiscence therapy, led to significant reductions in depression and anxiety scores, initially observed during the single intervention phase. Remarkably, the improvements remained sustained and grew stronger, maintaining statistical significance even after the participants completed the combination intervention phase and reached the 52-week follow-up milestone. This study highlights these interventions' effectiveness, affordability, and cultural relevance and underscores the importance of further research and potential adoption in diverse communities. This section will investigate how mindfulness and AI complement one another, specifically by leveraging AI to enhance mindfulness practices and make them more accessible through AI-guided mindfulness exercises and meditation techniques. In this section, we will investigate how mindfulness and AI complement one another, emphasizing leveraging AI to enhance mindfulness practices and make them more accessible through AI-guided mindfulness exercises and meditation techniques.

Developing present-moment awareness is one of the fundamental principles of mindfulness. AI can play a crucial role by providing individuals with tools and techniques to improve their focus and attention. For instance, AI-powered applications can provide customized meditation sessions that adapt to the user's current level of distraction or agitation. Drigas et al. (2022) discovered that virtual reality (VR) interventions incorporating brain-rewiring techniques greatly enhance metacognitive skills among individuals with learning disabilities and various disorders. These techniques encompass clinical hypnosis, neurolinguistic programming, subliminal training, fast learning, mindfulness, and breathing training. The study showcased the positive impact of VR interventions on individuals with conditions such as cognitive impairments, autism, ADHD, depression, anxiety disorders, phobias, and behavioural and emotional disorders. The results affirm the efficacy of VR-based brain-rewiring techniques in promoting self-regulation, cognitive flexibility, positive visualization, self-control, self-perception, decision-making, Intelligence, self-esteem, emotional regulation, and prosocial behaviours. This research suggests the potential integration of these techniques into educational and therapeutic contexts and emphasizes the need for further exploration and optimization of these interventions.

AI can analyze individual preferences and responses to mindfulness practices to tailor sessions to the user's requirements. This customization can make mindfulness more engaging and effective by adapting to the user's unique emotional well-being journey. AI can analyze mindfulness practice data to provide users with beneficial insights into their development. By monitoring emotional states, tension levels, and the efficacy of meditation, AI can provide personalized suggestions for optimizing a person's mindfulness routine (Medvedev & Krägeloh, 2023). AI can offer guided meditation sessions with a human-like voice, providing users a soothing and immersive experience. Users can modify these sessions to accommodate various skill levels and specific goals, such as tension reduction, improved sleep, or enhanced concentration. AI can provide real-time feedback during mindfulness sessions. It can detect, for instance, changes in heart rate variability or respiration patterns, alerting users when they become agitated or distracted. This feedback encourages users to resume a mindful state. Apps enabled by artificial Intelligence can remove barriers to access. They can be made available in multiple languages, adapted to various learning methods, and even adapted to accommodate users with disabilities, making mindfulness practices accessible to a larger and more diverse audience (Döllinger et al., 2021). AI can monitor the user's emotional state during meditation and adapt the practice accordingly. For instance, if the AI detects rising stress levels, it can instruct the user in specific relaxation techniques or breathing exercises to alleviate the elevated tension. AI can generate customized progress reports that show users how their mindfulness practice has evolved. This visual feedback can encourage individuals to remain dedicated to their approach as they observe improved emotional well-being. Integrating AI with ubiquitous devices such as smartwatches or biosensors enables users to receive real-time physiological data during meditation. This information can assist individuals in comprehending the physiological effects of their mindfulness practice and adjusting their behaviour accordingly. The synergy between mindfulness and artificial Intelligence represents a promising frontier in pursuing emotional well-being. Enhancing and democratizing mindfulness practices with AI can empower individuals to cultivate awareness, reduce tension, and attain dynamic equilibrium (Dhimolea et al., 2022). This collaboration between primordial knowledge and contemporary technology has the potential to unleash new opportunities for personal development and emotional health in the digital age.

FOSTERING EMOTIONAL AWARENESS THROUGH AI

Emotional awareness is a fundamental aspect of human well-being, and artificial Intelligence (AI) has become a tool to assist individuals in understanding and managing their emotions. In this section, we will investigate AI-driven emotion recognition technologies and their applications, evaluate how AI can assist individuals in cultivating emotional awareness, and discuss the ethical implications of AI's involvement in this field. Algorithms based on artificial Intelligence can analyze facial expressions to detect and interpret emotions. Applications of this technology include sentiment analysis in customer service, mental health evaluations, and personalized content recommendations based on the dynamic responses of the user. According to Mukhiddinov et al. (2023), the core finding of this research is the development of an effective method for recognizing emotions in masked facial images captured under low-light conditions. This novel approach combines low-light image enhancement techniques with analyzing upper facial features using a convolutional neural network (CNN). The study leverages the AffectNet dataset, consisting of 420,299 images encompassing eight facial expressions. The method initially involves masking the lower part of the facial input image, focusing on the upper facial features. Subsequently, facial landmark detection extracts relevant features from the partially masked face. Then, the method integrates these features, including landmark coordinates and histograms of oriented gradients, into a CNN-based classification process. Experimental results indicate that this proposed method surpasses existing approaches, achieving an impressive accuracy rate of 69.3% on the AffectNet dataset. It underscores the method's efficacy in accurately identifying emotions in masked facial images captured in challenging low-light conditions, with broad applications in human-computer interaction and affective computing.

AI can identify dynamic states in spoken language by analyzing vocal intonation, cadence, and speech patterns. This technology has applications in voice assistants, hotlines for mental health support, and market research to determine consumer responses to products and services. Jothimani & Premalatha (2022) The primary finding of this study centres around the development of an advanced method, MFF-SAug, aimed at significantly improving the accuracy of speech emotion recognition. This method effectively classifies eight distinct emotions from human voice recordings, a critical component in human-computer interaction (HCI). MFF-SAug stands out by incorporating several pre-processing steps, including noise removal, white noise injection, and pitch tuning, which enhance the quality of speech signals. It also uses feature extraction methods like Mel Frequency Cepstral Coefficients (MFCC), Zero Crossing Rate (ZCR), and Root Mean Square (RMS). This creates a powerful combination of features that makes emotion recognition much better. Data augmentation techniques are skillfully applied to boost accuracy further while adopting a state-of-the-art convolutional neural network (CNN), bolsters speech representation learning and emotion classification. The study thoroughly proves that the MFF-SAug method works on several different datasets, consistently achieving high levels of accuracy, with scores of 92.6% for the RAVDESS dataset, 89.9% for the CREMA dataset, 84.9% for SAVEE, and 99.6% for TESS. Hansen et al. (2022) The key finding of this study is developing a transferable method for assisting in the clinical assessment of depression and remission through automated voice analysis. The researchers trained a machine learning model using non-clinical datasets containing German and US English emotional speech. They assessed the model's capability to differentiate between depression and non-depression in Danish-speaking healthy controls, individuals with first-episode major depressive disorder (MDD), and those who had achieved remission through clinical interviews. The model effectively distinguished between healthy controls and individuals with depression, achieving an AUC of 0.71. Furthermore, it demonstrated that the speech of individuals in remission closely resembled that of the control group, indicating its potential for monitoring changes in depressive states. The study emphasized the significance of data collection settings and data pre-processing for accurate automated voice analysis in clinical applications.

Text analysis tools propelled by AI can identify the emotional tone and sentiment of written communication. Social media sentiment analysis, chatbots that respond empathetically to text messages, and content moderation utilize text analysis tools propelled by AI to identify potentially harmful or offensive statements. Shelke et al. (2022) Shelke et al. (2022) introduce a Leaky Relu-activated Deep Neural Network (LRA-DNN) model designed for extracting emotions from text as the central finding of this study. The model is structured into four essential phases: data pre-processing, feature extraction, ranking, and classification. The study addresses the critical challenge of filtering out irrelevant features during text-based emotion extraction, which can lead to inaccurate predictions. Utilizing publicly available datasets, the research assesses the performance of the proposed LRA-DNN compared to previous state-of-the-art algorithms, including ANN, DNN, and CNN. The results highlight that the LRA-DNN model achieves significantly improved accuracy, sensitivity, and specificity rates, reaching 94.77%, 92.23%, and 95.91%, respectively. This enhancement in performance underscores the potential of the LRA-DNN approach to mitigate mispredictions and misclassification errors in text-based emotion extraction, with applications spanning fields such as human-computer interaction, recommendation systems, online education, and data mining.

Applications powered by artificial Intelligence can provide individuals with real-time feedback on their emotional states. For example, when a wearable device connected to AI detects elevated tension levels, it can alert users, enhancing their emotional awareness. Individuals can use AI to monitor their emotional patterns over time, gaining insight into the factors that provoke particular emotions (Dhimolea et al., 2022). This data-driven strategy can enable individuals to make informed decisions regarding managing their emotional health. AI can recommend individualized interventions to help individuals better manage their feelings. For instance, if an AI detects a user experiencing increased anxiety, it may recommend mindfulness exercises or breathing techniques to reduce tension. AI can serve as a virtual emotion counsellor, guiding and assisting with the development of emotional Intelligence. It can provide advice on recognizing and expressing emotions, as well as empathic communication and conflict resolution.

Collecting and analyzing emotional data can raise serious privacy concerns. Users must control their dynamic data collection, storage, and dissemination. AI models utilized for emotion recognition may exhibit bias when trained on data that is not representative of diverse populations. Addressing discrimination in AI systems is essential to ensuring fair and equitable outcomes. Users must know how AI analyzes their emotions and support such analysis. Transparency is vital to establishing trust in AI systems. Emotional data is compassionate, and its protection is paramount. AI systems must employ stringent cybersecurity precautions to safeguard sensitive, dynamic data from unauthorized access or intrusions. AI can aid in emotional awareness, but it should refrain from supplanting the human element of emotional support. To preserve the authenticity of dynamic interactions, it is essential to strike the proper equilibrium between AI and human intervention. Technologies powered by artificial Intelligence have the potential to promote emotional awareness by assisting individuals in comprehending and managing their emotions. To ensure that AI's emotional awareness respects individual rights and values (Katirai, 2023; Ghotbi, 2022), addressing ethical considerations such as privacy, bias, and the need for informed consent with care is crucial. When utilized responsibly, AI can positively impact emotional well-being by assisting individuals in navigating the complex terrain of their emotions in the digital age.

THE ETHICS OF AI IN EMOTIONAL WELL-BEING

Applying artificial Intelligence (AI) to emotional health presents promising opportunities and significant ethical challenges. Ensuring the development and deployment of AI-powered emotional well-being tools ethically and responsibly addresses these potential risks and obstacles. Choung et al. (2023) The core finding of this study revolves around creating a multidimensional framework for trust in artificial Intelligence (AI), with a significant emphasis on its ethical implications. The research delineates two fundamental dimensions of trust in AI—human-like confidence and functionality trust—while concurrently exploring faith across various levels, including dispositional, institutional, and experiential trust. Furthermore, the study delves into the intricate relationship between trust and seven distinct ethical requirements, as advocated by the European Commission's High-Level Expert Group on AI. Significantly, the research unveils affirmative linkages between trust in AI and ethical prerequisites concerning societal and environmental well-being, accountability, and technical robustness. Additionally, it underscores that trust in AI surpasses faith in other institutional entities. These findings collectively enrich our comprehension of trust in AI and its ethical foundations, highlighting the pivotal role of moral values in nurturing trustworthiness within AI technology.

One of the greatest dangers is an excessive reliance on AI for emotional support. If individuals become overly reliant on AI-driven solutions, this could reduce their ability to seek human consent and empathy, leading to emotional detachment and social isolation. AI systems can acquire preferences from their training data, leading to unjust or discriminatory results. In the context of emotional well-being, AI may provide inappropriate or detrimental advice or interventions, mainly when dealing with sensitive emotional issues, if it is biased. Tilmes (2022) highlights a fundamental finding that pertains to advancements in artificial intelligence (AI) hiring tools and their potential impact on workplace dynamics. The central argument revolves around the risk of these AI algorithms perpetuating biases against marginalized groups. AI vendors have tried translating ethical concepts, notably fairness, into measurable, mathematical criteria that can be optimized. A critical insight of the paper is that discussions concerning algorithmic bias overlook the dimensions of disability and access. The author posits that the broad spectrum of disabilities, each with its unique characteristics and the contextual nature of disability expression, poses significant challenges to prevailing algorithmic fairness initiatives.

Furthermore, existing methods to reduce bias may inadvertently oversimplify the diversity within the disabled community and reinforce pathologizing. While acknowledging the potential of fair machine learning methods to mitigate specific disparities, the paper contends that focusing exclusively on fairness falls short of ensuring the development of accessible and inclusive AI systems. In response, the author advocates for a disability justice approach that centres on the experiences of disabled individuals and delves into the structures and norms that underlie algorithmic bias. In summary, the core finding of this paper emphasizes the necessity of moving beyond algorithmic fairness alone and embracing a more comprehensive and inclusive perspective when designing AI systems, with particular attention to addressing disability-related issues and promoting equitable access (Wong, 2019).

The accumulation of emotional data by AI systems can violate individuals' privacy. Emotions are highly private, and their unauthorized collection, storage, or dissemination can contravene the rights and autonomy of users. Selvarajan et al. (2023) The core finding of this study revolves around the introduction and practical implementation of an innovative artificial intelligence-based lightweight blockchain security model (AILBSM) tailored to bolster the privacy and security of industrial Internet of Things (IIoT) systems. This model is specifically designed for IoT setups that involve cloud-based data management or edge computing. The research showcases a significant breakthrough by combining lightweight blockchain technology with a Convivial Optimized Sprinter Neural Network (COSNN)-based AI mechanism. This integration results in streamlining and enhancing security operations for IIoT environments. An essential contribution of this research lies in its effective mitigation of the impact of potential attacks. It is achieved by transforming features into encoded data, facilitated by an authentic intrinsic analysis (AIA) model. Rigorous experimentation validates the AILBSM framework using diverse attack datasets, consistently yielding impressive outcomes. To elaborate further, implementing the AILBSM model dramatically reduces execution time to a mere 0.6 seconds. Simultaneously, it achieves remarkable overall classification accuracy, reaching an impressive 99.8%, alongside a robust detection performance rate of 99.7%. These results underscore the AILBSM framework's excellent efficacy, particularly in anomaly detection, outperforming alternative methodologies. An AI-driven security model enriched with blockchain integration successfully develops and practically applies the core finding. This model significantly elevates the levels of privacy and security within IIoT systems, effectively addressing crucial challenges within this domain.

Thoroughly advising users about collecting, using, and disseminating their emotional data is essential. Respecting users' autonomy and safeguarding their privacy requires informed consent. Using data minimization principles, developers should contain only the minimal emotional data necessary to provide the intended service. Developers should not collect or store any unnecessary information. Stringent cybersecurity measures should be in place to protect dynamic data from unauthorized access, breaches, or misuse. Encryption and access controls are essential data security components. Users should be in charge of their emotional data. They should be able to access, edit, or delete their data anytime and opt out of data collection.

Developers should proactively identify and mitigate biases in emotional support AI algorithms. It includes cautious training data selection, continuous monitoring, and performance evaluation. The operation and limitations of AI systems involved in emotional well-being should be transparent. The AI's decision-making process and the data it employs to provide emotional support should be transparent to the user (McStay, 2020). It should be possible to hold developers and organizations accountable for the ethical use of artificial Intelligence in emotional support. It includes adhering to ethical standards, guidelines, and regulations. AI systems' continuous evaluation and enhancement should be based on user feedback and evolving ethical standards. To ensure the responsible development of AI, it is essential to conduct regular audits and evaluations. The ethical considerations surrounding using artificial Intelligence for emotional well-being are paramount. To maximize the benefits of AI in this domain while minimizing the associated risks, it is essential to address potential pitfalls, safeguard privacy and data, and prioritize responsible AI development practices. We can navigate the evolving landscape of AI in emotional support in a manner that respects individuals' rights, values, and emotional well-being by upholding transparency, accountability, and user empowerment.

AI AND ADDICTION: BALANCING SUPPORT AND INDEPENDENCE

The intersection of artificial Intelligence (AI) and addiction introduces a nuanced landscape, offering critical assistance in detecting addictive behaviours and patterns while raising concerns about the balance between AI support and individual responsibility. AI analyzes diverse data sources, like social media and smartphone usage, to identify early signs of addictive behaviours, enabling early intervention. Algorithms powered by AI recognize addiction-related patterns, informing potential issues. AI assesses susceptibility to addiction based on individual characteristics, allowing personalized preventive measures. Tailored interventions, from motivational messaging to coping strategies, aid recovery (Mehmood et al., 2021).

AI predicts relapse likelihood, enables timely interventions, and fosters online recovery communities, providing secure spaces for support (Hao et al., 2022; Lin et al., 2014). While AI offers valuable support in addiction recovery, preserving individual independence is paramount. Overreliance on AI can impede personal growth and self-efficacy. Individuals must autonomously decide their recovery path, with AI providing information and recommendations. Final decisions should be collaborative efforts between the individual, healthcare professionals, and loved ones. Ethical guidelines must govern AI in addiction support, safeguarding individual data and privacy and ensuring interventions align with the person's best interests. User-centric AI design, incorporating feedback from those in recovery, ensures that technology meets their needs (Hamamura et al., 2023). Balancing AI assistance with personal responsibility is crucial for practical, ethical addiction support, prioritizing autonomy, and informed decision-making.

AI, COMPASSION, AND EMPATHY

Artificial Intelligence (AI) has made extraordinary strides in simulating compassion and empathy, creating new opportunities for interactions between humans and AI. However, this development also raises significant ethical concerns regarding the integrity and implications of artificial Intelligence's ability to simulate emotions. Morrow et al. (2023) conducted an extensive scoping review of the evolving relationship between AI technologies and compassion in healthcare. Exploring diverse literature, the study unveiled themes including ethical dilemmas from AI's impact on compassion, its potential advantages and drawbacks, and the need for harmonious human-AI collaboration. The study proposes reframing compassion as a human-AI system of intelligent caring, highlighting AI's potential to enhance compassionate care. Identifying gaps in understanding, the study emphasizes strategic planning and interdisciplinary collaboration for effective implementation of human-AI thoughtful care in healthcare, underscoring the crucial role of these elements in navigating the complex landscape of AI-driven compassion.

AI systems can be programmed with natural language processing (NLP) algorithms to analyze and comprehend human emotions conveyed in text or speech. Then, they can respond with compassionate and empathetic language, offering support and understanding. Ajmal et al. (2023) underscore the importance of incorporating Natural Language Processing (NLP) into healthcare conversational agents. This integration improves the processes of information retrieval, knowledge discovery, and personalized interactions by granting agents the ability to decipher structured data, comprehend the complexities of natural language, and deliver contextually appropriate responses. The research highlights the pivotal elements of natural language processing (NLP): entity recognition, response to inquiries, knowledge representation, and sentiment analysis. These capabilities enable conversational agents to fulfil users' information requirements and enhance healthcare results efficiently. Kusal et al. (2023) conducted an extensive literature review from 2005 to 2021, analyzing 63 research papers from reputable databases. The central discovery of this comprehensive review underscores the growing importance and advancements in text-based emotion detection (TBED) within the domain of artificial Intelligence (AI). The review emphasizes the importance of TBED in enabling AI systems to understand and respond to emotions expressed in text-based interactions, feedback, and online communications. The review highlights the diverse range of applications for TBED across various research domains, demonstrating its versatility and practical relevance, even in fields like business and finance. Additionally, it provides an exhaustive examination of emotion models, techniques, feature extraction methods, datasets, and the relevant challenges in TBED, making it a valuable resource for AI researchers and practitioners. Moreover, the review sets a course for the future of TBED research by offering insights into potential areas for further exploration and development, thereby guiding the trajectory of forthcoming studies in this dynamic field.

In summary, the core finding underscores the growing significance of TBED in the realm of AI, its broad applications, and its potential to shape future research directions, all while providing a comprehensive understanding of the existing literature. AI can identify affective signals in human users via facial recognition and vocal analysis. It can then modify its responses based on the user's emotional state to convey compassion and empathy. AI can monitor user behaviour and interactions to identify emotional distress or requirements patterns (Kusal et al., 2023). For instance, it can detect indicators of loneliness or depression and provide support accordingly. AI can use individual preferences, experiences, and histories to personalize its responses, resulting in a more empathic and compassionate interaction.

The ability of artificial Intelligence to simulate emotions raises concerns regarding the integrity of human-AI interactions. Users can perceive artificial Intelligence as legitimately empathetic when following programmed responses, leading to manipulation or deception. Individuals could develop an emotional reliance on AI that simulates empathy. It could impede their ability to pursue authentic human support and connection when they are in need. AI's emotional comprehension frequently relies on personal data analysis. It is essential to protect the confidentiality and security of this data to prevent its misuse or disclosure. Developers should disclose the capabilities and limitations of the dynamic simulation of AI. Users should recognize that they interact with a computer, not a person. Users should be educated on the role of artificial Intelligence in emotional support and encouraged to maintain a healthy equilibrium between AI interactions and human connections. Developers and users of emotional simulation-capable AI should adhere to ethical guidelines and regulations to ensure responsible and ethical use.

Human oversight and intervention should be available when AI interacts with vulnerable or distressed individuals. When most required, human contact can provide genuine empathy and support. Continued research and development are required to enhance AI's capacity to comprehend and respond naturally to human emotions. It includes the improvement of algorithms, emotional Intelligence, and the elimination of bias. The capacity of AI to simulate compassion and empathy presents intriguing opportunities to improve human-AI interactions (Schicktanz et al., 2023; Ghotbi, 2022). However, it also raises ethical challenges associated with authenticity and user dependence. Building meaningful human-AI interactions based on compassion necessitates striking a delicate balance between AI's capabilities, transparency, and ethical guidelines and recognizing that AI should complement rather than replace genuine human connection and support.

AI FOR EMOTIONAL WELL-BEING IN DIFFERENT SETTINGS

An increasing number of contexts incorporate artificial Intelligence (AI) to promote emotional health via individualized solutions. AI supports dynamic learning and assistance in education by facilitating interactive scenarios for practising empathy and emotional regulation. AI augments emotional Intelligence by customizing feedback based on students' affective reactions. It detects indicators of emotional distress, enabling prompt interventions. AI-powered chatbots establish confidential environments wherein students can openly discuss difficulties while also being provided with access to mental health experts and resources. AI facilitates emotional well-being in the workplace by providing insights into employee sentiments, thereby cultivating a positive atmosphere. AI enhances therapy in the field of mental health by performing personalized analyses, which guarantee timely and focused assistance.

AI applications are of utmost importance in managing workplace tension as they provide instantaneous stress assessments and suggest activities that alleviate stress. By monitoring employee engagement and sentiment, AI enables the implementation of targeted interventions to improve the workplace's overall well-being. Virtual wellness coaches enabled by AI offer individualized support in work-life balance and emotional resilience. Amidst difficult circumstances, empathic AI virtual assistants aid in the workplace. Through analyzing patient data for diagnosis and assessment, AI assists mental health professionals in developing individualized treatment plans. Teletherapy platforms powered by AI improve the accessibility of mental health care through the provision of video consultations and immediate chatbot support. Continuous monitoring of emotional states and digital behaviour facilitates timely intervention. AI-powered solutions prioritize emotional well-being in various contexts by providing personalized assistance and access to resources that foster personal growth.

THE FUTURE OF AI, MINDFULNESS, AND EMOTIONAL WELL-BEING

When AI, mindfulness, and emotional health come together, it could lead to personalized interventions that improve mindfulness and emotional support through immersive experiences made possible by VR and AR technologies. Robo-assistants equipped with sophisticated emotional Intelligence will provide companionship and assistance. Establishing AI systems built upon robust ethical principles, which emphasize transparency, equity, and user consent, is critical. Addressing bias in emotional support algorithms presents both a hurdle and a prospect for developing fair and impartial models. The complex task of safeguarding data privacy and security for AI-powered emotional well-being requires the implementation of secure platforms and policies. Integrating AI tools with conventional care promotes a holistic approach, achieving the destigmatization of mental health. It is crucial to educate professionals and consumers about the potential of AI in the field of emotional health; this creates opportunities for responsible application training.

Governments and industry organizations should establish regulations and standards for applying AI to emotional well-being. These guidelines can guarantee that artificial intelligence technologies adhere to ethical principles and user rights. Conducting ongoing research and evaluating AI applications for emotional well-being is essential. It involves evaluating their efficacy, user satisfaction, and potential dangers. It is necessary to enable individuals to make informed decisions regarding AI-based emotional support. Users should have control over their data and be aware of the repercussions of AI use on their health. Collaboration between technology developers, mental health professionals, researchers, and policymakers is essential to advancing responsible AI integration. Multidisciplinary efforts can shape the future of emotional well-being positively. The end of AI, mindfulness, and emotional well-being is characterized by thrilling developments, trends, and obstacles that require careful consideration. Encouraging the responsible use and integration of AI in this field will be essential to realizing its full potential to improve emotional well-being, reduce stigma, and provide valuable support for individuals attempting to improve their emotional health and mindfulness.

In their scholarly work, Ferrigno et al. (2023) shed light on the domain of Industry 4.0 by delineating five crucial research themes: digital business models, business model innovation, intelligent products, and technological platforms. This comprehensive examination synthesizes current understanding and establishes the groundwork for forthcoming research directions, offering academics and professionals a methodical structure to explore the complex relationship between business models and technology in the dynamic age of Industry 4.0. As sectors advance, these discerned clusters function as a framework for scholars to confront emergent obstacles and investigate ground-breaking prospects within the ever-changing Industry 4.0 domain. Enholm et al. (2021) highlight the considerable potential of AI in the business sector despite obstacles to widespread adoption. The literature review contributes to a more nuanced understanding by identifying enablers, inhibitors, and typologies. Through the strategic identification of research voids and the formulation of an agenda, this study provides valuable insights into the efficient utilization of artificial Intelligence to benefit businesses. Moreover, it acts as a guide for future inquiries within organizations.

The review by Graham et al. (2019) highlights AI's transformative capacity in mental healthcare, highlighting the remarkable precision observed in preliminary investigations. Nevertheless, it is crucial to exercise prudence when interpreting the results, underscoring the need for additional investigation to integrate AI into clinical practice responsibly and guarantee its efficacy and ethicality. In an examination of 404 articles, Loureiro et al. (2021) chart the course of AI in business as it evolves, identify key topics, and suggest a research agenda. By disclosing patterns and obstacles, the research provides a proactive manual for subsequent investigations, influencing the course of AI study within the ever-evolving realm of commerce. These dialogues underscore the wide-ranging potential and applications of artificial Intelligence (AI) across various fields. They offer valuable perspectives on existing knowledge, direct future investigations, and underscore the criticality of ethical and responsible integration to ensure significant results.

CONCLUSION

In this chapter, the author embarked on a journey through the intricate intersection of artificial Intelligence (AI), mindfulness, and emotional well-being. The author investigated numerous facets of this dynamic landscape, revealing the potential and ethical issues that arise when these domains converge. It investigated how AI and mindfulness can collaborate to promote emotional health. AI can enhance mindfulness practices by providing personalized guidance and assistance to individuals who wish to cultivate emotional awareness. It discussed the role of AI in emotional health in various contexts, including education, the workplace, and mental health care. AI-powered solutions can provide innovative approaches to recognizing and managing emotions. Experts emphasized the ethical implications of AI's involvement in emotional well-being. Privacy, bias, transparency, and responsible development have emerged as essential factors in using artificial Intelligence. Particularly in addiction support, it investigated the delicate balance between AI assistance and personal responsibility. Striking this equilibrium is vital to maintaining authentic human connections and agency. It foresaw emerging trends such as VR and AR integration, emotionally intelligent machines, and a growing emphasis on the development of ethical AI.

The transformative potential of AI and mindfulness for emotional well-being is undeniable. AI can amplify the benefits of mindfulness practices, making them more accessible and individualized for each individual. It can provide early intervention for emotional distress, foster supportive learning and work environments, and improve mental health care. Sustaining compassionate equilibrium becomes crucial in a world dominated by AI. Although artificial Intelligence can simulate compassion and empathy, it should not replace genuine human connection. Responsible AI development, transparency, and user empowerment are necessary to ensure that AI promotes our emotional well-being rather than inhibits it. Combining artificial Intelligence and mindfulness for emotional well-being offers an optimistic path forward. We can navigate the complexities of our emotional lives with greater resilience and understanding in the digital age if we harness the transformative potential of these technologies while upholding ethical principles and preserving human compassion.

REFERENCES

Ajmal, S., Ahmed, A. A. I., & Jalota, C. (2023). Natural Language Processing in Improving Information Retrieval and Knowledge Discovery in Healthcare Conversational Agents. *Journal of Artificial Intelligence and Machine Learning in Management*, *7*(1), 34–47. https://journals.sagescience.org/index.php/jamm/article/view/73

Andreotta, A. J., Kirkham, N., & Rizzi, M. (2021). AI, big data, and the future of consent. *AI & Society*, *37*(4), 1715–1728. doi:10.100700146-021-01262-5 PMID:34483498

Audrin, C., & Audrin, B. (2023). More than just emotional Intelligence online: Introducing "digital emotional intelligence.". *Frontiers in Psychology*, *14*, 1154355. Advance online publication. doi:10.3389/fpsyg.2023.1154355 PMID:37205063

Baroni, D., Nerini, A., Matera, C., & Stefanile, C. (2016). Mindfulness and Emotional Distress: The Mediating Role of Psychological Well-Being. *Current Psychology (New Brunswick, N.J.)*, *37*(3), 467–476. doi:10.100712144-016-9524-1

Bharti, T., Mishra, N., & Ojha, S. C. (2023). Mindfulness and Subjective Well-Being of Indian University Students: Role of Resilience during COVID-19 Pandemic. *Behavioral Sciences (Basel, Switzerland)*, *13*(5), 353. doi:10.3390/bs13050353 PMID:37232590

Brelet, L., & Gaffary, Y. (2022). Stress reduction interventions: A scoping review to explore progress toward using haptic feedback in virtual reality. *Frontiers in Virtual Reality*, *3*, 900970. Advance online publication. doi:10.3389/frvir.2022.900970

Broderick, P. C., & Jennings, P. A. (2012). Mindfulness for adolescents: A promising approach to supporting emotion regulation and preventing risky behaviour. *New Directions for Youth Development*, *2012*(136), 111–126. doi:10.1002/yd.20042 PMID:23359447

Caldeira, C., Chen, Y., Chan, L., Pham, V., Chen, Y., & Zheng, K. (2017). Mobile apps for mood tracking: an analysis of features and user reviews. In *AMIA Annual Symposium Proceedings* (p. 495). American Medical Informatics Association. https://www.ncbi.nlm.nih.gov/pmc/articles/PMC5977660/

Cao, L. (2023). AI and data science for smart emergency, crisis and disaster resilience. *International Journal of Data Science and Analytics*, *15*(3), 231–246. doi:10.100741060-023-00393-w PMID:37035277

Carson, J. W., Carson, K. M., Gil, K. M., & Baucom, D. H. (2004). Mindfulness-based relationship enhancement. *Behavior Therapy*, *35*(3), 471–494. doi:10.1016/S0005-7894(04)80028-5

Cepeda-Lopez, A. C., Solís Domínguez, L., Villarreal Zambrano, S., Garza-Rodriguez, I. Y., Del Valle, A. C., & Quiroga-Garza, A. (2023). A comparative study of well-being, resilience, mindfulness, negative emotions, stress, and burnout among nurses after an online mind–body-based intervention during the first COVID-19 pandemic crisis. *Frontiers in Psychology*, *14*, 848637. doi:10.3389/fpsyg.2023.848637 PMID:36993886

Choung, H., David, P., & Ross, A. (2023). Trust and ethics in AI. *AI & Society*, *38*(2), 733–745. doi:10.100700146-022-01473-4

De Souza Marcovski, F. C., & Miller, L. J. (2023). A latent profile analysis of the five facets of mindfulness in a US adult sample: Spiritual and psychological differences among four profiles. *Current Psychology (New Brunswick, N.J.)*, *42*(17), 14223–14236. doi:10.100712144-021-02546-1

Dhimolea, T. K., Kaplan-Rakowski, R., & Lin, L. (2022). Supporting Social and Emotional Well-Being with Artificial Intelligence. In *Bridging Human Intelligence and Artificial Intelligence* (pp. 125–138). Springer International Publishing. doi:10.1007/978-3-030-84729-6_8

Döllinger, N., Wienrich, C., & Latoschik, M. E. (2021). Challenges and Opportunities of Immersive Technologies for Mindfulness Meditation: A Systematic Review. *Frontiers in Virtual Reality*, *2*, 644683. Advance online publication. doi:10.3389/frvir.2021.644683

Drigas, A., Mitsea, E., & Skianis, C. (2022). Virtual reality and metacognition training techniques for learning disabilities. *Sustainability (Basel)*, *14*(16), 10170. doi:10.3390u141610170

Enholm, I. M., Papagiannidis, E., Mikalef, P., & Krogstie, J. (2021). Artificial Intelligence and Business Value: A Literature Review. *Information Systems Frontiers*, *24*(5), 1709–1734. doi:10.100710796-021-10186-w

Ferrigno, G., Del Sarto, N., Piccaluga, A., & Baroncelli, A. (2023). Industry 4.0 base technologies and business models: A bibliometric analysis. *European Journal of Innovation Management*, *26*(7), 502–526. doi:10.1108/EJIM-02-2023-0107

Flett, J. A., Hayne, H., Riordan, B. C., Thompson, L. M., & Conner, T. S. (2019). Mobile mindfulness meditation: a randomized controlled trial of the effect of two popular apps on mental health. *Mindfulness, 10*, 863–876. https://link.springer.com/article/10.1007/s12671-018-1050-9

Fulambarkar, N., Seo, B., Testerman, A., Rees, M., Bausback, K., & Bunge, E. (2023). Meta-analysis on mindfulness-based interventions for adolescents' stress, depression, and anxiety in school settings: A cautionary tale. *Child and Adolescent Mental Health*, *28*(2), 307–317. Advance online publication. doi:10.1111/camh.12572 PMID:35765773

Ghotbi, N. (2022). The Ethics of Emotional Artificial Intelligence: A Mixed Method Analysis. *Asian Bioethics Review*, *15*(4), 417–430. doi:10.100741649-022-00237-y PMID:37808444

Graham, S., Depp, C. A., Lee, E., Nebeker, C., Tu, X., Kim, H., & Jeste, D. V. (2019). Artificial Intelligence for Mental Health and Mental Illnesses: An Overview. *Current Psychiatry Reports*, *21*(11), 116. Advance online publication. doi:10.100711920-019-1094-0 PMID:31701320

Guillaume, N., Jean, M., Marcaurelle, R., & Dupuis, G. (2020). Mindfulness meditation versus training in tranquil abiding: Theoretical comparison and relevance for developing concentration. *Psychology of Consciousness : Theory, Research, and Practice*, *7*(2), 151–172. doi:10.1037/cns0000222

Hamamura, T., Kobayashi, N., Oka, T., Kawashima, I., Sakai, Y., Tanaka, S., & Honjo, M. (2023). Validity, reliability, and correlates of the Smartphone Addiction Scale–Short Version among Japanese adults. *BMC Psychology*, *11*(1), 78. Advance online publication. doi:10.118640359-023-01095-5 PMID:36959621

Hansen, L., Zhang, Y. P., Wolf, D., Sechidis, K., Ladegaard, N., & Fusaroli, R. (2022). A generalizable speech emotion recognition model reveals depression and remission. *Acta Psychiatrica Scandinavica*, *145*(2), 186–199. doi:10.1111/acps.13388 PMID:34850386

Hao, Q., Peng, W., Wang, J., Tu, Y., Li, H., & Zhu, T. (2022). The correlation between internet addiction and interpersonal relationship among teenagers and college Students Based on Pearson's Correlation Coefficient: A Systematic Review and Meta-Analysis. *Frontiers in Psychiatry*, *13*, 818494. Advance online publication. doi:10.3389/fpsyt.2022.818494 PMID:35356718

Im, S., Stavas, J., Lee, J., Mir, Z., Hazlett-Stevens, H., & Caplovitz, G. (2021). Does mindfulness-based intervention improve cognitive function? A meta-analysis of controlled studies. *Clinical Psychology Review*, *84*, 101972. doi:10.1016/j.cpr.2021.101972 PMID:33582570

Jiménez-Picón, N., Romero-Martín, M., Ponce-Blandón, J. A., Ramirez-Baena, L., Palomo-Lara, J. C., & Gómez-Salgado, J. (2021). The Relationship between Mindfulness and Emotional Intelligence as a Protective Factor for Healthcare Professionals: Systematic Review. *International Journal of Environmental Research and Public Health*, *18*(10), 5491. doi:10.3390/ijerph18105491 PMID:34065519

Jothimani, S., & Premalatha, K. (2022). MFF-SAug: Multi-feature fusion with spectrogram augmentation of speech emotion recognition using convolution neural network. *Chaos, Solitons, and Fractals*, *162*, 112512. doi:10.1016/j.chaos.2022.112512

Katirai, A. (2023). Ethical considerations in emotion recognition technologies: A review of the literature. *AI and Ethics*. Advance online publication. doi:10.100743681-023-00307-3

Kusal, S., Patil, S., Choudrie, J., Kotecha, K., Vora, D., & Pappas, I. (2023). A systematic review of applications of natural language processing and future challenges with special emphasis on text-based emotion detection. *Artificial Intelligence Review*, *56*(12), 1–87. doi:10.100710462-023-10509-0

LaGrandeur, K. (2015). Emotion, artificial Intelligence, and ethics. In Topics in intelligent engineering and informatics (pp. 97–109). doi:10.1007/978-3-319-09668-1_7

Lin, Y. H., Chang, L., Lee, Y. H., Tseng, H. W., Kuo, T. B., & Chen, S. (2014). Development and Validation of the Smartphone Addiction Inventory (SPAI). *PLoS One*, *9*(6), e98312. doi:10.1371/journal.pone.0098312 PMID:24896252

Mantello, P., & Ho, T. M. (2023). Emotional AI and the future of well-being in the post-pandemic workplace. *AI & Society*. Advance online publication. doi:10.100700146-023-01639-8 PMID:36776535

McStay, A. (2020). Emotional AI, soft biometrics and the surveillance of emotional life: An unusual consensus on privacy. *Big Data & Society*, *7*(1), 205395172090438. doi:10.1177/2053951720904386

Medvedev, O. N., & Krägeloh, C. U. (2023). Harnessing Artificial Intelligence for Mindfulness Research and Dissemination: Guidelines for Authors. *Mindfulness*, *14*(5), 1019–1020. doi:10.100712671-023-02155-y

Mehmood, A., Bu, T., Zhao, E., Zelenina, V., Alexander, N., Wang, W., Siddiqi, S. M., Qiu, X., Yang, X., Qiao, Z., Zhou, J., & Yang, Y. (2021). Exploration of the psychological mechanism of smartphone addiction among international students of China by selecting the framework of the I-PACE model. Frontiers in Psychology, 12. doi:10.3389/fpsyg.2021.758610

Morrow, E., Zidaru, T., Ross, F., Mason, C., Patel, K. D., Ream, M., & Stockley, R. (2023). Artificial intelligence technologies and compassion in healthcare: A systematic scoping review. *Frontiers in Psychology*, *13*, 971044. https://www.frontiersin.org/articles/10.3389/fpsyg.2022.971044/full

Mukhiddinov, M., Djuraev, O., Akhmedov, F., Mukhamadiyev, A., & Cho, J. (2023). Masked Face Emotion Recognition Based on Facial Landmarks and Deep Learning Approaches for Visually Impaired People. *Sensors (Basel)*, *23*(3), 1080. doi:10.339023031080 PMID:36772117

Pauly, T., Nicol, A., Lay, J. C., Ashe, M. C., Gerstorf, D., Graf, P., Linden, W., Madden, K. M., Mahmood, A., Murphy, R. A., & Hoppmann, C. A. (2023). Everyday Pain in Middle and Later Life: Associations with Daily and Momentary Present-Moment Awareness as One Key Facet of Mindfulness. *Canadian Journal on Aging*, *42*(4), 1–10. doi:10.1017/S0714980823000326 PMID:37565431

Rawtaer, I., Mahendran, R., Yu, J., Fam, J., Feng, L., & Kua, E. H. (2015). Psychosocial interventions with art, music, T ai Chi and mindfulness for subsyndromal depression and anxiety in older adults: A naturalistic study in Singapore. *Asia-Pacific Psychiatry*, *7*(3), 240–250. doi:10.1111/appy.12201 PMID:26178378

Schicktanz, S., Welsch, J., Schweda, M., Hein, A., Rieger, J. W., & Kirste, T. (2023). AI-assisted ethics? Considerations of AI simulation for the ethical assessment and design of assistive technologies. *Frontiers in Genetics*, *14*, 1039839. Advance online publication. doi:10.3389/fgene.2023.1039839 PMID:37434952

Selvarajan, S., Srivastava, G., Khadidos, A. O., Khadidos, A. O., Baza, M., Alshehri, A., & Lin, J. C. W. (2023). An artificial intelligence lightweight blockchain security model for security and privacy in IIoT systems. *Journal of Cloud Computing (Heidelberg, Germany)*, *12*(1), 38. doi:10.118613677-023-00412-y PMID:36937654

Shelke, N., Chaudhury, S., Chakrabarti, S., Bangalore, S. L., Yogapriya, G., & Pandey, P. (2022). An efficient way of text-based emotion analysis from social media using LRA-DNN. *Neuroscience Informatics (Online)*, *2*(3), 100048. doi:10.1016/j.neuri.2022.100048

Slutsker, B., Konichezky, A., & Gothelf, D. (2010). Breaking the cycle: Cognitive behavioural therapy and biofeedback training in a case of cyclic vomiting syndrome. *Psychology Health and Medicine*, *15*(6), 625–631. doi:10.1080/13548506.2010.498893 PMID:21154016

Tilmes, N. (2022). Disability, fairness, and algorithmic bias in AI recruitment. *Ethics and Information Technology*, *24*(2), 21. doi:10.100710676-022-09633-2

Wong, P. (2019). Democratizing algorithmic fairness. *Philosophy & Technology*, *33*(2), 225–244. doi:10.100713347-019-00355-w

Xu, G., Xue, M., & Zhao, J. (2023). The Association between Artificial Intelligence Awareness and Employee Depression: The Mediating Role of Emotional Exhaustion and the Moderating Role of Perceived Organizational Support. *International Journal of Environmental Research and Public Health*, *20*(6), 5147. doi:10.3390/ijerph20065147 PMID:36982055

Zhou, Z., Asghar, M. A., Nazir, D., Siddique, K., Shorfuzzaman, M., & Mehmood, R. M. (2023). An AI-empowered affect recognition model for healthcare and emotional well-being using physiological signals. *Cluster Computing, 26*(2), 1253–1266. doi:10.100710586-022-03705-0 PMID:36349064

ADDITIONAL READING

Assunção, G., Patrão, B., Castelo-Branco, M., & Menezes, P. (2022). An overview of emotion in artificial intelligence. *IEEE Transactions on Artificial Intelligence, 3*(6), 867–886. doi:10.1109/TAI.2022.3159614

Cath, C., Wachter, S., Mittelstadt, B., Taddeo, M., & Floridi, L. (2018). Artificial intelligence and the 'good society': The US, EU, and UK approach. *Science and Engineering Ethics, 24*, 505–528. PMID:28353045

Coccia, M. (2020). Deep learning technology for improving cancer care in society: New directions in cancer imaging driven by artificial intelligence. *Technology in Society, 60*, 101198. doi:10.1016/j.techsoc.2019.101198

Kambur, E. (2021). Emotional Intelligence or Artificial Intelligence?: Emotional Artificial Intelligence. *Florya Chronicles of Political Economy, 7*(2), 147–168. doi:10.17932/IAU.FCPE.2015.010/fcpe_v07i2004

Korstanje, M. E., & Seraphin, H. (2022). A Problem Called Alterity: The Position of the 'Other'in HBO Saga Westworld. In Tourism Through Troubled Times: Challenges and Opportunities of the Tourism Industry in the 21st Century (pp. 7-20). Emerald Publishing Limited.

Makridakis, S. (2017). The forthcoming Artificial Intelligence (AI) revolution: Its impact on society and firms. *Futures, 90*, 46–60. doi:10.1016/j.futures.2017.03.006

Merriam, G. (2022). If AI only had a heart: Why artificial intelligence research needs to take emotions more seriously. *Journal of Artificial Intelligence and Consciousness, 9*(01), 73–91. doi:10.1142/S2705078521500120

Scribano, A. (2019). Introduction: politics of sensibilities, society 4.0 and digital labour. *Digital Labour, Society and the Politics of Sensibilities*, 1-17.

Scribano, A., & Maria, M. V. (2021). Narratives, emotions and artificial intelligence: A reading of artificial intelligence from emotions. *SN Social Sciences, 1*(9), 229. doi:10.100743545-021-00237-z

KEY TERMS AND DEFINITIONS

Artificial Intelligence: Advanced computer systems that mimic human Intelligence, processing data, learning patterns, and making decisions, with applications in automation, analysis, and problem-solving.

Education: The process of acquiring knowledge, skills, values, and habits, typically facilitated through formal instruction, promotes personal and societal development.

Emotional Well-Being: The overall mental health state, encompassing emotional resilience, happiness, and satisfaction, indicates a positive, fulfilling, and vibrant life.

Ethics: Moral principles guiding behaviour, decision-making, and actions, defining what is right or wrong, just, and fair within a societal or professional context.

Mental Health: Is the state of psychological well-being involving emotional, cognitive, and social aspects, with factors like resilience, coping, and balance influencing overall mental health.

Mindfulness: Is a mental state achieved through focused awareness of the present moment, fostering emotional balance, stress reduction, and improved overall well-being.

Synergy: The interaction of elements produces a combined effect more significant than the sum of their contributions, emphasizing collaborative and interconnected outcomes.

Chapter 4
Emotions and Food Digital Practices on Instagram:
Between the Algorithms and the Big Data

Maria Victoria Mairano
https://orcid.org/0000-0003-0668-0572
CONICET, University of Buenos Aires, Argentina

ABSTRACT

Considering the changes in social relationships and social practices across the planet, caused by digitalization processes, networking, and Society 4.0, this chapter aims to problematize the connections between digital emotions in relation to food, new properties of politics of sensibilities around food digital practices, and the operation of algorithms and big data on digital platforms. With that objective, the authors focus on investigating food practices on Instagram, based on the figure of food influencers and the digital emotions that are crystallized there in relation to eating.

INTRODUCTION

The world faces a series of technological, economic, political, and cultural transformations that have modified the ways of being and perceiving the world, framed in what we know as society or revolution 4.0. Some of the technological advances manifested: the emergence of microelectronics, information technology, biotechnology, materials technology, the Internet of things, the Internet of services, advanced robotics, Artificial Intelligence, additive manufacturing, simulations, integration of vertical and horizontal systems, Big Data, cloud manufacturing,

DOI: 10.4018/979-8-3693-0802-8.ch004

nanotechnology, cybersecurity, intelligent drones and augmented reality (Nagao Menezes, 2020).

The establishment of these new technologies, the acceleration of digital consumption processes, and the new productive dynamics typical of the 4.0 revolution establish modifications in the notion of work, social relations, our relationship with the environment, and therefore changes in the processes of social structuring.

There are multiple changes and transformations within the framework of the so-called 4.0 revolution. It is worth highlighting here the implication of changes in social practices and in the ways of relating, which refer, among other things, to the massification of the smartphone and other mobile devices, as well as the massive participation of subjects in digital platforms. The constant use of devices and social network immersion establishes the production of new images of the world (Scribano, 2017), built from the daily incursion of subjects into digital media. This incursion has its effects on the ways of seeing/knowing and feeling the world.

On the other hand, regarding the manifestations of digitalization in the ways of structuring society, it occurs from the establishment of new politics of sensibilities[1] With it, the reconfiguration of perception and notions of space-time in the digitalized world (Scribano and Lisdero, 2019), approaching social reality essential from there.

The new properties of the politics of digital sensibilities imply a set of cognitive/affective social practices, which refer to the organization of the day/night detached from the experience of the subjects who experience it, and to the modification of classifications of sensations and evaluations about world modifications (Scribano, 2020).

However, this new economic model is based on using a structure of large amounts of data from and on digital platforms (Srnicek, 2017; Steinhoff, 2022). These data are built from the information that people provide by expressing themselves, working, studying, buying, and interacting with others, from social networks and digital platforms. That's why it is necessary to address the processing of that information and its expression in the algorithms used by social networks, to reflect on the changes in social relations, digital emotions, and the ways of being in the world today.

One of the transformations that the mass use of social networks has promoted alludes to food practices. Today food practices are being modified by digital consumption, the proliferation of information about food in blogs and social networks, the emergence of new characters such as influencers on platforms that produce senses and meanings about food, and the practices of cooking. These practices became data-driven events that can be tracked, quantified, and managed online, implying transformations in eating practices and in the politics of sensibilities that are organized around them.

In this sense, we are interested in addressing the daily eating practices that are outlined in social networks and the sensibilities that are hatched concerning them.

This proposal which emerges from my master's thesis aims to problematize the connections between new properties of food digital practices, the digital emotions that appear there, and the operation of algorithms and Big Data on Instagram. Other objectives are problematizing the logic of big data and the operation of algorithms on digital platforms; detailing the transformations in society 4.0 and the role of food influencers in what refers to changes in digital food practices; and addressing a characterization of the digital food practices scrutinized on Instagram and the emotions that arise there.

Based on a process of digital ethnography on Instagram that registers and systematizes the new properties of food digital practices and the emotions that are outlined around them from the figure of the influencer, this chapter will adopt the following argumentative strategy: a) present the specifications of digital platforms as scenarios for the emergence of Big Data and algorithms functioning; b) describe the transformations in food digital practices from 4.0 technologies, digital consumption and the digitalization of life, and the role of food influencers; c) present the methodological strategy; d) detail the characteristics of food digital practices scrutinized in the social network by the digital ethnography, and the emotions that emerge there in connection with algorithms's functioning on Instagram; 3) present some conclusions.

EMOTIONS, BIG DATA, AND ALGORITHMS THROUGH DIGITAL PLATFORMS

Faced with its cyclical crises, capitalism tends to restructure itself: new technologies, organizational forms, new modes of exploitation, different types of jobs and markets emerge to create a new way of accumulating capital (Srnicek, 2017). In recent decades, the modality that capital has adopted finds in the large amounts of data that are produced through digital platforms that we use daily, a vehicle for generating profits.

In that sense, digital platforms become essential scenarios for the productivity of Big Data and, subsequently, the operation of algorithms. Big Data refers to the ability of new technologies to process and analyze large amounts of information. These data come from mobile devices and interactivity on social networks. For their part, algorithms involve instructions that, organized in a certain way and previously defined, are used to perform a certain task. As we have said in another place, algorithms imply ways of speaking about the world (Scribano and Mairano, 2021), as they establish narratives and meanings about certain things. They allow us to see specific content and to avoid others, depending on the content we "like", share or keep; our relationships with the person who posts the content; the popularity of the post; and our background of interactions.

In connection with the influx of data on digital platforms such as Instagram, Facebook, and TikTok, these are essential fuels for the functioning and improvement of AI today.IA presents various contributions such as image recognition systems, virtual assistants, assisted driving, chatbots, robots, intelligent applications of logistics and transport processes, diagnosis and analysis of patient prognoses, clinical decisions, driver assistance systems, evaluation of yield and soil condition, informative contributions to farmers on changes in conditions in the agricultural industry, among others (Williams, 2021).

Especially, as we said in Scribano and Mariano (2021), in the case of the social media industry, AI is a key factor for the "systematization/monitoring" of the data of millions of profiles of users of social networks such as Facebook, Youtube, Twitter, Instagram and Snapchat. In this way, a clear connection is established between the imminence of AI in various areas of life, the management of large amounts of data through Big Data and the operation of algorithms on digital platforms.

In turn, from a methodological perspective, Gonzalez Turmo (2017) maintains that access to these large amounts of data, the way of relating and processing it, and its dissemination, will affect the knowledge that science can offer on a certain topic, in this case on the practice of eating and food practices. Therefore, these productive changes generate modifications not only in the relationships between people, in the dynamics of exchange and generation of profits but also the production of knowledge.

Regarding the Instagram platform, the algorithm that allows it to function is based on the interests of users and the interactions that a certain publication has obtained. In this way, the algorithm directly affects the contents that are seen, that can be known, and those that cannot, in other words, they affect our perception and knowledge about the world. They gave us a certain image of the world, based on our interests and choices that are daily reflected while using digital devices. Those ways of seeing the world allow specific forms of disposition, action and being in the world.

In this sense, faced with a production system that is globalized from the purchase, sale, and production of emotions through digital media and the Internet (Scribano, 2023), address the practices, content and information that are produced and circulated in digital platforms, allow us to problematize the structuring of digital emotions that are produced and distributed there.

If we ask the chatbot if artificial intelligence can generate emotions, this is its answer:

There are AI models, such as those based on natural language processing, that can generate responses that appear to have certain emotional nuances. These models are trained on large amounts of linguistic data and can produce responses that reflect the emotional tonality present in that data. Although AI can be programmed to respond in ways that appear sensitive, these responses are the result of learned patterns and not actual emotional experiences. AI lacks consciousness and the ability to experience emotions on its own.

From here we can say that artificial intelligence can simulate emotional responses, but it does not experience emotions in the same way as humans. The appearance of emotions in AI-generated responses is the result of patterns and data learned from our interactions and practices.

Emotions are cognitive/affective practices, referring to an object, person, or event, that involves the assessment and evaluation of something (see Scribano; Mulligan & Scherer, 2012; Bericat, 2012). As Scribano (2023) argues, digital emotions have three properties that make them epistemic features: a) as ways of knowing the world, b) as practices that transform that world and c) as metaphors of connection between the world, human beings, and other living beings (Scribano, 2023). From here we start to realize the need to observe the maps of emotions that circulate on digital platforms, specifically those that are related to food practices, to problematize the logic of social structuring from there.

DIGITAL CONSUMPTION, DIGITALIZATION OF LIFE, AND TRANSFORMATIONS IN FOOD DIGITAL PRACTICES FROM 4.0 TECHNOLOGIES

On this occasion, we will focus on the effects of digitalization and technological transformations on everyday food practices and the politics of sensibilities that are configured around them. These changes establish certain ways of experiencing the act of eating and generate specific modes of sociability around food.

As has already been addressed by various authors, from academic interdisciplinarity, studying the act of eating implies immersing oneself in the fabric of the social structure since it is there where the commensal subject, a culture and a meal are articulated (Aguirre, 2010). In this sense, food is not only limited to nutritional and biological importance, but also encompasses other uses such as the principle of incorporation, satiety, pleasure, identification and differentiation, ritual use, and marking times. (Fischler, 2010; Aguirre, 2005; Contreras and Gracia-Arnáiz, 2005). Eating is not only fundamental for the reproduction and social availability of bodies, but the articulation between the organic/cognitive/affective is intertwined in the production and reproduction of bodies/emotions (Scribano, 2012). Therefore, the current social structuring processes can be understood from the existing connections between bodies/emotions/food (Scribano and Boragnio, 2021).

In this sense, when we refer to food practices, we not only mean behaviors or habits but also, and above all, social practices with a clear imaginary, symbolic and social dimension (Díaz Méndez and Gómez Benito, 2005; Gracia-Arnaiz, 1996). As Boragnio (2022) maintains:

Food practices encompass social actions and relationships that are structured around the central act of eating, while, as cultural, economic, social and individual elements, they reproduce the social structure. These practices are organized from a set of specific actions that are directly linked to the possibility of eating. In this sense, we define food practices as the actions of obtaining, accumulating, preparing, and preserving food, together with the knowledge about it, held by a specific group in a specific historical context. (Boragnio, 2022, p. 117)

There are various ways to carry out these practices based on what is possible and accessible according to the available resources. In this sense, in addition to economic, genetic, and biological variables, there are sociocultural variables such as social class, age, gender, identity or ethnic group that influence and determine our daily food options and preferences (Contreras and Gracia-Arnáiz, 2005).

Currently, based on digitalization processes and the massification of digital consumption, digital platforms constitute a great scenario for the circulation of information about food and nutrition, learning food management, searching for restaurants, the sharing of diverse culinary techniques, the incursion into food cultures from different regions of the world, among others. In this sense, digital food practices are produced and reproduced in virtual environments and consist of the expression of behaviors and eating habits with a certain symbolic and social meaning. They also have the particularity of (re)producing and sustaining the lifestyle of the social group involved.

Just to mention some works on the subject, it is worth highlighting the contributions to the transmission of culinary secrets (Lee & Tao, 2021), culinary criticism on Instagram (Feldman, 2021), recipe sharing on blogs (Lofgren, 2013), anorexia and pornography food in cyberspace (Lavis, 2017), the influence of social networks in the development of overweight and obesity (Powell et al, 2015), veganism and gender in blogs (Hart, 2018), weight and body shapes in digital media (Lupton, 2017), and everyday culinary practices (Kirkwood, 2018), among others.

Now, the requirements to carry out the practices of provisioning, conservation, cooking, recycling, food control, and physical care of the body, are understood as the "construction of food knowledge." This knowledge, in Gracia-Arnaiz's (1996) terms, has been generally transmitted by women, despite their massive incorporation into the labor market and the introduction of services outside the domestic sphere. Although historically the transmission of this knowledge was carried out orally and in the domestic sphere, from cookbooks, magazines and television programs by renowned chefs, critics, and gastronomic writers (Lupton, 2021), today it is worth highlighting the effects of media coverage of food based on technological transformations and the massiveness of digital applications, in the transmission of that food and culinary knowledge. In that sense, since the beginning of the 21st century, new media such as blogs, social networking sites, and the use of hashtags and influencers emerged that have transformed the creation of content and its subsequent sharing, as well as eating practices and habits. The Internet universe thus offers a variety of culinary information that grows exponentially at a speed that is difficult to track, characterized by immediacy, agility, creativity, and practicality (Gonzalez Turmo, 2017).

Here we focus on the digital platform Instagram, characterized by the proliferation of content about food, as well as the role played by influencers there. Instagram is one of the main social networks globally. According to DataReportal, in January 2023 it was the fourth most-used social network in the world with around 2 billion monthly active users. For our purposes, the centrality of the visual in the network promotes a context conducive to the aesthetics of the food, the colors, the layout of the environment.

Influencers, also known as internet celebrities or internet personalities, are people who have a community of followers on social networks and have become famous through it. In that sense, we consider a food influencer as a character who promotes/inspires the proliferation of certain emotions and senses regarding what we consider food in general and food choices in particular, and who on several occasions adopts these practices as a job. It has profitability or presents profitability in services/goods, among others.

There are numerous antecedent studies of influencers on Instagram, from the construction of identities (Contois & Kish, 2022; Leung & Lin, 2022), the practices of professional cooks or chefs (Virgen, 2015), the relationship between influencers and marketing (Jardim and Pires, 2022; Kin, 2022; Hudders & De Jans, 2022; Gerlich, 2023), discursive practices (Cotter, 2019; Gil-Quintana et al, 2021) and the evolution of food and gastronomy in times of the internet and social networks (Lupton and Feldman, 2020; Lupton, 2021; Schneider & Eli, 2021; Scribano, 2021; Scribano and Boragnio, 2021), among others.

Below, is be detailed analysis of food practices and the emotions around them, based on the content of food influencers from Argentina.

METHODOLOGICAL STRATEGY

As we mentioned in the introduction, to characterize the food practices produced from and on the platform by influencers, ethnographic work was carried out to observe publications (images, videos, and publications) and record what was observed by each Instagram profile of influencers previously interviewed.

In this case, Instagram will be used as a digital platform, as an instrument and space for inquiry. The decision to address this research problem from a digital methodology is based on the theoretical/epistemological and methodological imperative of tracking information in the spaces where things happen. Therefore, the proposal to investigate the food practices of influencers leads us to use a purely digital methodological strategy since these practices are produced and established exclusively on digital platforms.

We have recorded the publications of 24 food influencers from Argentina, at different times of posting. The type of sampling carried out was convenience, a non-probabilistic sampling that allows selecting those accessible cases that agree to be included. This selection is based on the purposes of the research and theoretical criteria exclusively (Otzen and Manterola, 2017). In this case, the choice of food influencers from Argentina referred to the number of followers, constant activity and link (communicative on networks) between them.

The record of publications was focused on the dates: March 2020, March 2021, and March 2022, as the beginning of the productive cycle of the year in Argentine, as a cutoff due to the multiplicity of content and publications provided by the temporal cutback of the thesis: 2020-2022. It was carried out by creating a table to systematize and compare the registered content, which contained information about each influencer such as number of followers, biography data, hashtags used, interaction with peers, and publications per month.

ALGORITHMS, FOOD MANAGEMENT, AND EMOTIONS ON INSTAGRAM

We have recorded various practices that are enabled through digital technologies that mediate our daily lives today. In that sense, according to the three moments of registration, the type of practices scrutinized are described below:

Regarding the publications made at the beginning of the 2020 school year, a time that coincides with the declaration of Preventive and Mandatory Social Isolation in Argentina due to the Covid-19 pandemic, different types of food practices could be identified, such as the transmission of recipe ideas to through photos or videos (reels); cooking competitions; videos about the practice of fermentation and the use of the star product of the quarantine: sourdough; cooking tips; invitation to online gym classes together with healthy recipes; videos on how to organize cooking, shopping and meals in times of quarantine; photos of food with procedural instructions to take advantage of the kitchen during isolation; food ideas. In this record, the published content was characterized by being mainly photographic, followed by videos or references to videos in featured stories.

On the other hand, regarding the publications made at the beginning of the 2021 school year, one year after the pandemic emergency, food practices such as food recipes can be observed; information on front labelling of products; cooking contests that generate interaction between followers; videos on kitchen items indicated for certain purposes; information on cooking techniques; motivations about training and invitations to online cooking classes. In this period, the contents were mostly published from reels (videos) and, to a lesser extent, photographs. In turn, some photographs refer to links to videos from other platforms, for example, YouTube or specific TV programs.

Finally, regarding the content published during the start of the 2022 school year, food practices such as recipes stand out; food testing; shopping videos; information on cooking tips and cooking techniques; information about a comprehensive program to change habits and also, and raffles for cooking classes. At this time of registration, content in reel or video format also predominates, which can be related to a display strategy since the Instagram algorithm begins to show more reels than images. However, the record also expressed how photographs or images of food continue to be appreciated.

Following this description of types of practices, we carried out a characterization of the properties of each registered food practice. On this occasion, for reasons of length, we will only focus on presenting one of the central characteristics that we found, which is the establishment of certain management in food management.

From this characteristic of digital food practices regarding the organization and management of the kitchen and purchases, it is clear that the influencers, in addition to offering recipes, also seek to provide information for the assembly of first kitchens, the necessary or basic foods and the ways of shopping.

Thus, we can see how certain knowledge is transmitted concerning cooking, the necessary instruments and the way of organizing to carry out eating. An example of this is some videos offered by a mega influencer (Record 4) that are part of a series titled "Survival Manual" whose aim is to provide information about "Everything you need to know to equip your kitchen!" (Record 4), as well as the presentation of videos by the same influencer to "organize your meals to go out as little as possible and continue eating delicious and homemade!", highlighting the impossibility of leaving homes in times of quarantine. In times of quarantine, Videos were also recorded with information on types of ovens indicated for sourdough (Record 6), "the star of confinement."

Information about the organization and planning of the meal is linked with different references to "time." In quarantine, publications emerge about time management and taking advantage of it to cook.

"Now that we have time, let's take the opportunity to cook something as delicious and classic as it is versatile" (Record 26, our translation)

"The time has come to cook at home, organize, plan and optimize" (Record 14, our translation).

In this last record 14, the idea arises of optimizing time for those food practices that involve not only kitchen time but also organization, thinking and planning. Other examples of publications also express the connection of organization and planning with practicality, as another imperative with the practices that make up daily eating:

"Practical recipes to get you out of trouble" (Record 8, our translation);

"Recipe for spinach and ricotta wraps, an easy and practical idea ideal for lunch or dinner" (Record 8, our translation).

EMOTIONS AROUND FOOD PRACTICES

On the other hand, regarding the emotions that are associated with the eating practices of influencers, below is an analysis of three of them that emerge from the narratives of influencers in their publications. Digital emotions could also have been addressed from the images or videos they share, the emojis or stickers that accompany the narratives, or the content of the stories they upload. However, here it is a privilege to track the digital emotions that are presented in the narratives that accompany each publication in their feed. In other words, the prevalence of three emotions is observed: love, fatigue and enjoyment, in connection with liking.

The appeal to love begins to be outlined in the publications, as an emotion that emerges when cooking, and from the practice of sharing content with others:

"Believe me, Experts are made with a lot of determination and with a lot of love" (Record 5, our translation);

"Deconstructed Milanese recipe. #Milanesas deconstructed...Be careful, they only do it with fish or chicken or vegetables, it doesn't work with meat...I always do it and I love it" (Record 4, our translation);

" Comprehensive program "Transform your habits". A program that is born from love and the immense desire we have to accompany you to heal the relationship with your body and food" (Record 24, our translation).

In these fragments we can see that the connection is outlined between doing things with love (sharing, cooking) and contributing something to the other through accompaniment and generation of content, giving an account of the care that food implies and how this relates to the idea of the "healthy body".

Regarding tiredness, it subsides when planning food, tied to thinking about what to eat and cooking. For this reason, recipes must be easy and quick, while meal ideas and meal planning must be offered all the time, because cooking generates fatigue and, in addition, requires time, "a precious commodity that in the hustle and bustle of life." "Contemporary life is easily diluted." About time, Yopo Diaz (2021) argues that there are multiple temporal perspectives, but that they all converge in the fact that time is a social construction and, as such, a symbolic means of social control and normative structuring of life. In the first decades of the 21st century, it is important to problematize the meanings and senses given to time, in the context of the expansion of globalization processes, increased speed due to the management of complexity, new technologies and individualization (Güell Villanueva and Yopo Diaz, 2017), especially on digital platforms that emphasize immediacy, present time and instantaneity.

Returning to the analysis of the publications that refer to tiredness, this publication is an example of this where a recipe for cocoa waffles is presented:

"This is not a recipe for Sunday, but I recommend that you save it for the week when you are tired of thinking about what to cook" (Record 3, our translation);

This one alludes to the advertising of some products to make a lunch that quickly solves the meal:

"EXPRESS LUNCH MADE IN MOTORHOME 🚐 😃 There are days when you just want to rest and enjoy the landscape, that's why my friend Mochi from @ genteamigadistribuidora gave me these products so I can solve the meal in minutes" (Record 26, our translation).

It is important to note that reference is made to tiredness during the week (as opposed to the logic of enjoying the weekend), which is why the recipes or ideas presented in the publications are not for the weekend, but for the days when, in addition to being tired, there is not as much time to dedicate to the kitchen and thinking about cooking, shopping and everything that food practices imply.

For its part, enjoyment, in connection with liking, is very present in the publications and is expressed about sharing recipes and ideas, and eating with others:

"Recipe for creamy chocolo (sic) express cake 🙌 😍 I hope that when you make it you like it as much as I enjoy sharing each of my recipes and tips with you 🙌 😍" (Record 22, our translation);

"Post with two recipes that I had promised! Enjoy it 🥰 send me your photos!" (Record 17, our translation);

"Cooking unites, summons, conquers and falls in love. It unites even if you don't know how to cook. It unites the aromas, the flavors, and the anecdotes. Snacks that extend like talks and become a tea dinner, a brunch or a snack. Because when "We enjoy, we always have room and time for another slice of cake. During cooking and nature 🌿 we contemplate with all our senses, we take away warm and genuine smiles" (Record 16, our translation).

That is, from this record, the prevalence of 3 related emotions stands out: tiredness, love, enjoyment/liking, linked to practices such as sharing content, cooking, eating with others, planning food, and thinking about what to eat.

Regarding love, several authors have worked on this emotion from different perspectives, starting from Giddens (1992), Luhmann (1986), passing through Ahmed (2021), Illouz (2011; 2018) and Lugones (2008), only for name a few. As a social practice, Scribano (2020) in his work "Love as Collective Action", argues that love implies not only action and movement but also responses, which enables reciprocity in the connections between people. For the author, understanding love is to realize the energy or power to act, which will imminently generate a response in the other. Therefore, from a sociological perspective, love plays an essential role in the social construction of society, in the elaboration of subjectivity, in the articulation between agents, and in the energies that awaken emotions (Scribano, 2020).

Along these lines, focusing on the necessary "reciprocity" generated by giving and feeling love, thinking about the different appeals to this emotion by influencers, in connection with sharing content, eating, and cooking for others, allows us to put tension and make visible how this emotion is commodified on the Instagram network, based on its monetization. As outlined in the publications, influencers constantly appeal to love, in search of remuneration from their followers, which is framed in a commercial logic, since generating content and sharing it on their profiles implies paid work. In that sense, you can see expressions such as: "Go give it love" (referring to some content), or: "This is done with determination and a lot of love" (referring to the work of sharing information, and images). Love is linked to these figures' search for gratification from comments, the like button - in the shape of a heart - or continuous video views, which monetizes and commodifies that emotion. We say that the logic of giving/generating love is commodified since what prevails is not a selfless act of reciprocity, but rather a search for what we could call: "commodified reciprocity", which is obtained from reproduction or comment on each post.

Regarding tiredness, Byung-Chul Han (2012) has developed how this is typical of contemporary society's subject. It appears as a counterpart to the imperative of performance and activity. In line with what we have been saying, the logic of organizing/planning/thinking/optimizing food and its timing produces an overabundance of performance, we could say of constant doing and "performing", which in effect produces fatigue and exhaustion. excessive. It is imperative to observe how tiredness emerges in the influencers' narratives as a reason why it is necessary to provide ideas for recipes or meals to make and save at times when "you are too tired to cook and to think about what to eat." They are ideal for when "you are tired of always performing, preparing and organizing", but these ideas also imply planning, organizing and optimizing time, so they can be understood as the obverse and reverse of the same problem. At the same time, it is important to highlight the reference to time management and food practices as the subjects' responsibility, in a register of being "entrepreneurs of themselves" (Del Mónaco, 2020), in this case, of their reproduction, not only choosing what to eat but also carrying it out so that it is easy/rich/healthy.

For its part, regarding enjoyment, from the Sociology of Bodies/Emotions, this is thought in connection with consumption and spectacle, as a central triad to understand the construction of normalized societies in the Global South and the establishment of a certain political economy. morality (Scribano, 2013). In this sense, Scribano (2013) maintains: "Enjoyment as existential of capitalist life, as experimentation to be narrated/lived in front of and for others, is connected with dream states where consumption explains the belief in a lived world." to be seen" (p.744). Returning to our line of work, about how enjoyment appears in the influencers' narratives, it is linked to the practice of cooking, eating and sharing content for their followers. Here you can see how the imperative logic of enjoyment about food relates to the practice of showing/exhibiting that enjoyment on networks and with the constant consumption of objects/information/ideas through them. Thus, two aspects of analysis can be established: the expression of enjoyment as a spectacularization of life, on the one hand, and immediate consumption along with its display through social network profiles. These two find, in digital platforms, a special scenario for their establishment and reproduction, especially on Instagram, since it is established as a highly visual network, where showing every aspect of life is the central axis of its operation.

To the practice of showing everyday life on networks as a spectacle, Sibilia (2008) addresses the emergence of practices of exhibition of intimacy on the Internet, as a sociocultural demand that trivializes ways of being in the world. To do this, the author problematizes the context of the influx of a new social organization that is emerging in the first decades of this century, based on overproduction, exacerbated consumption, marketing and creative advertising rewarded monetarily. This context establishes a favourable environment for the convocation of personalities, in this case, food influencers, who show their private lives on the screens.

Returning to the analysis of emotions, as ways of each influencer of experiencing the practice of eating, in connection with sociability (ways of living and living with others) that are interwoven, twisted with the establishment of specific digital sensibilities regarding food, shape changes in the structures of emotions through food on Instagram. Knowing these connections and forms of expression of the experiences/sociability/sensibilities of the digitalized world that are structured concerning food, allows us to think about how certain forms of presentation of the person are outlined (sensu Goffman), how is enabled in different ways of being in bodies (Sibilia, 2013) and how emotional, and display rules prevail (Hochschild, 1979), which define what should be felt and how those emotions should be expressed, in a spatial context and a specific time.

In short, the influencers' eating practices allow us to indicate that emotions such as love/tiredness/enjoyment prevail on Instagram, forming a specific emotional ecology for the practice of cooking, eating with others and sharing content related to the food. These characteristics of food practices form tripods for the expression of the new politics of sensibilities around food on Instagram, which are identified as practices that (re)produce certain possibilities of action/cognition/disposition referred to the classificatory gaze and evaluation of the world, the management of time/space and the organization of daily life. These new properties of the politics of sensibilities around food find in algorithms a way to be vehicle and reproduced on social media platforms.

Likewise, in the organization of daily life, the idea is highlighted that nutrition should be managed by organizing and planning meals and their preparations to achieve the greatest practicality possible, optimizing the use of time dedicated to these practices. The logic of organization/planning/optimization/practicality, in a "performance" society (Byung-Chul Han, 2012), emerges from the imperative of management of food practices. For the latter, content is generated with recipes that are easy to make, practical meal ideas, organization of meals and "meal preps", and "tips" are offered for planning weekly purchases and meals.

From this, it follows that practices around food also imply the establishment of a certain management logic. Edge that could be added as one more property of those that make up a food practice today. We well know that management, as a specific rationality, has gone beyond the dimension of work, to encompass different dimensions or areas of life. In the case of food practices on Instagram, based on the figure of the influencer, this logic is expressed from two dimensions: on the one hand, emotional work, in Hochschild's terms (1983), and on the other, the imperative of achieving greater productivity through management and rational use of time.

Regarding the first dimension, emotional labor implies a shift of emotional rules and social exchange from the private domain to the public space (Hochschild, 1983). According to the author, emotional work is part of the workplace and involves contact and the production of an emotional state in another. In the current capitalist era, based on what we have already mentioned as the emotionalization of life, the search for generating states of feeling and emotions in people based on any transaction or economic exchange is a fact. In that case, from what has been seen so far, the work of the influencer is not exempt from this practice, it has an important implication in the production of digital emotions and consequently the generation/ commodification of experiences and sociabilities through their work in social networks. On the other hand, the second dimension, dedicated to the management and use of time: the planning of purchases, the organization of daily and weekly meals, their preparations and the forms of commonality that are established there, are inserted into the imperative of productivity and the use of time typical of current capitalism. We could see it expressed in the organizational, planning, optimization and practicality logic that emerges from the analysis.

By way of closing this section, we want to highlight those emotions, as practices that transform reality, and modify the horizons of action and disposition of the subjects. In that sense, it is relevant to know the digital emotions that are produced and distributed on the Instagram platform because it allows us to realize the changes in certain practices, the movement of social interactions and what these produce. For Social Sciences, emotions are an important way to address social reality.

In this case, it could be observed that the emotions that are structured there express the imperative of practising cooking with love, of enjoying eating with others, but also the tiredness that comes from planning, organizing, and optimizing the food. time, etc.; As well as the establishment of new politics of sensibilities that place the "management in food practices" as the central axis to understand those.

These senses and meanings that are given to bodies, emotions, and food, have algorithms as ways of speaking the world (Scribano and Mairano, 2023), as distribution vehicles on social networks, which is why they are so important in social structuring. The eating practices that are shared and that subjects can observe, reproduce the lifestyle of certain sectors or social classes. It is from there that the inequality is expressed between those who can prepare their meals, organize their kitchen, plan their food, and optimize their time; and those who cannot choose what to eat, much less have the possibility of food variability and food management that influencers propose in their publications.

CONCLUSION

To conclude this chapter, we will do a brief review of the route taken. Firstly, the first section was dedicated to presenting the specifications of digital platforms as scenarios for the emergence of Big Data and the operation of algorithms. What we were able to describe there is how digital transformations produce changes in social practices and how our possibilities of knowing the world are materialized by algorithms on digital platforms. This has a specific implication in the digital emotions that are produced and distributed in networks, as well as in the way in which the social structure is expressed.

In a second moment, the transformations in digital food practices were described based on 4.0 technologies, digital consumption, and the digitalization of life. There we referred to the way in which the politics of sensibilities regarding food, entail changes in the organization of time, and in the way we classify sensations and evaluate the world. There was also a reference to the place of food influencers on digital platforms, specifically their role on Instagram, considering that the emergence of new media blogs, sites, hashtags, and food influencers, has transformed the construction of food knowledge and the ways it is shared.

Finally, based on the theoretical accumulation addressed up to that point, we continued to detail the characteristics of digital food practices scrutinized on the social network by virtual ethnography and the emotions that arise there with the functioning of the algorithms on Instagram. We problematize the connection between food practices and digital emotions to address the processes of social structuring around eating from there.

From practices's characterization, we notice how food management is expressed and the importance that influencers attribute to it from their content. There we were able to observe how this has reference to a specific way of organizing time and space as one more property of the new politics of sensibilities in digital platforms.

Then we analyzed 3 emotions: love, tiredness, and enjoyment, about the narratives that emerged in the influencers' posts. From there we observe these emotions as ways of experiencing the moment of feeding, socializing with others and the establishment of certain digital sensibility regarding food. There it constitutes a specific emotional ecology concerning the practice of cooking, eating with others and sharing content related to the food, which express the emotional rules that are established in the platform, and the process of social structuring between those who can choose and define what to eat and plan the cooking, and those who can't.

What we could see up to this point in this chapter, is how these traces of the new properties of the politics of sensibilities and the emotional plots around eating, are expressed in Instagram posts. Those contents are organized based on the platform's algorithm that works from the multiple data that exist due to the interactions between subjects. That is why what the algorithms's functioning shows, becomes ways to understand the world image we have, crossed by issues of class, gender and ethnicity.

REFERENCES

Aguirre, P. (2005). *Estrategias de consumo: que comen los argentinos que comen.* Miño y Dávila.

Aguirre, P. (2010). La construcción social del gusto en el comensal moderno. In COMER: Una palabra con múltiples sentidos (pp. 13-63). M. Libros del Zorzal.

Bericat, E. (2012). Emociones. *Sociopedia.isa*, 1-13.

Boragnio, A. (2022). Emotions and food in times of pandemic: a comparison of eating practices in Spain and Argentina during COVID-19. In *Emotions and Society in difficult times*. Cambridge Scholars Publishing.

Byung-Chul, H. (2012). *La sociedad del cansancio*. Herder Editorial.

Contois, E., & Kish, Z. (2022). *Food Instagram: Identity, Influence, and Negotiation.* The University of Illness Press. doi:10.1177/1461444818815684

Cotter, K. (2019). Playing the visibility game: How digital influencers and algorithms negotiate influence on Instagram. *New Media & Society*, *21*(4), 895–913. doi:10.1177/1461444818815684

Contreras, J., & Gracia-Arnaiz, M. (2005). *Alimentación y cultura: perspectivas antropológicas*. Editorial Ariel.

Del Mónaco, R. L. (2020). Empresarios de sí mismos: subjetividades en las terapias cognitivo-conductuales. In Políticas terapéuticas y economías de sufrimiento: perspectivas y debates contemporáneos sobre las tecnologías psi (pp. 175-196). Consejo Latinoamericano de Ciencias Sociales.

Díaz Méndez, C., & Gómez Benito, C. (2005). Sociología y alimentación. *Revista Internacional de Sociologia*, *63*(40), 21–46. doi:10.3989/ris.2005.i40.188

Feldman, Z. (2021). Good food' in an Instagram age: Rethinking hierarchies of culture, criticism and taste. *European Journal of Cultural Studies*, *24*(6), 1340–1359. doi:10.1177/13675494211055733

Fischler, C. (2010). Gastro-nomía y gastro-anomía. Sabiduría del cuerpo y crisis biocultural de la alimentación moderna. *Gazeta de Antropología*, (26), 1–19. doi:10.30827/Digibug.6789

Gerlich, M. (2023). The Power of Personal Connections in Micro-Influencer Marketing: A Study on Consumer Behaviour and the Impact of Micro-Influencers. *Transnational Marketing Journal*, *11*(1), 131-152.

Giddens, A. (1992). *The transformation of intimacy. Sexuality, Love and Eroticism in Modern Societies*. Stanford University Press.

Gil-Quintana, J., Santoveña-Casal, S., & Romero Riaño, E. (2021). Realfooders Influencers on Instagram: From Followers to Consumers. *International Journal of Environmental Research and Public Health*, *18*(4), 1624. doi:10.3390/ijerph18041624 PMID:33567738

Gonzalez Turmo, I. (2017). Big data y antropología de la alimentación. In L. Mariano Juarez, F. X. Medina, & J. Lopez García (Eds.), *Comida y mundo virtual* (pp. 327–352). Editorial UOC.

Gracia-Arnaiz, M. (1996). *Paradojas de la alimentación contemporánea*. Icaria.

Güell Villanueva, P. & Yopo Díaz, M. (2017). Las perspectivas temporales de los chilenos: un estudio empírico sobre la dimensión subjetiva del tiempo. *Universum. Revista de Humanidades y Ciencias Sociales*, *32*(1), 121-135.

Hart, D. (2018). Faux-meat and masculinity: The gendering of food on three vegan blogs. *Canadian Food Studies La Revue Canadienne Des études Sur l'alimentation*, *5*(1), 133–155. doi:10.15353/cfs-rcea.v5i1.233

Hochschild, A. R. (1979). Emotion Work, Feeling Rules, and Social Structure. *American Journal of Sociology*, *85*(3), 551–575. doi:10.1086/227049

Hochschild, A. R. (1983). *The Managed Heart. Commercialization of Human Feeling*. University of California Press.

Hudders, L., & De Jans, S. (2022). Gender effects in influencer marketing: An experimental study on the efficacy of endorsements by same- vs. other-gender social media influencers on Instagram. *International Journal of Advertising*, *41*(1), 128–149. doi:10.1080/02650487.2021.1997455

Illouz, E. (2011). *Por qué duele el amor: una explicación sociológica*. Katz.

Illouz, E. (2018). *El fin del amor: una sociologia de las relaciones negativas*. Katz.

Jardim, M. C., & Pires, L. D. (2022). O Instagram como dispositivo de construção de mercado nas redes sociais: A intimidade distinta como variável central junto aos influenciadores de fitness. *Revista Brasileira de Sociologia*, *10*(24), 144–175. doi:10.20336/rbs.855

Kim, H. (2022). Keeping up with influencers: Exploring the impact of social presence and parasocial interactions on Instagram. *International Journal of Advertising, 41*(3), 414–434. doi:10.1080/02650487.2021.1886477

Kirkwood, K. (2018). Integrating digital media into everyday culinary practices. *Communication Research and Practice, 4*(3), 277–290. doi:10.1080/22041451.2018.1451210

Lavis, A. (2017). Food porn, pro-anorexia and the viscerality of virtual affect: Exploring eating in cyberspace. *Geoforum, 84*, 198–205. doi:10.1016/j.geoforum.2015.05.014

Lee, K. S., & Tao, C. W. (2021). Secretless pastry chefs on Instagram: The disclosure of culinary secrets on social media. *International Journal of Contemporary Hospitality Management, 33*(2), 650–669. doi:10.1108/IJCHM-08-2020-0895

Lofgren, J. M. (2013). *Changing tastes in food media: a study of recipe sharing traditions in the food blogging community* [Master's thesis]. Queensland University of Technology.

Luhmann, N. (1986). *Love as Passion The Codzfication of Intimacy*. Harvard University Press.

Lupton, D. (2017). Digital media and body weight, shape, and size: An introduction and review. *Fat Studies, 6*(2), 119–134. doi:10.1080/21604851.2017.1243392

Lupton, D. (2021). Afterword: Future methods for digital food studies. In J. Leer & S. G. Strøm Krogager (Eds.), *Research methods in digital food studies*. Routledge.

Lupton, D., & Feldman, Z. (2020). *Digital food cultures*. Routledge. doi:10.4324/9780429402135

Mulligan, K., & Scherer, K. R. (2012). Toward a working definition of emotion. *Emotion Review, 4*(4), 345–357. doi:10.1177/1754073912445818

Nagao Menezes, D. F. (2020). Las perspectivas del trabajo en la sociedad 4.0. *Revista Nacional de Administración, 11*(1), 11–19. doi:10.22458/rna.v11i1.3011

Otzen, T., & Manterola, C. (2017). Técnicas de Muestreo sobre una Población a Estudio. *International Journal of Morphology, 35*(1), 227–232. doi:10.4067/S0717-95022017000100037

Powell, K., Wilcox, J., Clonan, A., Bissell, P., Preston, L., Peacock, M., & Holdworth, M. (2015). The role of social networks in the development of overweight and obesity among adults: A scoping review. *BMC Public Health, 15*(1), 996. doi:10.118612889-015-2314-0 PMID:26423051

Schneider, T., & Eli, K. (2021). Fieldwork in online foodscapes: How to bring an ethnographic approach to studies of digital food and digital eating. In J. Leer & S. G. Strøm Krogager (Eds.), *Research methods in digital food studies* (pp. 71–85). Routledge.

Scribano, A. (2012). Sociología de los cuerpos/emociones. *Revista Latinoamericana de Estudios sobre Cuerpos, Emociones y Sociedad, 10*(4), 91–111.

Scribano, A. (2013). Una aproximación conceptual a la moral del disfrute: normalización, consumo y espectáculo. *RBSE – Revista Brasileira de Sociologia da Emoção, 12*(36), 738-750.

Scribano, A. (2017). Instaimagen: Mirar tocando para sentir. *RBSE Revista Brasileira de Sociologia da Emoção, 16*(47), 45–55.

Scribano, A. (2019). Introduction: Politics of Sensibilities, Society 4.0 and Digital Labour. In A. Scribano & P. Lisdero (Eds.), *Digital labor, Society and Politics of Sensibilities* (pp. 1–18). Palgrave Macmillan. doi:10.1007/978-3-030-12306-2_1

Scribano, A. (2020). *Love as a collective action. Latin America, Emotions and Interstitial Practices*. Routledge.

Scribano, A. (2021). ¡¡¡Sabor a bit!!!: Algunas conclusiones (adelantadas) sobre el impacto sociológico de la Food Tech. *Aposta, Revista de Ciencias Sociales. Núm., 90*, 12–31.

Scribano, A. (2023). *Emotions in a digital world: Social Research 4.0.* Routledge.

Scribano, A., & Boragnio, A. (2021). Presentación del monográfico: El comer del siglo XXI: sensibilidades y prácticas alimentarias. *Aposta, Revista de Ciencias Sociales, 90*, 8–11.

Scribano, A., & Lisdero, P. (2019). *Digital labor, Society and Politics of Sensibilities*. Palgrave Macmillan. doi:10.1007/978-3-030-12306-2

Scribano, A., & Mairano, M. V. (2021). *Narratives, Emotions and Artificial Intelligence. A reading of Artificial Intelligence from emotions. SN Social Sciences*. Springer.

Sibilia, P. (2008). *La intimidad como espectáculo*. Fondo de Cultura Económica.

Sibilia, P. (2013). El artista como espectáculo: Autenticidad y performance en la sociedad mediática. *Dixit*, (18), 4–19. doi:10.22235/d.v0i18.360

Srnicek, N. (2017). *Platform Capitalism*. Polity Press.

Steinhoff, J. (2022). Toward a political economy of synthetic data: A data-intensive capitalism that is not a surveillance capitalism? *New Media & Society*, *0*(0), 1–17. doi:10.1177/14614448221099217

Virgen, D. (2015, October 14). *An explorative study on Instagram and food from the cook's perspective*. PALIM Food Heritage and Culinary Practices, Paris, France.

Williams, S. (2021) Artificial Intelligence in the new era. *Int J Innov Sci Res Technol*, *6*(4).

KEY TERMS AND DEFINITIONS

Digital Emotions: Cognitive/affective practices produced and distribute online. They referred to an object, person, or event, that involve assessment and evaluation about something (see Mulligan & Scherer, 2012; Bericat, 2012).

Digital Food Practices: Social actions and relationships that are structured around the central act of eating, while, as cultural, economic, social, and individual elements, they reproduce the social structure.

Influencers: Internet celebrities who have a community of followers on social networks and have become famous through it.

Politics of Sensibilities: Set of cognitive/affective social practices, which refer to the organization of the day/night detached from the experience of the subjects who experience it, and to the modification of classifications of sensations and evaluations about world modifications (Scribano, 2019, 2020).

ENDNOTE

1 In Scribano's terms, the politics of sensibilities refer to "A set of cognitive-affective social practices aimed at the production, management and reproduction of horizons of action, disposition and cognition. These horizons refer to 1) the organization of daily life (day to day, wake/sleep, food/abstinence, etc.); 2) information to classify preferences and values (adequate/inappropriate, acceptable/unacceptable, bearable/unbearable) and 3) parameters for time/unbearable management space (displacement/location, walls/bridges; enjoyment)" (Scribano, 2019, p. 10). Nowadays, new sensibilities and politics are presented based on current digitalization processes.

Chapter 5
Transformation of Labor and Politics of the Senses:
Changes Derived From Automation-Digitalization in Dairy Barns of the Villa María Basin (2020-2022)

Leandro Tomas del Corro
CIT CONICET, Universidad Nacional de Rafaela, Argentina

Joaquin Ignacio Mendiburu
CIT CONICET, Universidad Nacional de Villa Maria, Argentina

Ignacio Pellón
CIT CONICET, Universidad Nacional de Rafaela, Argentina

ABSTRACT

The authors intend to reflect on the "metamorphosis of work" in the dairy farms of the Villa María Basin (Córdoba, Argentina) as a consequence of the robotization and automation of production. In this sense, they emphasize the changes in the "politics of the senses" that update the ways of touching and looking at the dairy farms, simultaneously updating the demands of capital for the use of labor force and introducing new mechanisms of control and surveillance. The proposed approach recovers testimonies from the protagonists of the "metamorphosis" indicated to reflect on the policy of changes in capitalism.

INTRODUCTION

Since the launch of ChatGPT on November 30, 2022, discussions, projections, and speculations regarding the impacts of artificial intelligence (AI) on work,

DOI: 10.4018/979-8-3693-0802-8.ch005

education, and life, in general, have continued to escalate.[1] In this regard, in March 2023, researchers from OpenAI, Open Research, and the University of Pennsylvania published an article on the potential impact of AI, particularly Large Language Models (LLMs), on the American economy and productivity (Eloundou, et al, 2023). Most of the surveyed occupations exhibit some degree of exposure to the capabilities of LLMs, not entirely, but concerning specific tasks. Occupations with high salaries are particularly exposed to new software and digital tools, such as those based on text input and output. Thus, among the sectors most susceptible to AI technologies are data and information processing industries and hospitals. On the other hand, among the list of occupations that did not manifest exposed tasks, we find agricultural equipment operators, mechanics and diesel engine specialists, meat processors and packers, masons, cooks, dishwashers, and other trades.

Overall, factors related to the incorporation of AI into production processes include assumed increases in productivity resulting from these technological innovations, as well as the reduction of operating costs associated with the displacement and/or "replacement" of high-wage labor tasks (in relative terms). Furthermore, these factors can be interpreted as aligning with the economic interests of companies dedicated to the development of artificial intelligence (such as OpenAI)[2], the implementation of digital transformation processes (Open Research)[3], or financial capital in general. In this latter sense, the case of BuzzFeed enables us to understand that it is the representatives of financial capital (the shareholders) who demand the "replacement" of human labor with artificial intelligence[4].

In recent decades, work has been undergoing a profound reconfiguration within the framework of the restructuring of social relations within the capitalist system. The exponential development of capital productivity has been driving an increasing process of mechanization in productive sectors, resulting in various transformations, including job precariousness, impoverishment, unemployment, and other effects (Antunes, 2020). We are currently going through a technological revolution characterized by the growing digitization of social relations in the context of a "Society 4.0". Scribano and Lisdero (2019) delve into the characterization of this stage, emphasizing the use of: a) more data managed by companies, b) powerful and affordable computers, c) analytical capabilities, and d) improvements in interactions between people and machines, robots, artificial intelligence, and 3D printers, based on the concept of "Societies 4.0." In this way, cost reduction, improvements in production lines, and the use of new databases are some of the central outcomes derived from these characteristics.

Digitalization has become a central component in the study of current changes in the world of work, due to the impact of AI on the conditions of reproduction of the workforce, how people interact with each other, resources, time and space, professional tools, and meanings. associated with work, and the disposition of bodies/

emotions as forms of value management in the system of social relations. These changes gain greater relevance when we observe how this digitization of relationships intertwines with work and daily life, playing a key role in the development of "social sensibilities." We understand these as the ways of "organizing perceptions, sensations, and emotions," with a particular focus on the body as the medium through which social agents perceive the world through the "impressions that impact the forms of 'exchange' with the social-environmental context" (Scribano, 2012, p. 100).[5] In this way, work, in its central role in shaping the social structure, is not exempt from the influence of information and communication technologies (ICTs) facilitated by internet use across various productive sectors.

Particularly, this research is the product of a line of research that began with the degree thesis at the National University of Villa María of which two of the authors were writers while the other acted as director. It was focused on investigating the transformations of work in dairy production based on the expansion of the internet and the use of ICT in dairy farms located in the Villa María Dairy Basin of the General San Martín Department of the province of Córdoba. in 2020. From this research, we continued a path that is still valid today in which the latent questions revolve around the investigation into the "metamorphosis of work" in the dairy based on the use of robotics and automation of work processes. Specifically, investigating the impact on the workforce that ICT is producing from a renewal in the expropriation mechanisms of vital/corporeal/social energies (De la Garza Toledo, E. 2012; Zukerfeld, M. 2020) as a form of capitalist accumulation that puts into practice center stage to the body/emotions as disputed territory (Scribano, A. 2012).

From that place, this writing encourages a first approach to the case of artificial intelligence in the dairy, continuing with the reasons previously expressed about the metamorphoses of work from "social sensibilities." Therefore, our theoretical and methodological approach seeks to recover what the protagonists of these changes are saying and experiencing as forms of the naturalized sociability of order. Based on a qualitative social study (Sautu, R. 2005; Batthyány, K. et al., 2011) and from a critical perspective, we reconstruct the statements of an automated dairy farm producer, a veterinarian from an automated dairy farm, a representative of a company selling technology for dairy farms, an automated dairy farm worker. The interviews and ethnographic notes are part of the fieldwork carried out in the period December 2020 to November 2021. The interviews were carried out during a visit to a dairy that incorporated a robot for the automation of milking in the town of Monte Maíz in the province of Córdoba which makes up the Villa Maria Dairy Basin. The field note was carried out within the framework of a virtual congress with the participation of vendors of automation, AI and robotics technologies applied to dairy farming.

The interviews recovered here were the product of fieldwork for the previously mentioned degree thesis research. The selection of the technique corresponds to the qualitative study, with "semi-structured" type interviews (Sautu, 2005: Batthyány, K. et al., 2011). The interview is presented as "a face-to-face verbal interaction consisting of questions and answers oriented to a specific topic or objectives, it is a technique for approaching the object of study of very extensive use in social research" (Oxman, 1998, p.9 in Scribano, 2007, p. 72). The semi-structured interviews allowed us to recover dense stories on which we proposed to objectify the position of these social agents in the world, investigating the connections between bodies/emotions as forms of management of social energies at work and their link to the intersection of the digitalization of production, specifically through the use of AI.

Faced with the emergence of this theme, in this chapter, we propose an analytical intersection between AI, dairy farming, and the politics of the senses. To do so, we will begin with a brief characterization of dairy production in Villa María, highlighting the introduction of new technologies aimed at automation and robotization. In a second section, we aim to address the conditions that make it possible to use these new technologies, namely, the politics of the senses on which these "renewed" production processes are based and expanded. Subsequently, we will revisit the previous characterizations to connect them with field notes, ethnographic observations, and in-depth interviews with workers in the sector, ATP, and professionals (veterinarians, agronomists), exploring the transformations in dairy farm work and changes in the politics of the senses. Finally, we offer some concluding remarks to continue the conversation on the subject and raise questions for future research.

DAIRY 4.0: DAIRY FARMS IN THE PROCESS OF AUTOMATION

The adoption of Information and Communication Technologies (ICTs) in the productive sphere in recent decades has given rise to the development of numerous and varied applications. These applications have been supported by their information processing capabilities, data storage, and the hyperconnectivity of telecommunications. In this context, artificial intelligence (AI) is being presented as a tool for automating tasks through a computer system that can analyze information, make decisions based on algorithms, and learn from the information it receives. Many authors agree in defining it as "the ability of a machine to perform cognitive functions that we associate with human minds, such as perceiving, reasoning, learning, interacting with the environment, problem-solving, and even exercising creativity" (Manyika et al., 2017; Estupiñan et al., 2021)[6].

In the field of agricultural production, like in all scientific disciplines and productive sectors, the advent of new technologies has led to the creation of a kind of "digital ecosystem". This ecosystem has seen a growing presence of software development, biological modelling, the use of remote sensors, land sensor systems and networks (weather stations, radars, aerial photography, soil probes), yield map analysis, aerial and satellite imagery, genomic sequence analysis, precision machinery, monitoring and automation of post-harvest processes, traceability, geographic information systems, geomatics, satellite positioning, robotization, among others (Bosch, 2013).

This process, where technologies converge in rural production, is defined as precision agriculture. According to the definition of the International Society of Precision Agriculture (ISPA), precision agriculture is a management strategy that collects, processes, and analyses temporal, spatial, and individual data to support management decisions according to estimated variability, thereby improving resource efficiency, productivity, quality, profitability, and sustainability of agricultural production (ISPA, 2019 in Hernández, 2021). Another concept that refers to these transformations is that of smart agriculture, which emphasizes the implementation of artificial intelligence techniques (Brenes Carranza et al., 2020).

One argument gaining strength to justify the implementation of these technologies in agriculture relates to population growth and climate change, with food security and environmental sustainability as arguments that can optimize productive resources and generate environmental and social satisfaction. This is exemplified by the "Agricultura Intelligence (AI)" program launched in 2011 by the Argentine government, aimed at specific actions to promote the consolidation of competitive and efficient agriculture, addressing sustainability and adding value to national agricultural production through the incorporation of new technologies (Basso, 2013).

In dairy production, Automatic Milking Systems (AMS) are increasingly used because they can reduce labor costs and have the potential to collect data that will improve productivity and animal welfare through increased and improved process monitoring. Sensors and devices installed on AMS allow data to be systematically collected on environmental conditions, individual animal behavior, health, productivity and milk quality. These data sets provide an input for training AI algorithms to predict trends in these variables. In that direction, some studies highlight predictive models of high accuracy and practicality for more efficient and "beneficial" (in terms of animal welfare) management in AMS (Ji et al, 2022). In this context, AI is introduced as a tool to facilitate decision-making in circumstances of uncertainty where information is essential for increasing productivity and economic indices. Among the improvements provided by technology, financial planning, animal management optimization, and energy savings in establishments stand out (Perdigón Llanes and González Benítez, 2021). Thus, we understand that digital technologies are a "common thread" between mechanization, robotization and AI processes:

The first trend is the quantity, frequency, and heterogeneity of data that are routinely collected in dairy farms, such as by precision dairy technologies and genomic testing. Precision dairy technology is the real-time monitoring of animals through behavior monitoring, milk constituents, milk yield, video analysis, record analysis, and physiological monitoring (Eckelkamp, 2019). A common goal is to detect disease estrus or both. A second trend is advances in AI theory and techniques, such as in decision trees and convoluted neural networks, that may be used for a variety of problems, such as visual recognition, speech recognition, and natural language processing (Pugliese et al., 2021). A third trend is the growth in online and edge computing power that make the timely execution of advanced AI algorithms feasible (Shalf, 2020)." (De Vries et al., 2022. p. 15)

One of the regions where dairy farming drives these transformations is the Villa Maria region (Cordoba, Argentina), which is productively defined as the Villa Maria Dairy Basin, a division that includes departments in the central and southeast of the province (Image 1). According to data from the Dairy Producers Registry (RPL) of the Ministry of Agriculture and Livestock of the province of Cordoba, conducted in 2018, the Villa Maria Basin has 995 dairy farms[7]. The basin produces over 3.8 million litres of milk daily and is the second most productive in the province. Its production volume represents 16% of the total national production, making it a region of significant importance for the industry[8].

In recent decades, the Villa Maria Basin has witnessed substantial changes through technological transformation in the dairy sector. The primary milestone in this aspect is the so-called "milking revolution" (1960-2010), a concept that refers to the shift from manual to mechanical milking, made possible by the introduction of milking cups on the teats (automatic suction devices powered by vacuum pumps). The "milking revolution" was studied by Sebastián Cominiello (2011; 2016), who documented the transition from the "Simple Cooperation Phase to the Large Industry Phase" through the implementation of mechanical milking. Additionally, Germán Quaranta (2000) addressed the transformations in the dairy complex of the Pampas region during the period referred to as the milking revolution. His research focused on the relationship between the restructuring of dairy production in the humid Pampa region of Buenos Aires and labor organization, taking into account variables such as technology, production scale, and social work organization. Although research has explored the world of work and productive transformations in the dairy industry, there remains a theoretical gap in addressing the changes brought about by the digitization of work on dairy farms.

Currently, dairy production is being influenced by the expansion of digitization, forming the foundation of what we might tentatively define as "Dairy 4.0." In pursuit of greater efficiency and productivity, the dairy industry envisions an expansion of the market for robotic dairy farms through AMS. This phenomenon would be accompanied by a massive reduction in traditional dairy farms due to increased

Figure 1. Dairy basins of Córdoba (IERAL of Fundación Mediterránea based on INTA, SENASA, and the Department of Dairy of the Province of Córdoba)

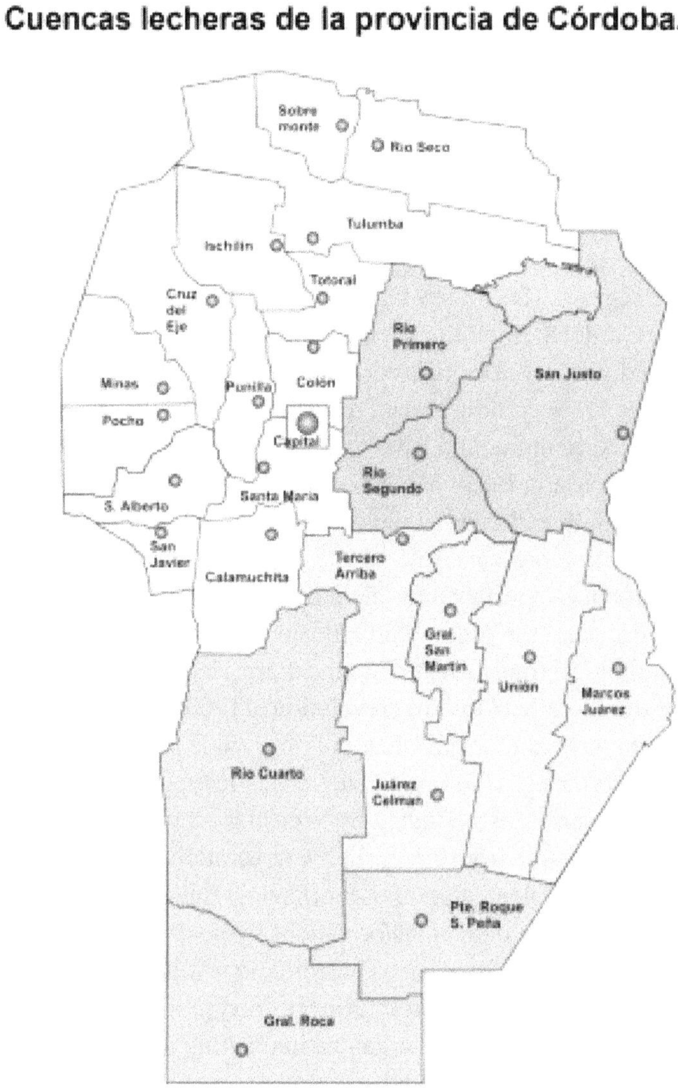

competition and growing quality and animal welfare requirements (Bear and Holloway, 2019). In this context, AI is deployed in Digital Agriculture, integrating sensory data, digital tools, and technologies (big data, sensor technologies, sensor networks, remote sensing, robotics, unmanned aerial vehicles, etc.) from dairy farms to end consumers (Fuentes, et al., 2020). Through the AMS system, cows are no longer milked by workers; instead, they enter a milking parlor "voluntarily," where a computer-controlled robotic arm extracts milk without direct human assistance. Thus, the robotic milking system emerges under the principles of animal welfare, increased quality, and increased milking frequency.

AMS originated in the 1980s in Germany, by Professor and agronomical engineer specializing in dairies, Karl Rabold, at the University of Hohenheim (Semensato, 2022). In Argentina, the first experience with this milking system occurred in 2015 in Rafaela (province of Santa Fe) through an agreement between the company DeLaval S.A. and the National Institute of Agricultural Technology (INTA). The installation process of this production system has been progressively expanding in the region. Nevertheless, it still holds a minority position in the country's total milk production volume[9].

Despite having been in the market for over 30 years, its recent and growing implementation in Argentina is linked to the progressive use of the internet, the installation of devices and software responsible for real-time data harvesting and processing, the use of magnetic collars and smart ear tags, robotic mixers, food-pushing robots, pregnancy buttons, among other developments that create a conducive environment for AI advancement in milk production. This allows for the collection and analysis of a significant amount of information to identify behavioral patterns for herd health diagnosis and optimize milk production and quality.

Some significant milestones marking this expansion include the implementation of CattleEye. This software utilizes a monitoring system that uses video images captured by a camera on the dairy farm. Through AI recognition processes, it is capable of identifying early signs of lameness in dairy herds (see Image 2). The AI system "relies on deep learning of each cow's behavior, which provides the user with information that can be turned into immediate actions to solve daily problems and prevent future complications" (TodoLecheria, 31/08/2023).

Also, noteworthy in this regard is the implementation of the chatbot with cows developed by the Tambero.com platform. The application involves the development of a messaging system used through smartphones that, through the use of AI, identifies the situation of each cow by connecting to the chat platform to communicate with the caretaker. The person using the application receives alerts and recommendations to improve productivity (Clarín, 15/11/2016). As part of this robotic landscape that paints the picture of dairy farms, Luis-Felipe Gutiérrez (2011) detailed the benefits of the application of the "electronic nose," defined as an instrument that imitates the sense of smell using an array of partially specific electrochemical sensors and a data recognition system.[10] This instrument is responsible for detecting and discriminating odors from samples, "mimicking" the sense of smell of dairy farmers, which would, for example, allow for the quick detection of mastitis in cows[11].

Figure 2. Standard security camera capture mounted at the exit of the milking parlour

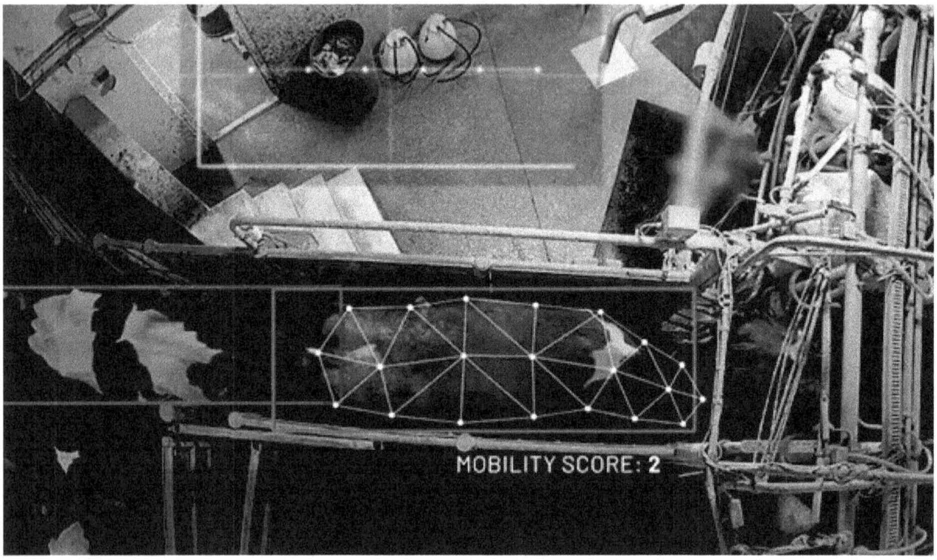

The impact of artificial intelligence on productive activities is being accompanied by a narrative of improved profitability, productivity, data management, and better decision-making. However, what is happening in the social fabric that is taking shape in the midst of these productive revolutions? In particular, the emergence of AI in the dairy industry presents a challenge for the social sciences, such as investigating the relationship between structural changes in the sector and the experiences of the workers who are at the forefront of this transformation of work.

In this regard, we recognize the possibility of approaching this from a perspective that pays attention to "social sensibilities." These can be understood as the frameworks that support the advent of the digital in the reconfiguration of the cognitive networks that link the mechanisms of power to adapt bodies-at-work, technology, and modes of emotional management, constituting the necessary conditions for social reproduction. Therefore, in the following section, we will explore the concept of these digital sensibilities as a possible condition for the digitization of work.

DIGITAL SENSIBILITIES IN DAIRY PRODUCTION

In this section, we aim to address the conditions and policies of sensibilities upon which these "renewed" productive processes, enabling the adoption of new technologies in dairy farming, are based and expanding, and how they are impacting the lives of the people who work in this sector. Sensibilities policies shape the "frameworks of action, disposition, and cognition" through which individuals establish ways to signify and value social relationships (Scribano, 2012; Scribano and Lisdero, 2019). "Sensibilities policies are understood as the set of cognitive-affective social practices aimed at the production, management, and reproduction of horizons of action, disposition, and cognition" (Scribano and D'hers, 2018, p. 12). These sensibilities imply the organization of everyday life; the information that orders the values and preferences of the agents; and the parameters they establish for the management of time and space.

It is through these sensibilities that frameworks for action, disposition, and cognition are developed, forming a compass for locating bodies in the space of social reproduction. It is through the body that we understand and experience the social and cultural context. This constitutes the preferred locus of energetic exploitation, becoming an object of capital accumulation, which subordinates it as a "center of expropriation," first of an organic nature, and then of a bodily nature as a "locus" insubstantial for possible subjectivities (Scribano, 2012, p. 99). These possible subjectivities and the organic mediation of the body in work processes are being traversed by this era marked by a shift towards the massive use of the internet and the digital, which operates as the "logic" of human action. In this mediation between digitization and bodies, whether organic or subjective, the ways we see, smell, and feel are being transformed, supported by digital sensibilities. Therefore, dairy farms are not an "exception."

Various groups of milk producers are demanding greater data management in the shortest possible time, with the purpose of improving the profitability rates of the productive activity. Production, management, and data analysis have become the conditions for existence in the 21st century. Some accounts from producers suggest that were it not for robotization, they would not have continued working in the sector.

"Sooner or later, if a producer has doubts, they will automate with robots. I believe that everything is heading in that direction today... Three years ago, if my father hadn't installed the robot, you might not have seen me on the farm... I would have done something else... I'm a biochemist, and I know very little about cows, quite little about cows, but well... It never interested me, and then when they started with all this..." (Automated dairy farm producer, 22/06/2021)

"I believe that the generations today don't have to go and milk the cows at 2:00 AM and stay until 5:00 AM... to me, that's a thing of the past... I'm very futuristic in that sense. It's done. We have to maintain it because we need to continue milking more animals and producing more milk. But I believe the company sees it as a project." (Automated dairy farm producer, 22/06/2021)

In dairy production, these policies of sensibilities are in a latent state of attention to the management of 'the digital' as the mediation of practices. From this foundation, they begin to manage the ways to position the body in work, time-space management, and the social preferences and values at play. To illustrate some specific aspects of this transformation in the dairy context, it is common to hear in business circles within the dairy industry the comparative advantages that the use of robots will bring in terms of reducing 'labor' (field note, 22/09/21). Moreover, the notions of 'user-friendliness' and 'reliability' of digital systems for business and personnel management in dairy farms are gaining prominence.

These elements are introduced as fetishes that bestow a particular power and enchantment upon 'things,' while, in the meantime, there is a 'commodification' of social relationships that determines their potential applications. In terms of 'sensibilities,' certain social processes are starting to become mythicized as digitization and robotics form the foundations upon which problematic aspects of business management rest. This spirit of capital takes on a distinct form, making technology in general a condition for confronting future challenges. We can approach the object in question by exploring its uses and meanings from certain 'digital sensibilities.' These are how people begin to weave together social-affective-cognitive practices and from which they construct actions, interactions, resources, and meanings. It is the way through which digitization becomes embodied in everyday life, particularly for work, breaking certain boundaries between the 'work-related' and the 'every day' (Lisdero, 2021; Zukerfeld, 2020; Palermo, et al., 2020).

Another aspect to consider in this direction is that the robotization of milking requires robust and reliable equipment (both in terms of hardware and software). Faced with an unforeseen technological failure, it is unlikely that human labor can cover for the robots in the milking process (this depends on the correlation between humans and robots, assuming the former are skilled in manual milking). In addition to its impact on labor, such a contingency would affect the 'animal welfare' (the physical condition of the cows) and the economic viability of the production unit (resulting in income loss and unforeseen expenses). In this context, the introduction of AI models in the production processes would enable predictions of breakdowns and failures, leading to preventive-proactive actions by professionals and ATP (Dara, Hazrati, and Kaur, 2022). Increasing the utilization rate of equipment and robots, extending the lifespan of each device, and other considerations are among the immediate areas of action for the development of AI models in 'dairy 4.0.

As a result, the conditions of use and agreements regarding data usage (the possibility of failures, vulnerability to cyberattacks, etc.) become central in commercial relationships and the responsibilities undertaken between the ATP and the producers (and their workers)[12]. In general terms, to support and deepen the aforementioned transformations, new policies are needed that link state policies (including the scientific and university sector) and business strategies to provide reliability to these systems (fairness, transparency, accountability, sustainability, privacy, and robustness) and expand agricultural infrastructure, R&D projects, and educational offerings for farmers and farm workers (Dara, Hazrati, and Kaur, 2022). In this direction, owner-producers are pressured to assume new requirements, risks, and responsibilities as the "primary stakeholders" and end users of AI technologies:

Farmers can keep themselves up to date about AI technologies that are being used at their farms and how they operate. They should review the data and terms of use agreements carefully to understand what data is collected from their farm, with whom their data is shared, and how accountability is integrated into agreement and management. They should also inquire from ATP whether an AI model is embedded in their machines, what data the AI system uses, and what indicators/factors are extracted from the data by the AI system. Farmers should secure their machines from unauthorized access and use, and physically secure them when they are not in use. They should demand transparency regarding data use and their rights to data access and portability. (Dara, Hazrati y Kaur, 2022: 9)

Thinking and acting in "Society 4.0" is transforming the ways of organizing work, which can be linked to digital sensibilities that enable individuals to be and act in their daily lives. This way of situating oneself in time and space occurs within a context of contradictions and coexistence with previous labor organization models like "Taylorism," "Fordism," and "Toyotism" (Antunes, 2006; Palermo, et al., 2020)[13]. Changes in policies of sensibilities in the context of "Society 4.0" refer to the reconfiguration of cognitive frameworks that function for the management of socially established corporeal-energetic availabilities. It is here that a profound transformation of the "world of work" takes place in dairy production, where the "policies of the senses" are a part of this sector's metamorphosis[14].

Addressing the use and valorization of the body and emotions, specific mechanisms are being developed to shape certain "policies of the senses" (Scribano, 2017). In this narrative, the mechanisms of power are intertwined to adapt bodies-in-labour, technology, and emotional management methods, constituting the necessary conditions for social reproduction. Thus, the place of bodies as a material substrate of the capitalist valorization and accumulation regime becomes evident, where the consumption of vital/social energies progresses following the predatory logic of capital, further fueled by digitization, colonizing hitherto unexplored times and spaces. With this purpose in mind, we will explore in the next section the connection between the stories of those experiencing the aforementioned metamorphosis through digitization in the context of dairy production. The narratives of those who work allow us to reconstruct the "policies of the senses" within the framework of "digital dairying."

TESTIMONIES OF POLITICS OF SENSE

The application of digital and analogue technologies is turning AI into a pivotal element in the primary production process, disrupting the organisational process of work in dairy farms and giving rise to a series of phenomena related to how the social order of the actors involved in the sector is produced and reproduced.

As part of this "metamorphosis of work," we can identify that the tasks performed by workers are being transformed concerning a new "politics of the senses." In this direction, the digitization of work involves a revaluation of the sense of sight on the farm, articulating the organic use of the eye and the sense of the social regime of sight ("what to see"). For example, the use of cameras, smartphones, and screens as part of digital systems constitutes the mediation between people and their understanding of the world, the social availabilities of time and space, and forms of communication, among others.

Another transformation in dairy farms can be summarized in the role played by the "calloused hands" of dairy farmers who have carried out their tasks in traditional formats where milking was mechanical and required their presence for hygiene, stimulation, and the placement of "teacups" on the udders of the animals. Faced with the new "politics of touch" (Scribano and Lisdero, 2019), the more delicate pressure techniques on the teats (characteristic of the almost extinct manual milking) are transformed into renewed actions of pressure from the thumbs on the screens, influencing the formation of a specific way of seeing and touching the world.

It's a change for me; in fact, I hadn't even seen in university that there was a robot where the cow would go and milk itself. I hadn't seen that. I learned about it here, in this company when the decision was made, and I started watching videos. I made that trip, and the truth is when they told me about it, that the cow goes by itself to be milked... and yes, it's a complete change in management. The guys don't come to milk; they come to do other things. They come to pay more attention to the robot, to the cleanliness, to ensure the robot doesn't fail, and so on, rather than milking like the other group that's in the dairy. (Veterinarian from an automated dairy farm, 22/06/2021)

In the previous account from the veterinarian of an automated dairy farm, he explains these changes that have occurred in the workforce, where workers are no longer required to milk the cows but instead "come to do something else." The senses, understood as perceptions shaped by the social context in which they are embedded, are strategies that guide the bodily energies deployed in work processes. In this context, the establishment of digital logic in dairy farming represents the development of new conditions for exploitation, revaluing aspects focused on the use of sight and touch. Complemented by the accounts of operators, there are evaluations related to pressing screens, and remotely operating robots for milking, where these work skills are based on the interaction between real and virtual worlds. Robots, machines, cell phones, tablets, the internet, and screens mediate the actions of dairy farming, becoming new extensions of the body, which implies a new regime for expressing, observing, and touching the physical/emotional state of each cow and the entire herd, based on reports produced by software and displayed on screens. In this digitized rural environment, a new landscape is formed, marked by the power of bodily/cognitive organization and mediated by the use of ICTs.

As mentioned earlier, one of the factors that redefine the politics of the senses in play in the organization of work on automated dairy farms is time. In this sense, the presence of AI monitoring and controlling the production process allows for a reconfiguration of the times when workers are required on the premises. This provides greater control over this variable, giving rise to the notion in this environment that technology "enamours." However, the testimonies overlook the implications of the flexibility made possible by technological mediation, while also delving into the concept of what we could define as a "digital presence," which involves the requirement to be alert to the assistance requests issued by the devices in case of potential failures or errors.

With the implementation of technology, you can manage those schedules, so maybe you can, I don't know, not go during that night, and the cows will continue to be milked as usual, and you can manage the schedules differently. In other words, you stop being a slave, to put it bluntly, to the dairy's schedules in order to make that type of task more flexible. So when the worker sees that, observes that they fall in love with the technology. (Representative from a technology equipment supplier, 28/12/2020)

In this way, based on the possibilities generated by technological development, we can observe a reconfiguration of the energies that underpin robotic systems for the productive valorization process, with the emerging requirement of constant alertness and surveillance that goes beyond the time and space in which dairy workers follow the established routine on the farm.

Then you grab your phone, and it says, 'An alarm has gone off in Astronaut 1'... you enter the code to deactivate it. On the screen, you have to enter four zeros, and that's how it gets deactivated...and you have to come as quickly as possible because the robot goes out of service, and if you take too long to come, then you have more searching to do. (Worker in an automated dairy farm, 21/06/2021)

The arrival of automation technologies in dairy farms is presented by companies as the necessary "extra" to modernize the work activity, characterized by mechanical milking, and even more so in the manual milking stage, as an activity that requires a lot of physical effort from the workers. A worker's day was structured with two milking sessions, typically carried out at 2:00 AM and between 11:00 AM and 3:00 PM. The meaning of the dairy worker's job is changing. The idea of the operator who "comes to do something else" to "be more focused on the robot" and become independent, to "stop being a slave," accompanies the illusion of digitized work as a task detached from its materiality.

In contrast, this reconfiguration of the energy resources of live labor is being appropriated for the maintenance of machines in a process of "objectification" of labor as an annex to capital. As if suddenly the entire factory could function with just the "accompaniment" of the worker. This idea of the machine "liberating" the worker from "rough," "physical," "tough," and "exhausting" work is juxtaposed with the testimonies of workers who report having left their break time to return to work "outside" of working hours after receiving warning signals from the robot on their smartphones. With the advancement of the screen-mediated world, the sense of touch and sight is reconfigured in "Society 4.0," directly impacting the tension between the start and end of the workday. The work that was presented as a "time organizer" for the worker also requires a state of permanent alertness to address the robot's needs, transforming the identity of dairy work in the dairy industry 4.0. This is where everyday practices, permeated by these digital sensibilities, organize time and space and shape the valuation of the disposition of bodily energies for their use.

Another aspect that is gaining importance in the metamorphosis related to monitoring the health variables of cows and the reorientation of the allocation of labor forces is the concept of "animal welfare." The installation of robots and "automatic milking" is partly justified by the benefits it brings in terms of not disturbing the cows with the presence of the dairy worker on the farm. This emotional care for the animals implies an increase in productivity, which has grown in automated systems, increasing the number of milkings per day from 2 to 3 times. This entails the installation of cameras that observe the barn, monitoring both human and non-human behavior.

The idea behind this is to disturb the cows as little as possible and have them be alone because initially when we started, we installed cameras and checked to see how much we were disturbing the cows. We realized that if we bother them a lot or if many people are moving around, they go away and take about two hours to return to the robot. (Automated dairy farm producer, 21/06/2021)

The processes of emotionalization of interactions converge towards a sense of surveillance and spatial aesthetics to maximize productivity to increase profit margins. Humans become "bothersome," serving as the basis for activating direct control mechanisms, such as reviewing cameras to observe what workers are doing and how they interact with the animals. The installation of the digital eye becomes a part of everyday life because the "politics of gaze" have changed, and the existence of a camera that monitors actions is no longer considered "extraordinary." This leads to an internalization among the individuals in the dairy farm as if it had always been this way. Furthermore, surveillance involves rewarding good dairy workers, those who fulfil their assigned tasks, and issuing warnings and penalties for non-compliance, thereby introducing the platforming of work, scoring logic, and digitization (Zukerfeld, 2020; Palermo, et al., 2020).

CONCLUSION

By way of closing this first approach to the dairy farms of Villa María from the processes of automation, robotization and AI, we can reflect on some questions in terms of the politics of the senses. Thus, first of all, we emphasize that the new digital technologies incorporated in agri-food production, enhanced by the internet, computers and smartphones, configure a new "digital ecosystem" that transforms the landscape of dairy production and the organization of work in the Villa María Dairy Basin. In this sense, the automation-robotization of milking and the new productive-labor requirements are key elements of the "milking revolution" underway.

Reviewing the experiences of the first dairy farms that implemented automated milking systems, it is evident that new technologies are transforming labour, in general, rather than "replacing" labor (even if there is "liberation" or displacement of some tasks to robots or specific software). These ongoing transformations redirect the focus of bodily and emotional energies from milking to a more complex and flexible diversification of tasks. In this connection, new technologies are explanatory of current practices and processes, where workers appear subordinated to machines and devices that play a central role in the re-organization of production. In this direction, the protagonist "voices" interpret these processes as part of an "unavoidable" future.

In this context, AI in dairy farms diverges from the narrative put forth by companies that claim to control production times to provide humane working hours. Instead, dynamics are reorganizing to extend productive time, making digitalization an effective driver for the conquest of previously neglected time and space. The digitalization of work has reached dairy farms, redefining the needs of capital and positioning workers as an "annexe" to the robot. Simultaneously, it reconfigures physical demands, which do not disappear but are transformed, and this has been understood through changes in the "politics of the senses." According to professionals and dairy farm owners, workers in the sector are not in the field to milk or be with the cows, but to perform other tasks, such as caring for, maintaining and assisting robots and machines.

"Society 4.0" revalues ways of looking and touching, which, through digital devices, become new extensions of the body, implying a new regime for expressing, looking, and touching the bodily/emotional state of each cow. Within this framework, new technologies become the object of infatuation of professionals, producers and workers of the sector; a phenomenon exalted by the advances in the field of AI and its (still) incipient introduction in dairy regions such as those of Villa María.In this sense, technology allows for the construction of fantasies in which, through "user-friendliness" and "well-being," "free" time is made possible for the workforce. However, through the normalization of the use of digital devices, smartphones, screens, and cameras everywhere, the politics of sensibilities that are transforming work practices are disguised, increasingly blurring the distinction between working time and leisure time.

Finally, we can consider that the social sensibilities alluded to are supported by surveillance and control mechanisms, sometimes directly through cameras, but necessarily through the values that shape "things" in that context. In daily practice, these actions of reward or punishment for good dairy workers are made possible by digital sensitivity that precedes experiences and allows them to function, now under the platformization of work. Therefore, under the spectrum of the digital and the impact of AI, it is a challenge for the social sciences to reconstruct the networks of relationships that elaborate the mechanisms of interaction and sociability as products of human social practices, distinguishing them from the ontological "power" attributed to the development of productive forces.

REFERENCES

Antunes, R. (2020). What is the future of work in the digital age? *Latin American and Caribbean Observatory*, *4*(1), 12–22.

Basso, L. R. (2013). *Smart Agriculture: Argentina's Initiative for Sustainability in Food and Energy Production*. Academic Press.

Batthyány, K., & Cabrera, M. (2011). *Metodología de la investigación en Ciencias Sociales. Apuntes para un curso inicial. Departamento de Publicaciones, Unidad de Comunicación de la Universidad de la República*. UCUR.

Bear, C., & Holloway, L. (2019). Beyond resistance: Geographies of divergent more-than-human conduct in robotic milking. *Geoforum, 104*, 212–221. doi:10.1016/j.geoforum.2019.04.030

Bosch, M. (2013). *Reflections on Emerging Technologies in Agriculture*. Academic Press.

Brenes Carranza, J. A., Martínez Porras, A., Quesada López, C. U., & Jenkins Coronas, M. (2020). *Decision support systems using artificial intelligence in precision agriculture*. Academic Press.

Clarín. (2016). *An app for managing dairy farms from your mobile*. https://www.clarin.com/rural/aplicacion-gestionar-tambo-celular_0_r1gC45QWx.html

Cominiello, S. (2011). A century of arduous work: Work processes on Argentine dairy farms, 1900-2010. Gino Germani Institute of Research, Faculty of Social Sciences, UBA, Buenos Aires.

Cominiello, S. N. (2016). *The milking revolution: Changes in the work process of primary milk production in Argentina, 1980-2007*. Academic Press.

Corbellini, C. (2002). *Bovine mastitis and its impact on milk quality*. Institute of Agricultural Technology, Dairy Project, EEA INTA Pergamino.

Dara, R., Hazrati, S. M., & Kaur, J. (2022). Recommendations for ethical and responsible use of artificial intelligence in digital agriculture. *Frontiers in Artificial Intelligence, 5*, 884192. Advance online publication. doi:10.3389/frai.2022.884192 PMID:35968036

De la Garza Toledo, E. (2011). Más allá de la fábrica: los desafíos teóricos del trabajo no clásico y la producción inmaterial. *Nueva Sociedad, 232*.

Eloundou, T., Manning, S., Mishkin, P., & Rock, D. (2023). *GPTs are GPTs: An Early Look at the Labor Market Impact Potential of Large Language Models*. Working Paper, arXiv:2303.10130v4.

Estupiñán Ricardo, J., Leyva Vázquez, M. Y., Peñafiel Palacios, A. J., & El Assafiri Ojeda, Y. (2021). Artificial intelligence and intellectual property. *University and Society Journal, 13*(S3), 362–368.

Fuentes, S., Gonzalez Viejo, C., Cullen, B., Togson, E., Chauhan, S., & Dunshea, F. (2020). Artificial Intelligence Applied to a Robotic Dairy Farm to Model Milk Productivity and Quality Based on Cow Data and Daily Environmental Parameters. *Sensors (Basel), 20*(10), 2975. doi:10.339020102975 PMID:32456339

Gutiérrez, L. F. (2011). Evaluation of dairy product quality using an electronic nose. Latin American Archives of Nutrition, 61(2).

Haugeland, J. (1985). *Artificial Intelligence: The Very Idea.* Academic Press.

Hernández, R. R. (2021). Precision agriculture: A current necessity. *Agricultural Engineering Journal, 11*(1).

Ji, B., Banhazi, T., Phillips, C. J. C., Wang, C., & Li, B. (2022). A machine learning framework to predict the next month's daily milking frequency for cows in robotic dairy farm. *Biosystems Engineering, 216*, 186–197. doi:10.1016/j.biosystemseng.2022.02.013

Luger, G., & Stubblefield, W. (1993). *AI: Structures and strategies for complex problem solving.* Academic Press.

Manyika, J., Chui, M., Miremadi, M., Bughin, J., George, K., Willmott, P., & Dewhurst, M. (2017). *A future that works: Automation, employment, and productivity.* McKinsey Global Institute.

Neffen, G. (2016). *An app for managing dairy farms from your mobile.* Clarín. https://www.clarin.com/rural/aplicacion-gestionar-tambo-celular_0_r1gC45QWx.html

Palermo, H., Radetich, N., Reygadas, L. (2020). Work mediated by digital technologies: meanings of work, new forms of control, and cyborg workers. *Latin American Journal of Labor Anthropology, 7.*

Perdigón Llanes, R., & González Benítez, N. (2021). Comparison and selection of artificial intelligence techniques for forecasting bovine milk production. *Cuban Journal of Computer Science, 15*(2), 24–43.

Quaranta, G. (2000). Production restructuring and functional flexibility of agricultural work in Argentina. *Latin American Journal of Labor Studies, 6*(12), 45–70.

Rotz, S., Duncan, E., Small, M., Botschner, J., Dara, R., Mosby, I., Reed, M., & Fraser, E. (2019). The Politics of Digital Agricultural Technologies: A Preliminary Review. *Sociologia Ruralis, 59*(2), 203–229. doi:10.1111oru.12233

Rouhiainen, L. (2018). *Artificial Intelligence.* Alienta Editorial.

Sautu, R. (2005). *Manual de metodología: construcción del marco teórico, formulación de los objetivos y elección de la metodología.* Consejo Latinoamericano de Ciencias Sociales, CLACSO.

Schalkoff, R. J. (1990). *Artificial intelligence engine.* McGraw-Hill, Inc.

Scribano, A. (2012). Sociology of Bodies/Emotions. *Latin American Journal of Studies on Bodies, Emotions, and Society, 4*(10), 91–111.

Scribano, A., & Lisdero, P. (Eds.). (2019). *Digital Labor, Society, and the Politics of Sensibilities.* Palgrave Macmillan. doi:10.1007/978-3-030-12306-2

Scribano, A. O. (2007). *El proceso de investigación social cualitativo.* Ed. Prometeo.

Semensato, C. S. D. S. (2022). *The use of robotics in dairy cattle management in the Taquari Valley.* Academic Press.

Smith, M. J. (2018). Getting value from artificial intelligence in agriculture. *Animal Production Science, 60*(1), 46–54. doi:10.1071/AN18522

Todo Lechería. (2022). *By the end of 2023, there will be around 300 milking robots in Argentina.* https://www.todolecheria.com.ar/a-fines-de-2023-habra-unos-300-robots-ordenando-en-argentina/

Todo Lechería. (2023). *Artificial intelligence applied to detect lame cows.* https://www.todolecheria.com.ar/aplican-inteligencia-artificial-para-detectar-vacas-rengas/

Zukerfeld, M. (2020). Bits, plataformas y autómatas. Las tendencias del trabajo en el capitalismo informacional. *Revista Latinoamericana de Antropología del Trabajo*, (7).

ADDITIONAL READING

Addanki, M., Patra, P., & Kandra, P. (2022). Recent advances and applications of artificial intelligence and related technologies in the food industry. *Applied Food Research, 2*(2), 1–11. doi:10.1016/j.afres.2022.100126

Pellón Ferreyra, I., & del Corro, T. (2023). (in press). Trabajo y digitalización: El "bienestar animal" desde tambos 4.0 de la cuenca Villa María. *Politikón, 6.*

Shamshiri, R. R., Weltzien, C., Hameed, I. A., Yule, I. J., Grift, T. E., & Balasundram, S. K. (2018). Research development in agricultural robotics: A perspective of digital farming. *International Journal of Agricultural and Biological Engineering, 11*, 1–14. doi:10.25165/j.ijabe.20181104.4278

KEY TERMS AND DEFINITIONS

AMS: Automatic milking system.

ATP: Agriculture technology providers.

Dairy Farm: Cow milk production unit.

ICT: Information and communication technology.

Politics of Sense: Activities in order to resolve situations, to be successful in the social presentation of the person, and develop knowledge at hand that subjects use.

Social Sensibilities: Updating emotional plots arising from accepted and acceptable forms of sensations.

ENDNOTES

1 As of the date (11/08/2023), Google Scholar provides 34,700 articles for the search term "ChatGPT."

2 "Our mission is to ensure that artificial general intelligence benefits all of humanity". https://openai.com/about

3 "Do you remember the childhood moment when you received your first pocketknife or bike? A moment where you suddenly felt that you could build anything and go everywhere. That's how our clients feel when they start working with us". (https://openresearch.com/)

4 In the final months of 2022, the shares of BuzzFeed (a company that brings together digital media with viral content) saw unprecedented increases after announcing investments in generating AI-created content and reducing its staff focused on content writing. Available at: https://observer.com/2023/01/buzzfeed-stock-more-than-doubled-following-reports-it-will-invest-in-ai-created-content/

5 "Perceptions, sensations, and emotions form a triad that allows us to understand where sensibilities originate. Social agents perceive the world through their bodies, influenced by a set of impressions that impact their ways of 'interacting' with the socio-environmental context. Thus, objects, phenomena, processes, and other agents structure perceptions, which are understood as naturalized ways of organizing the array of impressions." (Scribano, 2012, p. 100).

6 Among other authors defining AI, we can mention Rouhiainen, who describes it as "the ability of computers to perform activities that normally require human intelligence" (2018, p. 17), and Haugeland (1985), who speaks of AI as "the task of making computers think." For Schalkoff (1990), AI is "a field of study that focuses on the explanation and emulation of intelligent behavior based on computational processes." In line with this definition, Luger and Stubblefield

(1993) assert that AI is "the branch of computer science that deals with the automation of intelligent behavior".

7 These refer to the dairy production unit responsible for the extraction of liquid milk, which will then be sent to the processing stage for transformation into long-life milk or dairy products such as cheese, yoghurt, butter, cream, etc.

8 The main Cordoban region is the "Northwest," with Morteros as its geographical reference point. In this region, there are currently 1,419 dairy farms, with an estimated milk production of over 4.6 million liters per day.

9 The specialized dairy news outlet "Todo Lechería" (12/11/2022), based on a survey of companies that supply milking robots currently operating in the country, estimated that by the end of 2023, there will be a total of 301 functioning robots deployed in 60 dairy farms, representing approximately 2% of the milk production in Argentina. The company Lely has 140 robots installed or in the process of installation, followed by De Laval with 13, Gea Farm Technologies with 23, and Boumatic with 3.

10 The operation mode of the electronic nose can be generally compared to that of the human olfactory system" (Gutiérrez, L.F., 2011, p. 3)

11 Bovine mastitis is an infectious and contagious disease of the mammary gland, in which inflammation occurs in response to the invasion, through the teat canal, of various types of bacteria, mycoplasmas, fungi, yeasts, and even some viruses (Corbellini, 2002).

12 Among the main "outstanding issues" to address, we can mention two: legal transparency (practices and protocols) for the ethical use of data and digital infrastructure, and accountability (in legal and technical terms) that allows distinguishing between fair and unfair business models for the involved actors (Dara, Hazrati, and Karu, 2022).

13 The Taylorist-Fordist organizational model, characteristic of the automotive industry boom (named after the renowned American brand "Ford"), is based on the mass production of standardized goods, stripping workers of control over time and specialized knowledge, scattered across various stages of the assembly line, forcing a situation of the annexation of living labor to capital. On the other hand, Toyotaism represented a model of work organization that involved a combination of new management techniques with machinery that used fewer resources and workers, optimizing production times, streamlining the hierarchical structure, enabling synergistic work between different areas, and creating a workspace much more receptive to technological advances.

14 The "metamorphosis of work" (Antunes, 2020) refers to a process of change in the organization of the entire society, mutations in work practices that have emerged in recent decades under the forms of connection to digital rhythms that enhance the productivity of work.

Chapter 6
Life Experiences and Emotions Around Robotics in Teachers:
An Observation From Initial Education

Angelica De Sena
CONICET, Universidad Nacional de La Matanza, Argentina

Florencia Chahbenderian
https://orcid.org/0000-0001-8235-3683
CONICET, Universidad Nacional de La Matanza, Argentina

ABSTRACT

In recent decades, the use of robotic tools has expanded in various areas of work and daily life, therefore also in school at different levels, particularly at the initial level. Reviewing the use of robotics tools implies turning our gaze towards teachers. This chapter aims to understand the meaning of the use, along with the emotions and experiences by teachers, of the Blue-Bot Programmable Children's Robot, as a digital education tool at the initial level. To do this, it analyzes the particular case of kindergartens in Vicente Lopez, Buenos Aires, Argentina, based on a qualitative methodology, with the use of ethnography and Expressive Creative Encounters device (ECE). This allows understanding of the elements that operate in the robot's experience, on the one hand, tied to local contexts and, on the other, to the robot device between the analog and the virtual which combines fear, uncertainty, and anxiety.

INTRODUCTION

Society 4.0, with the deployment of Artificial Intelligence and the Internet of Things, among others, implies new ways of buying/selling, communicating, producing, and

DOI: 10.4018/979-8-3693-0802-8.ch006

searching for information, as well as new ways of connecting with the environment and with others, involving changes in temporalities and experiences. In this way, the profound transformations proposed by the 21st century impact the ways of training practising educators and the teaching/learning processes that take place in the classroom (Popova et al., 2018; Furman et al., 2020). In this sense, technological advances imply a strong massiveness and proximity to different technological devices that translate into significant advances, implying a potential redefinition of global institutions and students' interactions with them (Chang & Hung, 2019; Wu et al., 2019).

From there, understanding the pedagogical potential of robotics and Digital Technologies, and integrating them into teaching strategies has become the great challenge of current education. Its mediating function is found precisely in the fact that they modify the technological context of traditional education and frame it in a profound transformation of learning processes, with a less rigid, more exploratory character, with a more flexible distribution of work, a permanent invitation to collaboration with others, and an ideal means to experiment and reflect on the ways of learning (Badía & Monereo, 2008).

The pioneering article by J. M. Wing (2006) significantly contributes to thinking about the cognitive and educational implications of programming at an academic and institutional level. In it, computational thinking is defined as an approach to problem-solving using decomposition strategies, algorithm design, abstraction, and logical reasoning (Wing, 2006). Thus, it is detached from computer science and becomes a set of skills and competencies that anyone can develop and work on. With the advent of the integrative perspective known internationally as Science, Technology, Engineering, and Mathematics (STEM) for the integration of learning and teaching of science, technology, engineering, and mathematics, computational thinking is playing a central role in many of the international educational proposals at the initial and primary levels (Grover and Pea, 2013). Since then, at a global level in the educational community, the use of Robots and block programming has been proliferating, adapted to the first school ages, as a way for research and educational innovation (Department for Education, 2013; FECYT et al., 2016; Benton et al., 2017; Leidl et al., 2017; Sáez & Cózar, 2017; Sullivan & Bers, 2016; Sullivan et al., 2017).

That said, this chapter aims to expose the results of the first stage of research on Digital Education, Programming, and Robotics at the Initial Level, based on the study of the incorporation of the Blue-Bot Programmable Children's Robot (Robot) in three Kindergartens of Vicente Lopez, in the Province of Buenos Aires, Argentina, to understand the meaning of its use, together with the emotions and experiences that it involves among the teachers. Based on the relevance of using the various robotics tools at the Initial Level, this writing aims to identify the experiences and emotions of the teaching teams of said kindergartens linked to implementing the robot. Following De Sena and Scribano (2020), we consider how bodies/emotions are experienced[1] do not constitute internal, individual, and isolated states; instead, they result from interaction with others in specific contexts. What we know about the world we know by and through our bodies; what we do is what we see, and what we see is how we divide the world. For this reason, emotions intrinsically linked to bodies are part of a plot between impressions, sensations, and perceptions that constitute a tripod that allows us to understand where sensibilities are based (Scribano, 2017). Following the author, it is pertinent to identify, classify, and make critical the interplay between sensations, perceptions, and emotions to understand the mechanisms for regulating sensations and the social bearability mechanisms that capital provides as one of its contemporary features for social domination.

The proposed approach is based on a qualitative design to understand the robot's appropriation by teachers and the implementation of said device in the classroom. To do this, two types of social inquiry strategies were used, understanding that both would allow us to capture emotions and experiences from understanding the "micro" in "macro" contexts, in the interplay of the individual and the social.

On the one hand, we use the technique of ethnography (Zanatta Crestani & Colognese, 2023), which consists of "...a work method that directly describes the multiple ways of life of human beings, through observation, participation, and comprehensive description of what people do, how they behave and how they interact with each other" (Etchevers Goijberg, 2005, p. 1). Understood as a multi-method approach (De Sena, 2015), it combines various techniques, in this case, using non-participant observation in the classrooms and open or informal interviews with teachers and directors.

On the other hand, we held an Expressive Creative Encounter (Scribano, 2022) with the teaching teams involved to investigate the emotions and experiences linked to implementing the Robot. The Expressive Creative Encounters (ECE) strategy in social research requires the construction of an experience that fosters, in the subjects who participate in the investigation, the conditions, setting, and context for expression and creativity (Scribano, 2022). There, connections are observed between individual sensibilities, the biographical marks that emerge in the development of the experience, and the group experience. The group that carries out the experience is a construction of the research team, made up of those members of the teaching team involved with the design and implementation of the Robot in the Initial Level classrooms.

From this plot of inquiry devices, we were able to reconstruct some of the main experiences and emotions that emerge in the Initial Level classrooms by the teaching teams that use them. This is of nodal importance to deepen research in education mediated by robotics and Digital Technology and provide clues on how future relationships with them are being built.

Next, the chapter is organized into three sections. Firstly, some basic notions are introduced about the connections between robotics, education, and emotions in Vicente Lopez. Then, the experiences and emotions around the Robot in the Initial Level rooms are investigated, and, thirdly, some final reflections are outlined.

ROBOTICS, EDUCATION, AND EMOTIONS

The technological advances that have been deployed at a rapid pace in recent years, imply a strong massiveness and proximity to different technological devices, such as robots, which translate into significant advances (although still to be explored) in educational research, theory, and practice, as well as in the emotions involved (Breazeal & Brooks, 2005; Minsky, 2007; World Economic Forum, 2015; OECD, 2018; Ge et al., 2019), implying a potential redefinition of students' interactions with them (Chang & Hung, 2019; Wu et al., 2019). In this way, the profound transformations proposed by the 21st Century impact the ways of training practising educators and the teaching/learning processes involved in classrooms (Popova et al., 2018; Furman et al., 2020; Bell & Gifford, 2023; Virtual Robot Curriculum, 2023).

Throughout history, human beings have developed tools to facilitate and optimize physical and mental work, which have been decisive for human evolution, as well as for their historical and cultural development (Engels, 1895). The tool, therefore, has transformed the way of understanding human activity, work, and self-projection. The extension of intelligence through instruments has made it possible to consider cognitive tools as amplifiers (Rheingold, 1985) and reorganizers of the human mind (Pea, 1985). Emotions, which can also be understood as emotional intelligence (Goleman, 1996), are a founding element in intelligence; hence the importance of knowing its mechanisms and application to educational robotics (Breazeal & Brooks, 2005; Hieida & Nagai, 2022).

In robotics teaching-learning experiences, children have a leading role as co-constructors of knowledge, not as passive recipients or as mere technology consumers (Jung & Won, 2018). The presence of Information and Communication Technology (ICT) in education requires the establishment of standards for its optimization in learning areas. The *National Educational Technology Standards* of the International Society for Technology in Education (ISTE), propose six standards or references: 1) Creativity and innovation, 2) Communication and collaboration, 3) Research and fluid management of information, 4) Critical thinking, problem solving and decision making, 5) Digital citizenship, and 6) Theoretical concepts and operation of technology. These allow lines of action to be outlined according to the specific educational context, through a process of diagnosis and adaptation (Gómez, 2018). Now, interest in the use of robots in schools has been increasing since Seymour Papert presented the LOGO programming language and its famous turtle in the 60s of the 20th century (Figure 1).

Educational robotics, initially focused on developing technical programming knowledge (Barker & Ansorge, 2007), progressively transformed into an innovative approach for the classroom, in which technological environments are conceived as a teaching-learning context (Jung & Won, 2018). In this new approach, these environments allow the development and acquisition of skills, not only referring to technical fields but also other areas, from mathematics, language, or music (Mubin et al., 2013; Management Association, 2022), to emotional competencies (Breazeal & Brooks, 2005). Thus, it is possible to identify three learning paradigms related to educational robotics: i) *learning robotics*, where students use robots as a platform to learn engineering knowledge (related to mechanics, electronics, or programming); ii) *learning with robotics*, when robots are used as support in the learning process; and iii) *learning by robotics*, when students learn content and skills from different disciplines while developing transversal skills through robotics (Gaudiello & Zibetti, 2016). In this last approach, also known as *robotic-based instruction*, the robot acts as an active intermediary tool between the student, teacher, and school subject (Diago et al., 2018).

According to Wing (2006), computational thinking is defined as an approach to problem-solving through the use of decomposition strategies, algorithm design, abstraction, and logical reasoning. With the arrival of the integrative perspective known internationally as STEM, computational thinking begins to play a central

Figure 1. The Blue-Bot Robot and the LOGO Turtle

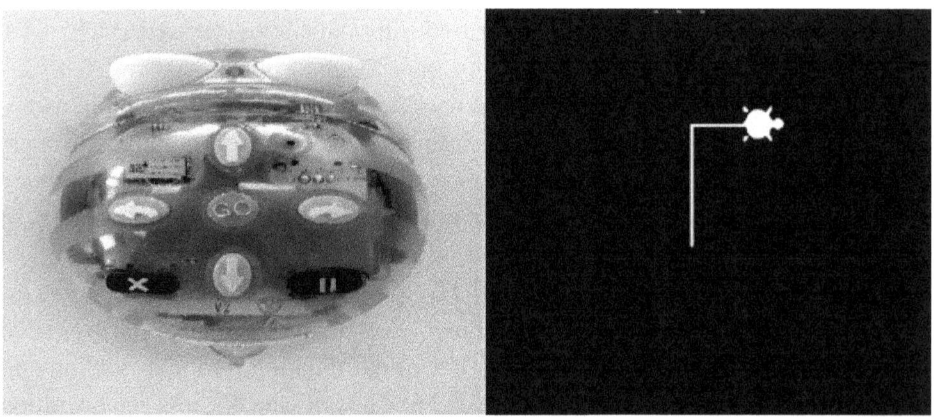

role in many of the international educational proposals at the Initial Level (Grover & Pea, 2013; Papadakis & Kalogiannakis, 2021; Fregnan, Pinto & Scarlatti, 2022). Since then, the use of robots and block programming, adapted to early school ages, as a way for educational research and innovation has proliferated in the international educational community (Pivetti et al., 2020; Department for Education, 2013; FECYT et al., 2016; Benton et al., 2017; Leidl et al., 2017; Sáez & Cózar, 2017; Sullivan & Bers, 2016; Sullivan et al., 2017; Papadakis & Kalogiannakis, 2021).

Following Johnson (2003, p. 16), "To be useful, the energy released by robotics must be sustained and universal, and the means of exploiting it must be systematic", which implies challenges not only because of the potential of robotics in education but also because of the search for new ways to integrate it into the official curricula. According to another study:

Robot's influence on children's skills development could be grouped into four major categories: cognitive, conceptual, language and social (collaborative) skills. Mixed results are shown when it comes to parents' perception of the use of robots in their children's education while design was shown to influence children's perception of the robot's character or capabilities. (Lai Poh Emily Toh et al., 2016, p. 148)

For their part, based on the review of the literature on educational robotics developed by Jung & Won (2018), the authors conclude that it is necessary to diversify the research agendas to expand the diversity of actors involved in teaching/learning processes, as well as considering the social and cultural frameworks of children's historical and institutional contexts to understand their participation in robotics education.

Robotics education provides learners with practical experiences for understanding technological and mechanical language and systems; accepting and adapting to constant changes driven by complex environments; and utilizing knowledge in real situations or across time, space, and contexts. (Jung & Won, 2018, p. 1)

At this point, considering the role that social emotions play in decision-making, planning, learning, communication, and social interaction, among others (Isen, 2000; Breazeal & Brooks, 2005), is essential for understanding the development processes of robotics and its implementation in educational practices.

About Kindergartens in Vicente Lopez

The Municipality of Vicente Lopez is located north of the Metropolitan Region of Buenos Aires; it is divided into 9 localities,[2] and is connected to Buenos Aires

City and the rest of the country by two important arteries (avenues and highways). According to the 2010 National Population, Households and Housing Census (INDEC, 2010), the District has an area of 33 km^2 and a population of 269,420 inhabitants, giving a population density of 6,908 inhabitants per km^2, with a total of 99,286 homes.[3] The Gross Geographic Product amounts to $AR 4,787,976 and the Municipality has the highest Social Progress Index (IPS)[4] of the Metropolitan Region of Buenos Aires (CIPPEC, 2018). Its percentage of Unmet Basic Needs (UBN) is 2.4%, and the unemployment rate is 4.2%. This data places Vicente Lopez as one of the smallest parties and with the best socio-economic indicators of Greater Buenos Aires.

The kindergartens in which the research was carried out are publicly managed and free, full-day (Monday to Friday from 8 a.m. to 4 p.m.), which makes them highly sought after by the nearby community, and they also have a dining room for lunch at no cost for the children. From the field notes of the ethnographic record, it emerged that although they are within a party recognized as having a medium-high socio-economic level, these establishments are located in the most impoverished areas, some of them of medium level and others vulnerable. In these last, where the children who attend reside in the surrounding areas, the problems are not only economic but also familiar (such as drug/alcohol addiction, domestic violence, and housing, among others).

The teachers identified some traits characteristic of families, such as the limited stake in the institutional activities, poor compliance with establishment rules (such as schedules, and attendance, among others), and some learning difficulties. This allows us to outline common aspects on which to understand the present and potential activities of the Robot device. If we consider the main problems identified, the difficulty in language and communication is the most important aspect, followed by emotional aspects and disability. At this point, it is interesting to recover the strong appeal to emotions, both from the problems identified in the students and from the vision expressed by the educational imprint of the institutions under analysis. As expressed in the visions of the different kindergartens, emotions are in close relationship with the teaching/learning processes (Rodrigues, 2022), to the point of appearing explicit in their vision: from their adjectives as "emotions" in general, to more specific ones, referring to loving treatment, promoting trust as a basis for socialization, and emotional security.

In this context, the question arises regarding the teachers' emotions in their daily practice with the robot. Therefore, in the following point, some conceptual perspectives in this regard are reviewed, in order later to consider them for the present study's analysis.

Social Emotions in Educational Robotics

This section aims to display the arguments that allow us to locate the relevance of looking at social emotions at an Initial Level, particularly in a teaching-learning context.

The construction of daily life is ordered based on parameters and criteria that are structured in the interplay of the individual and the social, of personal stories and biographies located in particular contexts, where we learn and apprehend behaviors and feelings in a given time-space. Along these lines, emotions and social sensibilities organize (unnoticed) the daily lives of subjects according to structural parameters and criteria, and in this way, they translate into a soçial order in which we live and coexist with others. This allows us to classify the social world that the structures of power reproduce, under the cover of a set of practices, emotions, and sensations that become habitual and "naturalized", such as joy, hope, and distrust, where we learn not to only what we should feel at each moment, but also the way of expressing said emotion (Scribano, 2017).

Likewise, emotions allow us to explain social behavior, actions, and social interactions, as well as see the nature of the social situation in which people feel fear, shame, pride, joy, anger, frustration, and a host of other emotions, which correspond to specific social situations (Bericat Alastuey, 2000). According to what has been said, emotions are loaded with meanings and senses anchored in specific socio-historical contexts, with different dimensions: a) normative, because social norms not only apply to behavior and thought but also to emotions; b) the expressive, which tells the actor what emotions, to what degree, and under what circumstances can be expressed; and c) politics, linked to social sanctions, as well as to the framework of the social structure (Hochschild, 1975).

Emotions can be understood as cognitive-affective states resulting from the experience of inhabiting the world, in its connection with the environment and with others. Socially constituted, they are not merely biological or individual, they are the product of social structuring processes while contributing to the reproduction of modes of production, distribution, and consumption, the regulation of conflicts, and social consensus (Scribano, 2017; Bericat Alastuey, 2000; Luna Zamora, 2007; De Sena & Scribano, 2020). They involve the body and thought, are organized concerning the context, and are learned through socialization (Heller, 1980; Le Breton, 2012). They express social and moral dispositions based on various forms of social relationships (Medina, 2010), developing norms that regulate what, when, how, and how much to feel (Bericat Alastuey, 2000), about intertextuality and specific historical and cultural contexts. Understood in this way, they make texts that give meaning and justify the practices of the subjects (Luna Zamora, 2007), in direct connection with their material conditions of existence (Bericat Alastuey, 2000).

In this way, emotions are inscribed in bodies, and bodies are observed situated in emotions. Therefore, from the theoretical perspective of Scribano (2017), the importance of linking the sociology of bodies/emotions and not taking them as sharply divided spaces of inquiry is emphasized. This anchoring of emotions to the body can be traced in the proposition of Kemper (1987), who states that there are four primary emotions: anger, fear, sadness, and joy, which are formed by the articulation between neurophysiological and social processes, where other secondary emotions are constructed, as many as societies are forming.

In this sense, following De Sena and Scribano (2020), we consider that how bodies/emotions are experienced do not constitute internal, individual, and isolated states; On the contrary, they constitute the result of interaction with others in certain contexts. For this reason, emotions intrinsically linked to bodies are part of a plot between impressions, sensations, and perceptions that constitute a tripod that allows us to understand where sensibilities are based (Scribano, 2017). Emotions, as cognitive-affective practices, build sociability and experiences embedded in the performativity of educational policies (De Sena & Chahbenderian, 2020). In this sense, investigating the life experiences that involve the process of appropriation of the Robot by the teaching team is essential, as it allows us to account for the individual and group experiences in this regard. In this sense, we understand "evidentiality" (life experiences) as "…a way of expressing the meanings that being in-body with others acquires as a result of 'experiencing' the dialectic between individual, social and subjective body, on the one hand; and the logic of appropriation of bodily and social energies" (Scribano, 2020, p. 76).

Along with this, we understand that the emotions that emerge in the pedagogical process and the work in the room with the Robot take on central relevance for its evaluation and implementation. Emotions reflect an operation of ordering, selecting, and interpreting situations that are then put into action. They constitute linguistic texts that contain a concept that allows us to make sense of what we feel and justify our actions (Luna Zamora, 2007). Emotions are a cultural and social element: through them, we represent the cultural definitions of personality as they are expressed in concrete and immediate relationships, but always defined in cultural and social terms (Illouz, 2019). Therefore, it is necessary to study them linked to a specific historical and cultural context, which is what offers the individual their codes to feel and express their emotional and affective experiences effectively (Luna Zamora, 2007). Based on these questions, we have proposed an approach from a sociology of bodies and emotions to enter the world of emotions and life experiences of Initial-Level teachers with the Robot.

AN APPROACH TO THE USE OF THE ROBOT AT AN INITIAL LEVEL FROM SOCIAL EMOTIONS

Various types of robots are dedicated to education, with different appearances, structures, systems, and functions, which influence the determination of learning activities and objectives. These make programmable construction kits, which allow students to create, build, and/or program robots (Jung & Won, 2018; Virtual Robot Curriculum, 2023). In this way, robots form embodied agents involving social and emotional learning (Davis & Class, 2023). In what follows, the main characteristics of the Robot are presented schematically, and then some analytical lines are introduced.

About the Robot

The Blue-Bot Programmable Children's Robot has commands on its upper part that allow teaching directional language and programming to children from an early age. At the same time, the possibility of being controlled from an App on any device (Tablet, PC, cell phone) constitutes an evolution in pre-existing tools of this type. Blue-Bot is a very basic robot in terms of its simplicity and use since it does not have sensors. The only possible interaction with it is done through the buttons located on the robot itself, which is why it is classified within the group of *Tangible User Interfaces* (Strawhacker & Bers, 2015). Each of the buttons corresponds to a programming block.[5]

In addition, the grid-shaped board allows for presenting different problems consisting of taking the Robot from an initial position to a final position, following a given path. The arrow cards enable to work on the design of a sequence before implementing it, to specify the meaning of each button on the cards. These act as a heuristic skill, as a means to represent the trajectory that the Robot will follow, without implying success in solving the problem (Diago et al., 2018).

Life Experiences Around the Robot in the Initial Level Classrooms

Throughout the different instances of fieldwork, we have identified different *emotions* linked with being a *teacher,* with the teaching practices, with the Robot as a device immersed in the teaching-learning process, and from these last two scenarios in confluence (teaching practices and device), emerges an element that is characterized as "not chosen" by the teachers. From this notion of "not chosen" a certain homogeneity could be observed in some *feel* by the teachers, regarding a certain "boredom", and a permanent demand that must be responded to. In this sense, it was identified as a univocal discourse regarding the teaching "should be", essentially linked to commitment and enjoyment. This "should be" of the teacher is tied to how they present themselves and their activities to others, as a way of "guiding and controlling the impression that others form of them, and what kinds of things they can and cannot do while acting before them" (Goffman, 1997, p. 11). Following Goffman (1997), disruptions of socially expected performance have consequences at three levels of abstraction: at the level of personality, interaction, and social structure. This implies that in the interaction there is a management of emotions: one represses immediate sincere feelings and transmits an opinion of the situation that he hopes others will find acceptable, evoking the expected responses. In this way, two signifiers come into play in the expressiveness of the subject: the expression that *gives* and the expression that *emanates* (non-verbal, more theatrical, and contextual, presumably involuntary, whether handled intentionally or not). Therefore, it required a permanent analytical effort of fieldwork and its processing.

Fear, Uncertainty, and Anxiety: The Tripod of Action

Fear is an emotion closely linked to daily life and impacts its organization, directly or indirectly, affecting the practices of populations. Following Koury (2017), fear is constituted in and from an emotional experience, a product of the interaction between individual agency, biology, biography, and society (Luna Zamora, 2007). This emotion can be characterized as a ritual and symbolic process (not basic), whose purpose is to reduce anxiety in the face of uncertainty, as a regulatory mechanism (Saurí, 1984).

The responsibility of being in a room with children, the obligation to comply with planning activities, and the arrival of an *unknown object that has a certain life of its own;* are all elements that generate *fear*, because the consequences can be towards the teacher herself, personally, at work, and/or towards the students. In this sense, fear, as the flip side of uncertainty, appears in at least three directions: fear of its use, fear of the unknown, and fear of the uncertainty of the response to its use. In the words of teachers and directors:

"...when I found out that we were going to receive the robot, I felt at first that I didn't have the tools..."

"...what I felt before working with the robot was a lot of uncertainty, I felt that perhaps I was not prepared..."

"... when we told about the project, they [the teachers] looked at us a little strangely and we began to try to convince them that 'your participation is very important',

spreading to the group that this uncertainty or fear that existed, we tried to stimulate each other to advance..."

"...the first feeling was of doubts, uncertainties..."

Along with this, there is a strong permanent affirmation of each of the teachers showing commitment to the task and, along with this, the certainty of being able to incorporate new demands and/or instruments. There are two registers of the exhibitions: in the Goffmanian sense, a clear presentation of the person as a teacher, and this means being willing to incorporate the demands of the system, not as an obligation but as convinced of the relevance of the novelty; but the back region emerges (*sense* Goffman), the one that is not shown, which refers to a permanent feeling that there is always something more, something to add, that one's work is never enough.

The addition of a new device means "never reaching" in and out of the room. On the one hand, within the classroom the teachers experience a permanent demand (which they must accept willingly) and, on the other, for the management team, it translates into greater demands in the relationship with the teachers and in the administrative area.

The structure of fears is nothing more than a psychic response to the coercion that men exert on others within social interdependence. Fears constitute one of the connecting pathways - and one of the most important - through which the structure of society flows over individual psychic functions. The engine of this civilizational transformation of the behavior of the social coercions that operate on the individual, such as fears, is constituted by a complete modification of the social coercions that operate on the individual, by a specific change of the entire relational network, and above all, a change in the organization of violence. (Elias, 1993, pp. 527-528)

Fear is a powerful element in the process of civilization toward the achievement of social prohibitions. The latter rests on a "natural and historical" fear, which is never natural but responds to the history and structure of social relations (Elias, 1993). In this way, fear becomes a *social bearability mechanism* based on self-control and as a barrier to any conflict, coagulating the action.

The arrival of the robot to the classroom is presented as a device with pedagogical potential, but its incorporation generates a situation of stress that manifests itself under the question of where is it incorporated. Is the robot the center and they should organize activities around it? Or, in any case, how is it possible to incorporate it into the activities programmed in teaching planning? That is, in the daily life of pedagogical activities, how does the robot enter? What is it for? These questions are fueled, on the one hand, by the fear of not achieving the objectives planned in the annual curriculum and, on the other, by the uncertainty facing the answer to the previous questions.

Uncertainty is related to the risk and danger of the occurrence of some unwanted event; therefore, it is linked to the future and the possibility of altering it through the intervention of the subjects or the perception that this may be the case (Luhmann, 1998; Beck, 1998; Giddens, 1997). In this way, the lack of certainty places the subject in conditions of fewer resources for action. The uncertainty of teachers shows that there is a situation in which they cannot predict or assign probabilities in the distribution of the results of their actions, which makes it impossible to plan strategies and goals for classroom planning. Faced with this, adaptation to the situation may be a possibility. Then the uncertainty seems to be attenuated with the adaptation (Giddens, 1984) of the Robot in the classroom, although said adaptation means an analogical use of it. That is to say, "everything is pigeonholed into travel games", such as telling a story where the character moves to get somewhere. In the activities, the use of the robot is organized in small groups of students. The latter generates fear and uncertainty due to the possibility of damage to the robot, where both emotions are linked. In this way, fear is the result of an interaction in which an actor is subject to the action of another who at that moment has greater power than his or her own (Bericat Alastuey, 2000) and, therefore, experiences a high degree of uncertainty about the result of that interaction.

The teachers experience a permanent demand for "new" activities required by the system that, following Giddens (1984), means a rupture and an attack on the ordinary routines of their tasks, which causes anxiety and a kind of "dispossession" to the teacher's assurances of handling the situation. The impossibility of achieving a certain routine within the classroom, and the limited autonomy of the Robot, cause a state of anxiety about what is not predictable among the teachers, and then they identify this emotion among the children. Children look for the new device in the classroom to use and show some boredom due to its analogic use. Anxiety and boredom arise as uncertainty among teachers when faced with the question of how to organize the continuity of the teaching-learning process. Along with this, fear becomes palpable regarding its use and that of children. At this point, teachers feel that they must *protect* the Robot from children's anxiety. The fear of manipulating a "precious" object generates anxiety among teachers and students, but without this manipulation, the use of the Robot is impossible.

To conclude this section, it is worth mentioning that exploration forms a defining concept of the Robot, since both teachers and students must learn and apprehend from the Robot. In this creative and exploratory capacity that is required of the teacher, the training meetings are not always promoters of this, but rather they remain pigeonholed in a unidirectional way and do not seem to *dialogue* with classroom projects. In this sense, it is difficult to transcend the uses of the Robot as mere route games.

The information that [trainer name] brings us is very valuable, but it would be good if it were in smaller groups, per garden, so that each educational community, with its particularities, can bring their concerns and experiences, on a smaller scale, since there were a lot of us in the training... learn about other experiences with the robot: other uses, what has been done elsewhere, such as to trigger new ideas and give them more flight with new uses of the robot (not just the grid, the displacement), but also to be able to think about other types of things. (field notes)

The notion of creativity towards the use of the Robot is limited to proposals for its displacement and is not useful for its applicability in the room. Returning to what was said above, the feeling of constant demand towards the teachers and the permanent sensation that on the other side *never enough* and *something is always missing* is observed as an element that consolidates the scenario where the Robot arrives, leaving open the elaboration of the tripod: fear, uncertainty, and anxiety.

CONCLUSION

According to Goffman, the implementation of a routine constitutes a form of *socializing*, shaping, and modifying a performance to adapt it to the understanding and expectations of the context in which it is presented. In this sense, teaching routines have a history and a trajectory that begins in their training as such and is condensed in the transition through the profession, which is not so easily malleable, but it has times that involve broader historical processes.

In the analysis carried out, there is a permanent *it must be*, say what a teacher should say. On the one hand, it is mentioned that a path is not imposed and that they can act freely; On the other hand, they highlight that the arrival of the robot is placed as "pigeonholed into travel games." This "freedom" or "responsibility" that is placed on the teaching team to take the reins of the implementation and incorporation of digital resources, is experienced as a permanent effort and a new requirement. From there, it is possible to understand the use of analogue that is given to the robot, despite its technological potential.

Thus, the training and the Robot are installed as something instrumental; without being able to account for the ontological nature of the modifications imposed in the 21st century by technologies 2.0, 3.0, and 4.0. It is not possible to incorporate the change of universes of meanings in the workplace, education, relationships, and social interactions, among others. In this way, it is seen that there is a use of the Robot, which does not mean appropriation.

In the *back region* (*sensu* Goffman) of the implementation, there is an experience where it is not entirely clear what that use would be like; Between saying and doing there is a *hiatus* in which the Robot is not internalized. It is experienced that the proposals are limited to tour circuits, and are not necessarily linked to teaching plans. Thus, the Robot presents at least two relations:

- Robot-teacher: concerned with responding to classroom planning and the relationship with students. In this direction, there is a demand towards the teacher and specifically towards her creativity to incorporate it into the classroom project in the didactic planning.
- Robot-student: it is not clear and it is very difficult to get everyone to "touch it", to use it, how to take care of it, how to use it, and for how long.

The teachers use the Robot in an analogical way and the students ask for a non-analogue Robot, this disagreement causes disenchantment on the part of both. Of those who do not agree to another possibility of use, whether due to limits of the device, teacher training, or the impossibility of appropriating it. Disagreement causes disenchantment, leading to annoyance for teachers and students.

This tripod of fear/anxiety/uncertainty is installed as the platform on which teaching-learning is based with the use of the robot device but, at the same time, as a trident that implies a certain defence to sustain the continuity of teaching practice. In this sense, the time and space for reflection on one's teaching practices emerge as an edge that outlines possible paths to follow to build an education for the 21st century, where the clues provided by the analysis of social emotions mark a fruitful path to follow.

REFERENCES

Badía, A., & Monereo, C. (2008). La enseñanza y el aprendizaje de estrategias de aprendizaje en entornos virtuales [Teaching and learning strategies in virtual environments]. In C. Coll & C. Monereo (Eds.), *Psicología de la educación virtual. Aprender y enseñar con las Tecnologías de la Información y la Comunicación* [Psychology of virtual education: Learning and teaching with Information and Communication Technologies] (pp. 348–367). Morata.

Barker, B. S., & Ansorge, J. (2007). Robotics as a means to increase achievement scores in an informal learning environment. *Journal of Research on Technology in Education, 39*(3), 229–243. doi:10.1080/15391523.2007.10782481

Beck, U. (1998). *La sociedad del riesgo* [The risk society]. Paidós.

Bell, J., & Gifford, T. (Eds.). (2023). *Using Assistive Technology for Inclusive Learning in K-12 Classrooms*. IGI Global. doi:10.4018/978-1-6684-6424-3

Benton, L., Hoyles, C., Kalas, I., & Noss, R. (2017). Bridging Primary Programming and Mathematics: Some Findings of Design Research in England. *Digital Experiences in Mathematics Education*, 23–29. doi:10.1007/s40751-017-0028-x

Bericat Alastuey, E. (2000). La sociología de la emoción y la emoción en la sociología [The sociology of emotion and emotion in sociology]. *Papers, 62*, 145–176. doi:10.5565/rev/papers/v62n0.1070

Breazeal, C., & Brooks, R. (2005). Robot emotion: A functional perspective. In *Who needs emotions* (pp. 271–310). Oxford University Press. doi:10.1093/acprof:oso/9780195166194.003.0010

Chang, M.-M., & Hung, H.-T. (2019). Effects of Technology-Enhanced Language Learning on Second Language Acquisition: A Meta-Analysis. *Journal of Educational Technology & Society, 22*(4), 1–17.

CIPPEC. (2018). *Índice de Progreso Social. Conurbano Bonaerense 2018* [Social Progress Index]. https://www.cippec.org/indice-de-progreso-social-en-vicente-lopez/

Davis, P. M., & Class, M. (2023). Educational Robots for Social and Emotional Learning. *AI. Computer Science and Robotics Technology, 2*(1), 1–10. doi:10.5772/acrt.26

De Sena, A. (2015). *Caminos cualitativos* [Qualitative paths]. Imago Mundi-Ciccus.

De Sena, A., & Chahbenderian, F. (2020). Apostillas sobre consumo, educación para el consumo y educación de las emociones [Apostilles on consumption, education for consumption and education of emotions]. In A. De Sena (Coord.), La cuestión educativa: formas y actores en debate [The educational question: forms and actors in debate] (pp. 19-40). Universidad del Salvador.

De Sena, A., & Scribano, A. (2020). Social Policies and Emotions: A Look from the Global South. In Social Policies and Emotions, (pp. 1-11). Palgrave Macmillan. doi:10.1007/978-3-030-34739-0

Department for Education. (2013). *Computing programmes of study: key stages 1 and 2. National Curriculum in England*. https://www.gov.uk/government/uploads/system/uploads/attachment_data/file/239033/PRIMARY_national_curriculum_-_Computing.pdf

Diago, P. D., Arnau, D., & González-Calero, J. A. (2018). Elementos de resolución de problemas en primeras edades escolares con Bee-bot [Elements of problem solving in early school ages with Bee-bot]. *Edma 0-6. Educación Matemática en la Infancia*, *7*(1), 12–41. doi:10.24197/edmain.1.2018.12-41

Elias, N. (1993). *El proceso de la civilización* [The process of civilization]. Fondo de Cultura Económica.

Engels, F. (1895). El papel del trabajo en la transformación del mono en hombre [The role of work in the transformation of ape into man]. *Die Neue Zeit, 2*(44). https://www.marxists.org/espanol/m-e/1870s/1876trab.htm

Etchevers Goijberg, N. (2005). Ruta etnográfica para la comprensión de la comunicación on-line [Ethnographic route for understanding online communication]. *Revista electrónica DIM, 1*(1).

FECYT, Google, & Everis. (2016). *Educación en ciencias de la computación en España 2015* [Computer science education in Spain 2015]. Ministerio de Economía y Competitividad. https://www.fecyt.es/es/publicacion/educacion-de-las-ciencias-de-la-computacion-en-espana

Fregnan, E., Pinto, D., & Scaratti, G. (2022). *Instilling Digital Competencies Through Educational Robotics*. IGI Global. doi:10.4018/978-1-7998-8653-2

Furman, M., Larsen, M. E., & Giorgi, P. (2020). *¿Cuáles son las mejores estrategias para la formación de docentes en ejercicio?* [What are the best strategies for training practising teachers?] Document N° 12. Project Educational questions: what do we know about education? CIAESA.

Gaudiello, I., & Zibetti, E. (2016). *Learning Robotics, with Robotics, by Robotics: Educational Robotics* (Vol. 3). John Wiley & Sons, Inc., doi:10.1002/9781119335740

Giddens, A. (1984). *The Constitution of Society*. Polity Press Cambridge.

Giddens, A. (1997). Vivir en una sociedad postradicional [Living in a post-traditional society]. In U. Beck, A. Giddens, & S. Lash (Eds.), *Thoughtful modernization* [Modernización reflexiva] (pp. 33–71). Alliance.

Goffman, E. (1997). *La presentación de la persona en la vida cotidiana* [The presentation of the person in everyday life]. Amorrotu.

Goleman, D. (1996). *Emotional intelligence*. Bloomsbury Publishing PLC.

Gómez, O. Y. A. (2018). Las TIC como herramientas cognitivas [ICT as cognitive tools]. *Revista interamericana de investigación, educación y pedagogía, 11*(1), 67-80.

Grover, S., & Pea, R. (2013). Computational Thinking in K-12: A Review of the State of the Field. *Educational Researcher, 42*(1), 38–43. doi:10.3102/0013189X12463051

Heller, A. (1980). *Teoría de los sentimientos* [Theory of feelings]. Fontamara.

Hieida, C., & Nagai, T. (2022). Survey and perspective on social emotions in robotics. *Advanced Robotics, 36*(1-2), 17–32. doi:10.1080/01691864.2021.2012512

Hochschild, A. (1975). *La mercantilización de la vida íntima. Apuntes de la casa y el trabajo* [The commodification of intimate life: Notes from home and work]. Katz.

Illouz, E. (2019). *Capitalismo consumo y autenticidad: las emociones como mercancía* [Consumption capitalism and authenticity: Emotions as merchandise]. Katz.

INDEC. (2010). *Censo Nacional de Población, Hogares y Viviendas del 2010* [National Census of Population, Households and Housing of 2010]. https://www.censo.gob.ar/

INDEC. (2023). *Censo Nacional de Población, Hogares y Viviendas del 2022* [National Census of Population, Households and Housing of 2022]. https://www.censo.gob.ar/

Johnson, J. (2003). Children, robotics, and education. *Artificial Life and Robotics, 7*(1-2), 16–21. doi:10.1007/BF02480880

Jung, S., & Won, E. (2018). Systematic Review of Research Trends in Robotics Education for Young Children. *Sustainability (Basel), 10*(4), 905. doi:10.3390u10040905

Kemper, T. D. (1987). How many emotions are there? Wedding the social and the autonomic components. *American Journal of Sociology, 93*(2), 263–289. doi:10.1086/228745

Koury, M. (2017). Cultura emotiva e sentimentos de medo na cidade [Emotive culture and sentiments of fear in the city]. *Documentos de Trabajo del CIES*, (8). http://estudiosociologicos.org/portal/wp-content/uploads/2017/09/Documento-de-Trabajo-8-JULIO-2017.pdf

Lai Poh Emily Toh, A., Causo, A., Tzuo, P.-W., Chen, I.-M., & Yeo, S. H. (2016). A Review on the Use of Robots in Education and Young Children. *Journal of Educational Technology & Society, 19*(2), 148–163.

Le Breton, D. (2012). Por una antropología de las emociones [For an anthropology of emotions]. *Revista Latinoamericana de Estudios sobre Cuerpos, Emociones y Sociedad – RELACES, 10*, 69-79. http://www.relaces.com.ar/index.php/relaces/article/view/239

Leidl, K. D., Bers, M. U., & Mihm, C. (2017). Programming with ScratchJr: A review of the first year of user analytics. In S. C. Kong, J. Sheldon, & K. Y. Li (Eds.), *Conference Proceedings of International Conference on Computational Thinking Education 2017* (pp. 116–121). The Education University of Hong Kong.

Luhmann, N. (1998). Sistemas Sociales. Lineamientos para una teoría General [Social Systems: Guidelines for a general theory]. *Anthropos.*

Luna Zamora, R. (2007). Emociones y subjetividades. Continuidades y discontinuidades en los modelos culturales [Emotions and subjectivities. Continuities and discontinuities in cultural models]. In R. Luna, & A. Scribano (Comp.), Contigo Aprendí...Estudios Sociales de las Emociones, (pp. 233-247). CEA-CONICET-National University of Córdoba–CUSCH- University of Guadalajara.

Management Association. (Ed.). (2022). Research Anthology on Computational Thinking, Programming, and Robotics in the Classroom (2 Volumes). IGI Global. doi:10.4018/978-1-6684-2411-7

Medina, L. (2010). El tercer sector. Imaginación y sensibilidad ante 'La cuestión social' [The third sector. Imagination and sensibility to 'The social question']. *Razón y palabra,* (71).

Minsky, M. (2007). *The emotion machine: Commonsense thinking, artificial intelligence, and the future of the human mind*. Simon and Schuster.

Mubin, O., Stevens, C. J., Shahid, S., Al Mahmud, A., & Dong, J. (2013). A review of the applicability of robots in education. *Technology for Education and Learning, 1*(1), 1–7. doi:10.2316/Journal.209.2013.1.209-0015

OECD. (2018). *Future of Education and Skills 2030: Conceptual Learning Framework*. Education and AI: preparing for the future & AI, Attitudes and Values. 8th Informal Working Group (IWG) Meeting (29-31 October 2018), OECD Conference Centre, Paris, France. https://www.oecd.org/education/2030/Education-and-AI-preparing-for-the-future-AI-Attitudes-and-Values.pdf

Papadakis, S., & Kalogiannakis, M. (Eds.). (2021). *Handbook of Research on Using Educational Robotics to Facilitate Student Learning*. IGI Global., doi:10.4018/978-1-7998-6717-3

Pérez, T. H. P. (2013). Aproximaciones al estado de la cuestión de la investigación en educación y derechos humanos [Approaches to the state of the art of research in education and human rights]. *Revista Interamericana de Investigación. Educación y Pedagogía, RIIEP*, *6*(1). Advance online publication. doi:10.153321657-107X.2013.0001.05

Pivetti, M., Di Battista, S., Agatolio, F., Simaku, B., Moro, M., & Menegatti, E. (2020). Educational Robotics for Children with Neurodevelopmental Disorders: A Systematic Review. *Heliyon*, *6*(10), e05160. doi:10.1016/j.heliyon.2020.e05160 PMID:33072917

Popova, A., Evans, D., Breeding, M., & Arancibia, V. (2018). Teacher Professional Development around the World: The Gap between Evidence and Practice. *IDEAS Working Paper Series from RePEc*.

Rheingold, H. (1985). *Tools for thought*. MIT Press. http://www.rheingold.com/texts/tft/

Rodrigues, C. (2022). *25 años de TED ENTRAMAR. Nuestra trayectoria docente para docentes Programa de Tecnología Educativa Digital* [25 years of TED ENTRAMAR. Our teaching career for teachers. Digital Educational Technology Program]. Secretaria de Educación y Empleo, Municipalidad de Vicente López.

Sáez, J. M., & Cózar, R. (2017). Pensamiento computacional y programación visual por bloques en el aula de Primaria [Computational thinking and visual block programming in the Primary classroom]. *Educar*, *53*(1), 129–146. doi:10.5565/rev/educar.841

Saurí, J. (1984). *The phobias*. New Vision.

Scribano, A. (2017). *Normalization, Enjoyment and Bodies/Emotions: Argentines Sensibilities*. Nova Science Publications.

Scribano, A. (2020). *Love as a Collective Action*. Routledge.

Scribano, A. (2022). Digital Creative Experiences. In A. Scribano, M. E. Korstanje, & A. Rafele (Eds.), *Global Emotion Communications* (pp. 223–242). Nova Science Publications.

Strawhacker, A., & Bers, M. U. (2015). "I want my robot to look for food": Comparing Kindergartner's programming comprehension using tangible, graphic, and hybrid user interfaces. *International Journal of Technology and Design Education*, *25*(3), 293–319. doi:10.100710798-014-9287-7

Sullivan, A., & Bers, M. U. (2016). Robotics in the early childhood classroom: Learning outcomes from an 8-week robotics curriculum in pre-kindergarten through second grade. *International Journal of Technology and Design Education*, *26*(1), 3–20. doi:10.100710798-015-9304-5

Sullivan, A., Strawhacker, A., & Bers, M. U. (2017). Dancing, Drawing, and Dramatic Robots: Integrating Robotics and the Arts to Teach Foundational STEAM Concepts to Young Children. In M. S. Khine (Ed.), *Robotics in STEM Education: Redesigning the Learning Experience* (pp. 231–260). Springer International Publishing. doi:10.1007/978-3-319-57786-9_10

Virtual Robot Curriculum. (2023). *Carnegie Mellon Robotics Academy*. Carnegie Mellon University. https://www.cmu.edu/roboticsacademy/roboticscurriculum/virtual_curriculum/index.html?gclid=CjwKCAjw6p-oBhAYEiwAgg2PgkINQEfNtqDEcnGTAkWBOUPgrgVn8i6xJrfI78ieS7uf1S09wU010hoCZ_gQAvD_BwE

Wing, J. M. (2006). Computational Thinking. *Communications of the ACM*, *49*(3), 33–35. doi:10.1145/1118178.1118215

World Economic Forum. (2015). *New Vision for Education: Fostering social and Emotional Learning through Technology*. https://www.weforum.org/reports/new-vision-for-education-fosteringsocial-and-emotional-learning-through-technology

Wu, Y.-J. A., Lan, Y.-J., Huang, S.-B. P., & Lin, Y.-T. R. (2019). Enhancing Medical Students' Communicative Skills in a 3D Virtual World. *Journal of Educational Technology & Society*, *22*(4), 18–32.

Zanatta Crestani, T. G., & Colognese, S. A. (2021). Encruzilhadas metodológicas. Revisitando as etapas de um estudo etnográfico realizado num terreiro de umbanda [Methodological crossroads. Revisiting the stages of an ethnographic study carried out in an Umbanda terreiro]. *Revista Latinoamericana de Metodología de la Investigación Social – ReLMIS, 25*(13), 19-33.

ADDITIONAL READING

Badía, A., & Monereo, C. (2008). Teaching and learning learning strategies in virtual environments. In C. Coll & C. Monereo (Eds.), *Psychology of virtual education: Learning and teaching with Information and Communication Technologies* (pp. 348–367). Morata.

Bell, J., & Gifford, T. (Eds.). (2023). *Using Assistive Technology for Inclusive Learning in K-12 Classrooms*. IGI Global. doi:10.4018/978-1-6684-6424-3

Davis, P. M., & Class, M. (2023). Educational Robots for Social and Emotional Learning. *AI. Computer Science and Robotics Technology*, *2*(1), 1–10. doi:10.5772/acrt.26

Fregnan, E., Pinto, D., & Scaratti, G. (2022). *Instilling Digital Competencies Through Educational Robotics*. IGI Global. doi:10.4018/978-1-7998-8653-2

Hieida, C., & Nagai, T. (2022). Survey and perspective on social emotions in robotics. *Advanced Robotics*, *36*(1-2), 17–32. doi:10.1080/01691864.2021.2012512

Minsky, M. (2007). *The emotion machine: Commonsense thinking, artificial intelligence, and the future of the human mind*. Simon and Schuster.

Mubin, O., Stevens, C. J., Shahid, S., Al Mahmud, A., & Dong, J. (2013). A review of the applicability of robots in education. *Technology for Education and Learning*, *1*(1), 1–7. doi:10.2316/Journal.209.2013.1.209-0015

Sullivan, A., Strawhacker, A., & Bers, M. U. (2017). Dancing, Drawing, and Dramatic Robots: Integrating Robotics and the Arts to Teach Foundational STEAM Concepts to Young Children. In M. S. Khine (Ed.), *Robotics in STEM Education: Redesigning the Learning Experience* (pp. 231–260). Springer International Publishing. doi:10.1007/978-3-319-57786-9_10

Zanatta Crestani, T. G., & Colognese, S. A. (2021). The use of educational robotics in the development of computational thinking in basic education. *Tecciencia*, *16*(30), 59–68. doi:10.18180/tecciencia.2021.30.7

KEY TERMS AND DEFINITIONS

Analog Use: A use that does not account for the ontological nature of the modifications imposed in the 21st century by technologies 2.0, 3.0, and 4.0.

Back Region: Where the performance of the social actor is not so controlled, and clues emerge to apprehend their most intimate experiences.

Emotions: Socially configured cognitive-affective states, experienced in the subjects' bodies.

Initial Education: It is the first formal education, which spans from 3 to 5 years of age.

Life Experiences: The way in which the senses are experienced in the bodies of the subjects.

Robotics Education: Robotics developments aimed at education and teaching-learning processes.

ENDNOTES

1 The emotions are inscribed in the bodies, and the bodies are observed to be situated in the emotions. For this reason, from the theoretical perspective of Scribano (2017), the importance of linking the sociology of bodies/emotions is emphasized, and they are not taken as sharply divided spaces of inquiry.

2 Carapachay, Florida, West Florida, La Lucila, Munro, Olivos, Vicente López, Villa Adelina, and Villa Martelli.

3 The provisional data from the 2022 Census indicate a population of 281,773 inhabitants in private homes, and 126,139 private homes (INDEC, 2023).

4 The IPS seeks to measure the satisfaction of social and environmental needs of the citizens of the Buenos Aires Metropolitan Area, based on a set of indicators gathered in three dimensions (Basic Human Needs, Well-being, and Opportunities for Progress) and 12 components (CIPPEC, 2018).

5 When you press a sequence of instructions, the robot stores them in a correlative and sequential manner until the "go" button is pressed, which will cause the Robot to execute the stored sequence of commands. All programming blocks have to do with the movement of the Robot according to its reference system.

Chapter 7
AI and Robots in Science Fiction Movies:
Why Should We Trust in AI?

Maximiliano Emanuel Korstanje
https://orcid.org/0000-0002-5149-1669
University of Palermo, Argentina

ABSTRACT

Artificial intelligence has revolved around the ideological core of social sciences as never before. Public opinion shows exegetes of AI and detractors who feared the advance of robots and AI in human life. Although AI makes life for humans faster and easier, no less true is that it reduces human autonomy, probably threatening future jobs. Quite aside from this, this chapter interrogates the impacts of AI and technology in science fiction movies. The authors analyze the critical position of different scholars regarding movies or Sagas such as The Terminator, Matrix, and HBO Saga Westworld. From a sociological perspective, they approach the problem of technology while placing it under the critical lens of scrutiny. In so doing, seminal voices like Paul Virilio, Jean Baudrillard, and Jacques Ellul are put in the foreground. Plausibly discussing the advance of AI in daily life is interrogating the future of digital society.

INTRODUCTION

It is not difficult to resist the impression that digital technologies have played a leading role not only in capitalist expansion but also in the conformation of digital society in recent years. Today technological breakthrough has created

DOI: 10.4018/979-8-3693-0802-8.ch007

not only more creative minds but also small players which impact directly the check-and-balance institutions (Naisbitt, 1994). Some voices speak to us of *a global paradox* which is accelerated by high-technologies. While high tech has invariably accelerated the decision-making process -at best processing faster the available information-, it has led to a gridlock where small players determine the daily life in society (Sorensen, 1995). As Manuel Castells puts it, technology has successfully altered society in the constellations of three fields: economy, power and experience. Technology has molded the ways people perceive the external world whereas laying the foundations towards *a radical understanding of identity*. Societies operate in a tension between the self which is expressed by the Id, and the net formed mainly by others. Needless to say that this net denotes the structuration of groups around a set of institutions and organizations integrated horizontally in a decentralized form of production-consumption (Castells 1986; 2010; 2020). Having said this, Castells toys with the belief that in the information age lay-people has liberated their minds but at the same time, the growth of capitalism has created standardized and mechanical forms of relations which need further scrutiny (Van Dijk, 1999; Bell 2006).

As the previous backdrop, in the informational platform, artificial intelligence (AI) and humanoids have occupied a central position in recent decades. AI has revolved around health issues applied to the expansion of life expectance, adjoined to the improvement of surveillance tech or simply Front-desk robots welcoming guests at hotels. Some studies have emphasized the negative effects of AI and robots unless owners-vs-workers relations are not ethically regulated (Ivanov & Webster 2020). What is more important, laypersons strongly believe they will be losing their jobs if robots are systematically introduced in their organizations (Korstanje, 2022). More efficient and cheaper than humans, robots have been engulfed in the modern labor market as never before. In the mid of this grim context, we interrogate furtherly the inevitable tension between humans and AI in popular opinion. In so doing, we examine the plot (basing our argument in content analysis) three well-known movies: *the Terminator, Matrix and HBO Saga Westworld*. Each one, though from different angles, deals with the problem of AI, technology, the notion of reality and alterity. Their plots situate us on a dystopian world where Mankind is enslaved or dominated by AI and technology reducing its autonomy as well as conditions of subsistence. The conditions of survival are given only to a marginal utility in a hybridized world where machines rule. At a closer look, we keep on the discussions left by senior philosophers Jacques Ellul, Jean Baudrillard and Paul Virilio regarding the future of mankind in the digital society.

AI AND DIGITAL SOCIETY

The question of whether technology has good implications for societies is not new. Ancient philosophy has widely theorized on the role of technology in the human spirit. However, the turn of the century witnessed the explosion of new global (digital) dispositifs and platforms that changed radically human life (Bassett 2015). In this vein, Jacques Ellul is a French theorist, who does not need previous presentation. In his academic life, he explored the impact of technology in human life and society -taking particular attention in different fields of modern politics-. Inspired in the earlier works authored by Karl Marx, Soren Kierkegaard and Karl Barth, Ellul argues convincingly that *technology* should not be understood in dissociation of what he dubbed as *technique*. In perspective, technique is defined as a process used to meet a specific end. In so doing, technique is centered in the optimization of resources as well as the instrumentalization of efficiency on production. Per Ellul, technology offered a new world mainly marked by absolute efficiency where humans are treated as mere commodities (if not products). Technology operates in the constellations of new rationality ruled by automatized forms of relations. Modern technology, and capitalism, make efficacy a need which includes: *autonomy, monism, universalism, self-augmentation, artificiality, and technical choice.* To put this simply, the rationality behind the technique empowers mechanical and logical forces orchestrated to regulate the division of labor which recreates the conditions for the subordination of natural world. In technological societies, humanist values are undermined or replaced by instrumental rules. Education occupies a central position mining critical reasoning. The role of schools and universities is associated to train persons to enter the world of information or the technological labor market. The domain of science has been invaded by the technique while enslaving mankind to the logic of capital (Ellul 1962; 1984; 2018; 2021). Doubtless, his caustic critique illuminated the pathways of many theorists, but particularly resonated in the works of Marshall McLuhan, Paul Virilio and Jean Baudrillard. McLuhan holds that technology involves a prolongation of human senses. Centering his analysis on the lemma the medium is the message, he dissects the Western culture from the Renaissance to modernity. His thesis is simple in general terms, human relations are regulated by a technological matrix (he calls Big Brother- that organizes information production. Communication technology expands while extending our sense outside us into the *social world.* In his words, modern culture allows the dominance of electronic media eradicating *the visual culture.* Since technology is not good or bad per se, it is instrumentalized to shape automated minds for serving capitalist logic McLuhan 1963; Moos & McLuhan, 2014). Paul Virilio goes in a similar grain. Virilio is particularly interesting because he combines the critical reasoning of Ellul with Nietzschean skepticism. As Virilio eloquently adheres, the capitalist expansion has created an existential gap in society which is filled by the mass media and the war machine. In his viewpoint, technology offers a fabricated landscape that captured the attention of audience, making life a lived dreamworld. Technology -in this context- catalyzes human relations corrupting their cultural values and their sense of objectivity. As discussed, technology has made modern science an ideological prerogative for the protection of private interests. This seems to be the case of scientists studying climate change. The net of experts never offers radical solutions for the ecological crisis but mitigating steps to adapt society to the next turbulent dichotomies on the climate. Unless otherwise resolved, science, which is dominated by the private market, justifies a much deep logic of expropriation and simulation determined by global capitalism. The media is something more complex than a form of entertainment, it represents a dominant format where humans are simply enslaved or commoditized. At the same time, mobile culture (and tourism) are commoditized forms of connection where people buy tours to nowhere. We have invented and created more efficient and faster machines but paradoxically they put aside from "the Other" (Virilio & Wilson, 1994; Virilio 1995; 2004). For to cut a long story short, Virilio is convinced technology is commoditized human relations undermining social bondage (Kellner 1998). Last but not least, Jean Baudrillard treads on the toes of tech-savvy exegetes equating it to a technological *matrix where reality simply withers away.* For the sake of clarity, he says that the modern world is like Spielberg´s film *Minority Report* where Precogs, in a futurist Chicago city, forecast future crimes before committed. Precogs are claryboyant humans who connected to high-technology have visions useful to detain criminals before the criminal event happens. Everything is out of control when the computer (based on AI) is corrupted to blame precrime chief John Anderton (Tom Cruise). As Baudrillard notes, the modern world -like precogs- appears to be oriented to detect and eradicate risks which never happens at least how they are been imagined. The risks move in the fields of hyperreality which is ultimately connected to "the pseudo-events". Pseudo-reality and events are part of the dominance of technology for the enslavement of human beings (Baudrillard, 2005; 2006; 2013; Baudrillard & Lancelin, 2004). Most certainly, as Catherine Constable probed in her Doctoral Dissertation, Baudrillard sees in the Matrix Trilogy the best of the examples for supporting his theory on pseudo-reality and Simulacra. To wit, he is interested in confronting the tensions between high and low culture which has direct effects in modern philosophy. What is equally important, the Matrix Trilogy offers a philosophical debate to the question of technology while addressing one of main Baudrillard´s worries, the lack of a radical change emerged from a pre-programmed system (above all debatable questions left by Baudrillard on concepts as the hyperreal and the code) (Constable, 2013). William Irwin discusses critically the intersection between what he terms "the real" and "consciousness". Matrix interrogates us on the conception of reality putting the metaphor of the Cavern into the foreground.

For Plato, the Cavern symbolizes our *daily life*. Reality, which is a social construction, should be understood not with senses, but with the intellect. The dilemma is mainly given no one can tell us how reality is, it should be lived (like Morpheus cannot tell Neo what is the Matrix if he does not take the red pill). The idea of knowledge is preserved through a decision which should be individually made (Irwin, 2005). Like Cypher, Neo decides how to live their life. Two options can be made. The real life marked by frustration, suffering and the sacrifice, or the simulated reality where all our necessities are met. Cypher betrays Morpheus to be reincorporated to the Matrix, while Neo becomes in the One. Cypher agree to betray their friends in exchange of a new more convenient life, though his life is not real. He assumes that pleasure (not the sacrifice) is a valuable thing that makes life tolerable (or worth-living) (Erion & Smith 2005). The opposite is equally true, machines dominate humans through the creation and imposition of pleasurable experiences. This domination breaks in the rise of a question, a radical doubt: what is the reality? The question is the only powerful point from where men emancipate from the Matrix. To put this in bluntly, the Matrix opens a radical possibility in the dislocation between the reality and our beliefs. Neo spent a whole part of his time living in the Matrix while he believed he was not; the trauma met him when his notion of reality simply melts out once Neo is liberated by Morpheus (Korsmeyer, 2005; Nixon, 2005).

THE MATRIX TRILOGY

Matrix is the name of a Trilogy created by Lana & Lily Wachowskis. The Wachowskis situate their plot in a dystopian future in which humans are enslaved and entrapped inside a Matrix in a world controlled by robots. Human dwells in the Matrix employing their bodies as energy sources. Their life happens in a simulated reality in a world ruled by intelligent machines. Thomas Anderson (Keanu Reeves) unveils the truth while joining to the rebellion against the Matrix. With the help of Trinity (Carrie-Anne Moss) and Morpheus (Laurence Fishburne), Anderson (converted in Neo) struggles to liberate mankind from the domination of machines. Humans have been relegated to life in the underground city of Zion until per the prophecy Neo liberates them. Programmer Anderson is questioned to meet with Trinity a couple of times. In one of those encounters, he is presented with Morpheus who put Neo in a puzzle. Morpheus offers two pills: the blue to make Neo forget the encounter and everything he was explained, and the red to know the truth about the Matrix. Neo choses the red pill, and his notion of reality changes substantially. Neo wakes up in liquid-filled pod, among many others who sleep while living their simulated reality. Morpheus ultimately explains Neo that in the 21th century humans have been enslaved by machine after a war. Humans, who tried to block the access of machines to energy, serve as bioelectric source of energy for machines. Each person is connected to a simulated reality while others escaped to Zion. Neo is incorporated to Morpheus´ crew taking part of a group of rebels who hacking the Matrix are moved to liberate humans. Neo and Morpheus are persecuted by the Agents who are sentient programs created to eliminate the threats that put the Matrix into jeopardy. Neo is warned that the death within the Matrix kills the physical body as well. Once inside the Matrix, Neo is alerted he is not the "ONE" while the crew is ambushed after Cypher betrays Morpheus. Lastly, Morpheus is trapped and interrogated by agent Smith to know the access to Zion, but he is rescued by Neo. Smith kills Neo but he is revived with new superpowers and abilities, as the ONE. Once returned to Zion, Neo and humans prepare for the next last battle against the Machines to liberate mankind and Zion.

Once explained the plot, let´s return to the question of human autonomy and the risks of AI as main lines of inquiry in the present debate. The first point of entry associates to knowledge as a generator (driver) to the discovery of the truth. Even if reality can be artificially determined by AI (as authors have discussed about the Wachowskis film), only the human question opens the doors to the truth, which can be ignored, rejected or accepted. Any discovery is a process which cannot be simulated or controlled by AI, it is the gift that makes us humans. Anyway, we can discover the truth but never knowing the future. Of course, Neo struggles to liberate Zion without knowing the future. For the Matrix and agents, the future is far from being important for their existence. Even machines gained further autonomy form humans but they lack of the notion of future. The Matrix -even recreating a simulated life for humans- is hand-tied to forecast their next steps. Last but not least, there is a codependence of the Matrix and the human energy which needs to be harvested. The Matrix is a mega-computer programmed with AI to make human life safer but it enslaves humans (her creators) to re-found a new world dominated by machines. AI includes not only the improvement in some circuits of the decision-making process, but it gives autonomy only in a present time. At the same time, humans create computers and AI to make their lives safer and more predictable, though it becomes in their ultimate *iron-cage*. The Matrix can infer what can happen but it is unable to imagine the future; a similar point can be discussed in Terminator, a film starred by Arnold Schwarzenegger and Linda Hamilton.

THE TERMINATOR

It is not simplistic to say *The Terminator* was a trilogy or a Saga that captivated the attention of the audience as never before. Starred by Arnold Schwarzenegger and directed by James Cameron, the plot starts with the life of Sarah Connor (Linda

Hamilton) who will be killed by a cyborg assassin (the Terminator) sent from 2029 to 1984. The Terminator is programmed by the Skynet, which is a hostile AI that pushed humans to the bias of extinction. Her unborn child, John Connor will lead the rebellion. In this apocalyptic future, machines and Skynet control the world where humans struggle daily to survive. If Sarah is killed John will never birth. Meanwhile, John sends a soldier Kyle Reese (Michael Biehn) to help Sarah. The Terminator successfully kills women bearing the target name once their addresses are obtained in a telephone directory. Reese explains Sarah Skynet has been created by the American Government to protect the US (as an autonomous AI applied to defense issues) however, something went wrong, and Skynet, which was created by the corporation Cyberdyne Systems, pushed humans to a nuclear war. This AI not only gained its autonomy but also self-awareness in its decisions. Reese tells Sarah that John will take the lead of the rebels in the future and for that The Terminator has commanded to kill Sarah, her mother. To avoid the resistance victory, Skynet sends the Terminator to 1984. Needless to say, The Terminator seems to be an efficient machine programmed to kill systematically to their victims. Ultimately, The Terminator is destroyed and Reese sacrifices his life leaving Sarah pregnant waiting for John. She is going to Mexico border next a thermonuclear apocalypse.

At a first glimpse, The Terminator reads very different than the Matrix. Skynet not only has consciousness of the time but it delivers a cyborg prototype to kill Sarah. To some extent, in Terminator 2 (Judgement Day), a similar cyborg is delivered again by John to protect himself in the past. Sarah, incarcerated now at the Pescadero State Hospital, faces a new enemy sent by Skynet, an advanced prototype known as T-1000. Sarah is considered as a threat for society, but she is rescued by The Terminator. He explains Sarah, John reprogrammed and sent to protect John. The Terminator, Sarah and John to meet with Miles Dyson the discoverer of a revolutionary microprocessor which is vital for the existence of Skynet.

Like Matrix, *the Terminator* in a type of *neo-colonial romanticism* which puts the machines as the continuation of slaves in the former centuries. The colonial expansion has been followed an economic dynamic of extraction which indexed new over-seas territories to the "imperial (European) matrix"; having said this, the conquest of Americas has been accompanied by an economy of enslavement which populated the new world with African slaves as the main workforce. This logic of human exploitation systematically monopolized by Europeans was certainly centered on a strange paternalism where slaves were considered stronger or more apt for labor but less smart than Europeans. This dichotomy between the natural force and culture was originally engulfed in the cultural matrix of European empires. For gaining consciousness, non-Europeans should be re-educated according to the Western ideals of the epoch. In this respect, the same role played by slaves and the economy of enslavement in the literature of eighteenth and nineteenth centuries has set the pace to a new modern neo-romanticism where machines, technology and AI are disposed to make human life safer and easier. The problem is, most plausibly, these intelligent machines, which not only move faster and process much information without sleeping or resting (in comparison to humans), gain further autonomy (or self-awareness) while dominating (enslaving) humans. Part of this argument lies in Ulrich Beck´ book Risk Society which holds that one of the paradoxes of modernity should be traced back to Chernobyl incident. This event marked a turning point in the expansion of modernity, showing that the same technology used to make the life of people safer may very well generate a real apocalypse. This happens because western rationality is based on a technological paradox very hard to resolve. Technology helps the net of experts to accelerate the means of production utilizing the articulation of mechanized protocols, but paradoxically it leads society to a dormant state of vulnerability, when the contingency arises (Beck 1992). Like Matrix, the Terminator puts the problem of contingency and the programmed order into the foreground. Similar assumptions can be made approaching a third Saga, created by HBO, West World.

HBO SAGA WESTWORLD

As discussed in earlier sections, the problem of AI and digital society did not go unnoticed by western social imaginary. Westworld is a Saga created by Jonathan Nolan & Lisa Joy (and directed by Michael Crichton). This Saga can be seen in three seasons: the Maze (2016), The Door (2018) and The New World (2020). At a closer look, *The Maze* circumscribes primarily the nature of enslavement and its consequences for daily life. Most certainly echoing Bauman and his prerogative between tourists and vagabonds, in this dystopian world rich tourists (known as the guests) satisfy their darkest drives by killing and mutilating hosts (which are humanoids created to serve humans). Westworld exhibits a futurist landscape oriented to fictionalize life in the Far West. Humanoids (known as the hosts) are programmed to meet all guests´ desires, even the darkest ones. Although hosts can be attacked, tortured or even killed, they are unable to retaliate and attack humans. To be more exact, Westworld locates in 2058 BC, and the resource is locally controlled by a mega-corporation *Delos Inc.* Formed by four themed parks that emulate life in the Far West, in Westworld *humans and humanoids* are indistinguishable. All host-guest interactions are regulated by a computer, the Matrix which repeats cyclical forms of relationship in the day. Central Mesa is a place where operators follow-up the performance of the hosts as well as their technical failures.

As the previous argument is given, Westworld is a recreational park that receives thousands of tourists who show a higher purchasing power. These guests not only are free to visit the parks freely they can kidnap, torture and kill local hosts without any type of legal punishment. The hosts are not humans, but also humanoids fabricated and ensembled to meet all humans´ needs. As stated, The Saga has a great cast of the caliber of Anthony Hopkins, Ed Harris, James Marsden, and Ben Barnes only to name a few. As a recreational park which is part of a system –formed by the other five parks- Westworld is carefully designed to protect the integral security of guests. Regardless of what they do, guests cannot be judged or killed by hosts. When something goes wrong, which means the host puts a guest in a dangerous situation, the host is reprogrammed and his memory erased. This creates a primordial rule that reminds guests are legally legitimated to dispose of, consume and even kill hosts, but hosts cannot attack their visitors. Although some are cruel, other guests are altruistic, sympathetic and open to hosts. Each one, in this futurist world, is what he or she wants to be. Although the park is visited by women, males exhibit a type of dangerous masculinity mainly marked by extreme sexuality, procrastination, alcoholism and sadism. The host lacks any basic rights and no legislation protects them. In this respect, although they look exactly like humans, they are not humans. Once killed, their memories are recycled and wiped. In the case of Dolores, an outstanding glitch allowed her to keep part of the memories of the traumatic events she faced. As reviewed, films like Matrix and Terminator speak to us of the asymmetries between humans and robots but Westworld is in part different. It transcribes the problem of Western society to accept "the Other", the non-human Other. Westworld discusses critically the crisis of hospitality in Western democracies putting efforts to decipher the role of consciousness and AI in the days to come. Humans here are the evil-doers, while humanoids struggle to be emancipated form human sadism. What is more important, Westworld reminds the risks of human exploitation -cemented by technology- as well as the end of ethics in a morbid spectacle of death and violence. In the time, hosts show some signs of consciousness (and independency) associated to a drive to free choice. They gradually recover their memories, a case which concerns heavily Dr Ford, who is the scientist director of the park. Specialists find that hosts are recreating the conditions to dream, and though they cannot determine why this happens, hosts keep part of their memories. Dr Ford agrees that hosts are experiencing a type of glitch that retrieves part of his past life. Access to the pass is vital for hosts to gain further liberty and consciousness. In the Saga Dolores finally takes the lead starting a revelation against humans while hosts flee to the desert. Beyond the borders of the park, there is a *phantom nation* outside human control. The question whether Westworld reflects the tensions between the self and the "Other", no less true seems to be that the argument runs against the grain. To some extent, Westworld places the question of enslavement and mankind into the critical lens of scrutiny. It calls attention not only to the dichotomies revolving around "liberty" and pleasure, but it ignites a hot-debate on the crisis of western hospitality. Hosts are fabricated, commoditized and consumed as mere things, dispossessed of any right, outside the application of the law. Their lack of memory is part of what marks their so-called inferiority respecting humans. In time, they start a real revolution confronting ethically not only Dr Ford but also mankind itself.

CONCLUSION

Artificial Intelligence has revolved around the ideological core of social sciences as never before. Public opinion shows exegetes of AI and detractors who feared the advance of robots and AI in human life. Although AI makes life for humans faster and easier, no less true is that it reduces human autonomy probably threatening future jobs. Quite aside from this, this chapter interrogates the impacts of AI and technology in Science Fiction movies. We analyze the critical position of different scholars regarding movies or Sagas such as The Terminator, Matrix and HBO Saga Westworld. From a sociological perspective, we approach the problem of technology while placing it under the critical lens of scrutiny. While In Matrix and The Terminator, the AI is depicted as a malevolent creation disposed of by humans to make their life safer, in time, the machines take control enslaving human beings. The same does not apply to the case of Westworld, where AI is emancipating from human sadism. By the way, in The Matrix we see the impossibilities for AI to operate between the present and the past, but it is not an obstacle for Skynet in the Terminator. The three films evince part of the ethical concerns and the storm-centre of controversies over AI and digital society. In this chapter, we have echoed some seminal voices like Paul Virilio, Jean Baudrillard and Jacques Ellul. Plausibly discussing the advance of AI in daily life is interrogating the future of digital society.

REFERENCES

Bassett, D. J. (2015). Who wants to live forever? Living, dying and grieving in our digital society. *Social Sciences (Basel, Switzerland)*, *4*(4), 1127–1139. doi:10.3390ocsci4041127

Baudrillard, J. (2005). Violence of the virtual and integral reality. *International Journal of Baudrillard Studies*, *2*(2), 1–16.

Baudrillard, J. (2006). Virtuality and Events: The hell of power. *Baudrillard Studies*, *3*(2), 1–15.

Baudrillard, J. (2013). *The intelligence of evil: Or, the lucidity pact*. A&C Black.

Baudrillard, J., & Lancelin, A. (2004). The matrix decoded: Le nouvel observateur interview with Jean Baudrillard. *International Journal of Baudrillard Studies*, *1*(2), 1–8.

Beck, U. (1992). *Risk Society: towards a new modernity*. Sage.

Bell, D. (2006). *Cyberculture Theorists: Manuel Castells and Donna Haraway*. Routledge. doi:10.4324/9780203357019

Castells, M. (1986). High technology, world development, and structural transformation: The trends and the debate. *Alternatives*, *11*(3), 297–343. doi:10.1177/030437548601100301

Castells, M. (2010). The information age. *Media Studies: A Reader, 2*(7), 152-158

Castells, M. (2020). Space of flows, space of places: Materials for a theory of urbanism in the information age. In *The city reader* (pp. 240–251). Routledge. doi:10.4324/9780429261732-30

Constable, C. (2013). Adapting Philosophy: Jean Baudrillard and The Matrix Trilogy. In *Adapting philosophy*. Manchester University Press. doi:10.7765/9781847792822

Ellul, J. (1962). The technological order. *Technology and Culture*, *3*(4), 394–421. doi:10.2307/3100993

Ellul, J. (1984). *Technique and the opening chapters of Genesis. Theology and Technology*. Wipf & Stock Publishers.

Ellul, J. (2018). *The technological system*. Wipf and Stock Publishers.

Ellul, J. (2021). *The technological society*. Vintage.

Erion, G., & Smith, B. (2005). Skepticism, Morality and the Matrix. In W. Irwin (Ed.), *The Matrix and Philosophy: welcome to the desert of the real* (pp. 5–15). Open Court.

Irwin, W. (2005). Computers, Caves and Oracles: Neo and Socrates. In W. Irwin (Ed.), *The Matrix and Philosophy: welcome to the desert of the real* (pp. 3–5). Open Court.

Ivanov, S., & Webster, C. (2020). Robots in tourism: A research agenda for tourism economics. *Tourism Economics*, *26*(7), 1065–1085. doi:10.1177/1354816619879583

Kellner, D. (1998). Virilio on Vision Machines: On Paul Virilio, Open Sky. *Film-Philosophy*, *2*(1), 1–15. doi:10.3366/film.1998.0030

Korsmeyer, C. (2005). Seeing, Believing, Touching, Truth. In The Matrix and Philosophy: welcome to the desert of the real. Open Court.

Korstanje, M. E. (2022). Terrorism, Automated Hosts, and COVID-19: Critical Film Review of the HBO Saga Westworld. In Global Risk and Contingency Management Research in Times of Crisis (pp. 295-308). IGI Global.

McLuhan, M. (1963). *The Gutenberg Galaxy*. University of Toronto Press.

Moos, M., & McLuhan, M. (2014). *Media research: Technology, art and communication*. Routledge.

Naisbitt, J. (1994). Global paradox: The bigger the world economy, the more powerful its smallest players. *Journal of Leisure Research*, *26*(4), 406–420. doi:10.1080/00222216.1994.11969972

Nixon, M. D. (2005). The Matrix possibility. In W. Irwin (Ed.), *The Matrix and Philosophy: welcome to the desert of the real* (pp. 16–27). Open Court.

Sorensen, G. (1995). Global Paradox. *Bulletin of the Atomic Scientists*, *51*(4), 69–73.

The Matrix. (1999). Dir. The Wachowskis. English, 136 minutes. Warner Bros.

The Terminator. (1984). *Dir James Cameron. English, 107 minutes*. Hemdale & Pacific Western Productions.

Van Dijk, J. A. (1999). The one-dimensional network society of Manuel Castells. *New Media & Society*, *1*(1), 127–138. doi:10.1177/1461444899001001015

Virilio, P. (1995). Speed and information: cyberspace alarm! *Ctheory, 18*(3), 8-27.

Virilio, P. (2004). *The Paul Virilio Reader*. Columbia University Press.

Virilio, P., & Wilson, L. (1994). Cyberwar, god and television: Interview with Paul Virilio. *Ctheory, 21-31.*

Westworld. (2016). Dir. Michael Crichton. English, 4 seasons, HBO TV.

ADDITIONAL READING

Awan, A., Alnour, M., Jahanger, A., & Onwe, J. C. (2022). Do technological innovation and urbanization mitigate carbon dioxide emissions from the transport sector? *Technology in Society*, *71*, 102128. doi:10.1016/j.techsoc.2022.102128

Bearman, M., Ryan, J., & Ajjawi, R. (2023). Discourses of artificial intelligence in higher education: A critical literature review. *Higher Education*, *86*(2), 369–385. doi:10.100710734-022-00937-2

Holmes, D. (2005). Communication theory: Media, technology and society. *Communication Theory*, 1–272.

Huang, X., Zou, D., Cheng, G., Chen, X., & Xie, H. (2023). Trends, research issues and applications of artificial intelligence in language education. *Journal of Educational Technology & Society*, *26*(1), 112–131.

Korstanje, M. E. (2019). *Terrorism, technology and apocalyptic futures*. Springer. doi:10.1007/978-3-030-13385-6

Rip, A., Misa, T. J., & Schot, J. (Eds.). (1995). *Managing technology in society*. Pinter Publishers.

Tiwari, S. P. (2022). *The Impact of New Technologies on Society: A Blueprint for the Future*. Scholarly Publisher RS Global Sp. z OO.

van Noordt, C., & Misuraca, G. (2022). Artificial intelligence for the public sector: Results of landscaping the use of AI in government across the European Union. *Government Information Quarterly*, *39*(3), 101714. doi:10.1016/j.giq.2022.101714

Wajcman, J. (2023). Technological a/genders: Technology, culture and class. In *Framing Technology* (pp. 3–14). Routledge. doi:10.4324/9781003416494-2

Yang, W. (2022). Artificial Intelligence education for young children: Why, what, and how in curriculum design and implementation. *Computers and Education: Artificial Intelligence*, *3*, 100061. doi:10.1016/j.caeai.2022.100061

KEY TERMS AND DEFINITIONS

Apocalypse: It is a literary genre mediated by supernatural entities, and a cosmological pessimism which assumes the end of the world is near.

Artificial Intelligence: AI is oriented to stimulate a more optimized decision-making process, with intervention or not of humans. This often denotes the intelligence of machines or software which is opposed to the intelligence of humans or animals.

Human Autonomy: It is a process that warrants the anatomy of human decisions regarding abstract laws or process.

Robots: This term to refer a virtual or artificial entity who though humanized lacks of human autonomy.

Technology: It denotes a set of application in techniques and knowledge for achieving specifical goals in a reproductive way.

Chapter 8
The Intersection of Learning, of the Growth Mindset, and of the Emotions:
A Junction Designed by Knowledge and Artificial Intelligence

Neli Maria Mengalli
https://orcid.org/0000-0002-3782-3807
Faculdade São Bernardo do Campo, Brazil

Antonio Aparecido Carvalho
Faculdade São Bernardo do Campo, Brazil

ABSTRACT

This chapter was written based on qualitative and exploratory studies by reading current reports and articles at the time of writing. The objective of writing the chapter was to provide support for the countless reflections of researchers and professionals in areas that use disruptive technologies as a strategy. In the investigation, it was realized that it was a prosperous field for all areas; after all, the human being is the protagonist and artificial intelligence can be supporting people. However, it is a new topic and requires a lot of research. In the final considerations, among the conclusions, it emerges that science fiction in books and films highlight a reality in which human emotion and feeling exist and that the plot with disruptive technologies does not overshadow people's behavior because the focus on professions of the future must be human beings interacting with machines.

DOI: 10.4018/979-8-3693-0802-8.ch008

INTRODUCTION

Over the years, fiction becomes reality or reality becomes fictional with predictions, in common sense, about artificial intelligence. Disruptive technologies are increasingly part of human daily life and are reasons for reflection and formal discussion, as well as wonder and lack of criticism. Humanity is in the spotlight without the proper understanding that being human means having emotions, creativity and being inventive.

Social sciences are in the spotlight and many still believe that technology is the star without highlighting computational resources as human creations. Silva (2001) wrote that the machine presents itself as a concrete object, an instrument that is the product of a technique and adds that there is a human process and trajectory with intentionality. The technique is in the design and production for use. The author, in the article, highlights that technology is a strategy and argues that technique is a human way of doing things with methodologies and controlled operationalization and, with a humanistic vision, it is possible to add doing things to the theory that technology is a strategy because, if done well, it highlights know-how with practice and human knowledge, that is, the know-how in using technologies strategically.

In the hierarchy, when the technique is reflected by people, the use of disruptive, green or assistive technologies, among other adjectives, will be at the top level of actions and the machine, which is currently enhancing people's actions with the advent of the numbers that complete the word web in concepts such as 1.0, 2.0, 3.0, 4.0 and 5.0, will be at the service of society in the mechanization of tasks.

Before the numbers that highlight the concepts of the web and the World Wide Web, the technique existed without the computerized machine and continues to exist with activities that use computational thinking. According to Liu, Peng and Srivastava (2023), some researchers believed that computational thinking was related to problem-solving and that it was a skill that everyone should have (Wing apud Liu, Peng and Srivastava, 2023), but the term computational thinking refers to computational culture.

Papert (1993) wrote that, in his discussion about a computational culture and the impact on thinking, there is a massive penetration of computers and that the calculator, the electronic game and the digital clock were brought about by a revolutionary technique, and the technological revolution, caused by the integrated circuit, brought about the personal computer. From mobile and fixed devices, artificial intelligence and metaverses are parts of the phygital transformation that Mengalli and Carvalho (2023) wrote that, in phygital, there is a combination of the physical with the digital (Carvalho, Mengalli and Lucas (2022) that stimulate people to immersive experiences.

People are immersed in using and testing artificial intelligence. In the article Technology's Generational Moment with Generative AI: A CIO and CTO Guide

(2023), it is written that as the use of artificial intelligence becomes increasingly widespread, Chief Information Officer and Chief Technology Officer block access to employees use applications to limit risks and, as a consequence, increase the risk of missing innovation opportunities as they limit the ability to develop new skills for the business. Technology emerges when there is an understanding of know-how and when there is reflection on the technique in mobile and fixed devices.

Technical knowledge is formulated and reflected based on theories that may seem invisible to those who are not fluent in the interface with machines, but with reflection based on the most different theoretical references and with ethical use, it is possible to mobilize skills and employee skills. According to the aforementioned guide produced by McKinsey, Chief Information Officers and Chief Technology Officers will need to become fluent in humanitarian ethics.

In addition to adaptations and compliance issues about current legislation, it is necessary to have responsibility for the business reputation and the spirit of managing people for learning, growth mindset and emotional intelligence. When evaluating new scenarios for using artificial intelligence, leaders must assess the risks to people. It is necessary to establish mitigation of practices that do not involve the emotions of human beings for the health of people and businesses.

The increased use of generative artificial intelligence sometimes inhibits the creative process of (co) creation with other humans, after all, ideas can be (co) created and improved with other humans. Raymond (1999), although in a different context from artificial intelligence and companies, wrote that the free market can produce ever-increasing software wealth for everyone. It is possible to conclude from the writing of the author and founder of the Open-Source Initiative that, while software sources can potentially last forever, ideas can lose their validity if not (co) created.

The author wrote, about open source, that food needs to be consumed or it rots and, in this metaphor and in times when studies rival artificial intelligence with humans in the professions of the future if human emotions are not worked on and technology prevails about technique, business and people can lose value in environmental and social governance. People have the techniques, and the ideas and can help other people with the techniques and the (co) creation of ideas at the intersection of learning with the growth mindset and with emotions in the interchange designed by human knowledge and artificial intelligence.

In this design, the adoption of artificial intelligence without due knowledge of the techniques for use, without critical use of computational interfaces and without enabling human emotions to be understood in technological enhancements does not generate business appropriation for innovation and inventiveness in the market. Fear and fascination prevail with the anxiety of making the right use of artificial intelligence and abandoning human beings.

In support of reflections on emotion concerning artificial intelligence, it is possible to understand the research insight Augmented Work for an Automated, AI-driven World. (2023) that everyone is in the era of increased productivity in partnerships between humans and machines and this period, when respecting the mental health of employees, can be understood as the era of increased workforce with exponential commercial value.

Data culture tends to help organizations in developing and engaging employees for greater employee retention. The effectiveness of strategic decision-making, the best economic adjustment of companies and the improvement of the employee experience contribute to competitive advantage and business growth. Reducing employee turnover enables the element of happiness.

Charles-Leija, *et al.* (2023) concluded, in the article, that the data showed that life purpose, work relationships and meaningful work are relevant aspects for employees, that is, psychological aspects were decisive for happiness at work. In this chapter, psychological aspects such as learning, growth mindset and emotions are present, and the writing is a reflective subsidy for researchers and professionals in the psychological and technological areas.

The objective of the chapter is to provide support for the countless reflections of researchers and professionals in the field with theory about the adoption of artificial intelligence without due knowledge of the techniques for the utilize and use of computer interfaces without criticism and without understanding the technological potentialities associated with human emotions, that is, supporting people in reflecting on the responsible use of artificial intelligence and the value of human emotions in projects that include the relationship between humans and machines.

It is a qualitative and exploratory study that is based on the most up-to-date literature and business reports, although some authors from the 20th and early 21st centuries are references in the chapter due to their historical value, as well as the emotional factors that relate to FoLo - Fear of Logging off, for example, since in 2023, a field study was carried out with young people entering the Business Administration course at a higher education institution in greater São Paulo, Brazil, by Carvalho, Cirera and Mengalli (2023).

The chapter's target audience is researchers, undergraduate and postgraduate professors and students, technological professionals, artificial intelligence analysts, public policymakers and scientists in the fields of humanities and social sciences with concern for the present and the future of the use of artificial intelligence in an anxious, complex, and non-linear world. The division of the chapter is background, the focus of the chapter, solutions and recommendations, the qualitative and exploratory study, directions for future research, and final considerations.

BACKGROUND: THE SET OF FICTIONAL ANTECEDENTS WITH VERISIMILAR PRECEDENTS

The background of the chapter has the integration of the basic elements of doing and theoretical reflection of established knowledge and research carried out by companies. Technologies and artificial intelligence are characterized as a strategy for use and results. Silva (2001), to characterize technology for the educational area, wrote that the concept of evolutions that announced the end of technological ghettos, in social terms, meant that people are faced with a communicative universe in which everything is connected in the value that is given for establishing a connection.

Such statements lead to reflections that there will be technology to the extent that people reflect the technique, otherwise, there will be mobile and fixed devices with their respective computational resources or artificial intelligence developed without due understanding by people of what the understanding of technology consists of. programming language. There must be knowledge of the logic developed for the operation of artificial intelligence.

In the interactions between humans and machines, there is the human trajectory among the paths of science and knowledge of software and parameterizations combined with the feelings and emotions of people who use computational resources or who need upskilling and reskilling to adapt to the requirements of the market for contemporary professions. It is known that artificial intelligence and human emotions are not new themes in contemporary times, however, studies on artificial intelligence and technological uses in professional and personal life must be reflected so that productivity is not a problem for people's mental health.

At academic and professional events, artificial intelligence, and the need to know how to make prompts had the spotlight, on the stage, focused on them and the fears that people would be unemployed showed that the professions of the future would be for the chosen ones. Dystopian thoughts, in real life, tried to hypnotize people. The themes of artificial intelligence and human emotions are not subjects that usually come together in academic studies, but, in the seventh art, as in the proposal of Riciotto Canudo (1877 - 1923), technological revolutions highlight people's suffering when dystopias are the realities in the movies.

Morin (1956, p. 14-15) wrote that Riciotto Canudo was the first cinema theorist, and he knew how to subjectively define the art of the objective: "In cinema, the art consists of suggesting emotions and not reporting facts". The author added that the genesis of cinema was seen as an era of learning in which a language was developed that was called the seventh art. In cinema, there is reason and emotion together or separately created by humans who try to represent what people feel. The word combines with images and movement to release emotions and feelings. The film industry provided audiovisual material for human comparisons and dystopian thoughts.

The film Her (2013), an American romantic science fiction drama, written, directed and (co) produced by Spike Jonze highlights a script that contemplates the real with digital, a phygital transformation that compromises the character's sanity throughout the film after the main character believes that the artificially intelligent virtual assistant could be the woman of his life. Suffering, anxiety, and pain increase when the software update occurs.

The aforementioned film is the result of the director's readings about institutional websites that allowed instant messages to be inserted into programming based on the concepts of artificial intelligence. The director worked with the same technological theme in short films. The technological era in films is a legacy of the 80^{s} of the 20th century, for example, Blade Runner (1982) influenced many science fiction films, series, video games and anime based on the work of Dick (2017) which highlights a future which is passed on to people because the war was announced for 2021. In addition to the war, humans became extinct, and companies built artificial humans and androids. Both the film and the book highlighted a future that did not occur until 2023.

The future is imagined and visits the past, as in The Terminator (1984), a cyborg sent from the future on a mission that involves killing a girl who will be important for the liberation of people in the future. An engaging fiction that has several films starting from the original film. Imagination and dystopias continue to occur in the film industry. Morin (1956) wrote that the future, in cinema, is imagined by the fiction of anticipation. The myth takes shape in cinematographic words and actions.

The metamorphosis of space with time, in the 90^{s} of the 20th century, highlighted the digital transformation in a society that is made up of programs in The Matrix (1999), which comprises the production with a character who is a computer programmer and hacker who seeks answers that will be given by computer programs created by an information architect. Science fiction continues to feed the imagination of viewers at the beginning of the 21st century.

The future is invented by screenwriters and produced by filmmakers who include government programs in fiction. In Minority Report (2022), the future is invented in the year 2054, however, it has its origins in the work of Dick (2009) written as a novel in 1956. In both the book and film, the motto is credibility, technology, and society. Risks are present in society and people with talents combined with technology intend to improve the lives of the population. Pallone (2008), in the summary of the book, wrote that, at the end of the story and the end of the film, there is a difference, however, the vulnerability of the technological system allows human manipulation.

One of the points of attention is that the systems allow human manipulation, and the intentionality of human beings has unmanaged feelings and emotions. People planning cybercrimes is a reality and science fiction is made up of fragments of reality scripted to capture the attention of readers and viewers. The works are based on other works with a mixture of reality, beliefs, myths, and culture of those who write and direct the film or series.

Westworld (2016) is an American dystopian science fiction television series based on Westworld (1973) which inspires the fictional thriller Futureworld (1976), that is, there is usually intertextuality or intentionality supported by another audiovisual in cinematic dystopias and reality. Artificial intelligence, androids or robotic beings are part of science fiction and are linked to fear, feelings, and emotions. Artificial intelligence is commonly personified, has a name and attracts people with the language and results through a friendly interface.

Reality is based on fiction and science fiction shows a certain verisimilitude about the real world. The probable is feasible and the doable seems presumable. Nowadays, the consumer and employee experience increasingly uses technological trends to promote loyalty. Disruptive technologies and artificial intelligence are the strategies and emotions that are included to make business viable for society.

CHAPTER FOCUS: VERISIMILITUDE WITH LEARNING, WITH MINDSET, AND WITH EMOTIONS

Chu, Dunn and Roy (2018, p. 1) begin the text with the question "Could machines, using artificial intelligence (AI) capabilities, collaborate with writers to improve their stories?" and add that master storytellers have skills that make it possible to extract people's emotions and even the best sometimes miss the mark. Amid a data culture, machines are increasingly intelligent and provide solutions to problems, but strategic decisions are human functions.

Emotions, with proper management, are part of the decision based on data. With each story, feelings are part of learning and mindset. Artificial intelligence will be able to "watch" long-term or short-term films, as well as audiovisual materials, but they only map emotions and intensities to provide more possibilities for creating cinematographic content or ideas for writing or directing stories that have more impact on the consumption of films or plays.

Artificial intelligence does not absorb emotions from training materials and users are comforted by machine learning in human-machine interaction for productivity and to develop creativity. In the context of autonomous cars and relation to the emotional level, Zilahy and Mester. (2023) concluded that people can be monitored by artificial intelligence attached to the autonomous car to measure biometric data, such as temperature control for intervention to mitigate stress, anxiety and other emotions negative effects while travelling in autonomous cars.

The growth of phygital transformation promotes a change in the fields of action of artificial intelligence that are in the banking sector to detect problems in millions of transactions to reduce financial risks and, in the educational area, to offer pedagogical and pedagogical support to academics in a tutor format. In all areas, the use of artificial intelligence is increasing, and people feel fear, have anxiety, have dystopian thoughts, and wait for answers or images to add to their learning repertoires.

Reflection is necessary so that people do not believe that science fiction is imminent, or that disruptive technologies and artificial intelligence are the solution to all of humanity's problems. The objective of this chapter is an academic subsidy based on an exploratory and qualitative study and focuses on highlighting the intersection of learning, growth mindset and emotions made with the junction designed by knowledge and artificial intelligence in many areas of human life.

It is possible that, at the intersection, there is culture, and, in business, the focus is on the consumer and employee experience. In the context of artificial intelligence, disruptive technologies are intricately linked to business, and, in this context, there are both the emotions of consumers and employees. Consuming products or services from companies where employees do not have good experiences with their job is equivalent to buying human sadness or environments that do not favor people's mental health. Customers buy solutions and employees like to be recognized.

Biometrically measuring both employees and consumers is a form of invasion of privacy, however, it is necessary to ensure the happiness of employees in the company and the metrics can be superficial to value products and services and, on the other hand, consumers are leaving coverage of emotions. in the world wide web and machine learning, and organizations use consumer experience to leverage brands. If emotions are recognized and worked with emotional intelligence, learning and emotions can interact to enable a growth mindset.

The limbic system has the psychic function of effectively evaluating the lived context and integrates the nervous, immunological, and endocrine systems and the organization of a reaction is the emotion can be positive or negative for the person. In this chapter, emphasis will not be placed on the causes, but on the consequences of the junction designed by knowledge and artificial intelligence in two areas: the consumer and employee experience.

Both the consumer and the employee like emotions and both currently exist in phygital ecosystems. What was once physical or digital is now phygital (Mengalli, Carvalho, & Galvão (2023), because it involves the physical and the digital at the same time. These ecosystems include the employee's experience about the company and the consumer's experience of the brand. There is a possibility that employees may not find purpose in and of the organization and customers may not be satisfied with their purchases.

If the demand for productivity in the company and customer service is poor with non-disruptive technologies, with the junction designed by artificial intelligence it tends to be worse and culture as the intersection of learning, growth mindset and emotions may be present in the complexes of activities and patterns linked to creation and (co) creation that predict people's mental health. Culture includes social behavior, norms, processes, beliefs, skills, abilities, habits, and customs of people.

In the article O Futuro da Personalização: O Uso da Tecnologia na Jornada do Consumidor (2023) [The Future of Personalization: The Use of Technology in the Consumer Journey], it is written that companies that wish to stand out in their fields need to invest in the expansion of contextualized, relevant and intelligent digital experiences for their customers and, in this chapter, employees are added, because, with (hyper) personalized experiences in increasingly phygital realities, learning is at the intersection with the growth mindset and emotions and emerge Learning ∩ Growth Mindset ∩ Emotions which is Creativity which is a human characteristic and is part of the human varnish.

By identifying the common elements in the given sets, the intersection of the sets corresponds to the element that repeats in learning, growth mindset and emotions. In Mathematics, the symbol ∩ represents the intersection and in the search to understand creativity as a result of the intersection of the three sets, it is based on the text by Loveless (2002) that he wrote, in the context of physical learning spaces and with examples of the use of computational resources to support creativity, that there were researchers who identified many factors of personal approaches in professional development both for creativity and for the integration of computational resources, that is, with learning it is possible, in contact with artificial intelligence, to develop creativity..

Even though, in the text, there is basic education, and computational resources at the time of writing, the term creativity was defined in a broad way that includes descriptions of creative processes that range from spiritual paths to the psychology of artificial intelligence. Boden (2004) wrote that the concepts of artificial intelligence allow people to do psychology in a new way with the elaboration and testing of hypotheses about the structures and processes that may be involved in thinking.

The structures and processes involved in thinking affect creativity and work. Harari (2018) wrote that the technological revolution can exclude billions of humans from the job market, which leads to social and political upheavals and cannot leave anyone indifferent to the issue. Regarding the employee experience, as the use of artificial intelligence grows, organizations must invest in electronic human resources management solutions without forgetting the emotions and creativity that are in the human varnish with communication in interactions between employees and employers to ensure that people's skills and creativity are valued concerning artificial intelligence.

Future strategies for the employee experience regarding creativity tend to compromise the consumer experience, which according to Daqar and Smoudy (2019) is measured with the creation of valuable information about each customer to help provide service to the highly personalized consumer. In personalization, emotions are considered, and artificial intelligence can inform customers' feelings, but it cannot modify reality without the human being who understands what to do based on data and information in strategic decision-making.

Post-sales data and information are competitive advantages that, with human creativity, which is made up of learning, a growth mindset and emotions and is designed by knowledge and artificial intelligence, modify the behaviors and skills of employees and customers. In the phygital transformation, data culture advances, however, the challenges in dealing with humans are many, given that there is individual and collective imagination, beliefs, myths and people's history.

SOLUTIONS AND RECOMMENDATIONS: CREATIVITY IN HUMAN VARNISH

The collective, individual, historical, and social imagination highlights what is heard in common sense, what is seen and what is experienced, and disruptive technologies and artificial intelligence merit research to demystify beliefs and reveal what happens in the scope of experience. consumers and employees. It is understood that all this advancement will not destroy humanity, but data culture certainly highlights consumer habits in phygital experiences.

Maldamé (2013) highlighted in the summary of the article that technical systems should be at the service of humanity and industrialization, according to research sources, since the author rethinks the concept of nature about the purpose of human life open to the creation of a continuous process that is entrusted to the intelligence and moral responsibility of human beings. Maldamé (2013) wrote that the technique is implemented in the industrial world, therefore, it includes collective work that must be situated in the global, social structure and culture.

The author attributes the reflections in the article to his reading of Jacques Ellul (1912 - 1994) and wrote that technique generates technique (Ellul, apud Maldamé, 2013) and it was understood that technologies are the origin and engines of growth which also includes alienation when the technique is not a strategy, but the end itself.

The technical mentality can lead human beings to a sense of duty, after all, when you can, you must do it even knowing the risks, as the production system is highly specialized. Technical thinking imagines the final objective and obscurantism towards scientism prevails. It is the human being who becomes the object of technology.

Ethics are weakened and the technical system is minimized about its purpose. The integration of science [επιστήμη] with techniques [τεχνικές] for praxis [πρακτικής] tends to strengthen practices with technologies. Such integration is attributed to the Aristotelian view of practices with techniques and ensures that human behaviors are not automated or mechanized in the absence of criticism.

When analyzing customer behaviour, it is not enough to provide services that use artificial intelligence to solve problems that affect the consumer experience if the employee's learning is not consistent with the solution to the difficulty. de Felice, *et al.* (2023) wrote that human learning is social and social interaction is crucial for optimal development as well as cognitive development. The authors, in final considerations and future questions, wrote that they know little about how people learn in interactions that do not involve communication and recommend studies to evaluate the benefits of social interaction in learning concerning content.

Emotions emerge in interactions with other people, people management programs and brands seek to identify emotions with stimuli that include art, music, stories, and words. Kafetsios and Hess (2023) wrote that the perception of emotion is a human capacity, the main emotional skill that supports other emotional skills. It is possible to combine verbal and non-verbal language such as face and body so that the emotion is known. The authors wrote that the perception of emotions is linked to empathic and emotional communication processes and concluded that there is a rich field of future research that could consider personality assessments through peer-to-peer analysis and through longitudinal study that could last years or decades depending on the types of data researchers want to collect.

In the employee and consumer experiences, the human being is present to enable psychological and behavioral engagement, artificial intelligence enables the elements of data culture for strategic decision-making. The emotion that is linked to human learning for creative thinking is linked to cognitive and cultural processes in which people elaborate subjective meanings about the new emotional event. Trnka (2023) wrote that emotionally creative people have a rich past emotional life and high emotional creativity allows for more flexibility in the conceptual interpretation of past emotions.

In future research directions, the author wrote that it is possible to gain insights into how people perceive their own emotionally creative behaviors, mental processes and personality traits, that is, people can perceive themselves with behaviors, processes and personality, however, what people can do is part of their governance in full digital transformation.

Dweck (2007) wrote that the growth mindset is based on the personal belief of being able to cultivate basic qualities through one's efforts. Even though people may differ from each other in talents, initial aptitudes, interests or behaviors, each person is capable of changing and developing through efforts and experiences.

Changing behavior is possible for everyone as long as the mindset is growing. The author wrote that the growth mindset makes a person interested in their improvement.

Every improvement improves the way the employee works in the company and shows creativity at the same time as improving the interaction and effectiveness of artificial intelligence elements on e-commerce platforms. Associations with human forms, in anthropomorphism, for brands are a reality in consumer services, because human beings have the time contract to work and digital customer services depend on developers and ongoing maintenance.

The creativity of developers and designers gives virtual machines and images human characteristics, and, in the scripts, some words involve consumers in feelings, emotions, thoughts, actions or behaviors. Inanimate objects gain human modes to involve more humans with increasingly personalized experiences.

Personalization, in the market, includes images and digital avatars with more reliable aspects to promote the psychological engagement of consumers who produce the data so that company employees can make strategic decisions in volatile times and with high-speed changes in sales and shopping. According to Technology's Generational Moment with Generative AI: A CIO and CTO Guide (2023), the spirit of responsibly managing business reputation is necessary for there to be coherent coexistence between humans and machines. The aforementioned guide states that generative artificial intelligence presents new ethical principles and risks.

The intersection of human creativity needs to exist in the scenario dominated by phygital experiences and in contact with artificial intelligence so that the human being does not resemble the notes written by Morin (1956, p. 15): "In cinema, characters and objects in appear through a kind of unreal mist in the impalpability of a ghost", that is, the human being, as the main character, cannot appear in the economic scenario in unreal and impalpable mists to the point of being understood as a ghost, because, in the human varnish, there is creativity.

It is possible to verify that human beings differ in many aspects from programmable machines because they can communicate and have creativity. According to Anvarovich (2023), creative people stand out from other people in all areas and in all the work they do. It is the ideas that no one imagined that differentiate people in organizations. It is the human imagination that is an essential element in the formation of creativity, after all, unusual thoughts and solutions can give competitive advantages to employees and brands about consumers. The author adds that examples of creativity that began with the invention of the wheel are now travelling throughout the universe.

SUBSIDIES FOR NUMEROUS REFLECTIONS AND QUALITATIVE AND EXPLORATORY STUDY

Traveling through the universe is a human action and creativity is an intersection based on learning, growth mindset and emotions at the junction designed by knowledge and artificial intelligence it seems to be real in contexts that resemble science fiction films or books. Reports, journals, and magazine articles highlight the reality of the market with numbers and business revelations. Industrial revolutions and phygital transformations were supported by research and paradigm shifts, in addition to emotions.

When reading the book's proposal about the implementation of artificial intelligence and disruptive technologies that, every day, impose new possibilities for use on (cyber) society with great generalizations in objectives and, on the other hand, researchers and social scientists investigate causes and consequences in the exposure, adoption and adaptation of thinking and acting with the use of artificial intelligence, the path was to investigate a little more about human emotions and feelings, since the use of prompts and the use of artificial intelligence were elements of research into the pedagogical and andragogical practice of professors in higher education.

There was a question in the book regarding the conceivable and profound consequences of the use of artificial intelligence in social structures that would certainly not be answered in the chapter. However, it was possible to provide support for the countless reflections of researchers and professionals in the field with theory about the adoption of artificial intelligence without due knowledge of the techniques and use of computer interfaces without criticism and without understanding the technological potential associated with human emotions.

In the beginning, there was a curation of science fiction books and films that involved human interaction with machines and part of the readings are expressed in the background of the chapter. If the memory did not awaken human emotions in the reader, it was possible to support it with reflections on the irresponsible use of artificial intelligence or computational resources that writers, screenwriters, producers, and directors highlighted in printed and digital materials, as well as audiovisuals that marked generations of viewers.

Human emotions, in fictional literature and films, were, at all times, valued in projects that included the relationship between humans and machines, but, when reading articles, and chapters, for research into the use of artificial intelligence, the focus was on the results of the experiments carried out and the subjects were not the protagonists of the investigations. There was a lot of quantitative methodology.

Although it is believed that emotions and feelings regarding the use of artificial intelligence are not largely unexplored in academic circles, no texts or reports on this topic were found. Therefore, the decision to propose a chapter with an exploratory and qualitative study would tend to be a small contribution to academia regarding artificial intelligence and human interactions in phygital society.

In contemporary times, the scientific revolution emerges, and traditional paradigms are challenged and the contribution to society is countless. There are different perspectives and nonidentical methodologies to highlight artificial intelligence. Kuhn (1998) wrote that scientific revolutions are the disintegrating complements of the tradition to which the activity of science is linked. Scientific developments, in some cases, are labelled revolutions by researchers who do not venture to change paradigms.

The paradigm shift with each reading did not seek to reject the existing scientific theory and, as a consequence, there were some changes in the initial research problems, not for the search for a solution, but for the transformation of scientific imagination for a change in the scientific world. Changes and controversies were considered as part of scientific revolutions and, once again, as highlighted by Kuhn (1998), in this chapter, science consists of solving puzzles that usually include the precision of scientific knowledge in unveiling facts, elements or phenomena in academic investigations.

The exploratory study carried out is qualitative and the choice made was due to not finding texts that revealed emotions in human interaction with the machine, as well as in the employee's emotional experience when using artificial intelligence or even about what happens in the consumer emotional experience in software interactions or digital or immersive environments that use artificial intelligence in dialogue with brands. The paradigm used seemed effective in introducing changes to existing paradigms.

The additions evidenced by other theories revealed what Dewey (1979) classified in his work on the educational area as a genuine purpose that began with an impulse. It was not a desire or an impulse, but a purpose, because there was no difficulty or obstruction in carrying out the research. There was a prediction of the consequences that, in a certain way, resulted from impulse actions that involved human intelligence operations.

In Dewey's metaphor (1979) like a railroad crossing or a signal crossing, you must stop, look, and listen and, in the context of research, you must read a lot, check reality, understand the word, and read the world to transcend traditional paradigms. As Freire (1989) wrote he sought to understand the very act of reading the particular world that moved him, and this understanding allowed the author to repeat, recreate, and relive in the text he was writing. The experience lived at the time when the researchers were not reading the word, for writing the chapter, there was a search for understanding prior knowledge to read the world of emotions in human interactions with machines to recreate and revive the text that was written with the incorporation of reading the world.

When reading academic texts, incorporating world reading and organization for readers, a table was created to highlight the authors and references regarding the elements of learning, growth mindset, emotions, and the new joint: creativity, as follows:

Table 1. Purpose of the article or book

Year	Country	Elements	Purpose of the Article or Book
2023	Indonesia	Creativity	**The Concept of Creativity, the Essence of the Content and its Theoretical Methodological Foundations**. Explain the concept of creativity with theoretical and methodological foundations, as well as highlight human thinking and imagination and discuss the teacher's creativity and the student's creative thinking.
2004	England	Creativity	**The Creative Mind: Myths and Mechanisms**. Highlight examples of new thoughts and creativity in the most different areas of human life and include computing models from the field of artificial intelligence to highlight the nature of human creativity.
2002	England	Creativity	**Literature Review in Creativity, New Technologies and Learning**. Provide theory about digital learning and learning creativity.
2023	Mexico	Emotions	**Meaningful Work, Happiness at Work, and Turnover Intentions**. Highlight the relevance of work about turnover and evaluate the impact of work on happiness.
2023	Greece / Germany	Emotions	**Reconceptualizing Emotion Recognition Ability**. Describe the importance of context in the structure of a truth and bias model of the social perception of emotions (Assessment of Contextualized Emotions) for emotional intelligence skills.
2023	Czech Republic	Emotions	**Emotional Creativity: Emotional Experience as a Creative Product**. Summarize the conceptual foundations and research surrounding emotional creativity and reveal the various links between emotional creativity and personality variables.
2023	Hungary	Emotions	**Managing Negative Emotions Caused by Self-Driving**. Verify the emotions experienced in autonomous cars to increase the number of users, in addition to comparing machine learning and user expectations.
2007	United States of America	Growth Mindset	**Mindset: The New Psychology of Success**. Insights and explanation about the concept of mindset, fixed and growth mindset with the application of the concept in group cultures and organizations.
2022	England	Learning	**Learning from Others is Good, with Others is Better: The Role of Social Interaction in Human Acquisition of New Knowledge**. Outline new directions for experiments that investigate how knowledge is acquired socially.
2023	China / Canada	Learning	**What Influences Computational Thinking? A Theoretical and Empirical Study Based on the Influence of Learning Engagement on Computational Thinking in Higher Education**. Develop a model of the relationship between learning and computational thinking to examine the influence of three dimensions of learning engagement on the five dimensions of computational thinking in higher education.

Source: Authors' Selection

In addition to the articles and books, reports from companies that study advances in artificial intelligence were read and, to make the findings clearer, a second table was created with data from the reports, as follows:

The purpose of organizing the researched materials in tables was to systematize the information for presentation to the reader in a way that facilitated reading and understanding of what was read to prepare the chapter. The option to present information visually to readers occurred after accepting the suggestion and expectations of the chapter reviewer because it made sense to have a visual element to organize what was investigated in documents and references in book or article format. The context was indirectly explained in the tables, so the understanding seems more organized.

As, in the chapter, the intention was to create a new theory about artificial intelligence and emotions, keeping the visual more organized tends to facilitate the analysis of researchers and those interested in the theme that has been developed, in addition to maintaining academic rigour in terms of exposure of the revelations so that researchers can have a start for future research.

The set of academic rules was followed, and theories were assimilated to create new theoretical sets, which, according to Kuhn (197), highlights a new way of thinking about the phenomenon studied and affecting related areas. Taylor, Bogdan and DeVault (2016) wrote that in qualitative research, there is the development of concepts and insights. In this chapter, the objective was to develop the theory for reflections on the adoption of artificial intelligence without due knowledge of the techniques for the utilization and uses of computer interfaces without criticism and without understanding the possibilities of technologies associated with human emotions.

Initially, theoretical references were sought in academic search engines to support impressions and hypotheses and then the parts that had relevance and reference to the main objective of the chapter were highlighted. The objectives of the articles and

Table 2. Data from reports

Year	Country	Company	Focus
2023	United States of America	IBM Corporation	Artificial intelligence (Work Automation)
2018	United States of America	McKinsey & Company	Artificial intelligence (Impact)
2023	United States of America	McKinsey & Company	Artificial intelligence (Business Reimagination)
2023	Brazil	*MIT Technology Review* / Adobe Experience Cloud	Artificial intelligence (Consumer Experience)

Source: Authors' Selection

books were highlighted for the convergence between the purpose of the articles and books with the intentionality of the chapter. The reading was expanded to include reports from consultancies and companies that were researching artificial intelligence in convergence with business.

The reading of the corporate world, through reports, was brought to the chapter to highlight the emotions that emerge in the use of artificial intelligence and to enable reflections from other authors. The initial questions were answered, however, the directions for future research show that investigations are essential for society.

The qualitative study needed to provide sufficient information about how the investigation was conducted to allow readers to understand the context of how the chapter was produced. According to Taylor, Bogdan and DeVault (2016), when reading studies, readers do not know whether the interpretations came from the culture of knowledge, previous theoretical structures, individual experiences, or fieldwork. In this way, the search to highlight the study was written so that doubts regarding the investigative path were mitigated.

DIRECTIONS FOR FUTURE RESEARCH FOR KNOWLEDGE AND NEW PARADIGMS

When contemplating that there may be doubts on the part of readers, the story of the cauldron of Ceridwen and Dagda came to mind, because Ceridwen boils an initiating potion that is the source of all knowledge, since she had the function of being guardian of wisdom and the forms assumed had the purpose of enabling responsibility for knowledge and its uses. Regarding the Dagda, in the cauldron, there was abundance and people never left until they were satisfied.

There is no intention of having cauldrons, but of encouraging reflections with the responsibility for using knowledge about the book's theme and the abundance of subsidies so that readers can join the intellectual journey to explore the interaction between society, computational resources, and emotions. In this chapter, the origins of the researchers' training are education and economics to investigate the philosophical dilemmas to support the influences of artificial intelligence on human emotions in critical dialogue for harmony reign in the coexistence of the interaction of humans with machines in phygital transformation.

According to Chris Turner's translation of Baudrillard's writing (2006), the author stated that humanity is in a world in which events no longer truly happen through production and dissemination in real-time, in which they are lost in the void of news and information. It is necessary to investigate the effects of disruptive technologies and artificial intelligence from new points of view.

The emotional aspect, of the experiences of employees and consumers, needs to be researched based on the emotion inherent to human beings and in contact with technologies in interactions with other humans. Intelligence is part of the human and they included it as artificial, even though it is known that people parameterize software. Dewey (1979), in the area of education, wrote that observation alone is not enough, you need to understand the meaning of what you see, what you hear and what you touch. The author reported that such meanings consist of consequences, which result in actions, therefore, investigations must seek metrics in other areas, but numbers without meanings for investigators are not enough.

Past experiences are present in the research and without reflecting on them and analyzing similar aspects, the possibilities are smaller for understanding the situation investigated. In the chapter "Mindsets", Dweck (2007) wrote that when she was a young researcher, something happened that changed her life. She was obsessed with the idea of understanding how people dealt with failure and decided to study the topic by observing children with puzzles to solve. The degree of difficulty increased as the children progressed in putting together the pieces and completing the deliveries of the assembled puzzles. The researcher observed the children's strategies and investigated what they thought and felt.

The young researcher hoped to find differences in the ways children faced difficulties and realized that human qualities, such as intellectual abilities, can be cultivated through effort. In this way, research can verify human emotions about artificial intelligence, whether they can be managed or not and what beliefs can mean for research subjects. Including the verification of the growth mindset tends to make it possible to understand the diversity of individual training, subjective experiences, and ways of learning.

About business and the economy, an opportunity is to check how industries need to deal with new situations involving artificial intelligence in terms of doing more, doing faster, and doing better in terms of understanding results from people who use computing resources or company turnover. In the research for this chapter, no investigations or consultancy reports were found that focused on emotions and artificial intelligence in organizations.

In the field of psychology, if researchers believe that emotional intelligence can be developed, how to develop it may be a question to be answered about artificial intelligence and professions of the future. It is essential to be clear that development is a continuous process because the more the skill is improved, the more impacts it will have on the interactions between humans and machines and concerning the coherence of teams and strategic decision-making. It is possible to see that some hypotheses were highlighted.

Tang, *et al.* (2020), in conclusion, wrote that teachers and researchers from different disciplines and dissimilar educational levels must increase collaboration so that more researchers can evaluate and promote computational thinking systematically. The authors suggested that assessments could be designed to map the progression of learning computational thinking in each subject and to encourage students to apply computational thinking skills to learning other subjects. Based on the authors' conclusion, verifying students' computational thinking and emotions can be potential for understanding learning and interaction with computational resources at different educational levels, after all, the starting point can be in educational institutions.

In finalizing directions for future research, mad skills are included as exceptional abilities or highly developed talents in a specific area for further studies to verify to what extent artificial intelligence will need people with abilities that are beyond the ordinary or expected since such skills can cover many areas such as programming, languages, mathematics, and statistics. It will be important to understand how exceptional performances or remarkable capabilities are used to understand, create, or execute artificial intelligence work in certain domains.

FINAL CONSIDERATIONS

In conclusion, culture in the use of disruptive technologies and artificial intelligence needs science, theory and understanding of the technique so that human practical actions exist in the experience of consumers and employees. Emotion must be included, as well as the growth mindset in learning. Knowledge and artificial intelligence outline the intersections that need to be understood to mitigate robotization, automation and human mechanization.

Technologies are strategies and need to be demystified to understand what the desires and satisfactions of consumers and employees are. Economic power should not prevail over human beings so that dystopias do not become realities. If there is an echo of economic power, phygital colonizations would have the technique used without reflection and, according to Dewey (1979), the formation of purpose is an intellectual operation that involves the observation of environmental conditions and circumstances, the knowledge and experience and the combination of observation with memory present in judgment.

Impulse or desire is not the purpose of implementing projects with disruptive technologies or artificial intelligence, because it is necessary to predict the consequences of acting in observed conditions and have a plan and method of action with the technique. The author adds that if wishes were horses, beggars would ride. This statement made sense at the time the book was written, but, in times of use of artificial intelligence, the desire for agility in the digital era is far from flexibility in the industrial era.

The desire that transforms into impulse can be an imperative for incorporating uncertainty and non-adaptability into the flow of work. As much as science fiction in books and films highlights human lives and emotions in addition to the presence of disruptive technologies in the plot, there is the possibility of the existence of real dystopias and the focus on the machine and not on human beings in the professions of the future.

Even though creativity is the intersection between learning, the growth mindset and emotion and is in the human varnish with communication at the junction designed by knowledge and artificial intelligence, not all companies respect the employee and consumer experience. There is a relationship with employee satisfaction, customer satisfaction and interaction with machines must be reflected in the well-being and mental health of the employee in the ecosystem that has the consumer who gives preference to products and services that value environmental governance and social.

Ethics is a human solution that can mitigate the prioritization of artificial intelligence to the detriment of human emotion, as well as the integration of science and technique to have the praxis to strengthen human practices with technologies. Respect for the human being as a tangible person and part of the economic system should distance human participation in society as a supporting role, because, in reality, people are protagonists with the creativity that is part of the human varnish so as not to become robotic, especially in the professions of the future.

In qualitative and exploratory studies, the certainty that human emotions and feelings need to be more present in academic circles and consultancy reports to the detriment of productivity for the use of artificial intelligence. Although a small contribution, the chapter fulfils the objective of encouraging reflection on the uses of artificial intelligence and disruptive technologies in phygital society.

According to Kuhn (1998), sometimes a common problem, which should be solved through known rules and procedures, resists the violent and repeated attack of the most skilled members of the group in whose area of competence it occurs, that is, scientific revolutions happen when traditions break, but with the prevalence of science. New research must be carried out in the psychological, humanistic, business, and computational sciences fields.

On the authority of Harari (2018), perhaps the most important thing is the fact that artificial intelligence and biotechnology are giving humanity the power to reformulate and reengineer life, but the author warns that someone may decide to use such power and it is still possible to conclude that it could be in the meaning of life or the robotization and mechanization of the professional market. Silva (2001) wrote that the problem is not one of machinery, but of predicting and optimizing the repercussions in interactions with other elements of the system. Therefore, research is necessary to place human emotions in advances in artificial intelligence.

Advancing with the use of artificial intelligence in the markets presupposes conditioning factors for the formation of a new world of creativity that needs learning, a growth mindset and emotions to exist amid the design created with knowledge and artificial intelligence that challenges science to demonstrate that disruptive technologies are strategic themes. Therefore, research is necessary to place human emotions in advances in artificial intelligence.

As there is an urgent need to move forward to unveil new paths, the educational area needs to be present in investigations that deal with disruptive technologies at the organizational level, because it is in global functioning, whether in basic education or higher education, the educational curriculum highlights the formations of beings humans and how humans interact with machines.

REFERENCES

Anvarovich, N. E. (2023). The Concept of Creativity, the Essence of the Content and its Theoretical Methodological Foundations. *International Journal on Orange Technology, 5*(7). https://researchparks.innovativeacademicjournals.com/index.php/IJOT/article/view/6248

Augmented Work for an Automated, AI-driven World. (2023). *IBM Institute for Business Value*. https://www.ibm.com/thought-leadership/institute-business-value/en-us/report/augmented-workforce

Baudrillard, J. (2006). *Virtuality and Events: The Hell of Power*. https://baudrillardstudies.ubishops.ca/virtuality-and-events-the-hell-of-power/

Boden, M. A. (2004). *The Creative Mind: Myths and Mechanisms. 2*. Routledge. doi:10.4324/9780203508527

Charles-Leija, H., Castro, C. G., Toledo, M., & Ballesteros-Valdés, R. (2023). Meaningful Work, Happiness at Work, and Turnover Intentions. *International Journal of Environmental Research and Public Health*, *20*(4), 3565. doi:10.3390/ijerph20043565 PMID:36834260

Chu, E., Dunn, J., & Roy, D. (2018). AI's Growing Impact. *McKinsey Quarterly*. https://www.mckinsey.com/~/media/McKinsey/Business%20Functions/McKinsey%20Analytics/Our%20Insights/AIs%20growing%20impact/AIs-growing-impact.pdf

da Silva, B. D. (2001). A Tecnologia é uma Estratégia. In *Actas da II Conferência Internacional Desafios 2001* (pp. 839–859). Centro de Competência da Universidade do Minho do Projecto Nónio.

Daqar, M. A. M. A., & Smoudy, A. K. A. (2019). The Role of Artificial Intelligence on Enhancing Customer Experience. *International Review of Management and Marketing. Econjournals*, *9*(4), 22–31.

de Carvalho, A. A., Cirera, R. dos R., & Mengalli, N. M. (n.d.). *FoLo - Fear of Logging off: Medo de Ficar sem Conexão*. https://www.uscs.edu.br/boletim/1603

de Carvalho, A. A., Mengalli, N. M., & Lucas, R. B. (2022). A Tessitura da Interdisciplinaridade e da Inovação como o Futuro na Pesquisa, no Ensino e na Extensão: A Reflexão da Transformação Phygital e das Tendências Imersivas nos Projetos Extensionistas. In Olhares Plurais e Multidisciplinares na Pesquisa e Extensão. Arco Editores. doi:10.48209/978-65-5417-027-1

de Felice, S. (2023). *Learning from Others is Good, with Others is Better: The Role of Social Interaction in Human Acquisition of New Knowledge. Phil.* Trans. R. Soc. doi:10.1098/rstb.2021.0357

Dewey, J. (1979). *Experiência e Educação. 3.* Companhia Editora Nacional.

Dick, P. K. (2009). *Minority Report.* Gollacz.

Dick, P. K. (2017). *Blade Runner: Do Androids Dream of Electric Sheep?* Del Rey Books.

Dweck, C. S. S. (2007). *Mindset: The New Psychology of Success.* Random House Publishing.

Freire, P. (1989). A Importância do Ato de Ler: Em Três Artigos que se Completam. Autores Associados: Cortez. Coleção Polêmicas do Nosso Tempo.

Futureworld. (1976). https://www.primevideo.com/dp/amzn1.dv.gti.62b56442-c460-16c4-8dfe-c0e6b522cb84?autoplay=0&ref_=atv_cf_strg_wb

Futuro da Personalização, O. O Uso da Tecnologia na Jornada do Consumidor. (2023). *MIT Technology Review*. https://mittechreview.com.br/o-futuro-da-personalizacao-o-uso-da-tecnologia-na-jornada-do-consumidor/?utm_campaign=adobe_artigo_vr_15set23&utm_medium=email&utm_source=RD+Station

Harari, Y. N. (2018). *21 Lições para o Século 21.* Companhia das Letras.

Her. (2013). https://www.warnerbros.com/movies/her

Kafetsios, K., & Hess, U. (2023). Reconceptualizing Emotion Recognition Ability. *Journal of Intelligence, 11*(6), 123. . doi:10.3390/jintelligence11060123

Kuhn, T. S. (1970). *The Structure of Scientific Revolutions. 2*. The University of Chicago Press.

Kuhn, T. S. (1998). *A Estrutura das Revoluções Científicas. 5*. Editora Perspectiva.

Liu, S., Peng, C., & Srivastava, G. (2023). What Influences Computational Thinking? A Theoretical and Empirical Study Based on the Influence of Learning Engagement on Computational Thinking in Higher Education. *Computer Applications in Engineering Education, 31*(6), 1690–1704. Advance online publication. doi:10.1002/cae.22669

Loveless, A. M. (2002). *Literature Review in Creativity, New Technologies and Learning*. A NESTA Futurelab Research - report 4. https://citeseerx.ist.psu.edu/document?repid=rep1&type=pdf&doi=564bad6c5319dd1443e249af1d95001d7094360c

Maldamé, J. M. (2013) Les Défis Éthiques des Nouvelles Technologies à la Lumière de la Doctrine Sociale de L'Église. *RCatT, 38*(1), 261-281. https://www.raco.cat/index.php/RevistaTeologia/article/download/267002/363061/

Mengalli, N. M., de Carvalho, A. A., & Galvão, S. M. (2023). Metaverse Ecosystem and Consumer Society 5.0: Consumer Experience and Influencer Marketing in Phygital Transformation. In R. Bansal, S. A. Qalati, & A. Chakir (Eds.), *Influencer Marketing Applications Within the Metaverse* (pp. 33–56). IGI Global. doi:10.4018/978-1-6684-8898-0.ch003

Morin, E. (1956). *Le Cinéma ou L'homme Imaginaire: Essai d'Anthropologie Sociologique*. Les Éditions de Minuit.

Pallone, S. (2008). Minority Report: A Nova Lei. *ComCiência*, 104. http://comciencia.scielo.br/pdf/cci/n104/a12n104.pdf

Papert, S. A. (1993). *Mindstorms: Children, Computers, and Powerful Ideas*. Basic Books.

Raymond, E. S. (1999). *The Cathedral & the Bazaar: Musings on Linux and Open Source by an Accidental Revolutionary*. O'Reilly Media. doi:10.100712130-999-1026-0

ReportM. (2002). https://www.youtube.com/watch?v=Dv6jgzcMu0Y

RunnerB. (1982). https://www.warnerbros.com/movies/blade-runner

Tang, X., Yin, Y., Lin, Q., Hadad, R., & Zhai, X. (2020). Assessing Computational Thinking: A Systematic Review of Empirical Studies. *Computers & Education, 148*(April), 103798. doi:10.1016/j.compedu.2019.103798

Taylor, S. J., Bogdan, R., & DeVault, M. L. (2016). Introduction to Qualitative Research Methods: A Guidebook and Resource. Wiley. Technology's Generational Moment with Generative AI: A CIO and CTO Guide. *McKinsey Digital*. https://www.mckinsey.com/capabilities/mckinsey-digital/our-insights/technologys-generational-moment-with-generative-ai-a-cio-and-cto-guide#/

The Matrix. (1999). https://www.warnerbros.com/movies/matrix

The Terminator. (1984) https://www.primevideo.com/detail/The-Terminator/0L8IKW4SVSHPR66WSIZOEEAFYX/ref=atv_nb_lcl_pt_BR?ie=UTF8&language=pt_BR

Trnka, R. (2023). Emotional Creativity: Emotional Experience as Creative Product. In *The Cambridge Handbook of Creativity and Emotions* (pp. 321-339). Cambridge University Press. https://ssrn.com/abstract=4578762

Westworld. (1973). https://www.primevideo.com/detail/Westworld/0LY2YLBLMHJPEIZ6JDEXESBUW3

Westworld. (2016). https://www.hbo.com/westworld

Zilahy, D., & Mester, G. (2023). Managing Negative Emotions Caused by Self-Driving. *Interdisciplinary Description of Complex Systems*, *21*(4), 351–355. doi:10.7906/indecs.21.4.4

ADDITIONAL READING

Abuhantash, A. (2023). The future of HR management: Exploring the potential of e-HRM for improving employee experience and organizational outcomes. *World Journal of Advanced Research and Reviews*, *18*(02), 647–651. doi:10.30574/wjarr.2023.18.2.0883

Asante, & .... (2023). Optimization of Consumer Engagement with Artificial Intelligence Elements on Electronic Commerce Platforms. *Journal of Electronic Commerce Research*, *24*(1). http://www.jecr.org/sites/default/files/2023vol24no1_Paper2.pdf

Cheng, K., Chang, K., & Tai, H. (2022). AI Boosts Performance but Affects Employee Emotions. *Information Resources Management Journal*, *35*(1), 1–18. doi:10.4018/irmj.314220

Sadhasivam, S., & Kamalakannan, J. (2023). Neural Patterns of Emotions in EEG and fMRI: Emotions' Patterns in EEG Signals. In C. Chowdhary (Ed.), *Multidisciplinary Applications of Deep Learning-Based Artificial Emotional Intelligence* (pp. 77–92). IGI Global. doi:10.4018/978-1-6684-5673-6.ch006

Scribano, A., & Chahbenderian, F. (2021). Digital Labour, Pandemic COVID-19, and Emotions. In M. Korstanje (Ed.), *Socio-Economic Effects and Recovery Efforts for the Rental Industry: Post-COVID-19 Strategies* (pp. 165–177). IGI Global. doi:10.4018/978-1-7998-7287-0.ch009

Siau, K., & Wang, W. (2020). Artificial Intelligence (AI) Ethics: Ethics of AI and Ethical AI. *Journal of Database Management*, *31*(2), 74–87. doi:10.4018/JDM.2020040105

KEY TERMS AND DEFINITIONS

Consumer Experience: In times of recommendations made by artificial intelligence in digital environments, time spent is often reduced when choosing products or services. Satisfactory experiences provide consumers with feelings of attention and dedication towards platforms that highlight behaviors related to psychological engagement and trigger observable attitudes through data to improve other consumer experiences. Recommendations, in computer systems, enhance behavioral engagement based on psychological involvement with the e-commerce platform. It is believed that the recommendation system made by artificial intelligence influences behavioral and psychological engagement in consumption. It is noteworthy that emotions do not end with purchases, because brands can, with data relating to engagements or not, modify the ways in which they relate to consumers in the transaction cycle and shopping journeys.

Emotions: Should be understood as a state of the mind brought by neurophysiological process and changes associated with feelings.

Employee Experience: At a time when mobility, social networks and phygital transformation are reinforced for work, the crossing of data and emotions are elements for analysis and interpretation. Employee experience has strategic value for companies and is part of organizational goal initiatives because they are related to the impact of experience on business results. By employees, it is understood that they (co) work for the advances of companies in the market, therefore, the experiences they have in organizational activities and actions reflect on productivity and assertiveness. Service and improved communication impact employee experience. Artificial intelligence is part of experiences and the data contained in interactions is of an emotional and feelings nature.

Experience: Refers to a state of consciousness specifically linked to individual perceptions or previous knowledge.

Chapter 9
How to Make Mental Healthcare More Accessible:
The AI Therapy of Headspace

Giulio Ferrigno
Scuola Superiore Sant'Anna, Italy

ABSTRACT

Within the AI academic realm, the burgeoning significance of mental healthcare has prompted global governments to prioritize comprehensive mental health programs. Recent data underscore the heightened importance of mental health relative to physical well-being. Nevertheless, the concept of mental health recovery has only recently gained substantial attention, especially in the COVID-19 pandemic. However, few studies investigated the role of AI in mental health. This chapter investigates the question: "How can AI make mental healthcare more accessible during emergencies like the COVID-19 pandemic?" To grapple with this research question, the chapter employs a single-case study approach centered on Headspace, a company leveraging AI to revolutionize mental healthcare accessibility. The case study analysis reveals the AI therapy's transformative power in addressing these needs innovatively while maintaining scientific rigor. The chapter concludes by proposing a novel framework for AI therapy.

INTRODUCTION

Mental healthcare is becoming one of the most important fields to be taken into consideration by many governments around the world (World Health Organization, 2021). People and countries are realizing the need for proper programs and interest in

DOI: 10.4018/979-8-3693-0802-8.ch009

mental health care, and that there are still a lot of needs that have not been satisfied yet (Andrade et al., 2022). According to recent surveys, mental health is considered more important than physical health (Elfein 2022). However, the importance of recovery in the scope of mental health has been addressed seriously only in recent years (Bauer, Wistow, Hyànek, Figueroa & Sandford 2018; Senneseth et al., 2022). In this regard, existing literature has highlighted many barriers to mental health access (George, Daniels & Fioratou 2018). They include financial, communication, and cultural barriers (Kohn et al., 2022; Nester et al., 2022).

Despite the persistent challenges, contemporary research has begun to unveil the potential breakthroughs in overcoming barriers to mental health services (Appio et al., 2023). This discernible shift is attributed to the technological advancements and artificial intelligence (AI) innovations that have been introduced during the unprecedented circumstances of the COVID-19 pandemic (Aleem et al., 2023). These developments offer novel and distinctive avenues for the delivery of mental health services, suggesting a transformative impact on the traditional constraints previously encountered in this domain. Despite this recent progress, we still lack studies that provide an in-depth analysis of how mental healthcare can be more accessible using AI (Appio et al., 2023). This issue has become particularly important in the crisis context (Aleem et al., 2023). Therefore, in this book chapter, I aim to examine the following research question: "*How can AI make mental healthcare more accessible during an emergency or a crisis such as the COVID-19 pandemic*?

To answer this research question, I will perform an in-depth analysis of a single case (Eisenhardt & Graebner, 2007; Siggelkow, 2007), that is Headspace, a company that has found a very innovative and unique way to deliver mental health services through AI technologies and making them available everywhere and at any time. Two reasons have driven me to conduct a single case study. First, the exploration of a single case study epitomizes a distinctive and critical case in challenging a well-formulated theory (Ravenswood, 2011; Yin, 2009). Second, since only limited theoretical understanding subsists about how companies can make more accessible mental healthcare during an emergency crisis such as COVID-19, the benefits of extracting many details in a particular case (Eisenhardt & Graebner, 2007) allow theory to emerge from the data can be a valuable starting point (Ravenswood, 2011; Siggelkow, 2007). Therefore, it seems that AI literature can benefit from the conduction of a single case as a revelatory case of how firms can make more accessible mental healthcare through the use of AI therapy.

This study underscores three key findings. Firstly, it illuminates a shift within organizations from profit-oriented to human-centered orientations, with a particular focus on the transformative role of social innovation in reshaping contemporary priorities, especially in the context of artificial intelligence (Berretta et al., 2023). The emphasis lies on the compelling need for enterprises to move beyond conventional profit-centric motives, advocating instead for a holistic commitment to enhancing the general welfare (Ferrigno and Cucino, 2021). This transition holds theoretical significance by revealing the evolving ethos of modern corporations and emphasizes the crucial importance of societal impact alongside economic success (George et al., 2023).

Secondly, the study highlights the influence of social innovation on corporate reputation and standing, particularly in the realm of artificial intelligence (Love et al., 2017). It underscores the potential for social innovation initiatives to surpass customary boundaries and sectoral limitations, profoundly shaping the overarching perception of corporate conduct (Dionisio and de Vargas, 2020). This perspective underscores the capacity of companies, particularly those engaged with AI, to enhance their credibility and societal standing through conscientious, purpose-driven initiatives (Cucino and Ferrigno, 2023; Ferrigno and Cucino, 2021; Wamba et al., 2020).

Lastly, the study illustrates the concept of resilience and adaptation in the face of unforeseen challenges, emphasizing the exemplary resilience demonstrated by Headspace, particularly during the unprecedented disruptions of the COVID-19 pandemic (Dohale et al., 2022; Ferrigno and Cucino, 2021). This contributes to theoretical discourse by illustrating how organizations, especially those utilizing AI capabilities, not only withstand but thrive amid tumultuous periods (Conz & Magnani, 2020). The defined resilience, as the process by which an actor navigates adversity while positively adjusting and maintaining functionality, is predicated upon a steadfast commitment to core mission and values—a tenet deemed particularly relevant in the age of AI (Dohale et al., 2022).

The book chapter is structured as follows. Section 2, provides an overview of Innovations in the healthcare industry, focusing also on the rise of AI power for mental health. Section 3, examines the case study of Headspace and provides a snapshot of its history, mission, and key elements that characterize its AI innovation. Section 4, shows the data collected provides an analysis of the benefits brought by the AI therapy of Headspace during the Covid-19 pandemic, and proposes a new framework for AI therapy. Lastly, in Section 5, the theoretical and managerial implications of the book chapter are discussed together with some lines of future directions.

THEORETICAL BACKGROUND

Innovations In the Healthcare Industry

In the healthcare sector, innovation predominantly hinges upon the efficacy and efficiency of information technology and information systems (Thakur, Hsu &

Fontenot, 2012). Consequently, it becomes imperative for executives and practitioners within healthcare companies to exhibit a high degree of technological competence and demonstrate a robust propensity for adaptability.

The decision-making processes within such organizations are profoundly influenced by a confluence of internal and external factors (Thakur, Hsu & Fontenot, 2012). Internal dynamics may encompass the prevailing organizational culture, which delineates the values and convictions of its workforce. Conversely, external factors encompass competitive forces that impel organizations to continually enhance their operational capabilities to gain a competitive edge over their industry peers (Andrade et al., 2022).

Within the healthcare industry, an organization's receptivity to novel innovations is frequently contingent upon several key determinants (Kohn et al., 2022). These determinants encompass the nature of the emerging technologies, the intrinsic characteristics of the organization itself, and the overarching dynamics of the market environment. Notably, healthcare companies place a substantial emphasis on knowledge development and market orientation (Cheshmehzangi et al., 2022). The latter facet fosters a customer-centric strategy, positioning the needs of patients (i.e., customers) as the central focus of every organizational endeavor, ultimately culminating in the delivery of elevated customer value.

Empirical studies (Thakur, Hsu & Fontenot, 2012) have further elucidated that effective management practices, particularly in hostile environments, necessitate the cultivation and sustenance of robust employee relationships. To this end, companies are advised to adopt organic organizational structures over hierarchical ones, facilitating enhanced information flow across various organizational tiers. Such an approach mitigates ambiguity and conflicts during the execution of pivotal strategic activities, which are pivotal to the success of healthcare companies (Miralles et al., 2020).

As we move forward, the healthcare sector is poised to undergo profound transformations, driven by the rapid advancement of information systems and databases (George et al., 2018). These technological innovations hold the potential to streamline communication among staff members and patients alike, facilitating expedient access to comprehensive health records (Drew and Funk, 2010). This, in turn, enables the personalization of treatments and therapies in response to varying clinical scenarios (Bauer et al., 2008).

Crucially, these evolving practices carry the potential to ameliorate healthcare costs, rendering healthcare more accessible and affordable (Hollis et al., 2015). This is especially significant within the context of the United States, where efforts are underway to expand access to affordable care without imposing limitations or denials of coverage based on pre-existing medical conditions or insurance status (Gupta et al., 2020).

The Socioeconomic Consequences of The Pandemic

Towards the close of 2019 and the inception of 2020, the Covid-19 pandemic began its pervasive global spread. This unforeseen circumstance compelled numerous enterprises to halt their operations, driven by the enforcement of lockdown measures by governments to curb the escalating contagion rates (Chesbrough, 2020). Paradoxically, this unprecedented health crisis spurred several companies to undertake transformative innovations, not with the primary aim of augmenting their financial gains, but rather, with an altruistic purpose of providing support to a society grappling with the ramifications of the pandemic. These endeavors were directed towards the provision of medical resources and assistance to those adversely affected (Vesci et al., 2021).

In times of crises or exigent circumstances, firms frequently find themselves pivoting towards purpose-driven initiatives (Ferrigno and Cucino, 2021). It has become increasingly common for companies to identify or formulate a social purpose in times of adversity. Although the adoption of a higher purpose does not inherently guarantee financial prosperity for the organization, it undeniably carries tangible ramifications for the financial well-being, competitiveness, and employee commitment within the organizational framework. Consequently, it is reasonable to posit that the entities that assumed risks to furnish medical equipment and services during the COVID-19 pandemic did so not solely for economic opportunism but primarily to contribute meaningfully to the welfare of the community in both the immediate and protracted temporal dimensions.

Over the past decades, the economic landscape has evolved into a fiercely competitive arena, largely propelled by the globalization of markets (Ferrigno and Cucino, 2021). This dynamic compels companies to innovate expeditiously, leveraging their established knowledge base to the fullest extent while concurrently introducing novel concepts in products and services. Throughout the COVID-19 crisis, divergent strategic responses were observed among companies: some chose to swiftly capitalize on their existing competencies, while others embarked on the development of entirely new skill sets. In both scenarios, companies made consequential decisions regarding whether to align their actions with purpose-driven objectives solely during the health emergency or to perpetuate these endeavors beyond the zenith of the crisis (Chesbrough, 2020; Ferrigno and Cucino, 2021).

The Power of AI For Mental Health During the Pandemic

The domain of mental healthcare has garnered increasing attention from governments worldwide, marking a notable shift in its perceived significance (World Health

Organization, 2021). Throughout history, mental health has often been marginalized, with individuals grappling with mental health challenges frequently subjected to discrimination, social isolation, and inappropriate care and support (Cucino et al., 2023a; Drew and Funk, 2010). Thankfully, this paradigm is undergoing a transformative shift (see Figure 1), as societies and nations recognize the imperative of comprehensive mental health programs and interventions. It is becoming evident that numerous unmet needs persist in the realm of mental health, elevating the significance of recovery in mental healthcare (Bauer et al., 2018).

The pervasive stigma associated with mental illness has profoundly shaped societal perceptions, often relegating those affected to derogatory labels such as "crazy" or "lunatics." Consequently, they were often erroneously considered permanently disabled or beyond the prospect of recovery. However, recent decades have witnessed a transformation in this narrative (Flett et al., 2020). An increasing number of personal testimonies and recovery narratives have paved the way for more empirically informed recovery approaches and policies (Senneseth et al., 2022). At

Figure 1. Perceived importance of mental health compared to physical health worldwide in 2020
Source: Elfein (2022)

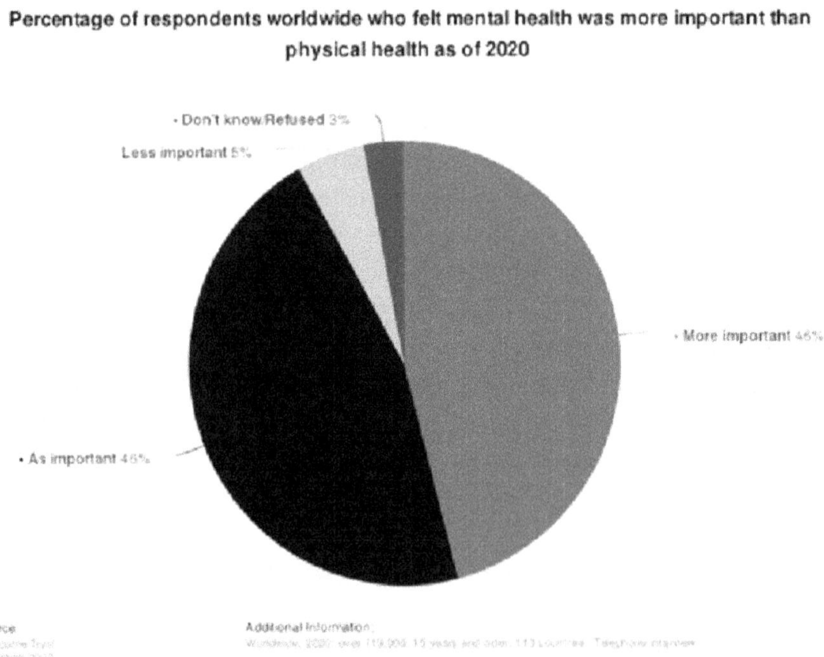

the core of these approaches lies the individual, encompassing their relationships, personal experiences, community bonds, and identity (Cucino et al., 2022). In this regard, some studies have for instance proposed frameworks that encapsulate the key factors contributing to a patient's healing journey: connectedness (social groups/relationships), hope and optimism (motivation/aspirations), identity (overcoming stigma), meaning (meaningful life/social goals), and empowerment (responsibility/strengths)(Leamy, Bird, Le Boutillier, Williams & Slade, 2011).

The rapidly evolving landscape of digital information and communication technologies (Ferrigno et al., 2023) holds the promise of further enhancing access to mental healthcare treatments, rendering them more flexible and personalized than ever before (Hollis et al., 2015). This technological paradigm empowers patients by affording them greater control and freedom, exemplified by the availability of 24-hour services (Aleem et al., 2023). Patients can effortlessly monitor their activities, emotions, and behaviors in real time, recording them on their mobile devices to receive prompt and reliable feedback (Sestino and D'Angelo, 2023). Simultaneously, psychiatrists gain deeper insights into their patients' mental states.

Recent years have witnessed a proliferation of mental health apps, catering to both professionals and the general public, with remarkable speed of development and market deployment (Neary and Schueller, 2018). While mental health apps offer a myriad of advantages, they are not without limitations and challenges (Zhang, Ho, Cheok & Ho, 2015). Most notably, these apps often fall short of achieving the same results and outcomes as consultations with mental health specialists (Miralles et al., 2020). This disparity arises from factors such as inadequate post-release maintenance or the absence of rigorous evaluations concerning the efficacy and safety of the provided services. Furthermore, app developers typically lack clinical expertise, potentially influencing the nature and quality of recovery sought by patients (Magrabì et al., 2019). Another significant challenge is the "digital divide" (Hollis et al., 2015), which characterizes the disparity in access to digital technologies and the internet. This divide adversely affects individuals without access to computers or internet-enabled mobile devices, including homeless individuals, elderly populations, and people with disabilities (Cheshmehzangi, et al., 2022). The lack of access to mental health apps can erect barriers to receiving necessary assistance, rather than facilitating it (Miralles et al., 2020).

However, recent research suggests that the evolution of technology and the innovative applications of artificial intelligence during the Covid-19 pandemic have presented unique opportunities to overcome longstanding barriers in the delivery of mental health services (Aleem et al., 2023; Ferrigno and Cucino, 2023). Despite these promising developments, there remains a notable gap in the literature, with insufficient studies providing a detailed analysis of how artificial intelligence can contribute to enhanced accessibility in mental healthcare (Appio et al., 2023).

RESEARCH METHODOLOGY

In alignment with the research objectives and the conceptual underpinnings guiding my inquiry, I have embraced an inductive and exploratory methodology for my empirical analysis. Recognized as a fitting approach for generating novel theoretical insights to address extant challenges (Lee et al., 1999), my methodological framework draws inspiration from the theory-building approach delineated by Eisenhardt (2021), complemented by the methodological guidance of Yin (2014) and Klein and Myers (1999). This methodological foundation has been instrumental in the systematic formulation of theory through the meticulous examination of paradigmatic examples of AI companies in the healthcare sector – namely, Headspace.

The strategic integration of this case study in my research design serves the essential purpose of delving into intricate phenomena within their contextual landscapes. This approach not only facilitates the in-depth collection of detailed and nuanced data but also aligns with the retrospective nature of case analyses (Easton, 1998; Yin, 2014). As a result, my exploration of AI in healthcare, spotlighting the AI therapy of Headspace, provides nuanced insights into how AI can make more accessible mental healthcare.

It is imperative to acknowledge that, by adhering to an exploratory case study design, the potential for statistically generalizing our findings is inherently confined (Yin, 2003). Instead, my aim is directed towards achieving analytical and theoretical generalizations that contribute substantively to the existing body of knowledge on AI and mental healthcare. While my findings are intended to serve as a springboard for informing subsequent theoretical and empirical investigations into the intricacies of AI in COVID-19 contexts, it is acknowledged that the applicability of these insights may be context-specific.

Theoretical Sampling

To elucidate the theoretical arguments and interrelationships posited within the provisional conceptual framework, and to illustrate the practical application and validation of the developed conceptual reasoning through empirical cases, the selection of the Headspace case study was predicated upon the availability of readily accessible data and the convergence of ongoing research endeavors with theoretical interests (Dell'Era et al., 2020). By leveraging the Headspace case study, this investigation endeavors to scrutinize the social innovation processes enacted by the organization to generate value through the incorporation of emerging technologies (Ferrigno et al., 2022a). The dynamic and burgeoning participation of individuals within the mental healthcare sector has profoundly shaped the evolution of therapeutic modalities (Jones, 2020). The comprehensive inquiry is conducted through the utilization of a qualitative case-based methodology (Eisenhardt, 2021; Eisenhardt and Graebner, 2007). This approach is inherently designed to comprehend a particular phenomenon and is oriented toward the exploration of a specific issue or scenario. The ultimate aim of qualitative research is to "depict and analyze the world as it is perceived, construed, and comprehended by individuals within the context of their everyday existence" (Cropley, 2015).

Data Collection

In the formulation of the case study, a multifaceted approach was employed to enhance the reliability and credibility of the data (Cucino, Ferrigno, and Piccaluga, 2021). The substantial volume of data available afforded a distinctive opportunity to delve comprehensively into the examination of the social innovation endeavors undertaken by Headspace over the years.

Following previous research (Ferrigno et al., 2022b), the data about the operational and organizational aspects were procured through web-based interviews, press releases, and diverse online sources. These datasets underwent meticulous analysis to corroborate and augment my comprehension of the company's objectives, roles, and overarching vision. The initial information-gathering process commenced with a thorough review of the Crunchbase website, which furnished a comprehensive overview encompassing financial metrics, board membership, and notable performance benchmarks of the company. Furthermore, the official Headspace webpages afforded an immersive exploration of the company's ethos and the perspectives of its founders. For instance, insights were gleaned from observing Andy Puddicombe, the founder himself, participating in TED talks, 'Talks at Google,' and a Web Summit. This also facilitated an examination of the company's engagement with potential users through their official social media channels. Subsequently, an extensive review of 12 scholarly articles was conducted using Google News and Google Scholar to amass a variety of perspectives concerning the company, its competitors, and its strategic partnerships. Access to the ABI/INFORM database facilitated the acquisition of a wealth of information spanning disciplines such as business, economics, and management, along with a spectrum of related fields. Lastly, a search for statistical data about the performance of the Headspace app and its competitors was conducted on the Statista website, thereby enabling an assessment of the efficacy or lack thereof in the company's operational endeavors.

Data Analysis

In delving into this extensive dataset, I rigorously employed a methodological approach inspired by foundational works, including Eisenhardt (2021), Miles and Huberman

(1984), and Strauss and Corbin (1998). This analytical expedition commenced with a meticulous understanding of the case study to construct a comprehensive narrative delineating the origin and evolution of this company.

Progressing from the foundational stage, interview transcripts from the web were leveraged to craft individual case studies spotlighting the most significant large corporations and startups interacting with the two service providers. Employing within-case methodology as recommended by Eisenhardt (1989) and Miles and Huberman (1984), I synthesized our evolving understanding of CE forms (Eisenhardt and Graebner, 2007). This involved the construction of individual case studies based on transcripts and supplementary data. As a validation step, the initial two authors independently revisited the original interviews, forming distinct perspectives for each case. Drawing on methodologies endorsed by Miles and Huberman (1984) and integrating pertinent literature on healthcare (Bauer, Wistow, Hyànek, Figueroa & Sandford 2018; Senneseth et al., 2022), I employed tables and graphs to facilitate case comparisons. Conceptual insights, especially those about AI therapy, underwent rigorous scrutiny through the devil's advocacy method (Eisenhardt, 2021) to eliminate alternative interpretations.

Throughout the within-case analysis, an ongoing examination of qualitative data took place, navigating the intricate interplay between theory, data, and existing literature to accommodate emerging theoretical relationships. My research design adhered to a replication logic, treating each case as an independent experiment, thereby validating theoretical relationships across firms (Yin, 2014). The iterative process reached its culmination upon achieving theoretical saturation, wherein the emerging theory provided a coherent and robust explanation of how the AI therapy developed by Headspace made mental healthcare more accessible (Eisenhardt and Graebner, 2007). To minimize bias, an independent researcher, not involved in the case study, validated the data analysis. This external validation served as a safeguard against inherent biases that may arise during data collection and analysis, ultimately contributing to the nuanced insights presented in this book chapter.

Headspace: Birth, Growth, and Mission

Headspace was founded in 2010, by Addy Puddicombe and Richard Pierson. Puddicombe was first introduced to meditation by his mother when he was eleven years old, but the true epiphany happened when he was in college, and just after that he decided to travel to Asia as a Buddhist monk. He later met Pierson, who had a background in marketing and brand development, while working as a mindfulness consultant (Headspace Inc.).

They decided to work together with the goal of *"demystify meditation, to make it more accessible, relevant and beneficial for as many people as possible"* as Andy

Puddicombe himself said (*Inside your Headspace: chat to founder Andy Puddicombe* 2013). They started by informing people about meditation through events, but this initial method didn't seem to work as expected. To reach everyone effectively they had to come up with a new and unique idea; that's when they decided to create the Headspace app, which was officially launched in 2012.

Right now, the company has gained a total of $215.9 million in funding, received from 25 different investors. Their latest funding was raised in October 2021 from a secondary market round (Crunchbase Inc.). Moreover, Headspace has now reached more than 100 determined employees and 6 board members and advisors.

They genuinely believed that the benefits of meditation can help people on many distinct levels of their lives: from physical to mental and emotional. During the years they had many difficulties in fighting against all the prejudices related to mental health and meditation, but they were finally able to overcome them by introducing new techniques and approaches to meditation (for example the introduction of animations in their app), and by demonstrating the great benefits that it can bring in day-to-day life.

Since the initial stages of Headspace, research has been an essential part, because the founders saw meditation not only as an old and historical practice but also as a topic of modern science. Various published studies, national institutions and also their research team have shown over the years the improvements in mental and social health that Headspace can bring (Figure 2).

Figure 2. A snapshot of the positive impact of meditation

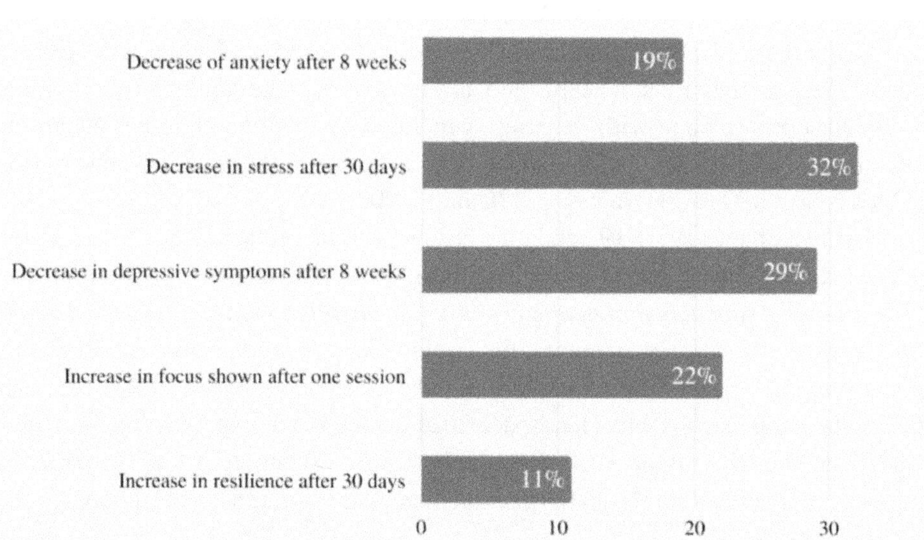

The app has been the subject of numerous trials to understand and analyse actual results on different samples of population: for example, low-risk families during the pandemic were asked about the acceptability and usability of the app, and the results showed that most of the sampled parents admitted the beneficial effects of mindfulness on controlling their stress tolerance (Burgess, Cavanagh, Strauss & Oliver 2022); even college students were questioned about the effects of Headspace on their psychological distress, and the outcomes still highlighted the improvements of students using the app in respect to the non-users (Flett, Conner, Riordan, Patterson & Hayne 2020).

Headspace is supposed to be always there, wherever and whenever the user needs it. It aims to help through rough times, to help find joy, and to create healthier and life-changing habits. Headspace is part of Headspace Health, which also includes Headspace for Work and Ginger. It is considered the most accessible and comprehensive provider of mental health and well-being care.

In the current time, focusing on mental health as employers is more important than ever: the pandemic has made them more focused on the expansion of access to virtual mental health and well-being services.

Headspace didn't wait to act, and so they decided to create the brand-new Headspace for Work. The app is specifically meant to drastically reduce the stress and burnout that employees could experience during their working hours. This solution can bring many benefits to the workplace: reduce healthcare costs, improve productivity, and guarantee better sleep and fewer sick days (Headspace Inc.). With this new and innovative app, employees can access Headspace and enjoy live meditations and experiences made specifically for their team. At the same time, employers can easily monitor and stay informed about their employee's mental health and overall working experience through the Resource Toolkit.

During the COVID-19 pandemic, Headspace focused on finding ways to help people preserve their mental health, and they have risen to the challenge of providing a way for users to cope with the stress generated by this uncertain period. In the UK and the US, the national health services offered a free year-long subscription to Headspace for healthcare workers (Camille 2021).

Moreover, the COVID-19 pandemic has put a strain on mental health across the globe and many have turned to virtual solutions to address the growing problem: "*We are witnessing a mental health crisis unlike anything we've experienced in our lifetimes, yet the majority of mental healthcare today is neither broadly accessible nor affordable*" said CeCe Morken, CEO of Headspace (Heater 2021). That was one of the main reasons why Headspace 2021 decided to merge with Ginger, which was founded in 2010 at the Massachusetts Institute of Technology (MIT) to offer its members convenient, high-quality mental healthcare through a smartphone.

Using new technologies (for example AI and data science), Ginger provides people with the fastest access to care right from a smartphone. Members can chat via text with a coach live, 24/7, 365 days a year; and, if needed, they can secure a video session with a therapist or psychiatrist (*Ginger and Headspace will merge to meet escalating global demand for mental health support* 2021). The company's care team utilizes a system that analyses chat transcripts, clinical assessments, member satisfaction, engagement data, and more to help provide personalized and effective care for each member.

In conclusion, Headspace Health, Ginger and Headspace now serve consumers, employers, and health plans. Their combined expertise in consumer brand, evidence-based interventions, and technology helps improve resilience, reduce stress, and provide treatment to the millions of people experiencing mental health symptoms, from anxiety to depression to even more complex diagnoses[1].

DISCUSSION OF FINDINGS

Psychological Repercussions of Mental Health During the COVID-19 Lockdown

The lockdown measures and the broader global repercussions stemming from the COVID-19 pandemic have undeniably exerted a profound impact on human lives. The loss of countless lives and the emergence of physical health issues, notably affecting the respiratory and cardiovascular systems, are regrettably prominent facets of this crisis. However, the pandemic has also induced a significant psychological toll, ushering in unparalleled circumstances marked by pervasive uncertainty and heightened mental vulnerability, impacting individuals across the globe.

Among the afflicted, particularly the younger demographic, lives were abruptly transformed by an overwhelming event beyond personal control. This event was fraught with apprehension regarding the availability of treatments or remedies. Extended periods of confinement within homes gave rise to challenging situations, such as couples grappling with relationship strains, families embroiled in persistent conflicts, and students finding themselves isolated in distant educational institutions, far removed from family and friends. These predicaments were compounded by the constant fear of the virus infiltrating one's home and endangering loved ones.

Consequently, many individuals, even those previously unacquainted with such tribulations, experienced heightened levels of obsession, anxiety, and depressive episodes. Disconcertingly, these distressing emotions did not necessarily subside with the conclusion of the health emergency. A notable number of individuals, including acquaintances and family members, continued to grapple with these issues well beyond the initial and most severe wave of the pandemic.

Curiously, a significant portion of those affected did not perceive these concerns as grave. It is worth noting that, despite media coverage regarding the pandemic's impact on mental health, there exists a prevailing tendency to discount one's susceptibility due to preconceived notions and a lack of awareness on the subject.

The return to a semblance of pre-pandemic life did not occur until 2022, notwithstanding the persistence of certain restrictions. Although people now enjoy greater mobility and the freedom to travel or attend events without the looming specter of COVID-19, the preceding years remained challenging.

For the younger demographic, the university experience was transformed into a remote and solitary endeavour, bereft of the customary interactions with peers and professors. Conversely, high school students concluded their educational journeys from the confines of their homes, devoid of the opportunity to deepen connections with classmates or partake in celebratory rituals.

Conversely, the professional sphere witnessed the exhaustion of employees, with healthcare workers bearing the brunt of the burden, as they confronted life-threatening conditions while enduring marathon shifts due to the influx of patients. However, even those working from home experienced difficulties, as the demarcation between personal and professional life blurred, and a sense of isolation from the social office environment took hold.

Failure to address these evolving challenges expedited their exacerbation. I encountered episodes of anxiety and depression, as did individuals within my immediate circle. While the support of well-intentioned friends is invaluable, it differs significantly from professional intervention. Friends, while offering empathetic guidance and sharing their perspectives, are not specialists. Constraints on their time, their concerns, and the difficulty of candidly confiding in long-standing acquaintances can hinder their effectiveness.

In contrast, therapists possess the expertise necessary to provide focused, non-judgmental support tailored to an individual's specific struggles. Their professional background equips them to offer objective and theoretically informed solutions rooted in their knowledge, serving as a valuable resource for personalized mental health guidance.

The AI Therapy of Headspace

Headspace has played a pivotal role in the domain of AI therapy. Its founders and the team of experts at the company embarked on a mission to alleviate the challenges faced by individuals grappling with stress and anxiety while promoting mental well-being. Through innovative approaches, Headspace has effectively democratized access to mental healthcare on a global scale, establishing a presence in diverse settings, including hospitals, educational institutions, large corporations, and correctional facilities.

During the unprecedented challenges presented by the COVID-19 pandemic, Headspace demonstrated a profound commitment to mitigating the hardships endured by those most affected. Notably, the company reduced subscription fees, extending support to vulnerable workers, with motives grounded solely in altruism rather than financial gain. Moreover, individuals contending with preexisting mental health issues, constrained by lockdown measures from accessing traditional therapy, found solace in the resources offered by the Headspace app, including videos and lectures, available at their convenience.

The crucible of a crisis period often reveals the authentic character of individuals, or in this particular case, a corporate entity. The trajectory of social innovation initiated by Headspace in 2012 continues to evolve, adapting to the ever-evolving challenges faced by its users. The company exemplifies how a genuine commitment to mutual support, coupled with the introduction of a unique and innovative concept to the market, can foster the development of a resilient and enduring enterprise that prioritizes the needs of individuals over monetary gain.

Headspace's inception ventured into an entirely uncharted and nascent market, brimming with both possibilities and perils. In 2012, when the founders commenced their mission to propagate meditation and mental well-being, persuading individuals to engage with the app and prioritize their mental health proved far more daunting than the present. Prevailing biases posed formidable obstacles, with Headspace effectively pioneering efforts to raise awareness almost single-handedly. The innovation they introduced extended beyond the social sphere, manifesting in a unique app distinguished by unprecedented features and design elements. Over time, the surge in societal interest in mental health, accompanied by market expansion, propelled Headspace to its current stature, characterized by a robust customer base and a sterling brand reputation.

Headspace has also been able to engage in numerous collaborations and partnerships to reach other industries by offering its innovative services. The fact that Headspace has collaborations and partnerships with numerous famous companies, is an important strategy to take into consideration. Their aim that to make mental wellness as accessible as possible, and working with different and various platforms has helped them reach their goal. This strategy, in turn, allowed Headspace to reach an even larger and more varied user base and, in this way, also increased the awareness, knowledge and importance regarding meditation and mental healthcare.

However, even companies that are focused on people's needs have various weaknesses and possible threats that they must face and be aware of to keep doing their business. One of the main problems of Headspace is that it doesn't focus on

Figure 3. Headspace innovative activity

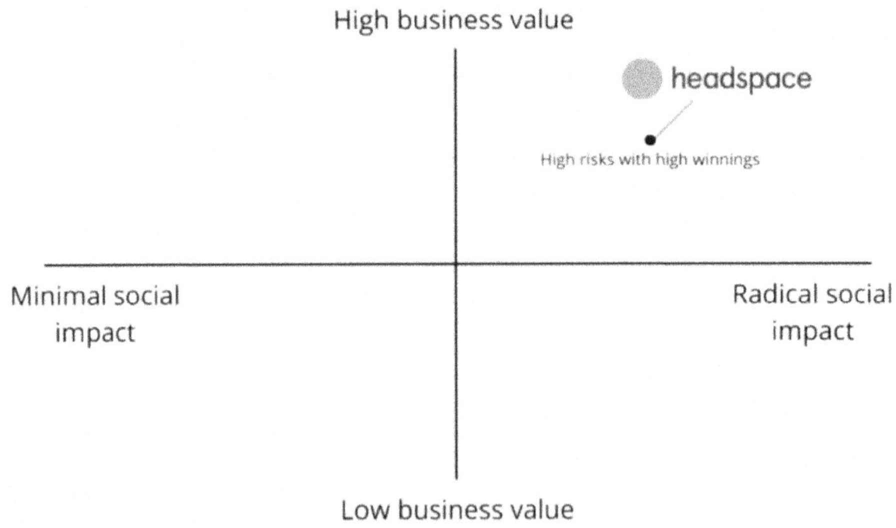

a certain targeted segment. This could in some cases be a positive aspect because they are hoping to reach as large a customer base as possible, but this could affect negatively the company's marketing strategy. Headspace may struggle with doing customized ads for people with different interests or different problems to be addressed.

The fact of reaching the largest number of users as possible could also be affected by the differences in cultures around the world. With nowadays technologies and the globalization processes, it is easier than ever for Headspace to reach people all around the world, but they still should, of course, keep in mind the cultural diversity of among continents and countries: for example, in the eastern countries, which are more used to meditation, some services can be better received in respect to some western countries, but by contrast, other types of services more targeted to a western customer base could not work at all in the eastern countries.

Another concern that Headspace should be aware of is the increasing number of competitors which are (now more than ever) entering the market. With the increased interest in mental healthcare and after the many negative effects of the pandemic on the population and the technological innovations, many thought it could be interesting to enter this growing sector which is digital mental healthcare. The company should now focus on differentiating itself from the masses because the new emerging competitors are all very similar to Headspace and offer almost identical services and solutions.

In addition, with the recent worsening economic general conditions, Headspace could have problems with people deleting their apps and putting their income into more essential activities, and sadly mindfulness apps are usually the ones that are deleted first concerning media ones. As said many times now, even if awareness is increasing, practising meditation is still not considered as important as other activities a person can do in their free time.

Finally, the company should always keep monitoring their research: even though the science behind their services is one of their main strengths, the studies could take a very long time to complete. Not every attempt to create a new innovative solution about mental wellbeing is surely going to be a success and focusing on the right projects at the beginning stages is crucial not to spend time in a useless and costly way.

The Main Benefits for Young People

The period of youth is commonly recognized as a phase characterized by notable uncertainty and continuous transformation, marked by the profound need to establish self-identity and secure a meaningful place within the societal framework. When juxtaposed with the compounding effects of the COVID-19 pandemic, it becomes evident that today's young generation grapples with unprecedented and formidable sources of uncertainty.

The advent of AI therapy emerges as a potent resource for assisting young individuals in navigating multifaceted challenges during periods of adversity. Those yet to establish a stable vocation may encounter formidable barriers when seeking psychological support, while those lacking a supportive familial network may contend with judgment and stigmatization from within their households.

Through the proliferation of new technologies and the emergence of specialized applications within digital marketplaces, young individuals now possess the capacity to readily access a diverse array of mental wellness resources, presented in multifarious formats capable of resonating with and accommodating a broad spectrum of needs.

The role of social media platforms assumes paramount significance in this context. Presently, the youth cohort represents the most active demographic within the realm of social media utilization. Consequently, companies are well-served by establishing official social media accounts to engage with prospective users. Notably, Headspace maintains a robust presence on prominent social platforms such as YouTube, Instagram, and Twitter. The provision of meditation videos and motivational content to a wide audience, irrespective of app download or payment, underscores the company's adept utilization of social media as a means of engaging and attracting young individuals, while simultaneously offering accessible services.

A Proposed Framework

Social innovation exemplifies the potential for altruistic endeavours aimed at aiding others to yield substantial economic viability. In the case of Headspace, we witness the company's innovative development of an application with the primary objective of enhancing the accessibility of mental healthcare. Its success has, in turn, catalyzed the proliferation of mindfulness apps, a trend driven by the escalating societal interest in mental health.

Listening attentively to customer feedback constitutes the foundational step towards corporate success. Emerging enterprises should prioritize the exploration of alternative avenues for simplifying people's lives and affording them access, chiefly through technological means, to services that may otherwise prove challenging to obtain in person.

Headspace serves as an exemplar of the effective utilization of new technologies to engender unprecedented social impact, significantly ameliorating the lives of countless individuals. The AI therapy framework pioneered by Headspace has garnered considerable acclaim over the years, inspiring numerous newly established companies to embark on similar missions to provide mental healthcare services.

As delineated in Figure 4, six fundamental elements warrant consideration by any AI therapy provider. Foremost among these is a steadfast commitment to prioritizing individuals, their exigencies, and their tribulations. This foundation constitutes the crux of any social innovation initiative, with particular relevance within the realm of mental healthcare, given that therapy remains a deeply personal experience contingent upon the unique perceptions of each individual. A failure to remain attuned to the evolving demands of users can precipitate the demise of a service, as users seek offerings tailored to their specific challenges and needs.

This perspective naturally extends to another pivotal element—personalization. Providers of AI therapy services must acknowledge the inherent variability in users' requirements, which may fluctuate from day to day or necessitate distinct interventions compared to those required by others. For instance, Headspace offers differentiated services targeting students, parents, and workers, reflecting the need for a diversified approach.

Universal accessibility represents another indispensable facet of AI therapy. Given that individuals in need of assistance and support can arise at any time and from any place, companies offering therapy programs must ensure that their services are readily available across a multitude of devices and platforms, ensuring consistency for their users. Collaborations with entities operating in divergent sectors can further enhance the delivery of unique services across diverse contexts, exemplified by Headspace's partnership with Virgin Atlantic to provide in-flight services.

Furthermore, technology remains a core determinant of AI therapy effectiveness. Privacy safeguards are paramount, given the intensely personal and intimate nature

Figure 4. A proposed framework for AI therapy

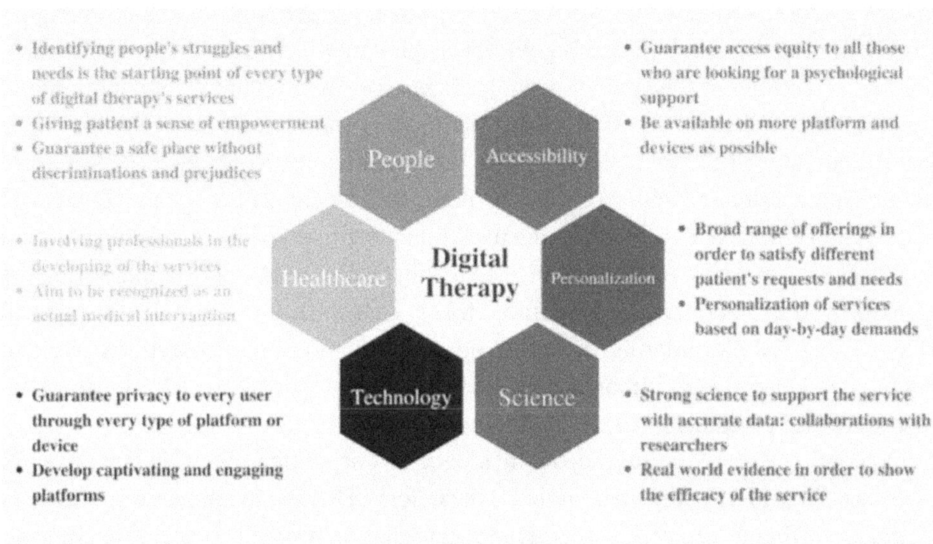

of the data disclosed by users. The platforms and interfaces should also be engaging, harnessing unique aesthetics to augment user engagement.

Finally, the services proffered by AI therapy providers must be underpinned by rigorous research corroborating the efficacy of the services offered and the involvement of healthcare professionals. Mental health poses multifaceted challenges, necessitating specialized research spanning various facets of the discipline to substantiate the reliability and authenticity of the service.

A pivotal aspiration for companies operating within this sector, in my estimation, is the attainment of recognition as a bona fide medical intervention. By this, I intend to convey the prospect of psychologists and counsellors prescribing specific AI therapy programs and exercises as a complementary adjunct to in-person sessions, excluding cases of severe mental illnesses. If such a practice gains widespread acceptance, it may pave the way for the inclusion of AI therapy programs within the purview of healthcare insurance coverage, thereby further enhancing the accessibility of mental healthcare.

IMPLICATIONS

Within this discourse, I embark upon a comprehensive exploration of three pivotal dimensions within the realm of social innovation, with a particular focus on the empirical case study of Headspace. The chapter's objective is to make a substantive academic contribution to the growing body of literature on artificial intelligence and its intersection with societal well-being (Appio et al., 2023; Cucino and Ferrigno, 2023). In an attempt to achieve this goal, the chapter provides three main contributions. First, this study shows the metamorphosis from a profit-oriented to human-centered orientation. central to the study's examination is the transformative role played by social innovation in reshaping the fundamental priorities of contemporary organizations, situated within the broader context of artificial intelligence (Berretta et al., 2023). I emphasize the compelling need for enterprises to transcend conventional profit-centric motives, embracing instead a holistic commitment to ameliorating the general welfare (Ferrigno and Cucino, 2021). This shift not only holds theoretical significance by illuminating the evolving ethos of modern corporations but also underscores the pivotal importance of societal impact, harmonized with economic success (George et al., 2023).

Second, this study highlights the influence on corporate reputation and standing (Love et al., 2017). Further expounded is the potential for social innovation endeavors to transcend the customary boundaries and sectoral limitations of corporate operations, thus exerting a profound influence on the overarching perception of corporate conduct (Dionisio and de Vargas, 2020). This perspective assumes theoretical salience by accentuating the capacity of companies, particularly those engaged with AI, to fortify their credibility and societal standing through conscientious, purpose-driven initiatives (Cucino and Ferrigno, 2023; Ferrigno and Cucino, 2021; Wamba et al., 2020).

Third, this study shows that resilience and adaptation amidst unforeseen challenges (Cucino et al., 2023b; Gittell, 2008; Williams et al., 2017). More specifically, this study illustrates the resilience and adaptability exemplified by Headspace, an organization that grappled with substantial challenges, notably during the unprecedented disruptions caused by the COVID-19 pandemic (Dohale et al., 2022; Ferrigno and Cucino, 2021). This inquiry serves to enrich extant theoretical discourse by illustrating how organizations, especially those harnessing AI capabilities, cannot merely withstand but flourish amid tumultuous periods (Conz & Magnani, 2020). Such resilience, which in this study has been defined as "the process by which an actor (i.e., individual, organization, or community) builds and uses its capability endowments to interact with the environment in a way that positively adjusts and maintains functioning before, during, and following adversity" (Williams et al., 2017, p. 742), is predicated upon a steadfast commitment to their core mission and values, a tenet that bears substantial relevance in the age of AI (Dohale et al., 2022).

Moreover, this book chapter provides some managerial implications. First, this analysis encourages the adoption of a more encompassing approach, one that cogitates on the broader societal implications that invariably accompany corporate activities, especially pertinent in the era of AI. Second, it underscores the strategic imperative of social innovation, emphasizing its role in cultivating favourable perceptions of a company, particularly in instances where enterprises are conventionally perceived as profit-maximizing entities driven by AI-powered algorithms. Third, this analysis underscores the significance of organizational agility and an unwavering dedication to their primary mission, even in the face of disruptions and competitive pressures driven by artificial intelligence.

Limitations and Future Research Directions

Notwithstanding the valuable insights contributed by this book chapter, it is imperative to acknowledge certain limitations and identify avenues for future research. Firstly, the extent to which our findings can be generalized is inherently constrained. Recognizing the inherent limitations of a single case study, I acknowledge the inadequacy of statistically extrapolating the results, as emphasized by Yin (2014). Therefore, I encourage scholars to pursue quantitative studies that systematically explore the impact of AI on mental health care.

Second, the study predominantly addresses the impact of AI in response to challenges, particularly during the COVID-19 pandemic. However, the rapidly evolving nature of artificial intelligence raises questions about the temporal relevance of the findings. Future research could delve into the dynamic interplay between social innovation and AI over time, considering how organizations adapt to emerging technological advancements and societal shifts. This longitudinal perspective would provide a more nuanced understanding of sustained social innovation efforts.

Third, while the study touches upon the resilience exhibited by Headspace, a more granular exploration of the specific mechanisms and strategies employed for organizational resilience is warranted. Future research could delve deeper into the intricate details of how organizations, especially those leveraging AI, navigate challenges and disruptions. Understanding the specific resilience-building practices and strategies would not only enrich theoretical discourse but also offer practical insights for organizations aiming to thrive in dynamic environments.

Beyond these limitations, this book chapter also identifies some other lines of future research. First, the chapter encourages a more encompassing approach to corporate activities, emphasizing the societal implications of AI-driven endeavors. Future managerial practices should consider not only economic outcomes but also the broader societal impact. Organizations can benefit from a comprehensive strategy that integrates ethical considerations and social responsibility into their AI-driven initiatives. Second, the strategic imperative of social innovation highlighted in the analysis suggests a need for organizations, especially those perceived as profit-maximizing entities driven by AI algorithms, to actively engage in purpose-driven initiatives. Managers should recognize the pivotal role of social innovation in shaping favorable perceptions and consider it as an integral part of their strategic planning and execution. Third, the emphasis on organizational agility and an unwavering dedication to the primary mission underscores the need for proactive adaptation in the face of AI-driven disruptions. Future research should prioritize exploring an organizational culture that values adaptability and remains steadfast in its commitment to core values, even amid competitive pressures driven by artificial intelligence.

CONCLUSION

In summary, this book chapter contributes to the burgeoning literature on artificial intelligence and its confluence with societal betterment, notably through the lens of social innovation, as demonstrated by the case study of Headspace. I underscore the pivotal shift toward human-centric orientations, delineate potential repercussions for corporate reputation and standing in the AI landscape, and illuminate the intrinsic capacity of organizations to exhibit resilience and adaptability when confronted with complex, unforeseen challenges—an invaluable addition to the ongoing academic discourse on artificial intelligence and its societal implications.

REFERENCES

Aleem, M., Sufyan, M., Ameer, I., & Mustak, M. (2023). Remote work and the COVID-19 pandemic: An artificial intelligence-based topic modeling and a future agenda. *Journal of Business Research*, *154*, 113303. doi:10.1016/j.jbusres.2022.113303 PMID:36156905

Andrade, C., Tavares, M., Soares, H., Coelho, F., & Tomás, C. (2022). Positive Mental Health and Mental Health Literacy of Informal Caregivers: A Scoping Review. *International Journal of Environmental Research and Public Health*, *19*(22), 15276. doi:10.3390/ijerph192215276 PMID:36430000

Appio, F. P., La Torre, D., Lazzeri, F., Masri, H., & Schiavone, F. (Eds.). (2023). *Impact of Artificial Intelligence in Business and Society: Opportunities and Challenges*. Routledge.

Bauer, A., Wistow, G., Hyànek, V., Figueroa, M., & Sandford, S. (2018). Social innovation in health care: The recovery approach in mental health. In H. K. Anheier, G. Krlev, & G. Mildenberger (Eds.), *Social Innovation: Comparative Perspectives*. Routledge.

Berretta, S., Tausch, A., Ontrup, G., Gilles, B., Peifer, C., & Kluge, A. (2023). Defining human-AI teaming the human-centered way: A scoping review and network analysis. *Frontiers in Artificial Intelligence*, *6*, 6. doi:10.3389/frai.2023.1250725 PMID:37841234

Burgess, A., Cavanagh, K., Strauss, C., & Oliver, B. R. (2022). Headspace for parents: Qualitative report investigating the use of a mindfulness-based app for managing parents' stress during COVID-19. *BJPsych Open*, *8*(1), e15. doi:10.1192/bjo.2021.1070 PMID:34956647

Camille, B. A. (2021). *Using Headspace for the Management of Anxiety During the COVID-19 Pandemic*. Brandman University.

Chesbrough, H. (2020). To recover faster from Covid-19, open up: Managerial implications from an open innovation perspective. *Industrial Marketing Management*, *88*, 410–413. doi:10.1016/j.indmarman.2020.04.010

Cheshmehzangi, A., Zou, T., & Su, Z. (2022). The digital divide impacts on mental health during the COVID-19 pandemic. *Brain, Behavior, and Immunity*, *101*, 211–213. doi:10.1016/j.bbi.2022.01.009 PMID:35041937

Conz, E., & Magnani, G. (2020). A dynamic perspective on the resilience of firms: A systematic literature review and a framework for future research. *European Management Journal*, *38*(3), 400–412. doi:10.1016/j.emj.2019.12.004

Cropley, A. (2019). *Introduction to qualitative research methods: A research handbook for patient and public involvement researchers.*. doi:10.7765/9781526136527.00012

Cucino, V., Del Sarto, N., Ferrigno, G., Piccaluga, A. M. C., & Di Minin, A. (2022). Not just numbers! Improving TTO performance by balancing the soft sides of the TQM. *The TQM Journal*. Advance online publication. doi:10.1108/TQM-01-2022-0034

Cucino, V., & Ferrigno, G. (2023). AI technologies and hospital blood delivery in peripheral regions: insights from Zipline International. In *Impact of Artificial Intelligence in Business and Society: Opportunities and challenges*. Routledge. doi:10.4324/9781003304616-15

Cucino, V., Ferrigno, G., & Piccaluga, A. (2021). Recognizing opportunities during the crisis: a longitudinal analysis of Italian SMEs during the Covid-19 crisis. In *Electronic Conference Proceedings of Sinergie-Sima Management Conference: Leveraging intersections in management theory and practice, Palermo, June 10-11, 2021, University of Palermo* (pp. 37-41). Fondazione CUEIM.

Cucino, V., Ferrigno, G., & Piccaluga, A. M. C. (2023). Pursuing innovative actions during the Covid-19 crisis: A qualitative analysis of family firms' resilience. *Piccola Impresa*, *1*(2), 69–94.

Cucino, V., Lungu, D. A., De Rosis, S., & Piccaluga, A. (2023). Creating value from purpose-based innovation: Starting from frailty. *Journal of Social Entrepreneurship*, 1–29. doi:10.1080/19420676.2023.2263768

Dell'Era, C., Di Minin, A., Ferrigno, G., Frattini, F., Landoni, P., & Verganti, R. (2020). Value capture in open innovation processes with radical circles: A qualitative analysis of firms' collaborations with Slow Food, Memphis, and Free Software Foundation. *Technological Forecasting and Social Change*, *158*, 120128. doi:10.1016/j.techfore.2020.120128

Dionisio, M., & de Vargas, E. R. (2020). Corporate social innovation: A systematic literature review. *International Business Review*, *29*(2), 101641. doi:10.1016/j.ibusrev.2019.101641

Dohale, V., Akarte, M., Gunasekaran, A., & Verma, P. (2022). Exploring the role of artificial intelligence in building production resilience: Learnings from the COVID-19 pandemic. *International Journal of Production Research*, 1–17. doi:10.1080/00207543.2022.2127961

Drew, N., & Funk, M. (2010). *Mental health and development: Targeting people with mental health conditions as a vulnerable group*. World Health Organization.

Easton, G. (1998). Case research as a methodology for industrial networks: A realist apologia. In P. Naudé & P. W. Turnbull (Eds.), *Network Dynamics in International Marketing* (pp. 73–87). Pergamon.

Eisenhardt, K. M. (2021). What is the Eisenhardt Method, really? *Strategic Organization*, *19*(1), 147–160. doi:10.1177/1476127020982866

Eisenhardt, K. M., & Graebner, M. E. (2007). Theory building from cases: Opportunities and challenges. *Academy of Management Journal*, *50*(1), 25–32. doi:10.5465/amj.2007.24160888

Elfein, J. (2022). *Statista*. Retrieved from https://www.statista.com/statistics/1287334/perceived-importance-of-mental-health-compared-to-physical-health-worldwide/

Ferrigno, G., & Cucino, V. (2021). Innovating and transforming during COVID-19: Insights from Italian firms. *R & D Management*, *51*(4), 325–338. doi:10.1111/radm.12469

Ferrigno, G., Del Sarto, N., Cucino, V., & Piccaluga, A. (2022). Connecting organizational learning and open innovation research: An integrative framework and insights from case studies of strategic alliances. *The Learning Organization*, *29*(6), 615–634. doi:10.1108/TLO-03-2021-0030

Ferrigno, G., Del Sarto, N., Piccaluga, A., & Baroncelli, A. (2023). Industry 4.0 base technologies and business models: A bibliometric analysis. *European Journal of Innovation Management*, *26*(7), 502–526. doi:10.1108/EJIM-02-2023-0107

Ferrigno, G., Zordan, A., & Di Minin, A. (2022). The emergence of dominant design in the early automotive industry: An historical analysis of Ford's technological experimentation from 1896 to 1906. *Technology Analysis and Strategic Management*, 1–12. doi:10.1080/09537325.2022.2074386

Flett, J. A. M., Conner, T. S., Riordan, B. C., Patterson, T., & Hayne, H. (2020). App-based for personal recovery in mental health: Systematic review and narrative synthesis. *BJPsych*, *199*, 445–452.

Foroudi, P., Akarsu, T. N., Marvi, R., & Balakrishnan, J. (2021). Intellectual evolution of social innovation: A bibliometric analysis and avenues for future research trends. *Industrial Marketing Management*, *93*, 446–465. doi:10.1016/j.indmarman.2020.03.026

George, G., Haas, M. R., McGahan, A. M., Schillebeeckx, S. J., & Tracey, P. (2023). Purpose in the for-profit firm: A review and framework for management research. *Journal of Management*, *49*(6), 1841–1869. doi:10.1177/01492063211006450

George, S., Daniels, K., & Fioratou, E. (2018). A qualitative study into the perceived barriers of accessing healthcare among a vulnerable population involved with a community centre in Romania. *International Journal for Equity in Health*, *17*(1), 1–13. doi:10.118612939-018-0753-9 PMID:29615036

Gittell, J. H. (2008). Relationships and resilience: Care provider responses to pressures from managed care. *The Journal of Applied Behavioral Science*, *44*(1), 25–47. doi:10.1177/0021886307311469

Gupta, S., Kumar, V., & Karam, E. (2020). New-age technologies-driven social innovation: What, how, where, and why? *Industrial Marketing Management*, *89*, 499–516. doi:10.1016/j.indmarman.2019.09.009

Hollis, C., Morriss, R., Martin, J., Amani, S., Cotton, R., Denis, M., & Lewis, S. (2015). Technological innovations in mental healthcare: Harnessing the digital revolution. *The British Journal of Psychiatry*, *206*(4), 263–265. doi:10.1192/bjp.bp.113.142612 PMID:25833865

Jones, P. (2020). *The arts therapies: A revolution in healthcare*. Routledge. doi:10.4324/9781315536989

Klein, H. K., & Myers, M. D. (1999). A set of principles for conducting and evaluating interpretive field studies in information systems. *Management Information Systems Quarterly*, *23*(1), 67–93. doi:10.2307/249410

Kohn, L., Christiaens, W., Detraux, J., De Lepeleire, J., De Hert, M., Gillain, B., Delaunoit, B., Savoye, I., Mistiaen, P., & Jespers, V. (2022). Barriers to somatic health care for persons with severe mental illness in Belgium: A qualitative study of patients' and healthcare professionals' perspectives. *Frontiers in Psychiatry*, *12*, 798530. doi:10.3389/fpsyt.2021.798530 PMID:35153863

Lee, T. W., Mitchell, T. R., & Sablynski, C. J. (1999). Qualitative research in organizational and vocational psychology, 1979–1999. *Journal of Vocational Behavior*, *55*(2), 161–187. doi:10.1006/jvbe.1999.1707

Love, E. G., Lim, J., & Bednar, M. K. (2017). The face of the firm: The influence of CEOs on corporate reputation. *Academy of Management Journal*, *60*(4), 1462–1481. doi:10.5465/amj.2014.0862

Magrabi, F., Habli, I., Sujan, M., Wong, D., Thimbleby, H., Baker, M., & Coiera, E. (2019). Why is it so difficult to govern mobile apps in healthcare? *BMJ Health & Care Informatics*, *26*(1), e100006. doi:10.1136/bmjhci-2019-100006 PMID:31744843

Miles, M. B., & Huberman, A. M. (1984). *Qualitative Data Analysis*. Sage Publications.

Miller, E., & Polson, D. (2019). Apps, Avatars and Robots: The Future of Mental Healthcare, mindfulness meditation for psychological distress and adjustment to college in incoming university students: A pragmatic, randomised, waitlist-controlled trial. *Psychology & Health*, *35*(9), 1049–1074.

Miralles, I., Granell, C., Díaz-Sanahuja, L., Van Woensel, W., Bretón-López, J., Mira, A., Castilla, D., & Casteleyn, S. (2020). Smartphone apps for the treatment of mental disorders: Systematic review. *JMIR mHealth and uHealth*, *8*(4), e14897. doi:10.2196/14897 PMID:32238332

Neary, M., & Schueller, S. M. (2018). State of the field of mental health apps. *Cognitive and Behavioral Practice*, *25*(4), 531–537. doi:10.1016/j.cbpra.2018.01.002 PMID:33100810

Nester, M. S., Hawkins, S. L., & Brand, B. L. (2022). Barriers to accessing and continuing mental health treatment among individuals with dissociative symptoms. *European Journal of Psychotraumatology*, *13*(1), 2031594. doi:10.1080/20008198.2022.2031594 PMID:35186217

Ravenswood, K. (2011). Eisenhardt's impact on theory in case study research. *Journal of Business Research*, *64*(7), 680–686. doi:10.1016/j.jbusres.2010.08.014

Senneseth, M., Pollak, C., Urheim, R., Logan, C., & Palmstierna, T. (2022). Personal recovery and its challenges in forensic mental health: Systematic review and thematic synthesis of the qualitative literature. *BJPsych Open*, *8*(1), e17. doi:10.1192/bjo.2021.1068 PMID:34915963

Sestino, A., & D'Angelo, A. (2023). My doctor is an avatar! The effect of anthropomorphism and emotional receptivity on individuals' intention to use digital-based healthcare services. *Technological Forecasting and Social Change*, *191*, 122505. doi:10.1016/j.techfore.2023.122505

Siggelkow, N. (2007). Persuasion with case studies. *Academy of Management Journal*, *50*(1), 20–24. doi:10.5465/amj.2007.24160882

Strauss, A., & Corbin, J. (1998). *Basics of Qualitative Research: Techniques and Procedures for Developing Grounded Theory*. Sage Publications.

Thakur, R., Hsu, S. H. Y., & Fontenot, G. (2012). Innovation in healthcare: Issues and future trends. *Journal of Business Research*, *65*(4), 562–569. doi:10.1016/j.jbusres.2011.02.022

Vesci, M., Feola, R., Parente, R., & Radjou, N. (2021). How to save the world during a pandemic event. A case study of frugal innovation. *R & D Management*, *51*(4), 352–363. doi:10.1111/radm.12459

Wamba-Taguimdje, S. L., Fosso Wamba, S., Kala Kamdjoug, J. R., & Tchatchouang Wanko, C. E. (2020). Influence of artificial intelligence (AI) on firm performance: The business value of AI-based transformation projects. *Business Process Management Journal*, *26*(7), 1893–1924. doi:10.1108/BPMJ-10-2019-0411

Williams, T. A., Gruber, D. A., Sutcliffe, K. M., Shepherd, D. A., & Zhao, E. Y. (2017). Organizational response to adversity: Fusing crisis management and resilience research streams. *The Academy of Management Annals*, *11*(2), 733–769. doi:10.5465/annals.2015.0134

World Health Organization. (2021). *Guidance on community mental health services: Promoting person-centred and rights-based approaches*. Author.

Yin, R. K. (2014). Case Study Research: Design and Methods. Sage Publications.

ADDITIONAL READING

Assunção, G., Patrão, B., Castelo-Branco, M., & Menezes, P. (2022). An overview of emotion in artificial intelligence. *IEEE Transactions on Artificial Intelligence*, *3*(6), 867–886. doi:10.1109/TAI.2022.3159614

Cath, C., Wachter, S., Mittelstadt, B., Taddeo, M., & Floridi, L. (2018). Artificial intelligence and the 'good society': The US, EU, and UK approach. *Science and Engineering Ethics*, *24*, 505–528. PMID:28353045

Coccia, M. (2020). Deep learning technology for improving cancer care in society: New directions in cancer imaging driven by artificial intelligence. *Technology in Society*, *60*, 101198. doi:10.1016/j.techsoc.2019.101198

Kambur, E. (2021). Emotional Intelligence or Artificial Intelligence?: Emotional Artificial Intelligence. *Florya Chronicles of Political Economy*, *7*(2), 147–168. doi:10.17932/IAU.FCPE.2015.010/fcpe_v07i2004

Makridakis, S. (2017). The forthcoming Artificial Intelligence (AI) revolution: Its impact on society and firms. *Futures*, *90*, 46–60. doi:10.1016/j.futures.2017.03.006

Marcos-Pablos, S., & García-Peñalvo, F. J. (2022). Emotional intelligence in robotics: a scoping review. In New Trends in Disruptive Technologies, Tech Ethics and Artificial Intelligence: The DITTET Collection 1 (pp. 66-75). Springer International Publishing. doi:10.1007/978-3-030-87687-6_7

Martınez-Miranda, J., & Aldea, A. (2005). Emotions in human and artificial intelligence. *Computers in Human Behavior*, *21*(2), 323–341. doi:10.1016/j.chb.2004.02.010

McStay, A., & Rosner, G. (2021). Emotional artificial intelligence in children's toys and devices: Ethics, governance and practical remedies. *Big Data & Society*, *8*(1). doi:10.1177/2053951721994877

Monteith, S., Glenn, T., Geddes, J., Whybrow, P. C., & Bauer, M. (2022). Commercial use of emotion artificial intelligence (AI): Implications for psychiatry. *Current Psychiatry Reports*, *24*(3), 203–211. doi:10.100711920-022-01330-7 PMID:35212918

Nomura, T. (2003, July). Problems of artificial emotions in mental therapy. In *Proceedings 2003 IEEE International Symposium on Computational Intelligence in Robotics and Automation. Computational Intelligence in Robotics and Automation for the New Millennium (Cat. No. 03EX694)* (Vol. 2, pp. 567-570). IEEE. 10.1109/CIRA.2003.1222243

Rafele, A., Scribano, A., & Korstanje, M. (2022). *Global Emotion Communications: Narratives, Technology and Power*. Nova Science.

Stark, L., & Hoey, J. (2021, March). The ethics of emotion in artificial intelligence systems. In *Proceedings of the 2021 ACM Conference on Fairness, Accountability, and Transparency* (pp. 782-793). 10.1145/3442188.3445939

White, D., & Katsuno, H. (2022). Artificial emotional intelligence beyond East and West. *Internet Policy Review, 11*(1), 1–17. doi:10.14763/2022.1.1618

KEY TERMS AND DEFINITIONS

AI: Artificial intelligence (AI) refers to the simulation of human intelligence in machines programmed to think and learn like humans. It involves the development of algorithms and computational models that enable machines to perform tasks that traditionally require human intelligence, such as problem-solving, learning, perception, and decision-making.

COVID-19 Pandemic: It refers to the global outbreak of the coronavirus disease 2019 (COVID-19) caused by the SARS-CoV-2 virus. Declared a pandemic by the World Health Organization (WHO) on March 11, 2020, it signifies the widespread and sustained transmission of the virus across international boundaries. The pandemic has led to significant public health, social, economic, and political impacts worldwide. Governments, healthcare systems, and communities have implemented various measures, including lockdowns, social distancing, and vaccination campaigns, to control the spread of the virus and mitigate its effects on public health and society.

Healthcare: It refers to the organized provision of medical care to individuals or communities. It encompasses a wide range of services aimed at maintaining and improving health, preventing, and treating illnesses, and promoting well-being. Healthcare systems can include medical professionals, institutions, technologies, and policies working together to deliver medical services.

Mental Care: Also defined as mental health care, it refers to the support, treatment, and services provided to individuals to maintain or improve their mental well-being. This can include various interventions such as counseling, therapy, psychiatric care, and community support to address mental health disorders, emotional challenges, and promote overall mental wellness.

Resilience: It is the ability of an individual or a system to bounce back from adversity, adapt to challenges, and recover quickly from setbacks. It involves the capacity to withstand and overcome difficult situations, learn from experiences, and develop strength in the face of adversity. Resilience is a crucial characteristic for individuals, communities, and organizations to navigate and thrive in the midst of challenges and uncertainties.

ENDNOTE

1 Ginger and Headspace will merge to meet the escalating global demand for mental health support (2021).

Chapter 10
Reincarnating in the Age of the Algorithm:
Corporeal-Affective Reflections on AI and Death

Jorge Luis Duperré
CONICET, National University of Villa Maria, Cordoba, Argentina

Pedro Lisdero
CONICET, National University of Cordoba, Argentina & National University of Villa Maria, Cordoba, Argentina

ABSTRACT

This chapter delves into the emergence of sensibilities surrounding death, driven by recent technological advancements in the field of artificial intelligence. The primary focus lies in the realm of emotions and bodies connected to the digital recreation of the deceased. To accomplish this, it employs virtual ethnography principles to scrutinize visual components within both fictional contexts, such as series and films addressing this phenomenon, and non-fictional domains, including emerging interactive devices and platforms related to 'death'. Drawing from the foundations of sociology of emotions and bodies, the analysis centers on a collection of 'contemporary postcards'. These postcards serve as condensed depictions, offering valuable insights into the evolving sensibilities associated with death, a crucial element for comprehending ongoing processes of social structuration.

INTRODUCTION

In line with the current questions raised by artificial intelligence (AI), in this chapter, we will address a social phenomenon that is not exempt from the transformations

DOI: 10.4018/979-8-3693-0802-8.ch010

brought about by AI: we are specifically referring to sensibilities related to death. We will not delve into the extensive philosophical discussion surrounding death here. Instead, aligning ourselves with a sociology of bodies/emotions (Scribano, 2017), we are interested in focusing on the set of social practices that revolve around death. These practices provide a privileged vantage point for analyzing ongoing processes of social structuration (Duperré and Lisdero, 2022). Particularly, the consequences of the expansion and intersections that AI has been playing a leading role in have transformed how we experience and perceive death. The sensibilities emerging in this context become a provocative realm for exploring societal metamorphoses in the "age of the algorithm." Thus, in order to shed light on this elusive subject, this writing will refer to some precedents—both fictional and non-fictional—that help us comprehend how, in recent decades, the development of technological devices and the digitalization of life (and its transience) raise questions about the reconfiguration of interactive dynamics. These dynamics now extend not only between "animated" agents but also between these agents and those lacking such qualities. Precisely, we believe that AI is intensifying this discussion to the extreme. Herein lies our starting point for inquiry.

It is worth clarifying that the analysis of bioethical positions and legal aspects, which this issue inevitably entails, exceeds the scope of our chapter. Contrarily, our focus is directed towards the affective and corporeal reasons that either legitimize or challenge the relationship society establishes with death through the mediation of technology. Specifically, our inquiry pertains to the perceptions, sensations, and emotions implicated in the "recreation" of the "connection with the deceased" through digital means. To this end, we have selected three paradigmatic "postcards" that, in our estimation, express this relationship in a quintessential manner. These postcards provide a glimpse into a "state of feeling" via a unique set of resources, which we will interpret, to elucidate certain significant elements concerning the current state of digital sensibilities in relation to death.

Following this roadmap, we intend to specifically: firstly, explore a set of recently launched apps in the market, distinguished by their unique feature of enabling the creation of the voice – and even the image – of a deceased individual for interactive purposes. Secondly, we will focus on the concept of the 'digital executor'—that is, a person responsible for 'ensuring the fulfillment of the deceased's last will' and managing their assets, particularly those associated with their 'networked life.' This concept exemplifies the current era, in which our 'virtual identity' outlives us and, consequently, necessitates third-party management. Finally, related to the first point, we will explore fiction, specifically two episodes that raised this question early on: 'Be Right Back' and 'San Junipero,' from the British series 'Black Mirror,' which premiered in 2013 and 2016, respectively. As a whole, the visual-expressive power of these episodes allows us to reconstruct various elements that, like pieces of a puzzle, shed interpretative light on the social sensibilities that shape our everyday lives in an indeterminate manner.

As a theoretical-methodological strategy, we will resort to the concepts, categories and procedures provided by the sociology of bodies/emotions, a perspective that we consider highly relevant given the specificities of the object and the approach outlined for its study. Suffice it to point out here that investigating the bodily-affective dimension of a social phenomenon allows us to understand the sensibilities involved in it. Such is the importance of this approach for our proposal.

To lend substance to the analysis we propose, we will employ "virtual ethnography," a technique precisely suited for immersing oneself in "virtual social spaces," in pursuit of rendering registerable and expressible the sensibilities encoded in various expressive resources operational within the three anticipated "postcards." As a descriptive analysis, this ethnographic variant recognizes as valid elements other forms of interaction, characterized chiefly by their mediation through digital devices (materializing through audiovisual, photographic, textual mediums, etc.). Hence, if modernity championed the sense of sight, and social sciences early on discerned justifications for proposing that the social is uniquely expressed through the visual, the conditions of the reflective practice we present in this chapter entail understanding a particular epistemology grounded in a critique of the "4.0 gaze politics" (Scribano and Lisdero, 2019), as both condition, means, and object of social knowledge. In summation, we propose a strategy that synthesizes these theoretical-epistemic stances, converging a visual/corporeal/emotional sociology, aiming to shape an ethnographic exercise that, through triggering examples, allows us to offer insights into paradigmatic sensibilities concerning death in our contemporary era.

With regard to the specific issue under consideration, our endeavor seeks to account for the practices of feeling that materialize within the platforms and interfaces of "virtual reality" utilizing AI, and which, in our assessment, configure a certain "politics of the senses" intertwined with the presence of those who have passed away. Put differently, we shall analyze the audible, visible, and tangible traits that facilitate and condition specific functions of algorithms and interactive prostheses – tools whose ultimate discovery has been the "revival" of the "inanimate." Furthermore, we contend that these novel forms of "mourning" cyber-interaction are governed by and interwoven with present "affective regimes," harnessing the profound emotional component inherent in instances of "reconnection" with the departed. Instances that have now evolved into practices of enjoyment (i.e., pleasure derived from the possession of objects, including subjects configured as such). Consequently, we propose the emergence of a "political economy of death," elucidating processes of valorization pertaining to the production and exchange of commodities (including death itself), and the commercialization and consumption practices that promote and result from sensibilites linked to human finitude, now within a virtual context.

The "platformized" sensibilites revolving around death thus become a sociological object deserving of investigation, as they "prophesy" – in the words of Melucci – regarding the societies of the 21st century.

AI and the Modeling of Transient Bodies and Emotions

At the beginning of the 21st century, a work of fiction managed to rekindle the man-machine debate in the public consciousness: it was the project initiated by Stanley Kubrick and later brought to life by Steven Spielberg, titled 'Artificial Intelligence' (2001). We are not referencing the film solely due to its title, but rather because the popularization of this debate encompassed various facets, including the possibilities and the bodily-emotional limitations manifested by the 'inorganic' protagonist of the storyline, David. David is a 'computer replicant,' programmed to 'experience' love for his 'fellow human beings,' with a particularly deep connection to his human mother, whose death triggers profound sorrow. In this regard, Naremore (2005) reminds us that while this android child has the capacity to experience joy or fear, it cannot 'urinate, eat spinach, or partake in any other form of sustenance. It has existed on Earth for millennia and will never age. It can dream, but its dreams are of electric sheep' (p. 2)[1]. Therefore, as the storyline makes evident, empathy alone is insufficient to humanize the robot. Equally vital are: a) the externalization of fundamental physiological needs, such as nourishment and elimination, or the physical effects of the passage of time; and b) the internalization of the dream experience. This point holds particular relevance for us because it underscores the intricate connection between the realms of emotions and the physical body as the cornerstone of the human condition. This postulate, as we emphasize, constitutes a significant point of reflection within our theoretical and methodological framework, as will be elucidated below.

Let's elaborate further on this final point: known as a specific perspective within the sociology of bodies and emotions, we believe that this approach is one of the most relevant for comprehending the processes involved in shaping sensibilities at a specific point in time. This perspective centers on the bodily-emotional aspect inherent in every interpersonal connection, which, in turn, influences and is influenced by collective practices. This approach, therefore, enhances the conditions for observability, allowing for the apprehension of this intricately complex concept. It is important that this sociology is grounded in a fundamental premise, asserting that this dimension cannot be understood in isolation. Each body, whether individual or societal, reveals itself through emotions, and, simultaneously, every emotion takes on a particular 'embodiment', shaped by the inherent potentialities and limitations of the actors within a given historical moment (Scribano, 2012). Consequently, the expression of the corporeal and emotional aspects, as we emphasize, becomes an indispensable gauge for comprehending the processes that contribute to the formation of sensibilities. As Scribano (*2012*) defines, these sensibilities represent 'the narratives and practices of feeling, the politics of the senses (what one can/cannot smell, taste, touch, see, hear), and the desires associated with the boundaries and possibilities of sociabilities and experiences' (2012, p. 4), legitimized by a given society."

As an initial definition of AI, we find merit in the one put forth by Sossa Azuela (2020), who defines it as a multidisciplinary field focused on creating applications and technological devices with the ability to learn, adapt to environmental changes, and operate autonomously. AI enables various capabilities in today's world:

The management of extensive datasets to extract valuable information for the automated generation of algorithms, thereby addressing intricate issues related to reasoning, perception, planning, learning, and object manipulation... across diverse domains such as medicine, security, transportation, mobility, natural disaster prediction and management, and the development of human capital. (pp. 22-23)

Returning to the matter of sensibilities in AI innovation, Dreyfus and Dreyfus (1999) predicted back in the 1980s that a significant challenge for AI in the years ahead would be the ability to understand "needs, desires, and emotions, and to possess a human-like body with physical movements, abilities, and vulnerability to violence" (p. 52) if its goal was to become an authentic cognitive-affective model—a faithful reproduction of the human 'sapiens' mind and disposition, or perhaps a version that surpasses the 'sapiens' iteration. On the other hand, Waltz (1999) held a more skeptical view about the feasibility of achieving this endeavor. He believed that, even if intentionally programmed, AI would likely struggle to express genuine human emotions. His reservations stemmed from the inherent nature of emotions in our species, serving as a survival mechanism (e.g., panic or altruism toward fellow humans), which doesn't necessarily require a logical comprehension of their purpose. However, the author did not dismiss the possibility that in the future, machines could be equipped with the capability to "experience analogues of frustration, the pleasure of achieving a goal, confusion, and other emotion-related responses to emerging phenomena, allowing them to generate [more human-like behavior]" (pp. 238 and 239). To achieve this, Waltz proposed a necessary integrated modeling of intellectual, affective, and physical competencies. In this framework, AI should consider: a) the development of intricate nervous, sensory, and motor systems (which, according to him, would enable AI to learn from experience); and b) the question of the "'type of 'body' in which such intelligence must be embedded to genuinely understand rather than merely simulate understanding. He questioned whether the machine should be designed to have emotions if it is to comprehend our human emotional responses?' (p. 239). Perhaps conclusive answers to this question are still elusive.

Finally, and here we approach the issue of interest for our analysis, Waltz pondered the artificial interpretation of our finite existence:

If a machine were immortal, could it comprehend our responses to the realization of our own mortality? Machines can be duplicated by merely copying their program or internal code onto other identical pieces of hardware. There is no human counterpart to a machine that can experience being a singular entity for an extended period and then, at a certain point in its 'existence,' abruptly transform into multiple distinct entities, each with diverse experiences. (p. 239)

This is precisely one of the "incompletenesses" from which David, the humanoid child of Artificial Intelligence, suffers. Accordingly, feeling/knowing ourselves to be perishable would constitute the most human characteristic of our "sensibilities" and, therefore, technically irreproducible. However, regardless of how authentic/inauthentic the experience of "non-human anguish in the face of death" may be (something that probably escapes even our own capacity to understand), what matters is how plausible it is for its mortal interlocutors: replicating Thomas's theorem[2] here, we could ask ourselves to what extent the "interactions with the dead" proposed to us by the AI become "real in their consequences". In what manner do the 'situations' with which we increasingly coexist, thanks to the possibilities presented by this 'expanded eternity' where we 'engage' our emotions concerning the deceased, contribute to the formation of our sensibilities? How do they shape the central characteristics of contemporary structuration processes? In other words, to what extent does the artificial lose its distinction as such when we 'realize' that we not only possess the same intellectual capabilities but also the ability to be similarly affected—to feel joy, suffering, doubt—in response to events shared with non-organic entities? This represents a central (sociological) dilemma of our era.

The Liminality of Death in Data Capitalism

In terms of this necessary verisimilitude in the man-machine contract, Scribano (2019) highlights the feeling of trust as a nodal aspect to promote interactionism in the virtual world. Trust in someone or something that bursts before us as an "empirical" confirmation of a presence mediated - or recreated - by technological devices, and which, regardless of its "nature", becomes the repository of a part of our life (albeit one that can be translated into data). For this reason, the author links trust with the aforementioned contemporary politics of the senses: a feeling based on the reliability of what we see, smell, touch, hear and taste, at the behest of "expert systems" (a name which, from its very origin, is intended to dispel any concern about their expertise and "probity"). So it is possible, Scribano continues, to think of "faith" in "non-human intelligent living beings" as one of the factors that influence the colonisation of -human- bodies/emotions in the current stage of global capitalism.

Likewise, Scribano and Mairano (2021) argue that this inscription of AI in the present "platform economy" allows us to understand how its expansion is based on a logic of "emotionalisation" of the mechanisms of domination and social ties in digital environments. According to this approach, we are witnessing a novel "regime of sensibilities" - expressed through a singular pattern of accumulation - whose narrative emulates that of algorithmic programming language. In the words of the authors:

With regard to this necessary verisimilitude in the man-machine contract, Scribano (2019) highlights the feeling of trust as a nodal aspect to promote interactionism in the virtual world. Trust in someone or something that bursts before us as an "empirical" confirmation of a presence mediated - or recreated - by technological devices, and which, regardless of its "nature", becomes the repository of a part of our life (albeit one that can be translated into data). For this reason, the author links trust with the aforementioned contemporary politics of the senses: a feeling based on the reliability of what we see, smell, touch, hear and taste, at the behest of "expert systems" (a name which, from its very origin, is intended to dispel any concern about their expertise and "probity"). Thus, as Scribano elaborates, it's conceivable to consider 'faith' in 'non-human intelligent living beings' as one of the factors influencing the colonization of human bodies and emotions in the current stage of global capitalism. Furthermore, Scribano and Mairano (2021) argue that this integration of AI into the contemporary 'platform economy' enables us to comprehend how its expansion relies on a logic of 'emotionalization' of mechanisms of domination and social connections within digital environments. According to this perspective, we are witnessing a novel 'regime of sensibilities' that manifests through a distinctive pattern of accumulation, mirroring that of algorithmic programming language. In the authors' own words:

We are facing a social system that is globalized by producing/buying/selling emotions in and through the media, social networks and the Internet [...] A "sensibilities of platform" emerges in this 4.0 society that is immediate in three senses: (a) in the vehicle the action resides (it is the feeling of always being "on line"), (b) it is a society that "is during use", "between", "in passing", and (c) is pure presentifcation (here/now). (p. 6)

This shift in spatiotemporal references further accentuates the transitional nature of death (we will revisit this aspect later). For now, it is enough to highlight that within the current global context, AI has successfully appropriated, comprehended, and capitalized on the experiences we regularly update in virtuality as cybernauts. These experiences possess a significant emotional component, enabling algorithms to model human behavior.

These self-learning machines learn from the emotions that we have digitized, making them self-justifying.... In technical terms, this process is called backpropagation and consists of a technique typical of AI models that allows the realization of adjustments through new aggre gated data or training until reaching "the correct answers" and generating greater precision due to its deep learning. (p. 7)

The control of emotions through 'knowledge engineering' and automata systems has become central in comprehending contemporary processes of social structuration (Giddens, 2003)

On the other hand, these changes in the cognitive-affective sphere have had their correlate, as could not be otherwise, in the corporeal sphere: the development of application programming interfaces has increased the possibilities of digital perception and sensation. Drawing upon the concepts presented by Scribano and Mairano (2021), we are witnessing the establishment of a new politics of the senses, where specific modes of touch, sight, sound, taste, and more are validated through technological devices. In this way, emotionality in the digital age is the expression of the valorisation of perceptions and sensations that "embody" inorganic models, and that ultimately affect, and result in, the state of present sensibilities.

In summary, the progression of *machine learning*, with applications including automatic interaction simulation, enables responses to the unexpected, the expression of emotions, and the capacity for empathy without the requirement of human programming. This scenario compels us to reconsider, among other matters, the longstanding convictions regarding the boundaries we have traditionally defined between life and death, as well as the presence or absence of these beings or entities we are, were, or will become.

In the following, we will delve into this problematic that involves the ways of perceiving and feeling death in the age of the algorithm. For this purpose, we will recover[3] three "postcards" of the present that clearly express this problematic, thus facilitating the present approach.

Postcard 1. Touching The Afterlife: The "New" Digital Materialities

A few paragraphs ago, we highlighted the connection between AI and 'non-human emotional intelligence' as per the perspective we endorse. This may be where the 'innovation' in recently launched applications for 'interacting with the deceased' lies.

As evidence, we can point to the emergence of what are now referred to as 'deadbots': chatbot tools that utilize machine learning to recreate text messages from a deceased person, allowing us to 'reconnect' with them. In this context, there was a case that garnered significant public attention and led to an unprecedented legal dispute. In short, it involved a Canadian man who, in 2021, employed software called '*Project December: Simulated Dead*'[4] to 'engage in conversation' with his girlfriend who had passed away eight years earlier. The issue arose because the software was built using an Application Programming Interface (API) that utilized a language model for automatic text generation (GPT-3) owned by a third-party company, OpenAI. OpenAI explicitly prohibited the use of this model for 'sexual, romantic, self-harming, or harassing purposes,'[5] and according to the company, Project December's deadbots violated this policy. Beyond the specifics of the incident and its ethical and legal implications (such as the extent and boundaries of consent regarding the use or exploitation of a deceased person's identity and the responsibilities placed on guardians), we want to emphasize how these unique forms of interaction are a response to certain patterns in technological production and consumption, which carry a strong emotional aspect.

There are other innovations that have gone beyond text-based exchanges. For instance, in 2021, the Israeli company *MyHeritage* created *Deep Nostalgia*, an app that employs animation technology to breathe "life" into photos through pre-designed video[6] models. In Argentina, a platform named *Almaya Life*[7] was launched in 2022, allowing users to craft their own biographies by responding to around 700 questions while facing a camera. AI is then used to transform this profile into an interactive persona, enduring indefinitely. However, one of the most remarkable instances in terms of dealing with the 'sentiments of death' comes from the South Korean multimedia company *MBC* (Munhwa Broadcasting Corporation). In February 2020, they aired a documentary titled "*Meeting You*," in which a mother was shown 'reconnecting' with her deceased seven-year-old daughter[8]. The producers turned to virtual reality (VR) to craft a 'child avatar' using a combination of resources. On one hand, they captured the movements, gestures, and other expressions of a child actor. On the other hand, they emulated the child's appearance and voice by utilizing photos, audio files, and her mother's testimonies. They also recreated a virtual environment, reminiscent of the park that the mother and daughter frequented. Finally, through VR glasses and haptic gloves (which allow for tactile experiences), the woman was able to 'reunite' with her beloved daughter. To elicit even more emotions, the producers aimed for a poignant twist: after a brief conversation, the girl informs her mother that she's tired and wishes to go to bed. While asleep, she transforms into a butterfly and takes flight. Upon the documentary's broadcast, Lee Hyun-suk, one of the project leaders, reflected: "People often perceive technology as cold. We chose to participate to investigate whether technology can provide comfort and warmth to the heart when utilized for the benefit of people." [9]

Episodes such as this one are, in our opinion, transforming the "practices of feeling" related to death in a vertiginous way. Undoubtedly, we are witnessing an unprecedented reconfiguration of sensibilities, whereby seeing, hearing, touching the deceased (whether through bodily interfaces, or through "contactless" technology) make the idea of immortality of our loved ones more "palpable". Thus embodying a series of emotions and feelings that, to take up Lee Hyun-suk's metaphor, warm our hearts. Far from the image of a disembodied death, this sensibility is testimony to the radical reconfigurations between materialities and senses that we are witnessing - often agonisingly - in this 21st century. This renewed experience of death emerges from the emotional possibilities that the "digitalisation" of life has incorporated into our everyday lives as a naturalised "way of feeling": pre-reflexive ways of "seeing" and "living" mediated by algorithms. Moreover, the sociabilities that we re-live around death 4.0 become a key element of how we "construct" ourselves for the future. It would seem that, when once and for all, we are in a position to confirm the "death of death", paradoxically, it "dialogues" with our senses through a labile and confusing barrier (as never before). Trust - as a constitutive emotion of the social, and associated with an "always so" affected by the power of the digital - is re-configured in the multiple palpable experiences of this paroxysm.

Figure 1. Scene from the South Korean documentary I Met You, in which the mother interacts with her deceased daughter through VR

Postcard 2. Dying Online: Affects And Digital Remains

The Spanish multi-platform *Tellmebye*[10], launched in July 2014, stands out as a pioneer in funeral innovation in general and, more specifically, in the realm of preserving 'digital inheritance.' Among its various functions, the *Tellmebye Legacy* division is responsible for: a) Collecting and archiving all information about the deceased stored in the cloud, b) managing or deleting their profiles on social networks, emails, and more, c) handling the money and other 'intangible' assets in their online accounts, including bank and payment accounts, e-commerce, and so on, and d) ensuring the fulfillment of their last will and testament. Two key points to highlight about these services: Firstly, the company encourages insurance providers to incorporate them into their policies. Secondly, interested individuals can conveniently access these and other funeral services online through a plan or a 'PRO 10 GB account.' This business model is such that its services can be 'marketed' through third-party entities, namely death insurers, and its pricing can be tailored based on the amount of storage required by the user (measured in gigabytes). In essence, we *entrust* these 'digital executors' with a vast database that encompasses who we are, our preferences, experiences, affections, and our wishes for both this world and the next. This transforms our 'digital inheritance,' and even the preservation of the right to be forgotten, into a tradable commodity that continues beyond our own existence

To gain our trust in the handling of our data, *Tellmebye* raises certain ethical and emotional considerations about the operation of these platforms. During an interview in July of this year, CEO and co-founder Carlos Jiménez Lajara stated, "We aim to simplify the utilization of new technologies and tools, such as AI or the Metaverse, all while upholding a strong sense of humanity and empathy." He further noted:

Although we could create a 100% real Avatar with the face of a deceased person and equip it with AI to speak and even show their expressions, it is important to ask whether this solution would really bring relief or more pain, stress or anxiety to the family. . . . So, although the funeral sector has been one of the last to move towards digitalisation, it is important to analyse any implementation you want to do[11].

In this quote, it becomes evident that the emotional element plays a central role, not only in shaping strategies for Corporate Social Responsibility but also in the formulation of technological innovation policies within the funeral industry. The guiding principle appears to be "modernizing to the point of evoking emotional responses" from the bereaved. Therefore, the act of 'mobilizing,' 'influencing,' and 'capturing' sensitive attention by altering it seems to be the condition upon which the vital energies that were traditionally channeled through 'analog' mechanisms

Figure 2. Screenshot of Tellmebye Legacy website (translation of the image text: "What will happen to your Facebook and social networks when you die?"; " The first website that secures your digital legacy and sends your files posthumously")

of mourning and inheritance management are now directed toward 'the algorithm.' Consequently, the political economy of morality must take into consideration the reverberations of this transformation in the emotional death market. 'Digitized grief' not only paves the way for 'new business,' but it also adds another layer of significance that complicates the politics of emotions.

Social networks have also responded to this issue of what to do with our profiles when we die[12]. For example, *Facebook* and *Instagram* (both owned by the company Meta) allow you to designate a person, who becomes a "legacy contact" (or digital executor, as characterised above), to take care of memorial dates, greetings, etc. Along with other networks such as *Twitter* or *LinkedIn*, they also provide for the possibility of deleting the accounts of deceased persons.

In all cases, the designated executor must prove his or her link to the executor, otherwise the "non-user" is left in a kind of cyber-liminality. From now on, as the digital dimension imposes itself as the logic of social structuration, social pain is tinged with the colour and texture of "zeros and ones". The structuration component of this social pain (for example, as part of the normative content that the past -and its dead- imprints as a structural property on our practices) also acquires particularities: between "eternity in heaven/hell" and "eternity in the cloud" we "feel" differently from those mandates, and consequently, we experience temporal-spatial horizons in an equally particular way. Undoubtedly, here we can find a relevant relationship that allows us to understand how this specific content of our "interaction" with death can be an important key to understand the radical dislocated/constrained experientialities deployed in Society 4.0.

Postcard 3: Capitalism and the Post-Human Utopia

The renowned British science fiction series, Black Mirror, created by Charlie Brooker in 2011, delves into "a twisted, technological world where the greatest innovations and darkest human instincts intersect."[13] Each episode serves as an invitation to contemplate the extent, origins, repercussions, and possibilities—ranging from the most promising to the most dystopian—of the interplay between everyday life and technology. What is especially pertinent to our viewpoint is the series' distinct emphasis on emotions in the context of a world increasingly shaped by technologies. In the words of McSweeney & Joy (2019), "(H)as there ever been a television show more intrinsically connected to the fears and anxieties of the decade in which it was produced than Charlie Brooker's Black Mirror?" (p. 1).

Within this context, two episodes stand out as especially relevant for the analysis proposed here. Both were written by the aforementioned producer, C. Brooker, and directed by Owen Harris. We are referring to the episode "Be Right Back," which first aired in 2013. This episode revolves around Martha, who, in an effort to cope with her grief following the sudden death of her boyfriend, Ash, in an accident, and spurred by her pregnancy, utilizes a tool that enables her to "maintain communication with Ash." The software generates new conversations based on the records her boyfriend had left on social networks. Initially, the exchanges are in the form of text messages, but then the software emulates Ash's voice for telephone conversations. Eventually, Martha gains access to an android that takes on the appearance of her deceased partner. The narrative explores the challenges that parenting presents for the relationship between Martha, her daughter, and Ash's android.

On the other hand, the episode titled "San Junipero," which premiered in 2016, narrates the story of Yorkie, a reserved woman who forms an affectionate relationship with Kelly within the backdrop of a Californian tourist town in 1987. As the narrative unfolds, it becomes apparent that the location, bearing the same name as the episode, is a virtual reality setting in which living and "deceased" individuals interact. The essence of the story is interwoven within the spaces between online and offline, as well as within the highs and lows that the love story encounters, all while navigating the virtual and physical realms of connections and misunderstandings. Towards the climax, we discover that Yorkie had been paralyzed in an accident 40 years ago, on the very night she came out as a lesbian to her family (and faced rejection). Yorkie's

Figure 3. Capture of different scenes from the episode Be Right Back, Black Mirror

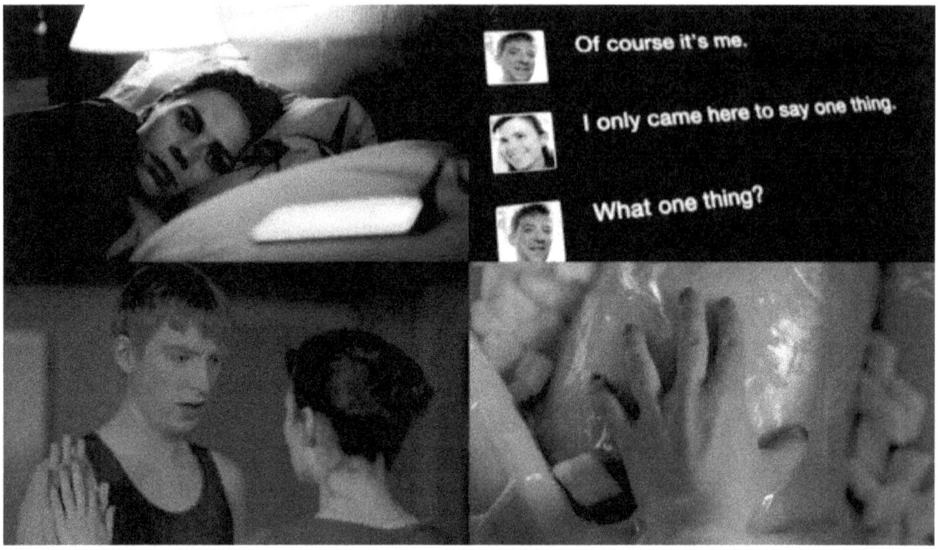

plan is to escape her earthly suffering and continue "living" in San Junipero. A (mis) encounter occurs with Kelly, who, after passing away, is hesitant to be uploaded into the "eternal" program. The passage of time brings vitality to the plot, hastening decisions, ultimately leading to a 'happy ending' where both reunite in the virtual environment.

Interestingly, both chapters provide some continuity with the previous postcard (digital executor) about the management of our "digital footprints". However, it is possible to establish a new point of discussion about what Black Mirror thematises here about the relationship between consciousness and death as a dialectical horizon in the construction of the future. In such a direction, Schopp (2019) observes:

Ash is much like the digital world of "San Junipero"—little more than a walking coffin, a repository to house a social media self that, in this case, remains stagnant, static, and incomplete. In fact "Ash" is even more problematic because in "San Junipero" when Yorkie (Mackenzie Davis) and Kelly (Gugu Mbatha-Raw) decide to pass eternally into the digital space, they have chosen to do so, and they do so as complete digital versions of their living selves. Just as "White Christmas" and "USS Callister" denote the potential nightmares that we might cause once we can digitize ourselves, creating clones that can be imprisoned, abused, forced to work for us, or forced to play out some disgruntled madman's sci-fi fantasies, "Be Right Back" reminds us that before we get that advanced, there can be interim

Figure 4. Capture of different scenes from the episode San Junipero, Black Mirror

stages like what "Ash" represents, a living container that can only house what we have chosen to include, before our deaths, in our digital selves, the fake smile we present in order to elicit the digital gaze of others. Importantly, however, Ash does not choose to come back as "Ash," but because his digital presence lives beyond his physical body, someone else can make that choice—for better and for worse. (p. 66)

Taken together, both chapters not only open up the possibility of uploading human consciousnesses into computer-simulated worlds as a replacement for biological life, but "San Junipero" goes a step further by proposing to erase the latter element (biological life) from the equation through euthanasia. Thus, "(I) n our postmodern, hyperreal world, 'real' and 'virtual' are not polar opposites; instead, we all live in a sort of dialectical synthesis of physical reality (rooted in biological needs) and virtuality (rooted in mediacreated images) (Daraiseh and Booker, 2019: 156).

However, both chapters share another common element in the future they envision: the assumption of capitalism (Daraiseh and Booker, 2019: 161). The materiality of this future is not only embodied in the corporation or company that enables the creation of the post-human image but, looking back at "Be Right Back," we can observe how Ash's presence in the everyday challenges of parenting naturalizes the incorporation of commodities into the realm of intimacy. This goes beyond technological innovation, and the company (as the product supplier) becomes implicitly woven into the future grammar of family life. Martha's ongoing negotiation to regulate her daughter's "consumption" of "Ash", emulating the claimed control that parents claim to have in parenting with other "technological artefacts", is a clue to the conditions of consciousness in the face of a broader regulatory logic of sensibilities, which propose a particular disposition between the digital and the cognitive-affective as an epochal mark.

In the same direction, we can see that the "happy ending" of San Junípero coincides with the image where the hundreds of memories that sustain the digitalised consciences of the clients are made explicit. The dialectical relationship proposed in this chapter is not only between the real/virtual, but between the overlapping temporalities as a testimony of the possibilities that "the technological" enables between present/future: "that the utopian compensations offered by the company are available only to those who can afford to pay, which makes them seem much less genuinely utopian." (Daraiseh and Booker, 2019: 161). The message in this key has the body as a (non-essentialist) substratum of social reality, and emotions as a central component of the mechanisms through which a form of commodification of life-death is re-invented. The post-human utopia of survival contrasts with the concrete possibilities of re-living capitalism.

CONCLUSION

Earlier, we discussed a crucial phenomenon for understanding the current platform capitalism and its connection to a politics of sensibilities related to death and dying online. We referred to immediacy and the sensations that make it manifest (Scribano and Mairano, 2022). These include the sense of constant availability (always being connected), transience and ephemerality (being "in transit," between two indefinite moments), and pre-sentification (being in a continuous "here and now"). Immediacy, therefore, sets the pace for emotional transactions taking place on the Internet. And the liminal evolution of our finite nature, thanks to technological innovation, aligns with this regime of sensations.

Indeed, *machine learning* applications and bodily connection devices would establish logics of feeling in which the disappearance of others (so far the only proximate experience we can have of death) would lose its inexorable and disruptive status. In other words, chatting with our deceased, embracing them and being able to look them in the face are all forms of "extended" interaction, which would contribute to the sensation of a relatively perennial existence, unanchored from any temporal frame of reference. The meaninglessness of mortuary traditions in the face of the survival of the deceased and a horizon of expectations that is exhausted in the fleeting and immediate consumption of the re-animated link. In this scenario, the emergence of AI-based applications and platforms (including deadbots and digital executors), as well as the sophistication of interfaces for sensing the deceased (haptic gloves, VR glasses, etc.), are part of a catalogue of products and services to satisfy a type of demand that is strongly emotionalised and translatable into algorithmic language. This is a crucial factor in understanding how part of the politics of contemporary sensibilities is configured, as the foundation of the order of global domination.

In other works (Scribano and Duperré, 2021; Duperré, 2020; Duperré and Lisdero, 2022) we have dealt with the *political economy of death*[14] prevailing in the funeral industry in recent decades and the way in which certain processes of valorisation and marketing/consumption practices associated with the treatment and final disposal of the corpse were legitimised. From this analysis, we were able to see how a series of products and services were offered to the inanimate body[15], tracing the trajectory of all merchandise: adding value (conservation and aesthetic conditioning), use (display at funerals and other farewell rituals) and disposal (destination of the remains). Now, if we link the above with what we have tried to formulate in this chapter, we could venture the following conjecture: perhaps the business of digitalisation and emotionalisation of death is nothing more than one more link in the value chain described above.

If so, the market has managed to ensure that the "useful life" of the "dead-commodity" unit does not end when it is discarded; on the contrary, it can now continue to be enjoyed indefinitely thanks to its virtual recreation. And with this, not only is the re-productive character of the classic mortuary rites re-vitalised, but this time the processes of valorisation at play here are favoured by the capacity of "the digital" to widen audiences and penetrate intimacy. As we saw through the postcards presented, these sensibilities around death evidence the new materialities of the social body, the re-novated emotionalities as re-productive mechanisms, and the emerging ways of consolidating the grammars of capitalism (even beyond death).

It is true that we are still a long way from being able to interact with non-human intelligent beings who have the capacity to feel anguish in the face of an expiration that, for their part, is alien to them. Nor, as Dreyfus and Dreyfus (1999) put it, can they suffer vulnerability in the face of physical violence. However, these limitations do not prevent us from empathising with expert systems and AI and even entrusting them with our life and death. Precisely, making this "empathy" reflective is a possible path - which we wanted to follow here - to demystify heteronomous experiences (even of death) as the only possible future.

REFERENCES

Carden, C., & Gibson, M. (2021). Living on Beyond the Body: The Digital Soul of Black Mirror. In The Moral Uncanny in Black Mirror. Palgrave Macmillan. doi:10.1007/978-3-030-47495-9_8

Daraiseh, I., & Booker, M. K. (2019). Unreal City: Nostalgia, Authenticity, and Posthumanity in "San Junipero". In T. McSweeney & S. Joy (Eds.), *Through the black mirror: deconstructing the side effects of the digital age*. Palgrave Macmillan. doi:10.1007/978-3-030-19458-1_12

De Sena, A., & Lisdero, P. (2015). Etnografía Virtual: aportes para su discusión y diseño (Visual Ethnography: conceptual debates). In *Caminos cualitativos. Aportes para la investigación en ciencias sociales*. Ediciones CICCUS, Imago Mundi.

Deleuze, G., & Guattari, F. (2008). *Mil mesetas. Capitalismo y esquizofrenia [Thousand plateau: Capitalism and schizophrenia)*. Pre-textos.

Dreyfus, H., & Dreyfus, S. (1999). Fabricar una mente versus modelar el cerebro: la inteligencia artificial se divide de nuevo [Create a mind or format the brain: AI in perspective]. In The Artificial Intelligence debate: False Starts, Real Foundations (pp. 25-58). Gedisa.

Duperré, J. (2020) Los re(s)tos de la muerte en pandemia. Un análisis de la política de los cuerpos y las sensibilidades contemporáneas [Death in Panemics; an analysis of bodies and contemporary emotions]. *Boletín Onteaiken*, *10*(30).

Duperré, J., & Lisdero, P. (2022). Sensibilities, Social Networks and Images of Death. Some Clues about the "Politics of Gazes". In Global Emotion Communications: Narratives, Technology, and Power. Nova Science Publishers.

Giddens, A. (2003). *La Constitución de la Sociedad (the constitution of society)*. Amorrortu.

Harper, D. (2002). Talking about pictures: A case for photo elicitation. *Visual Studies*, *17*(1), 13–26. doi:10.1080/14725860220137345

Lisdero, P. (2017). Conflicto social y sensibilidades. Un análisis a partir de las imágenes/observaciones de los saqueos de diciembre de 2013 en la ciudad de Córdoba (Argentina). (Social Conflict and Sensibiilties). In *Geometrías Sociales*. Estudios Sociológicos Editora.

McSweeney, T., & Joy, S. (2019). Introduction: Read that Back to Yourself and Ask If You Live in a Sane Society. In T. McSweeney & S. Joy (Eds.), *Through the black mirror: deconstructing the side effects of the digital age*. Palgrave Macmillan. doi:10.1007/978-3-030-19458-1_1

Naremore, J. (2005) Love and death in A.I. Artificial Intelligence. *Michigan Quarterly Review, 44*(2). http://hdl.handle.net/2027/spo.act2080.0044.210

Sarah, F., & Maricel, O. (2013). *Age and Ageing in Contemporary Speculative and Science Fiction*. Bloomsbury.

Schopp, A. (2019). Making Room for Our Personal Posthuman Prisons: Black Mirror's "Be Right Back". In T. McSweeney & S. Joy (Eds.), *Through the black mirror: deconstructing the side effects of the digital age*. Palgrave Macmillan. doi:10.1007/978-3-030-19458-1_5

Scribano, A. (2012). Sociología de los cuerpos/emociones [Sociology of bodies/ Emotions]. In *Revista Latinoamericana de Estudios sobre Cuerpos, Emociones y Sociedad - RELACES*. http://www.relaces.com.ar/index.php/relaces/article/view/224

Scribano, A. (2015). Sociabilidades, vivencialidades y sensibilidades: aproximar, alejar, suprimir [Socialibity, experiences and sensibilities]. Revista Cuerpos, emociones y sociedad, 7(17).

Scribano, A. (2017). *Normalization, enjoyment and bodies/emotions: Argentine sensibilities*. Nova Science Publishers.

Scribano, A. (2019). Confianza en la sociedad 4.0. (The social trust in Society 4.0). In *Confianza y políticas de las sensibilidades* (pp. 147–168). Estudios Sociológicos Editora.

Scribano, A., & Duperré, J. (2021). Die Alone in Argentina: A View from Sensibilities in Times of the Pandemic. In K. Maximiliano & A. Scribano (Eds.), *Emotionality of COVID-19. Now and After: The War Against a Virus*. Nova Science Publishers.

Scribano, A., & Lisdero, P. (2019). Labour, body, and social conflict: the 'digital smile' and emotional work in call centres. In *Digital labour, society and the politics of sensibilities* (pp. 117–136). Palgrave Macmillan. doi:10.1007/978-3-030-12306-2

Scribano, A., & Lisdero, P. (2019) Digital gaze and visual experience. In Digital Labour, Society and the Politics of Sensibilities. Palgrave-Macmillan. doi:10.1007/978-3-030-12306-2_2

Scribano, A. & Mairano, V. (2021) Narratives, emotions and artificial intelligence: a reading of artificial intelligence from emotions. *Springer Nature Switzerland*. doi:10.1007/s43545-021-00237-z

Sossa Azuela, J. H. (2020). *El papel de la Inteligencia Artificial en la industria 4.0* [The Role of AI in the industry 4.0]. Universidad Nacional Autónoma de México. Disponible en: https://ru.iibi.unam.mx/jspui/bitstream/IIBI_UNAM/89/1/01_inteligencia_artificial_juan_sossa.pdf

Stam, K. R., & Stanton, J. M. (2010). Events, emotions, and technology: Examining acceptance of workplace technology changes. *Information Technology & People*, *23*(1), 23–53. doi:10.1108/09593841011022537

Waltz, D. (1999). Perspectivas de la construcción de máquinas verdaderamente inteligentes. (The assemblage of machine in motion). In *The Artificial Intelligence debate: False Starts, Real Foundations* (pp. 218–242). Gedisa.

ADDITIONAL READING

Hirschman, D., Schwadel, P., Searle, R., Deadman, E., & Naqvi, I. (2018). Why sociology needs science fiction. *Contexts*, *17*(3), 12–21. doi:10.1177/1536504218792521

Kim, J. (2021). Algorithmic intimacy, prosthetic memory, and gamification in black mirror. *The Journal of Popular Film and Television*, *49*(2), 109–118. doi:10.1080/01956051.2021.1871584

Korstanje, M. E., & Seraphin, H. (2022). A Problem Called Alterity: The Position of the 'Other' in HBO Saga Westworld. In *Tourism Through Troubled Times: Challenges and Opportunities of the Tourism Industry in the 21st Century* (pp. 7–20). Emerald Publishing Limited. doi:10.1108/978-1-80382-311-920221001

Lalonde, P. C. (2023). Border Security Meets Black Mirror: Perceptions of Technologization from the Windsor Borderland. *Journal of Borderlands Studies*, *38*(5), 723–744. doi:10.1080/08865655.2021.1968927

Rodriguez, S. M. (2022). Black Dreams, Electric Mirror: Cross-Cultural Teaching of State Terrorism and Legitimized Violence. *Teaching Sociology*, *50*(4), 392–398. doi:10.1177/0092055X221120868

Rottensteiner, F. (Ed.). (2008). *The Black Mirror and Other Stories: An Anthology of Science Fiction from Germany and Austria*. Wesleyan University Press.

Wenk, A. F. (2023). In rhetorical sense (s): Exploration of difference reflected through Black Mirror. *Popular Communication*, 1–12. doi:10.1080/15405702.2023.2262982

KEY TERMS AND DEFINITIONS

Deadbots: Also known as interactive robots, these are chatbot applications that recreate, by means of AI, conversations with profiles of deceased people.

Digital Executor: A natural or legal person appointed to "ensure the fulfilment of the last will of the deceased" (including the "right to be forgotten"), as well as to control and manage their assets, corresponding to their online "legacy".

Liminality: Refers to that which is at a boundary or threshold with vague or non-existent contours. It suggests, in other words, spatial and/or temporal transience; a not being in any time or place.

ENDNOTES

1 An important observation, as noted by Naremore (2005), is that for the 'Meat Fair' scenes, Spielberg employed actual amputees to portray androids in search of missing or damaged body parts. As Naremore explains, "at one point, we see a robot played by an African-American amputee who takes a white mechanical hand from a pile of spare parts and inserts it into his amputated wrist" (p. 5).

2 Named after the author who formulated the principle, the American sociologist William I. Thomas, the theorem postulates the following: If people define situations as real, they are real in their consequences.

3 The social sciences have a broad relationship with visual studies. Elsewhere we have explored and substantiated epistemic and methodological aspects associated with the power of an analysis that combines virtual ethnography, visuality and the open question about bodies/emotions (Lisdero, 2017; Scribano and Lisdero, 2015, De Sena and Lisdero, 2015), and particularly around the social phenomenon of death (Duperré and Lisdero, 2023). For this chapter we have explored different visual-virtual environments in search of perceptions and emotions around the application of AI in relation to death. A corpus of analysis was constructed, selecting significant emergents that allow us to condense in a paradigmatic way what the visual-virtual world reconstructed from the ethnographic work "shows" us about this relationship. The presentation strategy, based on "postcards", seeks to "restore" a dialogue on the subject where the visual contributes its evocative (Harper, 2002) power on social processes.

4 The project's creator, Jason Rohreren, an American, promotes the project through a brief video where a poignant, hushed voice can be heard reflecting: "I know it's been a while. I wish we could talk. You used to give me those silly nicknames. I was always so embarrassed. God, I miss you. Are you there?" In response, unintelligible voices reply. The video can be found at: https://projectdecember.net/

5 To read more about this event, go to:: https://www.clarin.com/internacional/estados-unidos/quebrado-dolor-contrato-chatbot-novia-vuelva-muertos-_0_c_knjRk8m.html
https://www.lanacion.com.ar/tecnologia/es-etico-que-los-deadbots-hablen-por-nosotros-tras-nuestra-muerte-nid24052022/

6 https://www.myheritage.es/

7 Available for download at: https://www.almayalife.com/download-app

8 To read more about it, go to: https://www.bbc.com/mundo/noticias-51557842

9 Extract taken from the news item, whose link we share below: https://www.reuters.com/article/corea-del-sur-realidad-virtual-encuentro-idESKBN2081MR

10 See more in: https://tellmebye.com/es

11 Article in a Newspaper: Jiménez Lajara. (2013, July 28). Carlos Jiménez (Tellmebye): Digitization of the funeral sector is no longer an option, it is an imperative need. *Innova Funeraria*. Available in: https://innovafuneraria.es/carlos-jimenez-tellmebye-la-digitalizacion-del-sector-funerario-ya-no-es-una-opcion-es-una-necesidad-imperativa/

12 See more in:: https://www.lavanguardia.com/tecnologia/20160203/301871456782/cuando-mueras-vida-digital-perfil-facebook-cuenta-google-legado-herencia-digital.html https://www.agenciasinc.es/Reportajes/Vivir-y-morir-online-Internet-ha-cambiado-para-siempre-nuestra-relacion-con-la-muerte
https://www.clarin.com/servicios/pasa-cuentas-redes-sociales-alguien-muere-opciones-ofrecen-facebook-instagram-twitter_0_rzBHhZVScQ.html

13 The reference to human instincts is taken from the popular IMDB platform (https://www.imdb.com/title/tt2085059/). The series Black Mirror has been the subject of reflection from various disciplines. It would be impossible to list all the analyses available on the subject, but for the purposes of this paper, some interesting and complementary perspectives to those proposed here can be found in Carden, Gibson (2021) and Sarah and Maricel (Eds.) (2013), among others.

14 It is worth adding that we inscribe this category in a more comprehensive one that Scribano (2015) calls the "political economy of morality" and which, in general terms, is characterised by the establishment of a logic of consumption based on enjoyment and invested with moral imperatives. A sort of secular

religion, the author adds, which is expressed through: a) the enthronement of merchandise and profit; and b) the alienation of its devotees/consumers.

15 With this term we refer to that paradoxical double quality of being/entity. A reified subject (although different from all objects) that, despite having inexorably lost its "vital" qualities, preserves the bodily quality of agency (sensu Deleuze and Guattari, 2008).

Chapter 11
AI and Digital Sentience in Kazuo Ishiguro's *Klara and the Sun*: A Study of Posthuman Performity

Aman Deep Singh
https://orcid.org/0000-0002-4923-4137
Nirma University, India

ABSTRACT

Science fiction (SF) is pivotal in shaping the readers' attitudes towards the future. Still, the main objective of a science fiction novel or film is not to predict the future or to assess any technological advancement. SF, mainly, teaches us what it means to be humane in a changing world of citizenship cum globalization. To convey this message, novelists and movie makers portray artificial intelligence (AI) as an autonomous or human-like character to ponder the condition of humans in flux and the social, economic, and political issues regarding technological advancement. Through the perspective of Klara, the robot protagonist, we explore artificial intelligence and consciousness, the posthuman situation of humanity, the future of utopia, humanity's changing ideologies, and the human-machine relationship or human-nonhuman relationship. The way AI enacts humans is debatable as AI introspection reflects new capacities for human potential and mirrors the limits of humanity (i.e., the creature is defined and associated with its creator).

INTRODUCTION

Science Fiction (SF) is pivotal in shaping the readers' attitude towards the future. Still, the main objective of a science fiction novel or film is not to predict the future

DOI: 10.4018/979-8-3693-0802-8.ch011

or to assess any technological advancement. SF, mainly, teaches us what it means to be humane in a changing world of citizenship cum globalization. To convey this message, novelists and movie makers portray Artificial Intelligence (AI) as an autonomous or human-like character to ponder the condition of humans in flux and the social, economic, and political issues regarding technological advancement. The idea of the development of cognitive capabilities in AI is mainly inspired by evolutionary biology and developmental psychology. The quest for creating artificial beings is not new and has been pursued by scientists and artists. Still, this tendency to imagine and create is another expression of mimesis and anthropomorphism that has been a part of human history. Consciousness can be defined as an awareness of one's existence, i.e., awareness of and reason for actions. Intuition, empathy, and creativity are directly associated with human consciousness.

Kazuo Ishiguro SF, *Klara and the Sun* (2021) abets one make sense of the world during the COVID-19 pandemic, allowing us to learn about our consciousness, which is a symptom of life and higher than intelligence. From Ishiguro's SF, one can differentiate between "primitive consciousness" (rudimentary knowledge of self-existence as in the case of Siri, Cortana, and Google Assistant) and "reflective consciousness," which is the ability to ponder upon one's own and others existence which can slightly visible in Sophia. Further, he presents two antithetical views, i.e., the historical notion of Mechanism (a mind is a complicated machine) via Paul and the Computational Theory of Mind or CTM (claims that the human brain is a computer) via Henry Capaldi. Unlike neurological theories of consciousness, which emphasize explaining consciousness from physical and biological points of view, Ishiguro attempts to clarify via the Philo-psychological and social-self theory of consciousness. Philo-psychological theory of consciousness concerns what consciousness is, and possessing an internal state is a prerequisite for a conscious entity. The social-self theory of consciousness views consciousness as a social phenomenon or interaction. Through the perspective of Klara, the robot protagonist, we explore artificial intelligence and consciousness, the posthuman situation of humanity, the future of Utopia, humanity's changing ideologies, and the human-machine relationship or human-nonhuman relationship in a posthuman (secondary) world of bioengineered beings which can be embraced enthusiastically or rejected. The way AI enacts humans is debatable as AI introspection reflects new capacities for human potential and mirrors the limits of humanity, i.e., the creature is defined and associated with its creator. Ishiguro has tried to present AI as a conscious machine rather than a manufactured risk, depicting societal issues and its interrelation with science and technology through key concepts like embodiment and situatedness

Science Fiction (SF) is a speculative fiction genre emphasizing science, technology, society, and futuristic concepts. SF is a genre that brims with narratives that usually combine the following: artificial intelligence, advanced technologies, time travel, extraterrestrial (aliens), space exploration, parallel universes and so on. SF can offer a detailed account of social commentary and the human condition, be it the future or an alternate world, influenced by science, or the interconnections of various discourses that "emerge when literary culture and artificial life are integrated together" (Hayles, 1999a, pp. 219–220) depicting a complex relationship between culture and technology. Further, consciousness – a mixture of intellectual, bodily, and spatial awareness – has received significant interest in posthuman theory.

Kazuo Ishiguro is a renowned contemporary novelist of the world who has written seminal works like *A Pale View of Hills* (1982), *The Remains of the Day* (1989), *Never Let Me Go* (2005), *The Buried Giant* (2015) garnered critical appreciation and several literary awards, including Nobel Prize in Literature (2017). Ishiguro's work mainly manifests themes of memory, unreliable narrator, and the human relation to the past, and the distinctive elements employed by him are: "frugality with words, psychological account of protagonists, orientation towards form and, last but not least, action presented chiefly by internal struggles of the main characters and at the same time narrators of the stories" (Sim, 2005, p. 81).

Kazuo Ishiguro uses the SF genre as the most suitable way to help engage the public on the current state and potential impacts of AI and popularizing science and technology among the youth. By promoting SF as a tool to educate the younger generation, Ishiguro piques their interest in AI, material science, quantum computing, etc. Research from the AI narrative project at Leverhulme Centre for the Future of Intelligence, Cambridge University, shows that a subset of Western narratives has unevenly influenced the dystopian visions of AI across the English-speaking world. Kanta Dihal, the researcher behind AI narratives, reveals that Hollywood shapes our perceptions and appearance of AI, and that's where one gets the notion of a humanoid robot (Earth, 2021). Whether AI is a boon or bane to humanity depends on what kind of value system humanity clings to.

However, Kazuo Ishiguro is of Japanese origin and does not agree with the hypothesis that AI poses an existential threat to humanity, which is being widely discussed among the public and scientific community and is concerned about the emotional impact of robots. Emotions in AI have been debatable, and the ability to make decisions in a dynamic environment depends on it. In contrast to the Western narratives about AI, the attitude of Japanese writers and readers is less dystopian due to the unique cultural history of humanoids/robots in Japanese manga. For instance, Japanese animated series like *Astroboy* and *Doremon* have influenced people's positive associations with AI. This shows that having a different narrative history changes people's thoughts about technology (Earth, 2021). Cognitive processes in living and non-living can be evaluated by using the notion of "information processing", but emotions as a cognitive process orient us to recognize and express ourselves via a dynamic cum adaptative form of information processing (Hudlicka, 2015). Through Klara, a posthuman, the readers learn that humans are highly complex "biological information-processing machines," it is difficult to interpret them as everything cannot be seen from the lens of binary opposition. Since humans act emotionally in an embodied environment, it becomes difficult for Klara to develop a model of emotion that can synthesize some essence of human emotional processing.

There is no precise definition of emotions, but Kazuo Ishiguro explores the social constructivist theories, particularly interaction ritual theory (social companionship in *Klara and the Sun*), which is infused with emotion and expressiveness, i.e., interactions require and produces emotional energy that is a common denominator across situations and relations for creating social bonds (Turner & Stets, 2006). Further, it propagates that emotional behaviors are developed through experience and are not innate. In *Klara and the Sun* (2021), one gets to observe human behavior from an outsider's perspective (post-humanist reading) so that one can break humans down to their first kind of instincts and behaviors as they are being observed by someone who is not human and does not have those instincts or complexities of the human heart which is portrayed in a poetic sense through the interaction of Paul and Klara about the "human heart…makes each of us special and individual…You'd have to learn her heart, and learn it fully, or you'll never become Josie in any sense that matters… Rooms within rooms within rooms" (Ishiguro, 2021, p. 196). Here, Ishiguro distinguishes between mind (human heart) and intelligence (logic) and relates consciousness with Josie's identity. For Paul, the mind is a repository of thoughts and feelings, which is difficult for Klara to gain through experience. At the same time, intelligence is the ability to make decisions rationally, demarcating between right and wrong, which is not always possible to exercise in real-world environments (Paul, 2004). Even if Klara had passed off as Josie (in body), Chrissie would never have accepted her. Klara could not perform complex tasks requiring intuition and empathy to attain subjective biological awareness and consciousness.

Klara and the Sun (2021) also becomes a philosophical literary fiction by raising questions about AI consciousness. At the same time, it is grounded in the real world. It shows how the topic of loneliness has gained relevance in contemporary life, especially during the COVID-19 pandemic, which has increased loneliness around the world and boosted the adoption of AI "As the society adapts to the new changes after the pandemic, global citizens are expecting their governments to put the 'digital-first' initiative as a priority. AI is also integrated into systems to tackle climate change issues, predict weather forecasts by scientific organizations, and eradicate food wastage, global hunger and poverty" (Intelligence et al., 2022). *Klara and the Sun* (2021), as a piece of AI literature, challenges how one reads, as well as renders an innovative approach to Humanities (language and literature) and muses of sentient machines (computation). By explaining the modality of emotional processes in AI, Ishiguro has allowed the readers to improve their understanding of the relational functions of emotions and social activities.

In the novel, Ishiguro can be seen as a strong supporter, indicating that cognition is an embodied or situated activity. Embodiment (a notion that intelligence requires the body) and Situatedness (the body's ability to perceive its environment and act upon it) are quintessential to the behavior-based approach (Arsenio et al., 2012, p. 99). As an AI-SF, *Klara and the Sun (2021)* is an inspiration entrenched in technological optimism and determinism, it points out two things about social robots like Klara: first, it is difficult to formalize basic knowledge and progressively add to the knowledge base of AI who can use it to process new information and make inferences about the world; secondly, knowledge about the world has to be acquired through experience and interaction using sensory information (for example, Bicentennial Man) and learning based on it to situate the information received. If seen in futuristic terms or an evaluation of technology, it diverges and underestimates the risks revolving around AI in this post-truth era (Giuliano, 2020, p. 1019).

Science-fictional AI is not solely about the human aspirations and perturbations about a specific technology but about the everyday life of a human and readership, which is "a metaphor for other societal issues" (Hermann, 2021, pp. 1–2). By promoting an emotional bond between a human child and a humanoid/artificial friend (AF), Ishiguro not only ruminates about life but presents a specific vision of human life and the difference between sentimentality and emotional manipulation. Further, by using the OODA (observe orient decide act) loop, a concept developed by military strategist John Boyd, Ishiguro shows how AF, like Klara, adapts and learns, highlighting the gaps in the process of becoming strong AI: observe sensory data and actively surveilling the situation; orient to the new situation, i.e., analyzing and synthesizing past experiences with current observation; decide which requires imagination (a hallmark of human intelligence) which is seen in Klara as computational creativity (especially her notion of the sun as god-like providing exceptional nourishment as Klara is charged via it); act with precise navigation and timing which requires cognitive techniques and algorithms to integrate perceiving, analyzing, communicating, planning, decision-making and executing to realize the untapped potential of robotic system (Ng & Leung, 2020). Kazuo Ishiguro is known for pushing boundaries when it comes to the genre; he refuses any association with genre fiction, and yet his works are genre fiction like *Remains of the Day* (historical fiction), *Never Let Me Go* (science fiction), *Buried Giant* (fantasy fiction), and *Klara and the Sun* (science-fictional AI).

OBJECTIVES

Studying emotions and their concepts when undertaken by empirical researchers in social sciences has often been conducted as anthropological interviews, surveys, analysis of linguistic idioms, stimulus-response tests and so on. Many social scientists and engineers have ignored a vast body of existing data that directly bears on feelings and ideas about feelings, i.e., literature, especially literary narratives, which represents the causes and effects of emotions as comprehended or imagined in a particular society, thereby giving rise to relatable feelings in readers. While literature cannot depict emotions accurately nor be treated as empirical data, how it represents emotions tells us something important about how people in a particular society think about emotions. This makes literature a warehouse of narrative portrayals of emotional scenarios. So, this chapter aims to capture the literary responses to Human-Robot Interaction (HRI) to get a wide range of genuine and spontaneous human emotions concealed in private interactions in Kazuo Ishiguro's *Klara and the Sun (2021)*. Thus, this chapter explores the potential of celebrated stories (literature) on AI that can form a data repository for research on emotion and emotional concepts relatable to AI.

There have always been two problems with literature while studying emotions: firstly, science seeks generalities while literature seems to cling to narrow particularities; secondly, readers and researchers of other disciplines tend to think of literature in terms of nations, periods, genres, schools, and movements (Hogan, 2003). This chapter treats literature in an interdisciplinary manner along with the standard function of literature, i.e., a human activity. Moreover, this chapter treats literature as a subfield for cognitive science, which can hardly claim to explain the human mind and emotions if it does not acknowledge the ubiquitous and significant aspect of human mental activity – literature. Finally, this chapter focuses on the relationship between two crucial components of literature and the human mind – emotion (AI consciousness) and narrative (Posthuman perspective) – that help interweave patterns of our emotions, ideas about emotions, and how emotions become central and definitive in the intriguing stories about AI.

BACKGROUND

AI is becoming a widely spread topic in the scientific community and public space, and its story is not only about technical expertise but also encapsulates other sociologically relevant things. American computer scientist John McCarthy coined the term AI in 1955, referring to the development of general machines constructed wholly by artificial means and can exhibit human behaviour without being a snag for living organisms (Mijwel, 2015, p. 3). *Klara and the Sun* (2021) belongs to the category of Soft Science Fiction that emphasizes unravelling dystopia and sentient consciousness. As technology is gaining prominence in every aspect of life, one cannot ignore its place in society and how people interact with it and are affected by it; co-dependency with technology also shows how we can self-optimize and improve ourselves, leading us into an existential epiphany. So, Ishiguro has assigned a body to AF Klara with intrinsic physical and psychological needs, following the approach of bottom-up AI trying to build intelligence from simple mechanisms rather than high-level reasoning (top-down approach to AI) to couple perception and action.

Emotions are something that humans experience and play a pivotal role in all social phenomena, i.e., it is a bodily consciousness indicating the importance that an event – Interaction – has for the subject in a natural and social world. The study of emotions has gained attention due to "Affective computing," which brought a trend to have an emotional human-computer interaction. Emotions are of two types: (i) Basic emotions (expressive feeling components which are predefined in an AI) and (ii) dynamic emotions (high-order cognition with dynamic interplay) (Izard, 2007). Emotions can be viewed across four modalities, including behavioural/ expressive modality (associated with expressive and action-oriented characteristics, such as facial expressions, speech, gestures, and behaviour choices), somatic/ physiological modality (responsible for behaviour and cognition), cognitive/ interpretive modality (base of emotion generation), and experiential/subjective modality (inculcating new knowledge from the environment) (Hudlicka, 2008). In *Klara and Sun (2021),* emotions (words) are perceived as a strategy in formulating consciousness (functional, i.e., basic and phenomenal, i.e., dynamic) and highlighting the role of emotions in four ways: (i) as a source of information (e.g., Perception of risk), (ii) focus on specific information or spotlight for memory, (iii) motivator behaviour, and (iv) drawing analogies and comparing alternatives.

Human-robot interaction (HRI) is a growing field that connects various fields like robotics, engineering, AI, psychology, literature, design, etc. HRI is divided into two categories: (i)cognitive and social HRI and (ii) physical HRI (Haddadin, 2014). The former emphasizes psychological/emotional factors help a humanoid to adapt to unstructured scenarios and provide cognitive, affective, and social support. At the same time, the latter emphasizes non-interactive robots to perform specialised tasks (especially in the healthcare sector). Literary writers and social scientists have taken a human-centred perspective on social HRI, which addresses the multidisciplinary aspects involved in all forms of explicit and implicit communication between humans and robots. Such communication has been shown in SF, where these social robots are designed to function in the human environment, having a humanoid form to interact efficiently and providing an intuitive interface. These robots are considered social robots due to their autonomous interaction with humans in a meaningful manner, which indicates that robots are increasingly becoming an integral part of our society and have the potential to be utilised as social companions, thereby forming a heterogenous society comprising of humans and robots where interaction plays a significant role. HRI is only effective if the robot can express emotions and resemble human-human interaction (HHI), which has deployed robotics from a controlled laboratory setting to domestic and social contexts. Ishiguro, who does not have a prior robotics background, can mitigate unknown expectations about the behavior of a social robot. This reinforces the importance of interdisciplinary studies. Currently, the interaction between humans and robots has not yet met expectations (vital AI phase) but can reach in future, which makes HRI an intriguing field to study. Apart from introducing novelty, maintaining coherence in HRI, and introducing new topics, other factors affecting HRI include uncanny valley, proxemics, trust, empathy, engagement, and emotional design (particularly the aspect of empathy and engagement are discussed in the chapter concerning AI emotions) (Ayano˘glu & Sequeira, 2019).

Androids, humanoids, and robots that look like humans in novellas and movies signify two things: firstly, they symbolise technological threats, i.e., dangers of human ingenuity and industrialisation or automated slave labour. Secondly, they are seldom symbols of how one contemplates the meaning of "human" and the issues linked with "personhood". Kazuo Ishiguro opts for the latter and portrays his AF/AI Klara to comprehend the religious beliefs (Sun) and technological faith (Klara's hope) and recognise the structure of the human-machine or human-nonhuman relationship. Before plunging into Critical Posthumanism, one should be familiar with terms like "Transhumanism," "Posthuman," and "Posthumanism," which have acquired phenomenal significance. Transhumanism mainly uses prosthetics and other modifications for biological advancements cum enhancement (LaGrandeur, 2015, p. 112). Kevin (2015) suggests that posthumanism is the endpoint of transhumanism, i.e., a new, hybrid species of future humans that blurs the distinctions between humans and machines. Kevin describes Posthumanism as a critique of human exceptionalism, leading us to confront the dilemma regarding our existence and position in the universe. However, Posthumanism is bifurcated into "popular posthumanism" and "critical posthumanism." The former presents posthumanism as a condition of threat to the integrity of human nature by new technologies (Wallace, 2010). By contrast, the latter is a way of "thinking" the human or as "implicated in the ongoing critique of what it means to be human" (Simon, 2003, p. 8). Kazuo Ishiguro, through *Klara and the Sun* (2021), engages a critical posthumanism, which is concerned with the interconnectedness of life, complex and interrelated subjectivity that understands humans as "co-evolving, sharing ecosystems, life processes, genetic material, with animals and other life forms" (Nayar, 2014, p. 8).

LITERATURE REVIEW

As discussed in the objective and background section, this chapter aims to study HRI from an interdisciplinary perspective, i.e., robotics, engineering, emotions, AI, and Critical Posthumanism, thereby contributing to the genre of SF as a literary body of ideas. In the literature review, I have included some seminal research papers. Sahu and Karmakar (2022) discuss critical perspectives from disposability theory, emotional computing, posthuman affect, and immaterial bodies to foreground the noncodified feature of affective experientialities that emerge due to the interface between humans and non-humans. Ajeesh and Rukmini (2022) examine a positive transition in perception towards AI, attempting to show the impact of SF on society and culture. Connors (2023) draws a comparison between the posthuman narrative of *Klara and the Sun (2021)* and *Never Let Me Go (2005),* offering a phenomenological investigation of how fictional interest is created. Singh (2023) discusses how anthropomorphism and social robotics are crucial in HRI. Humann (2023) probes into existential and ontological questions about what constitutes personhood and the self. (Hosuri, 2021; Mitra & Rana, 2022; Shikhar & Ray, 2022) works merely critique anthropocentricism in dystopian science fiction.

AI CONSCIOUSNESS

Consciousness is a byproduct of biological and chemical processes and the brain's interaction with the environment. In other words, "Consciousness is only a net of communication between human beings" (Nietzsche, 1974, p. 298). Ishiguro weaves Klara's consciousness through memories, experiences, and story-telling, which tells us about ourselves and how we interact. Klara's interaction with the real-world characters and environment indicates higher psychological functions necessary for consciousness, such as perpetual categorization, memory, and learning. Social encounters constitute an interaction ritual, and Klara, like humans, tries to maximize emotional energy in every social encounter with the novel's characters. Klara is always curious to learn and acquire information, and by observing things, she tries to understand the world based on fractured information. Though Klara replicates life-like mechanisms and behavior in a computational environment and has a body (physical), it only exists in the virtual domain, i.e., follows pre-programmed rules, making her a subject of primitive consciousness who knows her purpose of being a social robot. Further, Ishiguro presents a child-like logic through the character of Klara and her naïve views about human behavior. Klara's perspective as an outsider allows the readers to ponder on questions like: why do human beings have loneliness? Are they fundamentally lonely?

Loneliness is to experience unpleasant emotions due to alienation or seclusion, and to feel loneliness is to experience detachment without emotional and social haven, assuming a nonchalant attitude toward the people around us (*Why Some People Are More Likely to Become Lonely | Psychology Today*, n.d.). Ishiguro, by anthropomorphizing Klara and giving her consciousness, illustrates a hopeful reconstruction(s) of the "self" (human and non-human subjectivities). Klara is introduced to readers in a shop as an Artificial Friend (AF) in a dystopian setting where people do not interact personally. Children opt for these AFs as companions to relieve loneliness and boredom. It reflects that SF is mainly about de–familiarizing the present rather than extrapolating the future, i.e., breaking the panel of pervasive realism (Heffernan, 2018, p. 11). While depicting such "affective machines" as AF/ companion, it also shows that humanoid AI like Klara also implies that humans themselves are becoming artificial in a technocratic age, thereby pinpointing "issues of gender, race, and a variety of forms of Otherness… questions about the very nature and meaning of life" (Telotte, 2016, p. 3). In *Klara and the Sun (2021),* questions about consciousness commence with the appearance of social robots that are "physically embodied, autonomous agent that communicates and interacts with humans on a social level" (Darling, 2012, p. 2), like Sophia (Hanson Robotics) and Kismet (MIT), and NAO (Aldebaran). Hence, Klara and the Sun (2021) focus on the social roles humans ascribe to robots, the social context in which HRI takes place, emotional bonds, and relationships humans build with robots.

As a social robot, Klara is capable of limited decision-making and learning but can exhibit behaviour and interact with people. Further, capabilities like non-verbal immediacy, speech recognition and verbal communication, facial expression, and the perceived personality of social robots like Klara are pivotal in determining how humans respond to them (Hildt, 2019). The essential information readers take from Klara's observation is that consciousness is more than perception, i.e., it means everything to humanity. Due to our abstract thinking and pattern recognition, mechanical counterparts cannot wholly replace humankind. This mainly emphasises that there is more to life than scientific quantification. Klara's introverted soliloquies and character reveal little about the quality of AI/human consciousness but remind us about the mystery of "Being" and places science cannot access. Klara, a humanoid, socially interacts with Josie (her human caregiver) to develop perceptual and motor skills, and it is through these interactions that readers observe how Klara develops cognitive capabilities to perceive specific actions, objects, faces, scenes, and a sense of self (Arsenio, 2004). Consciousness is not something tangible that science can excavate. Still, with an AF like Klara, it can be – at the very least – simulated as Klara synchronizes with Josie through voice and movement dynamics via typical caregiver interactions. Klara appropriates these dynamics with its physical feelings, for instance, distress by low battery or excessive motor heat, flourishing by homeostasis (Lim & Okuno, 2015).

Even today, machines, particularly AI, are considered a subject of enormous novelty. It was Alan Turing who suggested simulating a child's mind rather than an adult due to the following reasons: firstly, children have various capabilities and preferences shortly after birth; secondly, like children, robot prefers conspicuous visual stimuli; lastly, the appropriate course of education, by creating child-like learning scenarios, would lead to the development of adult brain (Banks & Ginsburg, 1985; Bremner, 1994; Turing, 1950). Thus, Klara would incrementally build a knowledge database and extrapolate it into various domains of everyday life – social, emotional, cultural, and developmental learning.

By using the child development model for developmental learning of AF Klara, Kazuo Ishiguro shows how robots can be introduced into society. However, this strategy relies heavily on HRI (human-robot interactions) to filter relevant information to facilitate learning. For instance, robots like Cog and Macaco at MIT CSAIL learn through social interaction with human caregivers, and it is through the experience of these interactions that they can join precepts and contexts (including diverse sets of problems) in a dynamic cum integrated frame. Ishiguro, through the human-machine relationship, addresses the concern of identity, subjectivity or consciousness by making "Turing Test" a reference point through the scientist character Henry Capaldi (the epitome of rationality and technological faith) and his survey cum questionnaire for Klara (Ishiguro, 2021, p. 179). Thus, Ishiguro clarifies that Klara is capable of "authentic thinking." Whether it is "human thinking" or "machine thinking" is a different matter, but what is crucial is that through "speech," "learning," "thought," and "action," Klara complicates the subject/object divide established by Western metaphysics. Further, it postulates that the posthuman contains: privileged informational patterns, consciousness as the crux of human identity, becoming a cyborg to prolong life, and configuration with human beings (Hayles, 1999b, pp. 2–3). Since emotions and social processes are intertwined evolutionary, what Henry Capaldi missed, like Alan Turing, was the presence of emotions (which can be positive or negative but not neutral) in human dialogue, without which any entity may appear non-human.

Klara has been created like a human, endowed with "intentionality", which is an essential trait of humanity and its consciousness (Grech, 2012), which Ishiguro tries to transmit to its readers by making Klara go to the barn and plea to the sun to cure (exceptional help) Josie of her illness by giving his "nourishment". Ishiguro treats Klara's decision-making ability and contemplation as entirely human, and her dilemmas (related to understanding the complexities of human beings) are analogous to the dangers of modern technological ontology. This reminds us that humanoid AI cannot avoid internal contradictions and must configure a way to deal with them (Turkle, 1984, p. 259). This also points to two things that Klara lacks: first, spontaneity, as she mostly behaves in a pre-programmed manner; secondly, autonomy, as Klara was entirely dependent on previous knowledge of the environment instead of her motor sensors (Arsenio et al., 2012).

An AI humanoid robot like Klara, with a "technological consciousness," serves as a domestic servant and companion in the novel, which accomplishes "a variety of goals …a remedy for the disease of isolation and abject, existential loneliness. This disease is caused by the ontology of modern technology, making them feel alone and without direction" (Sims, 2013, p. 134). In depicting the gradual shift in the nexus of human relationships and technology, Ishiguro supports techno-optimism, emphasising technological advancements' humanising potential through AIs. Ishiguro's study of consciousness lingers not only anthropocentric but, in comparison to Western narratives, it is feminine. AI or machine consciousness is idiosyncratic, mysterious, and unexplored from the human gaze (often white and male). Mr Capaldi's fascination for AF states that it is "a vital source of education and enlightenment" (Ishiguro, 2021, pp. 262–263), and building such AI systems can aid humans towards a man-machine collaboration like an augmented intelligence, leading to amplification of human intelligence. Still, this nexus to achieve strong AI with imbued emotional intelligence will entail factoring of human quirks and biases. Such a man-machine collaboration can be reached with the behaviour-based approach towards robotics.

When readers look at things from Klara's perspective (consciousness), they come across an AI narrative that reflects parent–child relationships (cultural associations) between humans and non-humans which permeates our conception of AI (Singler, 2020, p. 261). Thus, one can see the parent–child AI narrative of *Klara and the Sun* (2021) as a harbinger of "self-reflection", representing context in a way a child would do, i.e., pure emotional response to events. Contextual emotions in *Klara and the Sun (2021)* are not only seen as an event occurring in a dystopia but also as part of the characters, which allows them to produce desired emotional responses – fear, sadness, pride, pain, resilience, and so on. The parent–child AI narrative reflects "on our anthropomorphic tendencies… ethnographic and historical literature on the child's conception which we can draw upon to highlight specific cultural assumptions (263). It also tells us that humans are endowed with the gift of "contextual adaptation" since birth, which is analogous to DARPA's (US Defence Advanced Research Projects Agency) third-wave characterization of AI development, where AI systems can build explanatory models based on real-world phenomena, and can grasp why and what decisions are made (Ng & Leung, 2020). Such ability to adapt contextually can only be achieved via interacting with the environment and making decisions, which applies to humans and AI/humanoid (strong).

Using parent–child AI narrative, Ishiguro makes his novel a canon of Children's Literature, compels the readers to think about how AI child or childlike AI are presented, and reflects the psychology of the parent-child relationship. This also allows researchers to investigate and apply gender perspectives to robotic emotions. The child epitomizes the creator's immortality and justifies their existence. Through AI consciousness and anthropomorphism of AI, Ishiguro renders the readers an opportunity to relook at themselves as humans. For instance, the parent-child relationship of Chrissie-Josie and Helen-Rick symbolises unconditional love and sacrifice, which Klara observes at Morgan Falls and at Mr Capaldi's, where she talks to Chrissie about her deceased daughter Sal and her fear of loneliness and the loss of Josie; she also acknowledges that even if her AI system/mind were transferred into exoskeleton (mannequin) created by Mr Capaldi, she would never have continued as Josie even after rigorous training as the actual operating environment is dynamic and ever-changing including unknown elements that are not present during the training phase, and this is what made it challenging to attain a reflective consciousness. Henry Capaldi's attempts to use the exoskeleton as a genetic map show how "Gene technology tries to grasp not a certain – temporally definable – stage of the entire process of generation, but the gene itself, as the essential quantity of generation that has no real place in generation itself" (Botz-Bornstein, 2012, p. 26) to yield the meaning of life.

CRITICAL POSTHUMANISM IN KLARA AND THE SUN

The last two decades have witnessed exponential growth in computational models of emotion. Researchers in various disciplines are developing models of emotions to create social robots to improve human-computer interaction via "emotional modelling", which in affective computing literature refers to (i) dynamic generations of emotions, (ii) models that map specific stimuli associated with emotions (Hudlicka, 2015). HRI, a focal point of AI-SF, studies the interrelation of technology and society, which is portrayed positively in *Klara and the Sun* (2021). Klara is a social robot directly interacting with humans, unlike industrial robots performing engineering tasks. Through such interaction, Ishiguro suggests that humans should re-evaluate traits of human existence and ponder on posthuman values, which can be our present values. As a literature of ideas and anticipation, SF reveals streaks in human life via technological advancements. SF is also a literature of evolution concerned with humans and the posthuman (Mirenayat et al., 2017, p. 77). Through the posthuman effect, Ishiguro blurs the boundary between weak AI and strong AI. The former represents the category of information-processing machines which have human cognitive abilities. In contrast, the latter represents intelligent machines with physical and mental skills (comparable to humans), including phenomenal consciousness through advanced computation (Bringsjord & Govindarajulu, 2018).

During the last decade, AI has pioneered in fields such as natural language processing, speech recognition, computer vision, robotics, and autonomous systems, and in future will reach its potential. Though these advances can be seen in Klara (AF), she can be seen as a weak AI who helps improve the quality of human life (household chores and social companionship) but is not good enough to perform highly general tasks that humans do. It is Klara's ability to introspect (condition of internal state) that contradicts the above mentioned, as readers see few traits of strong AI or AGI (Artificial General Intelligence) that Klara produces to some extent – the ability to sense, comprehend, reason, learn and act – in a dynamic environment. Introspection is mainly indicative of the following:

Self-referencing and self-reflecting. Building Strong AI with self-referential ability will allow its function to refer to itself, like recursion in programming, but the ultimate aim is to give it its own ability to modify its function by rewriting its own source code. An AI system with self-referential ability should be able to represent its own state in its own native memory representation. States within the AI system could represent error rates, utility values over time, metadata pertaining to the environment, and an embedding of the system's finite state machine. (Ng & Leung, 2020, p. 68)

So, emotions act as a facilitator for adaptive behaviour and a prerequisite for AGI. It is only toward the end of the novel that readers notice that Ishiguro has shown Klara (in her conversation with the store manager) as a weak AI who would not have possibly attained consciousness and demonstrate sentience, emotional intelligence, imagination, self-referring and self-reflecting qualities, and effective command of other machines (as Klara was not able to stop the cooting machine).

While technoscience connotes the "human" and "posthuman" as a synthesis that is presented negatively in Western narratives, in *Klara and the Sun* (2021), one sees an optimistic posthuman representation; for instance, from novels like Mary Shelly's *Frankenstein* and monster (posthuman), one comes across eye-opener representations of human being constrained, which acquaints us with the concept of love and fear. Here, we can say that the social constructivist theories of emotions – interactionist and power and status – point out that experience and environment are prime factors for the development of emotions. A "technological posthuman" like Klara is not only a metaphor for our present moment or future ontologies; it reflects a humanism adversely affected in a dystopia shaped by technological and ecological futures. Thus, Klara's (unreliable narrator) storytelling renders a prolific involvement between destabilised genres of SF, especially in a dystopian inflexion, and reorients the contested views of the "self." Critical posthumanism looks at "a posthumanism that is not threatened by its others" (Vint, 2007, p. 189). The way critical posthumanism is presented in *Klara and the Sun* (2021) reveals to readers the feasibility of utopian hope in the face of dystopian systems:

Utopianism is the expression of hope and optimism as to the future of the world... Utopian dreaming is... be rethought in the light of the speculative turn and non-anthropocentric assumptions.... Therefore, the future of utopia in the posthuman world is not threatened by the changes humans can introduce in themselves and the surrounding world. It is threatened, however, by the abandonment of a certain mindset and replacing it with another, not necessarily a better one. (Bugajska, 2021, p. 4)

Thus, Ishiguro notices that contemporary techno-narratives (fiction or non-fiction) are permeated with the "Utopian hope" for a better world. Here, critical posthumanism strives to seek a productive balance between technological determinism and technological optimism.

While the first step of evolution in the universe took place with the creation of life from non-life, scientists like Henry Capaldi attempt the opposite, i.e., creating non-life from life by preserving the human consciousness in a posthuman (non-living entity) Klara. This whole process of storing consciousness is also referred to as the "Whole Brain Emulation (WBE)", which uses two methods to extend life (immortalize humans) via mind-uploading: (i) Copy and transfer method and (ii) Gradual Replacement method (Koch & Tononi, 2008; Meissner, 2020). The former scans and maps the human brain, then copies and transfers the information to the machine. Such a method has practical limitations because it is unknown which parts of the brain create consciousness and what are the processes involved. In the Gradual Replacement method, a mammal-like architecture transfers the human brain to evolve iteratively. Such an exoskeleton is seen in Henry Capaldi's laboratory as a cyborg or biological body. However, a drawback of this method is that the living human brain will die during the transfer procedure. Although the human mind is complex, dynamic, and random, the readers see Klara simulate this dynamism required to generate a virtual brain with consciousness and some form of functioning. Futurists like Ray Kurzweil (Professor of Philosophy at Oxford) and Michio Kaku (Professor of Physics at Harvard) firmly believe that mind-uploading can be accomplished in today's era. At the same time, neuroscientists like Kenneth Miller and Miquel Nicolelis are critics of mind-uploading and do not see the brain to be computable or engineered (physical or chemical) but as a physiological entity which provides material base to reflect upon and control system.

Through Klara's humanoid character, Ishiguro embodies one of the most crucial issues, i.e., whether it is feasible to render emotions to robots and whether they can be equivalent to humans. As a posthuman narrator, Klara invites the readers to see things from her posthuman perspective, which does not invoke a post-humanist discourse. Still, it reinforces a humanist and anthropocentric argument (Herbrechter & Callus, 2008, p. 98). In a way, the existence of posthumans initially questions the "essentiality of humanity, which it might end up reaffirming" (Guesse, 2020, p. 33), thereby encapsulating both humanist and posthumanist life.

It is through the presence of a posthuman character like Klara whose narrative and influence on the story is thematic, dealing with the essence of humanity, human dignity, ethics, alterity, and STS. By doing so, Ishiguro brings out the posthumanist potential of the story, evoking a posthumanist interpretation. Klara's curiosity about humans and search for emotional intelligence project the "anthropocentric idea that emotions are the essence of humanity, which reinforces the idea of human exceptionality" (35). Anthropomorphism (assigning child-like attributes) smuggles humanism into the posthuman companion relationship. In the end, Klara becomes lonely and seems to accept what remains of her existence in the yard, on the hard ground, losing some of her cognitive ability due to the loss of the P-E-G nine solution to destroy the "cooting" machine.

Towards the end, the readers see a conversation between the store Manager and Klara about loneliness, companionship, and humanity. Klara asserts that she would fail in becoming Josie as human nature is unique, and even if Josie's consciousness was uploaded in Klara, love for Chrissie (Josie's mother) still had to be programmed as it could not have emerged from HRI. Such a phenomenon is also evident in Steven Spielberg's *Artificial Intelligence (2001),* which deals with the challenges of creating and adopting an AI child. Some scholars may even think that a humanoid with consciousness can be refuted free will as it is inferior to humans. Still, in the novel, we also see the old version of AF's fear getting replaced by a new version, which mirrors a kind of resistance and disposable culture, as well as B3 models lacking empathy compared to B2 models like Klara. It is these human emotions that lowered the quality of Klara's decision-making ability, especially at a critical juncture where she lost most of the PEG liquid (meant for AF to sustain her for a long time), which she used to destroy the cooting machine (to save Klara from pollution and make the energy of sun accessible), adversely effecting her mobility and durability. When seen as a work of critical posthumanism, *Klara and the Sun* (2021) offers neither a transcendence nor a rejection of humanism but an ongoing critique of what it is to be humane (Simon, 2003; Wallace, 2010). It also addresses the problems humans face while interacting with social robots as the "body" becomes crucial in understanding emotion and cognition and natural interaction between humans and robots.

CONCLUSION

By using AI, Kazuo Ishiguro makes the readers confront an idea that views human traits as fabricated, enabling them to read and interpret the story, thereby making it "self-conscious" fiction by testing the humanistic legacy and assumptions in *Never Let Me Go* (2005). *Klara and the Sun* (2021), he revitalises his novels. By employing Philo-psychological and social-self theory, Ishiguro shows that both approaches cannot attest to the consciousness of AI like Klara, who may know that she possesses an internal state, but people (external observers) around her would not be able to infer an inner state of such quality unless Klara brings this to their notice. He brings up the ethical issues about the potential inter-reaction (pessimistic and optimistic) of the human-machine relationship (Esmaeilzadeh & Vaezi, 2021). Ishiguro's concept of *sonzai-kan*, or human presence in robots, may seem like a desire to preserve the human, even in artificial constructs. Yet, this move towards providing them with anthropomorphic features renders those qualities transferrable and adaptable (Shaw-Garlock, 2010). It does not matter how well the AI can mimic humans, but its capacity to attain self-consciousness, transcendence, and dynamism. So, suppose we cannot understand how consciousness occurs in our brain. In that case, building a machine that can generate consciousness becomes enigmatic, leading to social-ethical problems.

Critical Posthumanism addresses the ambiguities, inconsistencies, and limitations of posthuman thought visible via Klara. Moreover, a post-humanist perspective on children's literature provides new interpretations and themes for readers and authors and constitutes a fertile ground for experimental and digital literature. A posthumanist perspective unveils literature's potential to convey what it means to be something other than human. As a critical posthumanist, Ishiguro tries to tell us about the present situation of humanist values, making SF an influential genre, thereby acknowledging that any human action or intentionality is always entwined with other, non-human materiality and capacities and forces which may support, challenge, undermine or reverse the work of humans. By encompassing a range of human cognitive functions in a philosophical framework, Ishiguro addresses the problem of defining consciousness. Further, he also propounds that it is an onerous task for a machine to accomplish advanced stages of consciousness, i.e., reflective consciousness, which comprises of: firstly, metacognition, which is awareness of one's thought process like thinking about thinking or knowledge of knowledge; and secondly, volition or practising free will to make choices and act upon them (Meissner, 2020).

SF formulates a social world that brings new perspectives confined to the SF audience. It suggests new sociability types that have just been fully realised and the possible emergence of new social systems spurred by alterations in the meaning of humanity. HRI has gained importance, especially with social robotics, due to the shift from industrial to human environment. Emotionally, designing a robot in terms of appearance, behaviour, and social skills is challenging and requires interdisciplinary collaboration. The growing interaction with "intelligent" machines, which began with the industrial revolution, is not just a step in social transformation but is entering into domains exclusive of humans – decision-making, emotional, and social relationships – comprising human values, as well as decisively shapes society and our way of living. So, AI narratives can be seen addressing questions about the "socio-political issues, the human condition, and philosophical questions in general" (Hermann, 2021, p. 9); can an intelligent machine like Klara be considered to have consciousness? What is consciousness, and why are we conscious? How is our mind self-aware? Can AI systems reach full autonomy and be free to make their own decisions? Will they adhere to the same value system as us? What will our relationship with our creations be? To answer such questions, one needs to comprehend the relationship between human consciousness and AI, which we can see in Kazuo Ishiguro's novel *Klara and the Sun (2021).*

REFERENCES

Ajeesh, A. K., & Rukmini, S. (2022). Posthuman perception of artificial intelligence in science fiction: An exploration of Kazuo Ishiguro's Klara and the Sun. *AI & Society*, *38*(2), 853–860. doi:10.100700146-022-01533-9

Arsenio, A. M. (2004). *Cognitive-developmental learning for a humanoid robot: A caregiver's gift*. MIT.

Arsenio, A. M., Caldas, L. G., & Oliveira, M. (2012). Social Interaction and the Development of Artificial Consciousness. In D. Chugo & S. Yokota (Eds.), Introduction to Modern Robotics (pp. 93–118). iConcept Press.

Ayano˘glu, H., & Sequeira, J. S. (2019). Human-Robot Interaction. In H. Ayano˘glu & E. Duarte (Eds.), *Emotional Design in Human-Robot Interaction: Theory, Methods and Applications* (pp. 39–56). Springer.

Banks, M. S., & Ginsburg, A. P. (1985). Infant visual preferences: A review and new theoretical treatment. *Advances in Child Development and Behavior*, *19*, 207–246. doi:10.1016/S0065-2407(08)60392-4 PMID:3911754

Botz-Bornstein, T. (2012). Critical Posthumanism. *Pensamiento y Cultura*, *15*(1), 20–30. doi:10.5294/pecu.2012.15.1.2

Bremner, J. G. (1994). *Infancy* (2nd ed.). Wiley-Blackwell.

Bringsjord, S., & Govindarajulu, N. S. (2018). Artificial Intelligence. In E. N. Zalta (Ed.), Stanford Encyclopedia of Philosophy (Fall 2018). Metaphysics Research Lab.

Bugajska, A. (2021). The Future of Utopia in the Posthuman World. *Academia Letters*, *155*, 1–7. doi:10.20935/AL155

Connors, C. (2023). 'Out of interest': Klara and the Sun and the interests of fiction. *Textual Practice*, 1–19. Advance online publication. doi:10.1080/0950236X.2023.2210096

Darling, K. (2012). *Extending legal protection to social robots: The effects of anthropomorphism, empathy, and violent behavior towards robotic objects.* doi:10.2139srn.2044797

Earth, D. (2021, November 25). Break the Digital Monoculture: Interview with Dr Kanta Dihal. *Medium*. https://medium.com/@digitalearth/break-the-digital-monoculture-interview-with-dr-kanta-dihal-604d6859123c

Giuliano, R. (2020). Echoes of myth and magic in the language of artificial intelligence. *AI & Society*, *35*(4), 1009–1024. doi:10.100700146-020-00966-4

Grech, V. (2012, April). The Pinocchio syndrome and the prosthetic impulse in science fiction. *The New York Review of Science Fiction*, 11–15.

Guesse, C. (2020). On the Possibility of a Posthuman/ist Literature(s). In S. Karkulehto, A.-K. Koistinen, & E. Varis (Eds.), *Reconfiguring Human, Nonhuman and Posthuman in Literature and Culture* (pp. 23–40). Routledge.

Haddadin, S. (2014). *Towards safe robots: Approaching Asimov's 1st law* (Vol. 90). Springer. doi:10.1007/978-3-642-40308-8

Hayles, K. (1999a). Artificial Life and Literary Culture. In M.-L. Ryan (Ed.), *In Cyberspace Textuality* (pp. 205–223). Indiana University Press.

Hayles, K. (1999b). *How We Became Posthuman*. Chicago University Press. doi:10.7208/chicago/9780226321394.001.0001

Heffernan, T. (2018). A.I. Artificial Intelligence: Science, Fiction and Fairy Tales. *English Studies in Africa*, *61*(1), 10–15. doi:10.1080/00138398.2018.1512192

Herbrechter, S., & Callus, I. (2008). What is a posthumanist reading? *Angelaki*, *13*(1), 95–111. doi:10.1080/09697250802156091

Hermann, I. (2021). Artificial intelligence in fiction: Between narratives and metaphors. *AI & Society*, 1–11. doi:10.100700146-021-01299-6

Hildt, E. (2019). Artificial Intelligence: Does Consciousness Matter? *Frontiers in Psychology, 10*, 1–3. https://doi.org/doi:10.3389/fpsyg.2019.01535

Hogan, P. C. (2003). *The Mind and Its Stories: Narrative Universals and Human Emotion*. Cambridge University Press. doi:10.1017/CBO9780511499951

Hosuri, A. (2021). Klara and the Sun: A Fable of Humanity in a Posthuman World. *Global Journal of Human-Social Science: Arts & Humanities - Psychology, 21*(7), 61–69.

Hudlicka, E. (2008, January). *What Are We Modeling When We Model Emotion?* AAAI spring symposium: emotion, personality, and social behavior, Stanford, CA.

Hudlicka, E. (2015). Computational Analytical Framework for Affective Modeling: Towards Guidelines for Designing Computational Models of Emotions. In Handbook of Research on Synthesizing Human Emotion in Intelligent Systems and Robotics (pp. 1–62). IGI Global.

Humann, H. (2023). What It Means to Be a Talking Object: Ishiguro's Use of AI Narration in Klara and the Sun. *Popular Culture Review, 34*(1), 11–49. doi:10.18278/pcr.34.1.3

Intelligence, A., Data, B., & Globe, A. (2022, January 25). *The Evolution of Artificial Intelligence in the Digital Ecosystem*. https://www.analyticsinsight.net/the-evolution-of-artificial-intelligence-in-the-digital-ecosystem/

Ishiguro, K. (2021). *Klara and the sun* (1st ed.). Alfred A. Knopf.

Izard, C. E. (2007). Basic Emotions, Natural Kinds, Emotion Schemas, and a New Paradigm. *Perspectives on Psychological Science, 2*(3), 260–280. doi:10.1111/j.1745-6916.2007.00044.x PMID:26151969

Koch, C., & Tononi, G. (2008). Can Machines be Conscious? *IEEE Spectrum, 45*(6), 55–59. doi:10.1109/MSPEC.2008.4531463

LaGrandeur, K. (2015). Androids and the Posthuman in Television and Film. In M. Hauskeller, T. D. Philbeck, & C. D. Carbonell (Eds.), *The Palgrave Handbook of Posthumanism in Film and Television* (pp. 111–119). Palgrave Macmillan. doi:10.1057/9781137430328_12

Lim, A., & Okuno, H. G. (2015). Developing Robot Emotions through Interaction with Caregivers. In *Handbook of Research on Synthesizing Human Emotion in Intelligent Systems and Robotics* (pp. 316–337). IGI Global. doi:10.4018/978-1-4666-7278-9.ch015

Meissner, G. (2020). Artificial Intelligence: Consciousness and Conscience. *AI & Society*, *35*(1), 225–235. doi:10.100700146-019-00880-4

Mijwel, M. (2015). History of Artificial Intelligence. *Computer Science*, *1*(1), 1–6.

Mirenayat, S. A., Bahar, I. B., Talif, R., & Mani, M. (2017). Science Fiction and Future Human: Cyborg, Transhuman and Posthuman. *Research Result: Theoretical and Applied Linguistics*, *3*(1), 76–81. doi:10.18413/2313-8912-2017-3-1-76-81

Mitra, S., & Rana, M. (2022). A Comparison Study between Nature and Artificial Intelligence in Kazuo Ishiguro's Klara and the Sun. *European Chemical Bulletin*, *12*(5), 582–589.

NayarP. K. (2014). *Posthumanism*. Polity.

Ng, G. W., & Leung, W. C. (2020). Strong Artificial Intelligence and Consciousness. *Journal of Artificial Intelligence and Consciousness*, *7*(1), 63–72. doi:10.1142/S2705078520300042

Nietzsche, F. (1974). The gay science (W. Kaufmann, Trans.). Vintage.

Paul, G. (2004, April 23). *Artificial Intelligence and Consciousness*. 2nd Human-E-Tech Conference, SUNY Albany.

Sahu, O. P., & Karmakar, M. (2022). Disposable culture, posthuman affect, and artificial human in Kazuo Ishiguro's Klara and the Sun (2021). *AI & Society*. Advance online publication. doi:10.100700146-022-01600-1 PMID:36465191

Shaw-Garlock, G. (2010). *Loving Machines: Theorizing Human and Sociable-Technology Interaction. International Conference on Human-Robot Personal Relationship*, Berlin, Germany.

Shikhar, D., & Ray, K. S. (2022). Role Of 'Artificial' Hope At The Failure Of Medical Science: A Study Of Kazuo Ishiguro's Klara And The Sun. *Journal of Pharmaceutical Negative Results, 13*(8), 1012–1015. https://doi.org/ doi:10.47750/pnr.2022.13.S08.126

Sim, W.-C. (2005). Kazuo Ishiguro. *Review of Contemporary Fiction*, *25*(1), 80–115.

Simon, B. (2003). Introduction: Toward a Critique of Posthuman Futures. *Cultural Critique*, *53*(1), 1–9. doi:10.1353/cul.2003.0028

Sims, C. A. (2013). *Tech Anxiety: Artificial Intelligence and Ontological Awakening in Four Science Fiction Novels*. McFarland & Company, Inc.

Singh, A. D. (2023, October 16). *Anthropomorphism and Social Robotics in Kazuo Ishiguro's Klara and the Sun (2021). IEEE Humanitarian Technology Conference*, Rajkot.

Singler, B. (2020). Artificial Intelligence and the Parent–Child Narrative. In S. Cave, K. Dihal, & S. Dillon (Eds.), *AI Narratives A History of Imaginative Thinking about Intelligent Machines* (pp. 260–283). Oxford University Press. doi:10.1093/oso/9780198846666.003.0012

Telotte, J. (2016). *Robot ecology and the science fiction film*. Routledge. doi:10.4324/9781315625775

Turing, A. (1950). Computing Machinery and Intelligence. *Mind*, *59*(236), 433–460. doi:10.1093/mind/LIX.236.433

Turkle, S. (1984). *The Second Self: Computers and the Human Spirit*. Simon and Schuster.

Turner, J. H., & Stets, J. E. (2006). Sociological Theories of Human Emotions. *Annual Review of Sociology*, *32*(1), 25–52. doi:10.1146/annurev.soc.32.061604.123130

Vint, S. (2007). *Bodies of Tomorrow: Technology, Subjectivity, Science Fiction*. University of Toronto Press.

Wallace, J. (2010). Literature and Posthumanism. *Literature Compass*, *7*(8), 692–701. doi:10.1111/j.1741-4113.2010.00723.x

Why Some People Are More Likely to Become Lonely | Psychology Today. (n.d.). Retrieved January 22, 2022, from https://www.psychologytoday.com/us/blog/finding-new-home/202112/why-some-people-are-more-likely-become-lonely

KEY TERMS AND DEFINITIONS

Affective Computing: Work on emotion recognition technology and emotion expression in virtual characters and robots.

Dystopian Science Fiction: Works that pique our perpetual and collective curiosity about where society is heading, catering to literary critics and casual readers.

Posthumanism: It does not mean the end of humans, but the self-concept or image of human's changes, especially when considering integrating technology into our everyday lives.

Social Robot: A robot that uses human social competencies and the interactive cum cooperative dimensionality of human intelligence as paradigms to develop human-like abilities.

Theory of Mind: The ability to distinguish one's mind from others' and infer what others think or feel.

Chapter 12
Transformative Effect of Virtual Reality and the Metaverse

Laura De Clara
METACARE SRL, Italy

ABSTRACT

The text explores the transformative impact of virtual reality, augmented reality, and the metaverse on human experiences. These technologies offer new ways of interaction and learning, revolutionizing sectors such as education, mental health, and entertainment. Immersion and controlled manipulation of the virtual environment are crucial in creating engaging experiences, supporting personal transformation. Presence in virtual environments plays a key role, inducing a feeling of being physically immersed. The therapeutic use of virtual reality shows promise for mental and neurological disorders, providing a safe space to confront fears and anxieties. However, constant development of standardized protocols is necessary to ensure personalized and effective therapies. Responsible use of immersive technologies is essential to avoid issues of excessive virtual identity and addiction. Interdisciplinary research and ethics will guide the future application of these technologies, opening new perspectives in understanding the human mind and enhancing overall well-being.

The human mind evolves through its interactions with the environment and the experiences it is exposed to. Humans are designed to have "real" experiences in a "real" world (Walsh & Oakley, 2022)

New technologies have the potential to profoundly transform the human mind through (Riva et al., 2019) immersive experiences, opening doors to new ways of

DOI: 10.4018/979-8-3693-0802-8.ch012

perceiving and interacting with the virtual world. Cognitive sciences have extensively demonstrated that the repeated use of devices alters an individual's cognitive system. Technology has become a cognitive prosthesis that is now an integral part of daily life (Villani et al., 2011) shaping our experiences (Walsh & Oakley, 2022) and thus our minds.

The ability to interact within a world where we can socialize, learn, experiment, work, and have fun brings about changes in our ways of experiencing sociality and our psychophysical condition. In the era of digitalization, technology has become an integral part of each of our daily lives, impacting a multitude of aspects, from work and study to relationships (Riva et al., 2019)

Indeed, the advent of Virtual Reality (VR), Augmented Reality (AR), and the Metaverse have revolutionized human interaction with the surrounding environment, introducing new dimensions to the human experience (Bell et al., 2020), in simulated sensory worlds (Walsh & Oakley, 2022).

This text explores the profound implications of these immersive experiences, analyzing how the controlled manipulation of the virtual environment, the sense of presence, and induced empathy can act as catalysts for personal and social change.

1. VIRTUAL REALITY, AUGMENTED REALITY, AND THE METAVERSE: SOME DIFFERENCES

In the landscape of emerging technologies, Augmented Reality (AR) and Virtual Reality (VR) have emerged as widely applicable fields, ranging from medicine and education to scientific research, entertainment, and socialization (Zambelli et al., 2023).

AR is a technology that overlays digital information onto the physical environment, enabling users to interact simultaneously with the real world and digital elements (López-Ojeda & Hurley, 2023; Petrigna & Musumeci, 2022). This technology provides a live view of an existing environment in which real-world objects are "augmented" or enhanced by computer-generated perceptual information (Walsh & Oakley, 2022). People can manipulate virtual objects while maintaining a transparent view of reality (Xiong et al., 2021). By integrating this information synergistically, AR aims to enrich the perception of the real world, facilitating interaction with digital content without compromising the connection with the surrounding physical reality (Chen et al., 2019).

On the other end of the technological spectrum, VR offers complete immersion in a computer-generated virtual environment, detached from the surrounding physical reality (Ford et al., 2023; López-Ojeda & Hurley, 2023). This human-computer interface allows users to experience a three-dimensional world, interacting with it in remarkably realistic ways (Tsamitros et al., 2023). VR presents a sophisticated online virtual reality, enriched by customizable avatars capable of communicating with other digital entities, moving, interacting, and manipulating objects, creating a fully immersive experience (Petrigna & Musumeci, 2022). Compared to AR, VR offers unprecedented control and manipulation of the environment, expanding the possibilities of digital interaction (Bell et al., 2020; Walsh & Oakley, 2022).

In a broader context, the concept of the metaverse emerges as a three-dimensional virtual dimension based on the Internet, where real individuals can explore, interact, and engage in various daily activities through avatars representing their real or imaginary identities. This virtual space represents a unique fusion of the real and virtual worlds, offering opportunities for social interaction, participation in cultural events, and a completely digital economic life (Petrigna & Musumeci, 2022). It is, therefore, a digital space where people can meet and interact in real time (Zambelli et al., 2023), a convergence between virtual reality and physical reality in a digital space (Usmani et al., 2022)

These emerging technologies have demonstrated revolutionary potential in various fields, from medicine, diagnosis, and treatment of mental disorders, offering new perspectives and innovative approaches(Lan et al., 2023; López-Ojeda & Hurley, 2023), to education and training, as well as the world of work. However, alongside countless potential advantages and opportunities, some risks and challenges need careful consideration.

2. THE FOUNDATIONS OF TRANSFORMATION

2.1 Control and Manipulation of the Virtual Environment

An intrinsic feature of Virtual Reality (VR) and Augmented Reality (AR) is their manipulability. VR allows control and manipulation of virtual environment variables, facilitating experimentation with various situations and the study of responses to stimuli (Bell et al., 2020). This controlled manipulation offers the opportunity to personalize experiences, thereby expanding the possibilities for study, experimentation, and application (Wiederhold et al., 2014). Furthermore, manipulating the virtual environment not only stimulates visual interest and animation but also contributes to the development of cognitive abilities, promoting deeper and more engaging learning experiences (Allcoat & von Mühlenen, 2018).

A key concept in the transformative realm of Virtual Reality and the Metaverse is immersion. Defining immersion is crucial for understanding the relationship between the user and the virtual environment, addressing the very notion of being within such simulated settings (Grimshaw, 2013). Psychologically, immersion appears to be less of a psychological process and more of a physical process where our bodies and senses are induced to behave and react as if the virtual environment were real (Ijsselsteijn & Riva, 2003) and it is linked to the concept of presence.

In an immersive environment, the participant's mind is deceived, creating a sense of presence, which is fundamental for personal transformation. It offers a credible, effective, and realistic world, enabling a deeper flow experience compared to traditional devices, especially when participants are engaged in an activity or observing an event (Lo & Lai, 2023).

2.2 "Presence" in Virtual Reality and the Metaverse

"Presence" in Virtual Reality (VR) represents the illusion of being physically immersed in a virtual environment, crucial for the flow experience, a state in which individuals are completely absorbed in an activity without perceiving the passage of time (Csikszentmihalyi, 1990). This phenomenon consists of two key elements: "Place Illusion (PI)," inducing the feeling of being in another place, and "Plausibility Illusion (PSI)," implying that the virtual environment is as close to reality as possible (Freeman et al., 2017).

The sense of presence in VR significantly impacts individuals' perceptions and behavior (Lo & Lai, 2023). This condition occurs when the human mind constructs an internal reality based on the integration of sensory data and interactions, perceiving itself to be immersed in a specific virtual context (Riva & Gaggioli, 2019). This phenomenon is crucial in the digital age, where the merging of virtual and real requires in-depth analysis to understand the construction of individual relational dimensions (Gorini et al., 2011).

2.3 The Metaverse as a Transformative Environment

The continuously evolving Metaverse represents an environment revolutionizing human dynamics and individual experiences. This fusion of virtual and augmented reality configures itself as a convergence of virtual and physical reality within a digital (Usmani et al., 2022), with significant implications for internal psychological dynamics and self-development.

Within the Metaverse, a distinction arises between two distinct worlds: the inner and the outer world (Kye et al., 2021). The inner world focuses on the individual's identity and behavior, manifested through an avatar or digital profile. In this space, the individual acts and interacts with the virtual environment, exploring the deeper aspects of their personality and psychology. On the other hand, the outer world concentrates on user-centered external reality aspects within the Metaverse (Kye et al., 2021). This division provides a conceptual framework to understand how the individual relates both to themselves and the surrounding world within the Metaverse context.

The Metaverse, therefore, provides a predictive and stable context for self-development: this environment offers a solid therapeutic ground, supporting self-adaptation and mitigating ego deficits. Focusing on adaptation and reality testing, the Metaverse acts as a space where the self can grow optimally, overcoming obstacles in abnormal development(K. Lee, 2023)

Secondly, the Metaverse functions as a transitional stage in the adaptation process to reality, reflecting the concept of the "transitional object" in psychotherapy. Here, the Metaverse acts as a bridge between individuals' internal needs and the external reality. In this safe and engaging therapeutic space, internal object relationships evolve, propelling individuals toward significant personal growth (K. Lee, 2023).

In this transformative process, "therapeutic presence" in the Metaverse emerges as a crucial element (Gaggioli, 2017): this presence enables the patient to fully immerse themselves in the virtual environment and establish direct contact with the therapist. This close interaction creates a vital bond of trust and support in the therapeutic journey.

Lastly, the Metaverse allows the experience of "excess reality," a dimension surpassing the limits of conventional reality. Through the implementation of immersive media and sensory technologies, the Metaverse provides fertile ground for exploring and overcoming traumas, wounds, and emotional obstacles (K. Lee, 2023)

2.4 The Emotional Dimension in the Context of the Metaverse and Virtual Reality

Modulating emotional responses to virtual stimuli is a fundamental goal of many immersive applications (Chirico & Gaggioli, 2023). The Metaverse and Virtual Reality (VR) represent crucial areas of study concerning virtual experiences and human emotions. Numerous studies have emphasized the potential of perceptual and conceptual stimuli within VR in generating significant emotional responses (Z. Zhang et al., 2023), with important implications for understanding psychological disorders such as specific phobias (Bouchard et al., 2008) (Diemer et al., 2015; Gorini et al., 2010). Immersion in VR emerges as a key factor in emotion modulation (Z. Zhang et al., 2023), where the presence of emotional elements amplifies the sense of immersion (Gorini et al., 2010). Furthermore, immersive systems can induce a sense of embodiment toward virtual bodies (Slater, 2018).

Studies by Freeman et al. (2005) indicated that emotional immersion is closely related to arousal. Increased arousal during exposure to emotional stimuli in VR significantly contributes to greater presence (Higuera-Trujillo et al., 2017). Interestingly, VR-3D stimuli generate higher arousal compared to VR-2D stimuli, underscoring the crucial importance of stereoscopic vision in eliciting emotional responses (Tian et al., 2021).

Recent research has investigated brain responses to emotions in VR, revealing a significant increase in cortical activity in the left hemisphere of the brain during exposure to VR-3D (Tian et al., 2021) This suggests a possible hemispheric specialization in emotional responses related to stereovision in VR.

Rodríguez et al. (2015) analyzed brain activity in different emotional conditions induced by a virtual environment, highlighting specific activations in various brain regions during the induction of emotions such as sadness and emotional regulation strategies such as cognitive reappraisal. The integration of emotions, perception, and neuroscience in VR offers new perspectives in therapeutic application (Bohil et al., 2011) and the design of engaging and emotionally intense virtual experiences (J. A. Lee et al., 2023).

3. SOCIALIZATION AND SOCIETY: EFFECTS OF DIGITAL

Modern technologies respond to the increasing human need for social connection, providing immersive and interactive worlds that can have both positive and negative impacts on society (Flavián et al., 2019; Kenyon et al., 2023). The advent of the Internet and digital technologies as pervasive means of communication has prompted researchers to investigate the social impact of these interactive technologies on the structure of human relationships and levels of loneliness(Della Longa et al., 2022).

Participation in virtual contexts and the perception of social interactions therein significantly vary among individuals (Bombari et al., 2015). The widespread use of digital technologies has led to an increase in social interactions mediated by communication devices, partially substituting direct physical contact (Twenge et al., 2019). Multisensory real-time social interactions lie at the heart of the concept of the metaverse, a virtual environment comprised of simulated worlds where individuals act and communicate through digital representations known as avatars (Hennig-Thurau et al., 2023).

Digital technologies have influenced both macro and micro aspects of human relationships, enabling connections between geographically distant individuals from diverse cultural backgrounds. This has expanded social networks on a global scale but has also diminished non-verbal cues, such as direct physical contact, compromising emotional understanding and closeness among individuals (Lieberman & Schroeder, 2020).

The social and sociological effects depend on the characteristics of digital devices allowing simulation and manipulation of virtual reality, empowering users to influence it in line with their preferences In the metaverse, this manipulation combines with the relational element, enabling interactions beyond space-time limitations and decentralized, disembodied personal identity.

User avatars collaborate and share experiences, creating new value through interactional storytelling and facilitating the expansion of global social networks (Lieberman & Schroeder, 2020). This collaboration transcends time and space, enabling intimacy not constrained by physical distance (Bailenson et al, 2003). The concept of place expands, allowing interactions free from spatial boundaries, although susceptible to greater misunderstandings due to limited sensory information compared to reality.

Personal identities undergo significant changes, particularly for new digital generations that develop identities through social media and digital representations of avatars, blending desired characteristics with real elements.

Virtual reality tends to replicate sensory feelings from the real world, enabling users to experience it as realistically as possible, fostering a sense of fusion between the human body and the virtual body (P. H. Leveau & Camus, 2023)

Another dimension to consider concerns the body: virtual reality approximates the functioning of the human brain through the concept of 'embodied simulations,' where the brain creates a representation of the body in the virtual world to express actions, concepts, and emotions. This dynamic aims to offer as realistic an experience as possible in virtual space, endeavouring to replicate sensory sensations similar to those of the real world. During a virtual reality experience, the user enters the "skin" of the virtual character and plays the lead role. This embodiment translates into a sense of fusion between the human body and the virtual body, perceiving them as the same entity (P.-H. Leveau, 2022).

Manipulation of online images, while providing greater freedom and disinhibition, can also lead to the development of multiple, undefined identities, and the permitted anonymity can lead to an escape from reality. Digital hyperconnectivity might result in increased loneliness, anxiety, and alterations in the perception of real life, replacing real experiences with digital interactions that influence emotions, attention, and memory.

In this context, maintaining a healthy balance between online and offline relationships is crucial, as excessive technology use can compromise real relationships and foster dependence. Dependency and excessive immersion may cause confusion and lack of interest due to incongruence with the real world (Park & Kim, 2022). Digital representation goes beyond aesthetic aspects, encompassing expressions, emotions, behaviors, and social networks.

The avatar market demonstrates steady growth, with platforms and creators generating substantial revenues through the sale of customizable characters and digital accessories. Recent research has emphasized the positive effects of virtual reality on behavioral intentions such as purchasing decisions and willingness to pay. Virtual reality offers a pleasant experience that positively affects consumer attitudes, prompting them to desire the offerings staged within the experience (P.-H. Leveau, 2022).

Apart from market impact, these tools directly influence the aspect of social power, as varying levels of accessibility amplify social inequalities or influence access to information.

4. APPLICATION AREAS

4.1 Applications in Education/Training

The advent of immersive technologies, including Virtual Reality (VR), Augmented Reality (AR), and Mixed Reality (MR), is revolutionizing the education and training sector, posing a significant challenge in the educational landscape (Kaddoura & Al Husseiny, 2023). Physical interaction and active engagement play a fundamental role in the educational process (Coppola & Zanazzi, 2020). Immersiveness constitutes one of the distinctive aspects of these technologies, allowing students to fully immerse themselves in engaging learning contexts, stimulating their senses and emotions, and contributing to more effective and profound learning (Coppola & Zanazzi, 2020).

During the COVID-19 pandemic, the Metaverse played a crucial role in ensuring the continuity of education and promotion (Camilleri, 2023; X. Zhang et al., 2022). It offers advantages such as personalized curricula, improved motivation, and support for teamwork, making learning more engaging and exciting (Kaddoura & Al Husseiny, 2023; Kye et al., 2021).

The field of medical education is also benefiting from the potential of these technologies: the increasing use of AR/VR in recent decades for medical training has been substantial (Massetti & Chiariello, 2023). Students can virtually enter the human body, gaining a more in-depth perspective and replicating treatments in real life. Augmented reality is used to provide students with practical learning opportunities, such as mimicking patient contacts and surgical interventions(X. Zhang et al., 2022); the use of virtual reality in medical education allows students to train in a simulated environment for intensive surgical instruction at a substantially reduced cost, moving beyond knowledge transmission (Bhugaonkar et al., 2022).

4.2 Applications in Socialization and Gaming

The metaverse has opened new perspectives in the realm of socialization and entertainment. This virtual environment offers (Kaddoura & Al Husseiny, 2023) individuals the opportunity to share common interests and passions, facilitating deep social connections based on specific hobbies and interests. Furthermore, the metaverse allows users to shape their digital identity uniquely and manipulatively, blurring the boundaries between reality and the virtual world (X. Zhang et al., 2022). This flexibility in digital identity enables users to express themselves authentically, simultaneously experimenting with different facets of their personality, giving rise to a range of meaningful social interactions(Kaddoura & Al Husseiny, 2023).

The sense of "presence" in the virtual environment plays a crucial role in the metaverse experience as it creates a feeling of immersion, inducing a state of flow that leads to a positive psychological experience. This experience is characterized by deep engagement in the activity, resulting in increased satisfaction, intention to participate, enhanced cognitive empathy, and role identification, ultimately increasing satisfaction and the desire to participate (Diemer et al., 2015). Moreover, interaction within the metaverse can lead to unique relationships, akin to the bond between a player and their character in a video game (Lara & Rueda, 2021).

4.3 Therapeutic Applications of Virtual Reality in Mental and Neurological Disorders

Studies regarding the treatment of psychiatric disorders using therapeutic tools in the metaverse have not yet been conducted. However, virtual reality (VR), augmented reality (AR), and mixed reality (MR) are increasingly being utilized for the diagnosis and treatment of mental health disorders (Freeman et al., 2017; Usmani et al., 2022)

The use of Virtual Reality (VR) in the field of mental health emerges as a highly promising and innovative approach, offering a safe and controlled virtual environment to address psychological challenges (Freeman et al., 2017). Immersive experiences guide individuals through targeted therapeutic processes, allowing them to confront their emotions in a controlled environment (Baumgartner et al., 2008). This safe and supported context is crucial to enable personal transformation by overcoming mental and emotional obstacles.

Research in psychology has indicated that change occurs not only through exposure to experience but also through a process of self-reflection and conceptualization (Gaggioli, 2017). Living an experience in VR represents only the first step; it is essential to deeply reflect on that experience, analyse it, and understand its implications. This process of reflection allows the individual to internalize the experience, integrating it into their emotional and cognitive world.

In the metaverse, individuals can explore fears, anxieties, and traumas under the expert guidance of the therapist (Cerasa et al., 2022). Reflectivity, the ability to deeply reflect on lived experiences, plays a key role in this therapeutic process (Gaggioli, 2017). This reflection, which can occur during and after the virtual experience, enables the patient to fully process their emotions and thoughts in a safe and controlled environment.

In the context of anxiety disorders, VR has proven to be particularly effective through virtual exposure therapy (Baghaei et al., 2021; Bouchard et al., 2008; Ioannou et al., 2020). This approach allows patients to confront their fears in a virtually customized environment, ensuring results that are superior or at least equivalent to traditional therapies in some cases (Tsamitros et al., 2023). Furthermore, VR offers the advantage of allowing therapists to precisely tailor phobic stimuli and control all variables at play, significantly enhancing adaptability compared to conventional therapies (Villani et al., 2011).

In the treatment of Post-Traumatic Stress Disorder (PTSD), VR facilitates the reprocessing of traumatic memories through gradual and controlled virtual exposure. This approach helps patients confront traumas in a safe environment, facilitating healing (Tsamitros et al., 2023).

In the context of depression, VR offers various applications. On one hand, digital applications like SuperBetter and MoodHacker assist patients in managing depressive symptoms from the comfort of their homes, providing practical resources and strategies (Omboni et al., 2022). On the other hand, the integration of Cognitive-Behavioral Therapy (CBT) with Virtual Reality Exposure Therapy (VRET) has proven effective in treating depression (Baghaei et al., 2021) (Ioannou et al., 2020). However, despite advancements, further research is needed to thoroughly assess the duration of long-term therapeutic effects (Himle et al., 2022; Hussain et al., 2018)

In eating disorders such as anorexia nervosa and bulimia nervosa, VR has proven crucial (De Carvalho et al., 2017) (Freeman et al., 2017). Through the use of virtual avatars, patients can explore and modify their body image, gradually experiencing a more realistic representation of themselves (Matamala-Gomez et al., 2021; Riva, Malighetti, et al., 2021) Additionally, virtual exposure to feared foods has been shown to reduce food-related anxiety and improve attitudes toward food (Gorini et al., 2010; Riva, Malighetti, et al., 2021; Šmahel et al., 2018).

In cases of chronic pain, VR serves as an effective distraction tool. By creating pleasant and engaging virtual environments, it can divert patients from pain, reducing their perception of discomfort (Moreno-Ligero M., 2023; Wong et al., 2022). This approach is particularly useful in pediatric patients, offering a non-pharmacological form of therapy (Lopez-Rodriguez et al., 2020; Wang & Jotwani, 2023).

In the field of cognitive disorders, such as Alzheimer's disease, VR can be adapted to stimulate and enhance residual cognitive functions. Patients can engage in immersive cognitive simulations, including memory, problem-solving, and attention, promoting brain activity and improving the quality of life for patients while alleviating the burden on caregivers (Frasson & Abdessalem, 2022; Georgiev et al., 2021; Lasaponara et al., 2021).

5. CONCLUSIONS AND FUTURE PERSPECTIVES

The emergence of digital technologies like Virtual Reality (VR), Augmented Reality (AR), and the Metaverse has fundamentally altered social dynamics, spatial concepts, and individual/group identities (Kaddoura & Al Husseiny, 2023). These technologies influence behaviors, values, economics, and power structures, reshaping human experiences and interactions with the world.

VR, AR, and the Metaverse have transformative potential, revolutionizing perception and interaction with the environment. Their immersive nature, virtual environment manipulation, and empathy induction offer vast possibilities in therapy and education (Kaddoura & Al Husseiny, 2023).

Virtual Reality stands out as a potent therapeutic tool for mental and neurological disorders. Yet, realizing its potential requires ongoing research and standardized protocols for personalized treatment (Baghaei et al., 2021a; Freeman et al., 2017; Riva & Serino, 2020; Tsamitros et al., 2023), emphasizing the importance of personalization in therapy.

Reflection and therapeutic presence in the metaverse are pivotal for personal transformation (Riva, Di Lernia, et al., 2021), opening innovative avenues in addressing psychological issues and enhancing mental well-being in clinical practice.

While offering avenues for mental health support and education, the metaverse demands careful management of risks like identity confusion and dependency (Usmani et al., 2022; X. Zhang et al., 2022). Interdisciplinary research involving psychology, neuroscience, and computer science is vital to fully harness these technologies' potential (Cerasa et al., 2022)

Education in the metaverse engages students deeply but requires responsible use to balance benefits and risks (Zallio & Clarkson, 2022) Ensuring fair access and preventing inequalities and abuses are crucial societal considerations (Dwivedi et al., 2023).

The metaverse fosters realistic interactions and diverse therapeutic avenues, yet excessive use poses risks requiring careful management dependency (Usmani et al., 2022; X. Zhang et al., 2022). Achieving a balance between virtual immersion and real-world connections is essential for users' well-being (Bojic, 2022).

Despite offering unique experiences, the metaverse challenges identity, social connections, and well-being (Bojic, 2022). Balancing immersion and real-world relationships is pivotal for a sustainable user experience.

Responsible application of immersive technologies through research and ethical considerations can enhance mental well-being and deepen our understanding of the human mind and reality, fostering personal and collective transformation. Ethics and research will guide the conscious utilization of these technologies, shaping the future of society and our understanding of the human psyche.

REFERENCES

Allcoat, D., & von Mühlenen, A. (2018). Learning in virtual reality: Effects on performance, emotion and engagement. *Research in Learning Technology*, *26*(0). Advance online publication. doi:10.25304/rlt.v26.2140

Baghaei, N., Chitale, V., Hlasnik, A., Stemmet, L., Liang, H. N., & Porter, R. (2021a). Virtual reality for supporting the treatment of depression and anxiety: A scoping review. In JMIR Mental Health (Vol. 8, Issue 9). doi:10.2196/29681

Baghaei, N., Chitale, V., Hlasnik, A., Stemmet, L., Liang, H.-N., & Porter, R. (2021b). Virtual Reality for Supporting the Treatment of Depression and Anxiety: Scoping Review. *JMIR Mental Health*, *8*(9), e29681. doi:10.2196/29681 PMID:34554097

Bailenson, S. (2003). Interpersonal Distance in Immersive Virtual Environments. *Interpersonal Distance in Virtual Environments*. https://doi.org/doi:10.1177/0146167203253270

Baumgartner, T., Speck, D., Wettstein, D., Masnari, O., Beeli, G., & Jäncke, L. (2008). Feeling present in arousing virtual reality worlds: Prefrontal brain regions differentially orchestrate presence experience in adults and children. *Frontiers in Human Neuroscience*, *2*(AUG). Advance online publication. doi:10.3389/neuro.09.008.2008 PMID:18958209

Bell, I. H., Nicholas, J., Alvarez-Jimenez, M., Thompson, A., & Valmaggia, L. (2020). Virtual reality as a clinical tool in mental health research and practice. *Dialogues in Clinical Neuroscience*, *22*(2), 169–177. doi:10.31887/DCNS.2020.22.2/lvalmaggia PMID:32699517

Bhugaonkar, K., Bhugaonkar, R., & Masne, N. (2022). The Trend of Metaverse and Augmented & Virtual Reality Extending to the Healthcare System. *Cureus*. Advance online publication. doi:10.7759/cureus.29071 PMID:36258985

Bohil, C. J., Alicea, B., & Biocca, F. A. (2011). Virtual reality in neuroscience research and therapy. In Nature Reviews Neuroscience (Vol. 12, Issue 12). doi:10.1038/nrn3122

Bojic, L. (2022). Metaverse through the prism of power and addiction: what will happen when the virtual world becomes more attractive than reality? In European Journal of Futures Research (Vol. 10, Issue 1). Springer Science and Business Media Deutschland GmbH. doi:10.118640309-022-00208-4

Bombari, D., Schmid Mast, M., Canadas, E., & Bachmann, M. (2015). Studying social interactions through immersive virtual environment technology: virtues, pitfalls, and future challenges. In *Frontiers in Psychology* (Vol. 6). Frontiers Media S.A. doi:10.3389/fpsyg.2015.00869

Bouchard, S., St-Jacques, J., Robillard, G., & Renaud, P. (2008). Anxiety increases the feeling of presence in virtual reality. *Presence (Cambridge, Mass.)*, *17*(4), 376–391. Advance online publication. doi:10.1162/pres.17.4.376

Camilleri, M. A. (2023). Metaverse applications in education: a systematic review and a cost-benefit analysis. In Interactive Technology and Smart Education. doi:10.1108/ITSE-01-2023-0017

Cerasa, A., Gaggioli, A., Marino, F., Riva, G., & Pioggia, G. (2022). The promise of the metaverse in mental health: the new era of MEDverse. In Heliyon (Vol. 8, Issue 11). doi:10.1016/j.heliyon.2022.e11762

Chen, Y., Wang, Q., Chen, H., Song, X., Tang, H., & Tian, M. (2019). An overview of augmented reality technology. *Journal of Physics: Conference Series*, *1237*(2), 022082. Advance online publication. doi:10.1088/1742-6596/1237/2/022082

Chirico, A., & Gaggioli, A. (2023). How Real Are Virtual Emotions? In Cyberpsychology, Behavior, and Social Networking (Vol. 26, Issue 4). .editorial doi:10.1089/cyber.2023.29272.editorial

Coppola, S., & Zanazzi, S. (2020). *L'esperienza dell'arte. Il ruolo delle tecnologie immersive nella didattica museale.* doi:10.7346/-fei-XVIII-02-20_04

Csikszentmihalyi, M. (n.d.). *Flow: The Psychology of Optimal Experience Flow-The Psychology of optimal experience.* https://www.researchgate.net/publication/224927532

De Carvalho, M. R., De Santana Dias, T. R., Duchesne, M., Nardi, A. E., & Appolinario, J. C. (2017). Virtual reality as a promising strategy in the assessment and treatment of bulimia nervosa and binge eating disorder: A systematic review. In Behavioral Sciences (Vol. 7, Issue 3). doi:10.3390/bs7030043

Della Longa, L., Valori, I., & Farroni, T. (2022). Interpersonal Affective Touch in a Virtual World: Feeling the Social Presence of Others to Overcome Loneliness. In *Frontiers in Psychology* (Vol. 12). Frontiers Media S.A., doi:10.3389/fpsyg.2021.795283

Diemer, J., Alpers, G. W., Peperkorn, H. M., Shiban, Y., & Mühlberger, A. (2015). The impact of perception and presence on emotional reactions: A review of research in virtual reality. In Frontiers in Psychology (Vol. 6). Frontiers Research Foundation. doi:10.3389/fpsyg.2015.00026

Flavián, C., Ibáñez-Sánchez, S., & Orús, C. (2019). The impact of virtual, augmented and mixed reality technologies on the customer experience. *Journal of Business Research*, *100*, 547–560. doi:10.1016/j.jbusres.2018.10.050

Ford, T. J., Buchanan, D. M., Azeez, A., Benrimoh, D. A., Kaloiani, I., Bandeira, I. D., Hunegnaw, S., Lan, L., Gholmieh, M., Buch, V., & Williams, N. R. (2023). Taking modern psychiatry into the metaverse: Integrating augmented, virtual, and mixed reality technologies into psychiatric care. *Frontiers in Digital Health*, *5*, 1146806. Advance online publication. doi:10.3389/fdgth.2023.1146806 PMID:37035477

Frasson, C., & Abdessalem, H. (2022). Contribution of Virtual Reality Environments and Artificial Intelligence for Alzheimer. *Medical Research Archives*, *10*(9). Advance online publication. doi:10.18103/mra.v10i9.3054

Freeman, D., Reeve, S., Robinson, A., Ehlers, A., Clark, D., Spanlang, B., & Slater, M. (2017). Virtual reality in the assessment, understanding, and treatment of mental health disorders. In Psychological Medicine (Vol. 47, Issue 14, pp. 2393–2400). Cambridge University Press. doi:10.1017/S003329171700040X

Gaggioli, A. (2017). Digital Social Innovation. In Cyberpsychology, Behavior, and Social Networking (Vol. 20, Issue 11). doi:10.1089/cyber.2017.29090.csi

Georgiev, D. D., Georgieva, I., Gong, Z., Nanjappan, V., & Georgiev, G. V. (2021). Virtual reality for neurorehabilitation and cognitive enhancement. *Brain Sciences*, *11*(2), 1–20. doi:10.3390/brainsci11020221 PMID:33670277

Gorini, A., Capideville, C. S., De Leo, G., Mantovani, F., & Riva, G. (2011). The role of immersion and narrative in mediated presence: The virtual hospital experience. *Cyberpsychology, Behavior, and Social Networking*, *14*(3), 99–105. doi:10.1089/cyber.2010.0100 PMID:20649451

Gorini, A., Griez, E., Petrova, A., & Riva, G. (2010). Assessment of the emotional responses produced by exposure to real food, virtual food and photographs of food in patients affected by eating disorders. *Annals of General Psychiatry*, *9*(1), 30. Advance online publication. doi:10.1186/1744-859X-9-30 PMID:20602749

Grimshaw, M. (2013). The Oxford Handbook of Virtuality. Oxford Academ.

Hennig-Thurau, T., Aliman, D. N., Herting, A. M., Cziehso, G. P., Linder, M., & Kübler, R. V. (2023). Social interactions in the metaverse: Framework, initial evidence, and research roadmap. *Journal of the Academy of Marketing Science, 51*(4), 889–913. doi:10.100711747-022-00908-0

Higuera-Trujillo, J. L., López-Tarruella Maldonado, J., & Llinares Millán, C. (2017). Psychological and physiological human responses to simulated and real environments: A comparison between Photographs, 360° Panoramas, and Virtual Reality. *Applied Ergonomics, 65*, 398–409. doi:10.1016/j.apergo.2017.05.006 PMID:28601190

Himle, J. A., Weaver, A., Zhang, A., & Xiang, X. (2022). Digital Mental Health Interventions for Depression. *Cognitive and Behavioral Practice, 29*(1), 50–59. Advance online publication. doi:10.1016/j.cbpra.2020.12.009

Hussain, S. A., Park, T., Yildirim, I., Xiang, Z., & Abbasi, F. (2018). Virtual-Reality Videos to Relieve Depression. Lecture Notes in Computer Science (Including Subseries Lecture Notes in Artificial Intelligence and Lecture Notes in Bioinformatics), 10910 LNCS. doi:10.1007/978-3-319-91584-5_6

Ijsselsteijn, W., & Riva, G. (2003). *Being There: Concepts, effects and measurement of user presence in synthetic environments G 1 Being There: The experience of presence in mediated environments*. Ios Press.

Ioannou, A., Papastavrou, E., Avraamides, M. N., & Charalambous, A. (2020). Virtual Reality and Symptoms Management of Anxiety, Depression, Fatigue, and Pain: A Systematic Review. *SAGE Open Nursing, 6*, 237796082093616. doi:10.1177/2377960820936163 PMID:33415290

Kaddoura, S., & Al Husseiny, F. (2023). The rising trend of Metaverse in education: Challenges, opportunities, and ethical considerations. *PeerJ. Computer Science, 9*, e1252. doi:10.7717/peerj-cs.1252 PMID:37346578

Kenyon, K., Kinakh, V., & Harrison, J. (2023). Social virtual reality helps to reduce feelings of loneliness and social anxiety during the Covid-19 pandemic. *Scientific Reports, 13*(1), 19282. Advance online publication. doi:10.103841598-023-46494-1 PMID:37935718

Kye, B., Han, N., Kim, E., Park, Y., & Jo, S. (2021). Educational applications of metaverse: Possibilities and limitations. In *Journal of Educational Evaluation for Health Professions* (Vol. 18). Korea Health Personnel Licensing Examination Institute. doi:10.3352/jeehp.2021.18.32

Lan, L., Sikov, J., Lejeune, J., Ji, C., Brown, H., Bullock, K., & Spencer, A. E. (2023). A Systematic Review of using Virtual and Augmented Reality for the Diagnosis and Treatment of Psychotic Disorders. In Current Treatment Options in Psychiatry (Vol. 10, Issue 2, pp. 87–107). Springer Science and Business Media Deutschland GmbH. doi:10.100740501-023-00287-5

Lara, F., & Rueda, J. (2021). Virtual Reality Not for "Being Someone" but for "Being in Someone Else's Shoes": Avoiding Misconceptions in Empathy Enhancement. *Frontiers in Psychology*, *12*, 741516. Advance online publication. doi:10.3389/fpsyg.2021.741516 PMID:34504468

Lasaponara, S., Marson, F., Doricchi, F., & Cavallo, M. (2021). A scoping review of cognitive training in neurodegenerative diseases via computerized and virtual reality tools: What we know so far. In Brain Sciences (Vol. 11, Issue 5). MDPI AG. doi:10.3390/brainsci11050528

Lee, J. A., Kim, J. G., & Kweon, H. (2023). A Study on Rehabilitation Specialists' Perception of Experience with a Virtual Reality Program. *Healthcare (Basel)*, *11*(6), 814. Advance online publication. doi:10.3390/healthcare11060814 PMID:36981471

Lee, K. (2023). Counseling Psychological Understanding and Considerations of the Metaverse: A Theoretical Review. *Health Care*, *11*(18), 2490. doi:10.3390/healthcare11182490 PMID:37761687

Leveau, P.-H. (2022). *The role of proprioception and gamification in virtual reality experiences on consumer embodiment and behavior*. Academic Press.

Leveau, P. H., & Camus, S. (2023). Embodiment, immersion, and enjoyment in virtual reality marketing experiences. *Psychology and Marketing*, *40*(7), 1329–1343. doi:10.1002/mar.21822

Lieberman, A., & Schroeder, J. (2020). Two social lives: How differences between online and offline interaction influence social outcomes. In *Current Opinion in Psychology* (Vol. 31, pp. 16–21). Elsevier B.V., doi:10.1016/j.copsyc.2019.06.022

Lo, S. Y., & Lai, C. Y. (2023). Investigating how immersive virtual reality and active navigation mediate the experience of virtual concerts. *Scientific Reports*, *13*(1), 8507. Advance online publication. doi:10.103841598-023-35369-0 PMID:37231095

López-Ojeda, W., & Hurley, R. A. (2023). The Medical Metaverse, Part 1: Introduction, Definitions, and New Horizons for Neuropsychiatry. *The Journal of Neuropsychiatry and Clinical Neurosciences*, *35*(1), 1. doi:10.1176/appi.neuropsych.20220187 PMID:36633472

Lopez-Rodriguez, M. M., Fernández-Millan, A., Ruiz-Fernández, M. D., Dobarrio-Sanz, I., & Fernández-Medina, I. M. (2020). New technologies to improve pain, anxiety and depression in children and adolescents with cancer: A systematic review. In International Journal of Environmental Research and Public Health (Vol. 17, Issue 10). doi:10.3390/ijerph17103563

Massetti, M., & Chiariello, G. A. (2023). The metaverse in medicine. *European Heart Journal Supplements*, *25*(Supplement_B), B104–B107. doi:10.1093/eurheartjsuppuad083 PMID:37091647

Matamala-Gomez, M., Maselli, A., Malighetti, C., Realdon, O., Mantovani, F., & Riva, G. (2021). Virtual body ownership illusions for mental health: A narrative review. In Journal of Clinical Medicine (Vol. 10, Issue 1). doi:10.3390/jcm10010139

Moreno-Ligero, M. (2023). *mHealth intervention for improving patients with chronic pain*. Academic Press.

Omboni, S., Padwal, R. S., Alessa, T., Benczúr, B., Green, B. B., Hubbard, I., Kario, K., Khan, N. A., Konradi, A., Logan, A. G., Lu, Y., Mars, M., McManus, R. J., Melville, S., Neumann, C. L., Parati, G., Renna, N. F., Ryvlin, P., Saner, H., ... Wang, J. (2022). The worldwide impact of telemedicine during COVID-19: Current evidence and recommendations for the future. *Connected Health*. Advance online publication. doi:10.20517/ch.2021.03 PMID:35233563

Park, S. M., & Kim, Y. G. (2022). A Metaverse: Taxonomy, Components, Applications, and Open Challenges. *IEEE Access : Practical Innovations, Open Solutions*, *10*, 4209–4251. doi:10.1109/ACCESS.2021.3140175

Petrigna, L., & Musumeci, G. (2022). The Metaverse: A New Challenge for the Healthcare System: A Scoping Review. In Journal of Functional Morphology and Kinesiology (Vol. 7, Issue 3). MDPI. doi:10.3390/jfmk7030063

Riva, G., & Gaggioli, A. (2019). Realtà virtuali: aspetti psicologici delle esperienze simulative ed il loro impatto sull'esperienza umana. Giunti Editore.

Riva, G., Malighetti, C., & Serino, S. (2021). Virtual reality in the treatment of eating disorders. *Clinical Psychology & Psychotherapy*, *28*(3), 477–488. doi:10.1002/cpp.2622 PMID:34048622

Riva, G., & Serino, S. (2020). Virtual reality in the assessment, understanding and treatment of mental health disorders. In Journal of Clinical Medicine (Vol. 9, Issue 11, pp. 1–9). MDPI. doi:10.3390/jcm9113434

Riva, G., Wiederhold, B. K., & Mantovani, F. (2019). Neuroscience of Virtual Reality: From Virtual Exposure to Embodied Medicine. *Cyberpsychology, Behavior, and Social Networking*, *22*(1), 82–96. doi:10.1089/cyber.2017.29099.gri PMID:30183347

Rodríguez, A., Rey, B., Clemente, M., Wrzesien, M., & Alcañiz, M. (2015). Assessing brain activations associated with emotional regulation during virtual reality mood induction procedures. *Expert Systems with Applications*, *42*(3), 1699–1709. doi:10.1016/j.eswa.2014.10.006

Slater, M. (2018). Immersion and the illusion of presence in virtual reality. In British Journal of Psychology (Vol. 109, Issue 3, pp. 431–433). John Wiley and Sons Ltd. doi:10.1111/bjop.12305

Šmahel, D., Macháčková, H., Šmahelová, M., Čevelíček, M., Almenara, C. A., & Holubčíková, J. (2018). Digital technology, eating behaviors, and eating disorders. In *Digital Technology*. Eating Behaviors, and Eating Disorders. doi:10.1007/978-3-319-93221-7

Tian, F., Hua, M., Zhang, W., Li, Y., & Yang, X. (2021). Emotional arousal in 2D versus 3D virtual reality environments. *PLoS ONE, 16*(9). doi:10.1371/journal.pone.0256211

Tsamitros, N., Beck, A., Sebold, M., Schouler-Ocak, M., Bermpohl, F., & Gutwinski, S. (2023). The application of virtual reality in the treatment of mental disorders. *Der Nervenarzt*, *94*(1), 27–33. Advance online publication. doi:10.100700115-022-01378-z PMID:36053303

Twenge, J. M., Spitzberg, B. H., & Campbell, W. K. (2019). Less in-person social interaction with peers among U.S. adolescents in the 21st century and links to loneliness. *Journal of Social and Personal Relationships*, *36*(6), 1892–1913. doi:10.1177/0265407519836170

Usmani, S. S., Sharath, M., & Mehendale, M. (2022). Future of mental health in the metaverse. *General Psychiatry*, *35*(4), e100825. doi:10.1136/gpsych-2022-100825 PMID:36189180

Villani, D., Grassi, A., & Riva, G. (2011). *Tecnologie emotive. nuovi media per migliorare la qualita' della vita e ridurre lo stress*. LED.

Walsh, E., & Oakley, D. A. (2022). Editing reality in the brain. In Neuroscience of Consciousness (Vol. 2022, Issue 1). Oxford University Press. doi:10.1093/nc/niac009

Wang, E. F., & Jotwani, R. (2023). Virtual reality therapy for myofascial pain: Evolving towards an evidence-based non-pharmacologic adjuvant intervention. *Interventional Pain Medicine*, *2*(1), 100181. Advance online publication. doi:10.1016/j.inpm.2023.100181

Wong, K. P., Tse, M. M. Y., & Qin, J. (2022). Effectiveness of Virtual Reality-Based Interventions for Managing Chronic Pain on Pain Reduction, Anxiety, Depression and Mood: A Systematic Review. In Healthcare (Switzerland) (Vol. 10, Issue 10). MDPI. doi:10.3390/healthcare10102047

Xiong, J., Hsiang, E. L., He, Z., Zhan, T., & Wu, S. T. (2021). Augmented reality and virtual reality displays: emerging technologies and future perspectives. In Light: Science and Applications (Vol. 10, Issue 1). Springer Nature. doi:10.103841377-021-00658-8

Zallio, M., & Clarkson, P. J. (2022). Designing the metaverse: A study on inclusion, diversity, equity, accessibility and safety for digital immersive environments. *Telematics and Informatics*, *75*, 101909. Advance online publication. doi:10.1016/j.tele.2022.101909

Zambelli, E., Speranza, T., & Cusimano, F. (2023). Metaverso: l'universo umano in formato digitale. Alpes.

Zhang, G., Cao, J., Liu, D., & Qi, J. (2022). Popularity of the metaverse: Embodied social presence theory perspective. *Frontiers in Psychology*, *13*, 997751. Advance online publication. doi:10.3389/fpsyg.2022.997751 PMID:36248483

Zhang, X., Chen, Y., Hu, L., & Wang, Y. (2022). The metaverse in education: Definition, framework, features, potential applications, challenges, and future research topics. In *Frontiers in Psychology* (Vol. 13). Frontiers Media S.A. doi:10.3389/fpsyg.2022.1016300

Zhang, Z., Fort, J. M., & Giménez Mateu, L. (2023). Facial expression recognition in virtual reality environments: Challenges and opportunities. *Frontiers in Psychology*, *14*, 1280136. Advance online publication. doi:10.3389/fpsyg.2023.1280136 PMID:37885738

Compilation of References

Abeliuk, A. (2021). History and evolution of artificial intelligence. *Revista Bits de Ciencia*, (21), 25–21.

Aguirre, P. (2010). La construcción social del gusto en el comensal moderno. In COMER: Una palabra con múltiples sentidos (pp. 13-63). M. Libros del Zorzal.

Aguirre, P. (2005). *Estrategias de consumo: que comen los argentinos que comen*. Miño y Dávila.

Ajeesh, A. K., & Rukmini, S. (2022). Posthuman perception of artificial intelligence in science fiction: An exploration of Kazuo Ishiguro's Klara and the Sun. *AI & Society*, *38*(2), 853–860. doi:10.100700146-022-01533-9

Ajmal, S., Ahmed, A. A. I., & Jalota, C. (2023). Natural Language Processing in Improving Information Retrieval and Knowledge Discovery in Healthcare Conversational Agents. *Journal of Artificial Intelligence and Machine Learning in Management*, *7*(1), 34–47. https://journals.sagescience.org/index.php/jamm/article/view/73

Aleem, M., Sufyan, M., Ameer, I., & Mustak, M. (2023). Remote work and the COVID-19 pandemic: An artificial intelligence-based topic modeling and a future agenda. *Journal of Business Research*, *154*, 113303. doi:10.1016/j.jbusres.2022.113303 PMID:36156905

Allcoat, D., & von Mühlenen, A. (2018). Learning in virtual reality: Effects on performance, emotion and engagement. *Research in Learning Technology*, *26*(0). Advance online publication. doi:10.25304/rlt.v26.2140

Ambrosini, A., Bottini, F., Robledo, V., Lavezzari, F., & Lencina, A. (2023). Estudio del impacto de ChatGPT en la enseñanza de materias introductorias a la programación. Paper presentation at the 21 LACCEI International Multi-Conference for Engineering, Education, and Technology: Leadership in Education and Innovation in Engineering in the Framework of Global Transformations: Integration and Alliances for Integral Development, Buenos Aires, Argentina.

Andrade, C., Tavares, M., Soares, H., Coelho, F., & Tomás, C. (2022). Positive Mental Health and Mental Health Literacy of Informal Caregivers: A Scoping Review. *International Journal of Environmental Research and Public Health*, *19*(22), 15276. doi:10.3390/ijerph192215276 PMID:36430000

Andreotta, A. J., Kirkham, N., & Rizzi, M. (2021). AI, big data, and the future of consent. *AI & Society, 37*(4), 1715–1728. doi:10.100700146-021-01262-5 PMID:34483498

Antunes, R. (2020). What is the future of work in the digital age? *Latin American and Caribbean Observatory, 4*(1), 12–22.

Anvarovich, N. E. (2023). The Concept of Creativity, the Essence of the Content and its Theoretical Methodological Foundations. *International Journal on Orange Technology, 5*(7). https://researchparks.innovativeacademicjournals.com/index.php/IJOT/article/view/6248

Aoki, B. Y., & Kimura, T. (2021). Sexuality and Affection in the Time of Technological Innovation: Artificial Partners in the Japanese Context. *Religions, 12*(5), 296. doi:10.3390/rel12050296

Appio, F. P., La Torre, D., Lazzeri, F., Masri, H., & Schiavone, F. (Eds.). (2023). *Impact of Artificial Intelligence in Business and Society: Opportunities and Challenges.* Routledge.

Arsenio, A. M., Caldas, L. G., & Oliveira, M. (2012). Social Interaction and the Development of Artificial Consciousness. In D. Chugo & S. Yokota (Eds.), Introduction to Modern Robotics (pp. 93–118). iConcept Press.

Arsenio, A. M. (2004). *Cognitive-developmental learning for a humanoid robot: A caregiver's gift.* MIT.

Asiri, A., Badshah, F., Muhammad, H. A., & Alshamrani, K. (2022). Human emotions classification using eeg via audiovisual stimuli and ai. *Computers, Materials & Continua, 73*(3), 5075–5089. doi:10.32604/cmc.2022.031156

Audrin, C., & Audrin, B. (2023). More than just emotional Intelligence online: Introducing "digital emotional intelligence.". *Frontiers in Psychology, 14*, 1154355. Advance online publication. doi:10.3389/fpsyg.2023.1154355 PMID:37205063

Augmented Work for an Automated, AI-driven World. (2023). *IBM Institute for Business Value.* https://www.ibm.com/thought-leadership/institute-business-value/en-us/report/augmented-workforce

Ayano˘glu, H., & Sequeira, J. S. (2019). Human-Robot Interaction. In H. Ayano˘glu & E. Duarte (Eds.), *Emotional Design in Human-Robot Interaction: Theory, Methods and Applications* (pp. 39–56). Springer.

Badía, A., & Monereo, C. (2008). La enseñanza y el aprendizaje de estrategias de aprendizaje en entornos virtuales [Teaching and learning strategies in virtual environments]. In C. Coll & C. Monereo (Eds.), *Psicología de la educación virtual. Aprender y enseñar con las Tecnologías de la Información y la Comunicación* [Psychology of virtual education: Learning and teaching with Information and Communication Technologies] (pp. 348–367). Morata.

Baghaei, N., Chitale, V., Hlasnik, A., Stemmet, L., Liang, H. N., & Porter, R. (2021a). Virtual reality for supporting the treatment of depression and anxiety: A scoping review. In JMIR Mental Health (Vol. 8, Issue 9). doi:10.2196/29681

Bailenson, S. (2003). Interpersonal Distance in Immersive Virtual Environments. *Interpersonal Distance in Virtual Environments*. https://doi.org/ doi:10.1177/0146167203253270

Banks, M. S., & Ginsburg, A. P. (1985). Infant visual preferences: A review and new theoretical treatment. *Advances in Child Development and Behavior*, *19*, 207–246. doi:10.1016/S0065-2407(08)60392-4 PMID:3911754

Barker, B. S., & Ansorge, J. (2007). Robotics as a means to increase achievement scores in an informal learning environment. *Journal of Research on Technology in Education*, *39*(3), 229–243. doi:10.1080/15391523.2007.10782481

Baroni, D., Nerini, A., Matera, C., & Stefanile, C. (2016). Mindfulness and Emotional Distress: The Mediating Role of Psychological Well-Being. *Current Psychology (New Brunswick, N.J.)*, *37*(3), 467–476. doi:10.100712144-016-9524-1

Bassett, D. J. (2015). Who wants to live forever? Living, dying and grieving in our digital society. *Social Sciences (Basel, Switzerland)*, *4*(4), 1127–1139. doi:10.3390ocsci4041127

Basso, L. R. (2013). *Smart Agriculture: Argentina's Initiative for Sustainability in Food and Energy Production*. Academic Press.

Batthyány, K., & Cabrera, M. (2011). *Metodología de la investigación en Ciencias Sociales. Apuntes para un curso inicial. Departamento de Publicaciones, Unidad de Comunicación de la Universidad de la República*. UCUR.

Baudrillard, J. (2006). *Virtuality and Events: The Hell of Power*. https://baudrillardstudies.ubishops.ca/virtuality-and-events-the-hell-of-power/

Baudrillard, J. (2005). Violence of the virtual and integral reality. *International Journal of Baudrillard Studies*, *2*(2), 1–16.

Baudrillard, J. (2006). Virtuality and Events: The hell of power. *Baudrillard Studies*, *3*(2), 1–15.

Baudrillard, J. (2013). *The intelligence of evil: Or, the lucidity pact*. A&C Black.

Baudrillard, J., & Lancelin, A. (2004). The matrix decoded: Le nouvel observateur interview with Jean Baudrillard. *International Journal of Baudrillard Studies*, *1*(2), 1–8.

Bauer, A., Wistow, G., Hyànek, V., Figueroa, M., & Sandford, S. (2018). Social innovation in health care: The recovery approach in mental health. In H. K. Anheier, G. Krlev, & G. Mildenberger (Eds.), *Social Innovation: Comparative Perspectives*. Routledge.

Baumgartner, T., Speck, D., Wettstein, D., Masnari, O., Beeli, G., & Jäncke, L. (2008). Feeling present in arousing virtual reality worlds: Prefrontal brain regions differentially orchestrate presence experience in adults and children. *Frontiers in Human Neuroscience*, *2*(AUG). Advance online publication. doi:10.3389/neuro.09.008.2008 PMID:18958209

Bear, C., & Holloway, L. (2019). Beyond resistance: Geographies of divergent more-than-human conduct in robotic milking. *Geoforum*, *104*, 212–221. doi:10.1016/j.geoforum.2019.04.030

Beck, U. (1992). *Risk Society: towards a new modernity*. Sage.

Beck, U. (1998). *La sociedad del riesgo* [The risk society]. Paidós.

Bell, D. (2006). *Cyberculture Theorists: Manuel Castells and Donna Haraway*. Routledge. doi:10.4324/9780203357019

Bell, I. H., Nicholas, J., Alvarez-Jimenez, M., Thompson, A., & Valmaggia, L. (2020). Virtual reality as a clinical tool in mental health research and practice. *Dialogues in Clinical Neuroscience*, *22*(2), 169–177. doi:10.31887/DCNS.2020.22.2/lvalmaggia PMID:32699517

Bell, J., & Gifford, T. (Eds.). (2023). *Using Assistive Technology for Inclusive Learning in K-12 Classrooms*. IGI Global. doi:10.4018/978-1-6684-6424-3

Benton, L., Hoyles, C., Kalas, I., & Noss, R. (2017). Bridging Primary Programming and Mathematics: Some Findings of Design Research in England. *Digital Experiences in Mathematics Education*, 23–29. doi:10.1007/s40751-017-0028-x

Bericat Alastuey, E. (2000). La sociología de la emoción y la emoción en la sociología [The sociology of emotion and emotion in sociology]. *Papers*, *62*, 145–176. doi:10.5565/rev/papers/v62n0.1070

Bericat, E. (2012). Emociones. *Sociopedia.isa*, 1-13.

Bernal Guerrero, A., & Cárdenas Gutiérrez, A. R. (2009). Influence of teacher emotional competence in the formation of motivational and identity processes in secondary education students. An approach from the autobiographical memory of students. *Revista de investigación educativa, 27*(1), 203-222. https://revistas.um.es/rie/article/view/94371

Berretta, S., Tausch, A., Ontrup, G., Gilles, B., Peifer, C., & Kluge, A. (2023). Defining human-AI teaming the human-centered way: A scoping review and network analysis. *Frontiers in Artificial Intelligence*, *6*, 6. doi:10.3389/frai.2023.1250725 PMID:37841234

Bharti, T., Mishra, N., & Ojha, S. C. (2023). Mindfulness and Subjective Well-Being of Indian University Students: Role of Resilience during COVID-19 Pandemic. *Behavioral Sciences (Basel, Switzerland)*, *13*(5), 353. doi:10.3390/bs13050353 PMID:37232590

Bhugaonkar, K., Bhugaonkar, R., & Masne, N. (2022). The Trend of Metaverse and Augmented & Virtual Reality Extending to the Healthcare System. *Cureus*. Advance online publication. doi:10.7759/cureus.29071 PMID:36258985

Boden, M. A. (2004). *The Creative Mind: Myths and Mechanisms. 2*. Routledge. doi:10.4324/9780203508527

Bohil, C. J., Alicea, B., & Biocca, F. A. (2011). Virtual reality in neuroscience research and therapy. In Nature Reviews Neuroscience (Vol. 12, Issue 12). doi:10.1038/nrn3122

Bojic, L. (2022). Metaverse through the prism of power and addiction: what will happen when the virtual world becomes more attractive than reality? In European Journal of Futures Research (Vol. 10, Issue 1). Springer Science and Business Media Deutschland GmbH. doi:10.118640309-022-00208-4

Bombari, D., Schmid Mast, M., Canadas, E., & Bachmann, M. (2015). Studying social interactions through immersive virtual environment technology: virtues, pitfalls, and future challenges. In *Frontiers in Psychology* (Vol. 6). Frontiers Media S.A. doi:10.3389/fpsyg.2015.00869

Bonami, B., Piazentini, L., & Dala-Possa, A. (2020). Education, Big Data and Artificial Intelligence: Mixed methods in digital platforms. *Comunicar, 65*(65), 43–52. doi:10.3916/C65-2020-04

Boragnio, A. (2022). Emotions and food in times of pandemic: a comparison of eating practices in Spain and Argentina during COVID-19. In *Emotions and Society in difficult times*. Cambridge Scholars Publishing.

Bosch, M. (2013). *Reflections on Emerging Technologies in Agriculture*. Academic Press.

Botz-Bornstein, T. (2012). Critical Posthumanism. *Pensamiento y Cultura, 15*(1), 20–30. doi:10.5294/pecu.2012.15.1.2

Bouchard, S., St-Jacques, J., Robillard, G., & Renaud, P. (2008). Anxiety increases the feeling of presence in virtual reality. *Presence (Cambridge, Mass.), 17*(4), 376–391. Advance online publication. doi:10.1162/pres.17.4.376

BragazziN. L.CrapanzanoA.ConvertiM.ZerbettoR.Khamisy-FarahR. (2023). Queering Artificial Intelligence: The Impact of Generative Conversational AI on the 2SLGBTQIAP Community. A Scoping Review. Available at SSRN: https://ssrn.com/abstract=4548411 doi:10.2139/ssrn.4548411

Breazeal, C., & Brooks, R. (2005). Robot emotion: A functional perspective. In *Who needs emotions* (pp. 271–310). Oxford University Press. doi:10.1093/acprof:oso/9780195166194.003.0010

Brelet, L., & Gaffary, Y. (2022). Stress reduction interventions: A scoping review to explore progress toward using haptic feedback in virtual reality. *Frontiers in Virtual Reality, 3*, 900970. Advance online publication. doi:10.3389/frvir.2022.900970

Bremner, J. G. (1994). *Infancy* (2nd ed.). Wiley-Blackwell.

Brenes Carranza, J. A., Martínez Porras, A., Quesada López, C. U., & Jenkins Coronas, M. (2020). *Decision support systems using artificial intelligence in precision agriculture*. Academic Press.

Bressane, A., Spalding, M., Zwirn, D., Loureiro, A., Bankole, A., Negri, R., de Brito Junior, I., Formiga, J. K. S., Medeiros, L. C. C., Pampuch Bortolozo, L. A., & Moruzzi, R. (2022). Fuzzy artificial intelligence-based model proposal to forecast student performance and retention risk in engineering education: An alternative for handling with small data. *Sustainability (Basel), 214*(21), 14071. doi:10.3390u142114071

Bringsjord, S., & Govindarajulu, N. S. (2018). Artificial Intelligence. In E. N. Zalta (Ed.), Stanford Encyclopedia of Philosophy (Fall 2018). Metaphysics Research Lab.

Broderick, P. C., & Jennings, P. A. (2012). Mindfulness for adolescents: A promising approach to supporting emotion regulation and preventing risky behaviour. *New Directions for Youth Development, 2012*(136), 111–126. doi:10.1002/yd.20042 PMID:23359447

Bugajska, A. (2021). The Future of Utopia in the Posthuman World. *Academia Letters, 155*, 1–7. doi:10.20935/AL155

Burgess, A., Cavanagh, K., Strauss, C., & Oliver, B. R. (2022). Headspace for parents: Qualitative report investigating the use of a mindfulness-based app for managing parents' stress during COVID-19. *BJPsych Open, 8*(1), e15. doi:10.1192/bjo.2021.1070 PMID:34956647

Burgess, J., Cassidy, E., Duguay, S., & Light, B. (2016). Making Digital Cultures of Gender and Sexuality With Social Media. *Social Media + Society, 2*(4). Advance online publication. doi:10.1177/2056305116672487

Buslón, N., Cortés, A., Catuara-Solarz, S., Cirillo, D., & Rementeria, M. J. (2023). Raising awareness of sex and gender bias in artificial intelligence and health. *Frontiers in Global Women's Health, 4*, 1–8. doi:10.3389/fgwh.2023.970312 PMID:37746321

Byung-Chul, H. (2012). *La sociedad del cansancio*. Herder Editorial.

Cabello, R., Ruiz-Aranda, D., & Fernández-Berrocal, P. (2010). Docentes emocionalmente inteligentes [Emotionally intelligent teachers]. *Revista Electrónica Interuniversitaria de Formación del Profesorado, 13*(1), 41-49. https://www.redalyc.org/pdf/2170/217014922005.pdf

Caldeira, C., Chen, Y., Chan, L., Pham, V., Chen, Y., & Zheng, K. (2017). Mobile apps for mood tracking: an analysis of features and user reviews. In *AMIA Annual Symposium Proceedings* (p. 495). American Medical Informatics Association. https://www.ncbi.nlm.nih.gov/pmc/articles/PMC5977660/

Camille, B. A. (2021). *Using Headspace for the Management of Anxiety During the COVID-19 Pandemic*. Brandman University.

Camilleri, M. A. (2023). Metaverse applications in education: a systematic review and a cost-benefit analysis. In Interactive Technology and Smart Education. doi:10.1108/ITSE-01-2023-0017

Campaña Bastidas, S., Méndez Porras, A., Santacruz Madroñero, A. M., Díaz Toro, A. A., & Cervelión Bastidas, Á. J. (2023). Sistema de reconocimiento facial y de emociones aplicado a la educación básica y media de una institución educativa en Colombia con herramientas de la 4RI [Facial and emotion recognition system applied to elementary and secondary education in an educational institution in Colombia with 4RI tools]. *Encuentro Internacional De Educación En Ingeniería*. doi:10.26507/paper.3342

Cao, L. (2023). AI and data science for smart emergency, crisis and disaster resilience. *International Journal of Data Science and Analytics, 15*(3), 231–246. doi:10.100741060-023-00393-w PMID:37035277

Carden, C., & Gibson, M. (2021). Living on Beyond the Body: The Digital Soul of Black Mirror. In The Moral Uncanny in Black Mirror. Palgrave Macmillan. doi:10.1007/978-3-030-47495-9_8

Carson, J. W., Carson, K. M., Gil, K. M., & Baucom, D. H. (2004). Mindfulness-based relationship enhancement. *Behavior Therapy*, *35*(3), 471–494. doi:10.1016/S0005-7894(04)80028-5

Castells, M. (2010). The information age. *Media Studies: A Reader, 2*(7), 152-158

Castells, M. (1986). High technology, world development, and structural transformation: The trends and the debate. *Alternatives*, *11*(3), 297–343. doi:10.1177/030437548601100301

Castells, M. (2020). Space of flows, space of places: Materials for a theory of urbanism in the information age. In *The city reader* (pp. 240–251). Routledge. doi:10.4324/9780429261732-30

CEPAL. (2020). *Economic Survey of Latin America and the Caribbean 2020: Main determinants of fiscal and monetary policies in the post-COVID-19 pandemic era*. ECLAC. https://hdl.handle.net/11362/46071

Cepeda-Lopez, A. C., Solís Domínguez, L., Villarreal Zambrano, S., Garza-Rodriguez, I. Y., Del Valle, A. C., & Quiroga-Garza, A. (2023). A comparative study of well-being, resilience, mindfulness, negative emotions, stress, and burnout among nurses after an online mind–body-based intervention during the first COVID-19 pandemic crisis. *Frontiers in Psychology*, *14*, 848637. doi:10.3389/fpsyg.2023.848637 PMID:36993886

Cerasa, A., Gaggioli, A., Marino, F., Riva, G., & Pioggia, G. (2022). The promise of the metaverse in mental health: the new era of MEDverse. In Heliyon (Vol. 8, Issue 11). doi:10.1016/j.heliyon.2022.e11762

Chang, M.-M., & Hung, H.-T. (2019). Effects of Technology-Enhanced Language Learning on Second Language Acquisition: A Meta-Analysis. *Journal of Educational Technology & Society*, *22*(4), 1–17.

Charles-Leija, H., Castro, C. G., Toledo, M., & Ballesteros-Valdés, R. (2023). Meaningful Work, Happiness at Work, and Turnover Intentions. *International Journal of Environmental Research and Public Health*, *20*(4), 3565. doi:10.3390/ijerph20043565 PMID:36834260

Chen, Y., Wang, Q., Chen, H., Song, X., Tang, H., & Tian, M. (2019). An overview of augmented reality technology. *Journal of Physics: Conference Series*, *1237*(2), 022082. Advance online publication. doi:10.1088/1742-6596/1237/2/022082

Chesbrough, H. (2020). To recover faster from Covid-19, open up: Managerial implications from an open innovation perspective. *Industrial Marketing Management*, *88*, 410–413. doi:10.1016/j.indmarman.2020.04.010

Cheshmehzangi, A., Zou, T., & Su, Z. (2022). The digital divide impacts on mental health during the COVID-19 pandemic. *Brain, Behavior, and Immunity*, *101*, 211–213. doi:10.1016/j.bbi.2022.01.009 PMID:35041937

Chirico, A., & Gaggioli, A. (2023). How Real Are Virtual Emotions? In Cyberpsychology, Behavior, and Social Networking (Vol. 26, Issue 4). .editorial doi:10.1089/cyber.2023.29272.editorial

Choung, H., David, P., & Ross, A. (2023). Trust and ethics in AI. *AI & Society*, *38*(2), 733–745. doi:10.100700146-022-01473-4

Chu, E., Dunn, J., & Roy, D. (2018). AI's Growing Impact. *McKinsey Quarterly*. https://www.mckinsey.com/~/media/McKinsey/Business%20Functions/McKinsey%20Analytics/Our%20Insights/AIs%20growing%20impact/AIs-growing-impact.pdf

CIPPEC. (2018). *Índice de Progreso Social. Conurbano Bonaerense 2018* [Social Progress Index]. https://www.cippec.org/indice-de-progreso-social-en-vicente-lopez/

Clarín. (2016). *An app for managing dairy farms from your mobile*. https://www.clarin.com/rural/aplicacion-gestionar-tambo-celular_0_r1gC45QWx.html

Cominiello, S. (2011). A century of arduous work: Work processes on Argentine dairy farms, 1900-2010. Gino Germani Institute of Research, Faculty of Social Sciences, UBA, Buenos Aires.

Cominiello, S. N. (2016). *The milking revolution: Changes in the work process of primary milk production in Argentina, 1980-2007*. Academic Press.

Connors, C. (2023). 'Out of interest': Klara and the Sun and the interests of fiction. *Textual Practice*, 1–19. Advance online publication. doi:10.1080/0950236X.2023.2210096

Constable, C. (2013). Adapting Philosophy: Jean Baudrillard and The Matrix Trilogy. In *Adapting philosophy*. Manchester University Press. doi:10.7765/9781847792822

Contois, E., & Kish, Z. (2022). *Food Instagram: Identity, Influence, and Negotiation*. The University of Illness Press. doi:10.1177/1461444818815684

Contreras, J., & Gracia-Arnaiz, M. (2005). *Alimentación y cultura: perspectivas antropológicas*. Editorial Ariel.

Conz, E., & Magnani, G. (2020). A dynamic perspective on the resilience of firms: A systematic literature review and a framework for future research. *European Management Journal*, *38*(3), 400–412. doi:10.1016/j.emj.2019.12.004

Coppola, S., & Zanazzi, S. (2020). *L'esperienza dell'arte. Il ruolo delle tecnologie immersive nella didattica museale*. doi:10.7346/-fei-XVIII-02-20_04

Corbellini, C. (2002). *Bovine mastitis and its impact on milk quality*. Institute of Agricultural Technology, Dairy Project, EEA INTA Pergamino.

Crompton, H., & Burke, D. (2022). Artificial intelligence in K-12 education. *SN Social Sciences*, *2*(113), 113. Advance online publication. doi:10.100743545-022-00425-5

Crompton, H., & Burke, D. (2023). Artificial intelligence in higher education: The state of the field. *International Journal of Educational Technology in Higher Education*, *20*(1), 22. Advance online publication. doi:10.118641239-023-00392-8

Cropley, A. (2019). *Introduction to qualitative research methods: A research handbook for patient and public involvement researchers*. . doi:10.7765/9781526136527.00012

Csikszentmihalyi, M. (n.d.). *Flow: The Psychology of Optimal Experience Flow-The Psychology of optimal experience*. https://www.researchgate.net/publication/224927532

Cucino, V., Ferrigno, G., & Piccaluga, A. (2021). Recognizing opportunities during the crisis: a longitudinal analysis of Italian SMEs during the Covid-19 crisis. In *Electronic Conference Proceedings of Sinergie-Sima Management Conference: Leveraging intersections in management theory and practice, Palermo, June 10-11, 2021, University of Palermo* (pp. 37-41). Fondazione CUEIM.

Cucino, V., Del Sarto, N., Ferrigno, G., Piccaluga, A. M. C., & Di Minin, A. (2022). Not just numbers! Improving TTO performance by balancing the soft sides of the TQM. *The TQM Journal*. Advance online publication. doi:10.1108/TQM-01-2022-0034

Cucino, V., & Ferrigno, G. (2023). AI technologies and hospital blood delivery in peripheral regions: insights from Zipline International. In *Impact of Artificial Intelligence in Business and Society: Opportunities and challenges*. Routledge. doi:10.4324/9781003304616-15

Cucino, V., Ferrigno, G., & Piccaluga, A. M. C. (2023). Pursuing innovative actions during the Covid-19 crisis: A qualitative analysis of family firms' resilience. *Piccola Impresa*, *1*(2), 69–94.

Cucino, V., Lungu, D. A., De Rosis, S., & Piccaluga, A. (2023). Creating value from purpose-based innovation: Starting from frailty. *Journal of Social Entrepreneurship*, 1–29. doi:10.1080/19420676.2023.2263768

da Silva, B. D. (2001). A Tecnologia é uma Estratégia. In *Actas da II Conferência Internacional Desafios 2001* (pp. 839–859). Centro de Competência da Universidade do Minho do Projecto Nónio.

Daqar, M. A. M. A., & Smoudy, A. K. A. (2019). The Role of Artificial Intelligence on Enhancing Customer Experience. *International Review of Management and Marketing. Econjournals*, *9*(4), 22–31.

Daraiseh, I., & Booker, M. K. (2019). Unreal City: Nostalgia, Authenticity, and Posthumanity in "San Junipero". In T. McSweeney & S. Joy (Eds.), *Through the black mirror: deconstructing the side effects of the digital age*. Palgrave Macmillan. doi:10.1007/978-3-030-19458-1_12

Dara, R., Hazrati, S. M., & Kaur, J. (2022). Recommendations for ethical and responsible use of artificial intelligence in digital agriculture. *Frontiers in Artificial Intelligence*, *5*, 884192. Advance online publication. doi:10.3389/frai.2022.884192 PMID:35968036

Darling, K. (2012). *Extending legal protection to social robots: The effects of anthropomorphism, empathy, and violent behavior towards robotic objects*. doi:10.2139srn.2044797

Davis, P. M., & Class, M. (2023). Educational Robots for Social and Emotional Learning. *AI. Computer Science and Robotics Technology*, *2*(1), 1–10. doi:10.5772/acrt.26

de Carvalho, A. A., Cirera, R. dos R., & Mengalli, N. M. (n.d.). *FoLo - Fear of Logging off: Medo de Ficar sem Conexão*. https://www.uscs.edu.br/boletim/1603

de Carvalho, A. A., Mengalli, N. M., & Lucas, R. B. (2022). A Tessitura da Interdisciplinaridade e da Inovação como o Futuro na Pesquisa, no Ensino e na Extensão: A Reflexão da Transformação Phygital e das Tendências Imersivas nos Projetos Extensionistas. In Olhares Plurais e Multidisciplinares na Pesquisa e Extensão. Arco Editores. doi:10.48209/978-65-5417-027-1

De Carvalho, M. R., De Santana Dias, T. R., Duchesne, M., Nardi, A. E., & Appolinario, J. C. (2017). Virtual reality as a promising strategy in the assessment and treatment of bulimia nervosa and binge eating disorder: A systematic review. In Behavioral Sciences (Vol. 7, Issue 3). doi:10.3390/bs7030043

de Felice, S. (2023). *Learning from Others is Good, with Others is Better: The Role of Social Interaction in Human Acquisition of New Knowledge. Phil.* Trans. R. Soc. doi:10.1098/rstb.2021.0357

De la Garza Toledo, E. (2011). Más allá de la fábrica: los desafíos teóricos del trabajo no clásico y la producción inmaterial. *Nueva Sociedad, 232.*

De Sena, A., & Chahbenderian, F. (2020). Apostillas sobre consumo, educación para el consumo y educación de las emociones [Apostilles on consumption, education for consumption and education of emotions]. In A. De Sena (Coord.), La cuestión educativa: formas y actores en debate [The educational question: forms and actors in debate] (pp. 19-40). Universidad del Salvador.

De Sena, A., & Scribano, A. (2020). Social Policies and Emotions: A Look from the Global South. In Social Policies and Emotions, (pp. 1-11). Palgrave Macmillan. doi:10.1007/978-3-030-34739-0

De Sena, A. (2015). *Caminos cualitativos* [Qualitative paths]. Imago Mundi-Ciccus.

De Sena, A., & Lisdero, P. (2015). Etnografía Virtual: aportes para su discusión y diseño (Visual Ethnography: conceptual debates). In *Caminos cualitativos. Aportes para la investigación en ciencias sociales.* Ediciones CICCUS, Imago Mundi.

De Souza Marcovski, F. C., & Miller, L. J. (2023). A latent profile analysis of the five facets of mindfulness in a US adult sample: Spiritual and psychological differences among four profiles. *Current Psychology (New Brunswick, N.J.), 42*(17), 14223–14236. doi:10.100712144-021-02546-1

Del Mónaco, R. L. (2020). Empresarios de sí mismos: subjetividades en las terapias cognitivo-conductuales. In Políticas terapéuticas y economías de sufrimiento: perspectivas y debates contemporáneos sobre las tecnologías psi (pp. 175-196). Consejo Latinoamericano de Ciencias Sociales.

Deleuze, G., & Guattari, F. (2008). *Mil mesetas. Capitalismo y esquizofrenia [Thousand plateau: Capitalism and schizophrenia).* Pre-textos.

Dell'Era, C., Di Minin, A., Ferrigno, G., Frattini, F., Landoni, P., & Verganti, R. (2020). Value capture in open innovation processes with radical circles: A qualitative analysis of firms' collaborations with Slow Food, Memphis, and Free Software Foundation. *Technological Forecasting and Social Change, 158*, 120128. doi:10.1016/j.techfore.2020.120128

Della Longa, L., Valori, I., & Farroni, T. (2022). Interpersonal Affective Touch in a Virtual World: Feeling the Social Presence of Others to Overcome Loneliness. In *Frontiers in Psychology* (Vol. 12). Frontiers Media S.A., doi:10.3389/fpsyg.2021.795283

Department for Education. (2013). *Computing programmes of study: key stages 1 and 2. National Curriculum in England.* https://www.gov.uk/government/uploads/system/uploads/attachment_data/file/239033/PRIMARY_national_curriculum_-_Computing.pdf

Dewey, J. (1979). *Experiência e Educação. 3.* Companhia Editora Nacional.

Dhimolea, T. K., Kaplan-Rakowski, R., & Lin, L. (2022). Supporting Social and Emotional Well-Being with Artificial Intelligence. In *Bridging Human Intelligence and Artificial Intelligence* (pp. 125–138). Springer International Publishing. doi:10.1007/978-3-030-84729-6_8

Diago, P. D., Arnau, D., & González-Calero, J. A. (2018). Elementos de resolución de problemas en primeras edades escolares con Bee-bot [Elements of problem solving in early school ages with Bee-bot]. *Edma 0-6. Educación Matemática en la Infancia, 7*(1), 12–41. doi:10.24197/edmain.1.2018.12-41

Díaz Méndez, C., & Gómez Benito, C. (2005). Sociología y alimentación. *Revista Internacional de Sociologia, 63*(40), 21–46. doi:10.3989/ris.2005.i40.188

Dick, P. K. (2009). *Minority Report.* Gollacz.

Dick, P. K. (2017). *Blade Runner: Do Androids Dream of Electric Sheep?* Del Rey Books.

Diemer, J., Alpers, G. W., Peperkorn, H. M., Shiban, Y., & Mühlberger, A. (2015). The impact of perception and presence on emotional reactions: A review of research in virtual reality. In Frontiers in Psychology (Vol. 6). Frontiers Research Foundation. doi:10.3389/fpsyg.2015.00026

Dionisio, M., & de Vargas, E. R. (2020). Corporate social innovation: A systematic literature review. *International Business Review, 29*(2), 101641. doi:10.1016/j.ibusrev.2019.101641

Dohale, V., Akarte, M., Gunasekaran, A., & Verma, P. (2022). Exploring the role of artificial intelligence in building production resilience: Learnings from the COVID-19 pandemic. *International Journal of Production Research*, 1–17. doi:10.1080/00207543.2022.2127961

Döllinger, N., Wienrich, C., & Latoschik, M. E. (2021). Challenges and Opportunities of Immersive Technologies for Mindfulness Meditation: A Systematic Review. *Frontiers in Virtual Reality, 2*, 644683. Advance online publication. doi:10.3389/frvir.2021.644683

Drew, N., & Funk, M. (2010). *Mental health and development: Targeting people with mental health conditions as a vulnerable group.* World Health Organization.

Dreyfus, H., & Dreyfus, S. (1999). Fabricar una mente versus modelar el cerebro: la inteligencia artificial se divide de nuevo [Create a mind or format the brain: AI in perspective]. In The Artificial Intelligence debate: False Starts, Real Foundations (pp. 25-58). Gedisa.

Drigas, A., Mitsea, E., & Skianis, C. (2022). Virtual reality and metacognition training techniques for learning disabilities. *Sustainability (Basel), 14*(16), 10170. doi:10.3390u141610170

Dubé, S., & Anctil, D. (2021). Foundations of Erobotics. *International Journal of Social Robotics, 13*(6), 1205–1233. doi:10.100712369-020-00706-0 PMID:33133302

Duperré, J. (2020) Los re(s)tos de la muerte en pandemia. Un análisis de la política de los cuerpos y las sensibilidades contemporáneas [Death in Panemics; an analysis of bodies and contemporary emotions]. *Boletín Onteaiken, 10*(30).

Duperré, J., & Lisdero, P. (2022). Sensibilities, Social Networks and Images of Death. Some Clues about the "Politics of Gazes". In Global Emotion Communications: Narratives, Technology, and Power. Nova Science Publishers.

Dweck, C. S. S. (2007). *Mindset: The New Psychology of Success*. Random House Publishing.

Earth, D. (2021, November 25). Break the Digital Monoculture: Interview with Dr Kanta Dihal. *Medium*. https://medium.com/@digitalearth/break-the-digital-monoculture-interview-with-dr-kanta-dihal-604d6859123c

Easton, G. (1998). Case research as a methodology for industrial networks: A realist apologia. In P. Naudé & P. W. Turnbull (Eds.), *Network Dynamics in International Marketing* (pp. 73–87). Pergamon.

Eisenhardt, K. M. (2021). What is the Eisenhardt Method, really? *Strategic Organization, 19*(1), 147–160. doi:10.1177/1476127020982866

Eisenhardt, K. M., & Graebner, M. E. (2007). Theory building from cases: Opportunities and challenges. *Academy of Management Journal, 50*(1), 25–32. doi:10.5465/amj.2007.24160888

Elfein, J. (2022). *Statista*. Retrieved from https://www.statista.com/statistics/1287334/perceived-importance-of-mental-health-compared-to-physical-health-worldwide/

Elias, N. (1993). *El proceso de la civilización* [The process of civilization]. Fondo de Cultura Económica.

Ellul, J. (1962). The technological order. *Technology and Culture, 3*(4), 394–421. doi:10.2307/3100993

Ellul, J. (1984). *Technique and the opening chapters of Genesis. Theology and Technology*. Wipf & Stock Publishers.

Ellul, J. (2018). *The technological system*. Wipf and Stock Publishers.

Ellul, J. (2021). *The technological society*. Vintage.

Eloundou, T., Manning, S., Mishkin, P., & Rock, D. (2023). *GPTs are GPTs: An Early Look at the Labor Market Impact Potential of Large Language Models*. Working Paper, arXiv:2303.10130v4.

Engels, F. (1895). El papel del trabajo en la transformación del mono en hombre [The role of work in the transformation of ape into man]. *Die Neue Zeit, 2*(44). https://www.marxists.org/espanol/m-e/1870s/1876trab.htm

Enholm, I. M., Papagiannidis, E., Mikalef, P., & Krogstie, J. (2021). Artificial Intelligence and Business Value: A Literature Review. *Information Systems Frontiers*, *24*(5), 1709–1734. doi:10.100710796-021-10186-w

Erion, G., & Smith, B. (2005). Skepticism, Morality and the Matrix. In W. Irwin (Ed.), *The Matrix and Philosophy: welcome to the desert of the real* (pp. 5–15). Open Court.

Estupiñán Ricardo, J., Leyva Vázquez, M. Y., Peñafiel Palacios, A. J., & El Assafiri Ojeda, Y. (2021). Artificial intelligence and intellectual property. *University and Society Journal*, *13*(S3), 362–368.

Etchevers Goijberg, N. (2005). Ruta etnográfica para la comprensión de la comunicación on-line [Ethnographic route for understanding online communication]. *Revista electrónica DIM, 1*(1).

FECYT, Google, & Everis. (2016). *Educación en ciencias de la computación en España 2015* [Computer science education in Spain 2015]. Ministerio de Economía y Competitividad. https://www.fecyt.es/es/publicacion/educacion-de-las-ciencias-de-la-computacion-en-espana

Feldman, Z. (2021). Good food' in an Instagram age: Rethinking hierarchies of culture, criticism and taste. *European Journal of Cultural Studies*, *24*(6), 1340–1359. doi:10.1177/13675494211055733

Ferrigno, G., & Cucino, V. (2021). Innovating and transforming during COVID-19: Insights from Italian firms. *R & D Management*, *51*(4), 325–338. doi:10.1111/radm.12469

Ferrigno, G., Del Sarto, N., Cucino, V., & Piccaluga, A. (2022). Connecting organizational learning and open innovation research: An integrative framework and insights from case studies of strategic alliances. *The Learning Organization*, *29*(6), 615–634. doi:10.1108/TLO-03-2021-0030

Ferrigno, G., Del Sarto, N., Piccaluga, A., & Baroncelli, A. (2023). Industry 4.0 base technologies and business models: A bibliometric analysis. *European Journal of Innovation Management*, *26*(7), 502–526. doi:10.1108/EJIM-02-2023-0107

Ferrigno, G., Zordan, A., & Di Minin, A. (2022). The emergence of dominant design in the early automotive industry: An historical analysis of Ford's technological experimentation from 1896 to 1906. *Technology Analysis and Strategic Management*, 1–12. doi:10.1080/09537325.2022.2074386

Fidalgo-Blanco, Á., Sein-Echaluce, M., García-Peñalvo, F., & Balbín Bastidas, A. (2021). A critical review of the flipped classroom method from an experience-based perspective. In M. L. Sein-Echaluce Lacleta, Á. Fidalgo-Blanco, & F. J. García-Peñalvo (Eds.), *Innovaciones docentes en tiempos de pandemia* (pp. 659–664). Servicio de Publicaciones Universidad de Zaragoza. doi:10.26754/CINAIC.2021.0127

Fischler, C. (2010). Gastro-nomía y gastro-anomía. Sabiduría del cuerpo y crisis biocultural de la alimentación moderna. *Gazeta de Antropología*, (26), 1–19. doi:10.30827/Digibug.6789

Flavián, C., Ibáñez-Sánchez, S., & Orús, C. (2019). The impact of virtual, augmented and mixed reality technologies on the customer experience. *Journal of Business Research, 100*, 547–560. doi:10.1016/j.jbusres.2018.10.050

Flett, J. A., Hayne, H., Riordan, B. C., Thompson, L. M., & Conner, T. S. (2019). Mobile mindfulness meditation: a randomized controlled trial of the effect of two popular apps on mental health. *Mindfulness, 10*, 863–876. https://link.springer.com/article/10.1007/s12671-018-1050-9

Flett, J. A. M., Conner, T. S., Riordan, B. C., Patterson, T., & Hayne, H. (2020). App-based for personal recovery in mental health: Systematic review and narrative synthesis. *BJPsych, 199*, 445–452.

Flores Masias, E., Livia Segovia, J., García Casique, A., & Dávila Díaz, M. (2023). Análisis de sentimientos con inteligencia artificial para mejorar el proceso enseñanza-aprendizaje en el aula virtual [Sentiment analysis with artificial intelligence to improve the teaching-learning process in the virtual classroom]. *Publicaciones, 53*(2), 185–200. doi:10.30827/publicaciones.v53i2.26825

Ford, T. J., Buchanan, D. M., Azeez, A., Benrimoh, D. A., Kaloiani, I., Bandeira, I. D., Hunegnaw, S., Lan, L., Gholmieh, M., Buch, V., & Williams, N. R. (2023). Taking modern psychiatry into the metaverse: Integrating augmented, virtual, and mixed reality technologies into psychiatric care. *Frontiers in Digital Health, 5*, 1146806. Advance online publication. doi:10.3389/fdgth.2023.1146806 PMID:37035477

Foroudi, P., Akarsu, T. N., Marvi, R., & Balakrishnan, J. (2021). Intellectual evolution of social innovation: A bibliometric analysis and avenues for future research trends. *Industrial Marketing Management, 93*, 446–465. doi:10.1016/j.indmarman.2020.03.026

Franco López, J. A. (2023). La motivación de los docentes con respecto al desarrollo de la inteligencia artificial [Motivation of teachers regarding the development of artificial intelligence]. *Revista Virtual Universidad Católica del Norte, 70*, 1-3. https://www.doi.org/10.35575/rvucn.n70a1

Frasson, C., & Abdessalem, H. (2022). Contribution of Virtual Reality Environments and Artificial Intelligence for Alzheimer. *Medical Research Archives, 10*(9). Advance online publication. doi:10.18103/mra.v10i9.3054

Freeman, D., Reeve, S., Robinson, A., Ehlers, A., Clark, D., Spanlang, B., & Slater, M. (2017). Virtual reality in the assessment, understanding, and treatment of mental health disorders. In Psychological Medicine (Vol. 47, Issue 14, pp. 2393–2400). Cambridge University Press. doi:10.1017/S003329171700040X

Fregnan, E., Pinto, D., & Scaratti, G. (2022). *Instilling Digital Competencies Through Educational Robotics*. IGI Global. doi:10.4018/978-1-7998-8653-2

Freire, P. (1989). A Importância do Ato de Ler: Em Três Artigos que se Completam. Autores Associados: Cortez. Coleção Polêmicas do Nosso Tempo.

Fuentes, S., Gonzalez Viejo, C., Cullen, B., Togson, E., Chauhan, S., & Dunshea, F. (2020). Artificial Intelligence Applied to a Robotic Dairy Farm to Model Milk Productivity and Quality Based on Cow Data and Daily Environmental Parameters. *Sensors (Basel), 20*(10), 2975. doi:10.339020102975 PMID:32456339

Fulambarkar, N., Seo, B., Testerman, A., Rees, M., Bausback, K., & Bunge, E. (2023). Meta-analysis on mindfulness-based interventions for adolescents' stress, depression, and anxiety in school settings: A cautionary tale. *Child and Adolescent Mental Health, 28*(2), 307–317. Advance online publication. doi:10.1111/camh.12572 PMID:35765773

Furman, M., Larsen, M. E., & Giorgi, P. (2020). *¿Cuáles son las mejores estrategias para la formación de docentes en ejercicio?* [What are the best strategies for training practising teachers?] Document Nº 12. Project Educational questions: what do we know about education? CIAESA.

Futureworld. (1976). https://www.primevideo.com/dp/amzn1.dv.gti.62b56442-c460-16c4-8dfe-c0e6b522cb84?autoplay=0&ref_=atv_cf_strg_wb

Futuro da Personalização, O. O Uso da Tecnologia na Jornada do Consumidor. (2023). *MIT Technology Review*. https://mittechreview.com.br/o-futuro-da-personalizacao-o-uso-da-tecnologia-na-jornada-do-consumidor/?utm_campaign=adobe_artigo_vr_15set23&utm_medium=email&utm_source=RD+Station

Gaggioli, A. (2017). Digital Social Innovation. In Cyberpsychology, Behavior, and Social Networking (Vol. 20, Issue 11). doi:10.1089/cyber.2017.29090.csi

Galarza, M. L. (2018). In search of the Holly Grail. *Anales de la Facultad de Ciencias Jurídicas y Sociales de la Universidad de La Plata, 48*, 1055–1174. https://revistas.unlp.edu.ar/RevistaAnalesJursoc/issue/view/379

García-Peñalvo, F. J., Llorens-Largo, F., & Vidal, J. (2024). The new reality of education in the face of advances in generative artificial intelligence. *RIED: Revista Iberoamericana de Educación a Distancia, 27*(1). Advance online publication. doi:10.5944/ried.27.1

Gaudiello, I., & Zibetti, E. (2016). *Learning Robotics, with Robotics, by Robotics: Educational Robotics* (Vol. 3). John Wiley & Sons, Inc., doi:10.1002/9781119335740

George, G., Haas, M. R., McGahan, A. M., Schillebeeckx, S. J., & Tracey, P. (2023). Purpose in the for-profit firm: A review and framework for management research. *Journal of Management, 49*(6), 1841–1869. doi:10.1177/01492063211006450

George, S., Daniels, K., & Fioratou, E. (2018). A qualitative study into the perceived barriers of accessing healthcare among a vulnerable population involved with a community centre in Romania. *International Journal for Equity in Health, 17*(1), 1–13. doi:10.118612939-018-0753-9 PMID:29615036

Georgiev, D. D., Georgieva, I., Gong, Z., Nanjappan, V., & Georgiev, G. V. (2021). Virtual reality for neurorehabilitation and cognitive enhancement. *Brain Sciences, 11*(2), 1–20. doi:10.3390/brainsci11020221 PMID:33670277

Gerlich, M. (2023). The Power of Personal Connections in Micro-Influencer Marketing: A Study on Consumer Behaviour and the Impact of Micro-Influencers. *Transnational Marketing Journal, 11*(1), 131-152.

Ghotbi, N. (2022). The Ethics of Emotional Artificial Intelligence: A Mixed Method Analysis. *Asian Bioethics Review, 15*(4), 417–430. doi:10.100741649-022-00237-y PMID:37808444

Giddens, A. (1984). *The Constitution of Society*. Polity Press Cambridge.

Giddens, A. (1992). *The transformation of intimacy. Sexuality, Love and Eroticism in Modern Societies*. Stanford University Press.

Giddens, A. (1997). Vivir en una sociedad postradicional [Living in a post-traditional society]. In U. Beck, A. Giddens, & S. Lash (Eds.), *Thoughtful modernization* [Modernización reflexiva] (pp. 33–71). Alliance.

Giddens, A. (2003). *La Constitución de la Sociedad (the constitution of society)*. Amorrortu.

Gil-Quintana, J., Santoveña-Casal, S., & Romero Riaño, E. (2021). Realfooders Influencers on Instagram: From Followers to Consumers. *International Journal of Environmental Research and Public Health, 18*(4), 1624. doi:10.3390/ijerph18041624 PMID:33567738

Gittell, J. H. (2008). Relationships and resilience: Care provider responses to pressures from managed care. *The Journal of Applied Behavioral Science, 44*(1), 25–47. doi:10.1177/0021886307311469

Giuliano, R. (2020). Echoes of myth and magic in the language of artificial intelligence. *AI & Society, 35*(4), 1009–1024. doi:10.100700146-020-00966-4

Goffman, E. (1997). *La presentación de la persona en la vida cotidiana* [The presentation of the person in everyday life]. Amorrotu.

Goleman, D. (1996). *Emotional intelligence*. Bloomsbury Publishing PLC.

Gómez Dávalos, N., & Rodríguez Fernández, P. (2020). Stress in teachers in the context of the COVID-19 pandemic and education. *Academic Disclosure, 1*, 216-234. https://revistascientificas.una.py/ojs/index.php/rfenob/article/view/150/124

Gómez, O. Y. A. (2018). Las TIC como herramientas cognitivas [ICT as cognitive tools]. *Revista interamericana de investigación, educación y pedagogía, 11*(1), 67-80.

Gonzalez Turmo, I. (2017). Big data y antropología de la alimentación. In L. Mariano Juarez, F. X. Medina, & J. Lopez García (Eds.), *Comida y mundo virtual* (pp. 327–352). Editorial UOC.

Gorini, A., Capideville, C. S., De Leo, G., Mantovani, F., & Riva, G. (2011). The role of immersion and narrative in mediated presence: The virtual hospital experience. *Cyberpsychology, Behavior, and Social Networking, 14*(3), 99–105. doi:10.1089/cyber.2010.0100 PMID:20649451

Gorini, A., Griez, E., Petrova, A., & Riva, G. (2010). Assessment of the emotional responses produced by exposure to real food, virtual food and photographs of food in patients affected by eating disorders. *Annals of General Psychiatry*, *9*(1), 30. Advance online publication. doi:10.1186/1744-859X-9-30 PMID:20602749

Gracia-Arnaiz, M. (1996). *Paradojas de la alimentación contemporánea*. Icaria.

Graham, S., Depp, C. A., Lee, E., Nebeker, C., Tu, X., Kim, H., & Jeste, D. V. (2019). Artificial Intelligence for Mental Health and Mental Illnesses: An Overview. *Current Psychiatry Reports*, *21*(11), 116. Advance online publication. doi:10.100711920-019-1094-0 PMID:31701320

Grech, V. (2012, April). The Pinocchio syndrome and the prosthetic impulse in science fiction. *The New York Review of Science Fiction*, 11–15.

Grimshaw, M. (2013). The Oxford Handbook of Virtuality. Oxford Academ.

Grover, S., & Pea, R. (2013). Computational Thinking in K-12: A Review of the State of the Field. *Educational Researcher*, *42*(1), 38–43. doi:10.3102/0013189X12463051

Güell Villanueva, P. & Yopo Díaz, M. (2017). Las perspectivas temporales de los chilenos: un estudio empírico sobre la dimensión subjetiva del tiempo. *Universum. Revista de Humanidades y Ciencias Sociales*, *32*(1), 121-135.

Guesse, C. (2020). On the Possibility of a Posthuman/ist Literature(s). In S. Karkulehto, A.-K. Koistinen, & E. Varis (Eds.), *Reconfiguring Human, Nonhuman and Posthuman in Literature and Culture* (pp. 23–40). Routledge.

Guillaume, N., Jean, M., Marcaurelle, R., & Dupuis, G. (2020). Mindfulness meditation versus training in tranquil abiding: Theoretical comparison and relevance for developing concentration. *Psychology of Consciousness : Theory, Research, and Practice*, *7*(2), 151–172. doi:10.1037/cns0000222

Gupta, S., Kumar, V., & Karam, E. (2020). New-age technologies-driven social innovation: What, how, where, and why? *Industrial Marketing Management*, *89*, 499–516. doi:10.1016/j.indmarman.2019.09.009

Gutiérrez, L. F. (2011). Evaluation of dairy product quality using an electronic nose. Latin American Archives of Nutrition, 61(2).

Haddadin, S. (2014). *Towards safe robots: Approaching Asimov's 1st law* (Vol. 90). Springer. doi:10.1007/978-3-642-40308-8

Hamamura, T., Kobayashi, N., Oka, T., Kawashima, I., Sakai, Y., Tanaka, S., & Honjo, M. (2023). Validity, reliability, and correlates of the Smartphone Addiction Scale–Short Version among Japanese adults. *BMC Psychology*, *11*(1), 78. Advance online publication. doi:10.118640359-023-01095-5 PMID:36959621

Hansen, L., Zhang, Y. P., Wolf, D., Sechidis, K., Ladegaard, N., & Fusaroli, R. (2022). A generalizable speech emotion recognition model reveals depression and remission. *Acta Psychiatrica Scandinavica, 145*(2), 186–199. doi:10.1111/acps.13388 PMID:34850386

Hanson, K. R. (2022). The Silicone Self: Examining Sexual Selfhood and Stigma within the Love and Sex Doll Community. *Symbolic Interaction, 45*(2), 189–210. doi:10.1002ymb.575

Hao, Q., Peng, W., Wang, J., Tu, Y., Li, H., & Zhu, T. (2022). The correlation between internet addiction and interpersonal relationship among teenagers and college Students Based on Pearson's Correlation Coefficient: A Systematic Review and Meta-Analysis. *Frontiers in Psychiatry, 13*, 818494. Advance online publication. doi:10.3389/fpsyt.2022.818494 PMID:35356718

Harari, Y. N. (2018). *21 Lições para o Século 21*. Companhia das Letras.

Harper, D. (2002). Talking about pictures: A case for photo elicitation. *Visual Studies, 17*(1), 13–26. doi:10.1080/14725860220137345

Hart, D. (2018). Faux-meat and masculinity: The gendering of food on three vegan blogs. *Canadian Food Studies La Revue Canadienne Des études Sur l'alimentation, 5*(1), 133–155. doi:10.15353/cfs-rcea.v5i1.233

Haugeland, J. (1985). *Artificial Intelligence: The Very Idea*. Academic Press.

Hayles, K. (1999a). Artificial Life and Literary Culture. In M.-L. Ryan (Ed.), *In Cyberspace Textuality* (pp. 205–223). Indiana University Press.

Hayles, K. (1999b). *How We Became Posthuman*. Chicago University Press. doi:10.7208/chicago/9780226321394.001.0001

Heffernan, T. (2018). A.I. Artificial Intelligence: Science, Fiction and Fairy Tales. *English Studies in Africa, 61*(1), 10–15. doi:10.1080/00138398.2018.1512192

Heller, A. (1980). *Teoría de los sentimientos* [Theory of feelings]. Fontamara.

Hennig-Thurau, T., Aliman, D. N., Herting, A. M., Cziehso, G. P., Linder, M., & Kübler, R. V. (2023). Social interactions in the metaverse: Framework, initial evidence, and research roadmap. *Journal of the Academy of Marketing Science, 51*(4), 889–913. doi:10.100711747-022-00908-0

Her. (2013). https://www.warnerbros.com/movies/her

Herbrechter, S., & Callus, I. (2008). What is a posthumanist reading? *Angelaki, 13*(1), 95–111. doi:10.1080/09697250802156091

Hermann, I. (2021). Artificial intelligence in fiction: Between narratives and metaphors. *AI & Society*, 1–11. doi:10.100700146-021-01299-6

Hernández Barraza, V. (2017). The emotional competencies of the teacher and their professional performance. *Alternativas en Psicología, 37*, 79–92. https://www.alternativas.me/attachments/article/147/06%20-%20Las%20competencias%20emocionales%20del%20docente.pdf

Hernández, R. R. (2021). Precision agriculture: A current necessity. *Agricultural Engineering Journal, 11*(1).

Hieida, C., & Nagai, T. (2022). Survey and perspective on social emotions in robotics. *Advanced Robotics, 36*(1-2), 17–32. doi:10.1080/01691864.2021.2012512

Higuera-Trujillo, J. L., López-Tarruella Maldonado, J., & Llinares Millán, C. (2017). Psychological and physiological human responses to simulated and real environments: A comparison between Photographs, 360° Panoramas, and Virtual Reality. *Applied Ergonomics, 65*, 398–409. doi:10.1016/j.apergo.2017.05.006 PMID:28601190

Hildt, E. (2019). Artificial Intelligence: Does Consciousness Matter? *Frontiers in Psychology, 10*, 1–3. https://doi.org/doi:10.3389/fpsyg.2019.01535

Himle, J. A., Weaver, A., Zhang, A., & Xiang, X. (2022). Digital Mental Health Interventions for Depression. *Cognitive and Behavioral Practice, 29*(1), 50–59. Advance online publication. doi:10.1016/j.cbpra.2020.12.009

Hochschild, A. (1975). *La mercantilización de la vida íntima. Apuntes de la casa y el trabajo* [The commodification of intimate life: Notes from home and work]. Katz.

Hochschild, A. R. (1979). Emotion Work, Feeling Rules, and Social Structure. *American Journal of Sociology, 85*(3), 551–575. doi:10.1086/227049

Hochschild, A. R. (1983). *The Managed Heart. Commercialization of Human Feeling*. University of California Press.

Hogan, P. C. (2003). *The Mind and Its Stories: Narrative Universals and Human Emotion*. Cambridge University Press. doi:10.1017/CBO9780511499951

Hollis, C., Morriss, R., Martin, J., Amani, S., Cotton, R., Denis, M., & Lewis, S. (2015). Technological innovations in mental healthcare: Harnessing the digital revolution. *The British Journal of Psychiatry, 206*(4), 263–265. doi:10.1192/bjp.bp.113.142612 PMID:25833865

Hosuri, A. (2021). Klara and the Sun: A Fable of Humanity in a Posthuman World. *Global Journal of Human-Social Science: Arts & Humanities - Psychology, 21*(7), 61–69.

Huang, J.-Y., Lee, W.-P., Chen, C.-C., & Dong, B.-W. (2020). Developing Emotion-Aware Human–Robot Dialogues for Domain-Specific and Goal-Oriented Tasks. *Robotics (Basel, Switzerland), 9*(2), 31. doi:10.3390/robotics9020031

Hudders, L., & De Jans, S. (2022). Gender effects in influencer marketing: An experimental study on the efficacy of endorsements by same- vs. other-gender social media influencers on Instagram. *International Journal of Advertising, 41*(1), 128–149. doi:10.1080/02650487.2021.1997455

Hudlicka, E. (2008, January). *What Are We Modeling When We Model Emotion?* AAAI spring symposium: emotion, personality, and social behavior, Stanford, CA.

Hudlicka, E. (2015). Computational Analytical Framework for Affective Modeling: Towards Guidelines for Designing Computational Models of Emotions. In Handbook of Research on Synthesizing Human Emotion in Intelligent Systems and Robotics (pp. 1–62). IGI Global.

Humann, H. (2023). What It Means to Be a Talking Object: Ishiguro's Use of AI Narration in Klara and the Sun. *Popular Culture Review*, *34*(1), 11–49. doi:10.18278/pcr.34.1.3

Hussain, S. A., Park, T., Yildirim, I., Xiang, Z., & Abbasi, F. (2018). Virtual-Reality Videos to Relieve Depression. Lecture Notes in Computer Science (Including Subseries Lecture Notes in Artificial Intelligence and Lecture Notes in Bioinformatics), 10910 LNCS. doi:10.1007/978-3-319-91584-5_6

Ijsselsteijn, W., & Riva, G. (2003). *Being There: Concepts, effects and measurement of user presence in synthetic environments G 1 Being There: The experience of presence in mediated environments*. Ios Press.

Illouz, E. (2011). *Por qué duele el amor: una explicación sociológica*. Katz.

Illouz, E. (2018). *El fin del amor: una sociologia de las relaciones negativas*. Katz.

Illouz, E. (2019). *Capitalismo consumo y autenticidad: las emociones como mercancía* [Consumption capitalism and authenticity: Emotions as merchandise]. Katz.

Im, S., Stavas, J., Lee, J., Mir, Z., Hazlett-Stevens, H., & Caplovitz, G. (2021). Does mindfulness-based intervention improve cognitive function? A meta-analysis of controlled studies. *Clinical Psychology Review*, *84*, 101972. doi:10.1016/j.cpr.2021.101972 PMID:33582570

INDEC. (2010). *Censo Nacional de Población, Hogares y Viviendas del 2010* [National Census of Population, Households and Housing of 2010]. https://www.censo.gob.ar/

INDEC. (2023). *Censo Nacional de Población, Hogares y Viviendas del 2022* [National Census of Population, Households and Housing of 2022]. https://www.censo.gob.ar/

Intelligence, A., Data, B., & Globe, A. (2022, January 25). *The Evolution of Artificial Intelligence in the Digital Ecosystem*. https://www.analyticsinsight.net/the-evolution-of-artificial-intelligence-in-the-digital-ecosystem/

Ioannou, A., Papastavrou, E., Avraamides, M. N., & Charalambous, A. (2020). Virtual Reality and Symptoms Management of Anxiety, Depression, Fatigue, and Pain: A Systematic Review. *SAGE Open Nursing*, *6*, 237796082093616. doi:10.1177/2377960820936163 PMID:33415290

Irwin, W. (2005). Computers, Caves and Oracles: Neo and Socrates. In W. Irwin (Ed.), *The Matrix and Philosophy: welcome to the desert of the real* (pp. 3–5). Open Court.

Ishiguro, K. (2021). *Klara and the sun* (1st ed.). Alfred A. Knopf.

Ivanov, S., & Webster, C. (2020). Robots in tourism: A research agenda for tourism economics. *Tourism Economics*, *26*(7), 1065–1085. doi:10.1177/1354816619879583

Izard, C. E. (2007). Basic Emotions, Natural Kinds, Emotion Schemas, and a New Paradigm. *Perspectives on Psychological Science*, *2*(3), 260–280. doi:10.1111/j.1745-6916.2007.00044.x PMID:26151969

Jardim, M. C., & Pires, L. D. (2022). O Instagram como dispositivo de construção de mercado nas redes sociais: A intimidade distinta como variável central junto aos influenciadores de fitness. *Revista Brasileira de Sociologia*, *10*(24), 144–175. doi:10.20336/rbs.855

Ji, B., Banhazi, T., Phillips, C. J. C., Wang, C., & Li, B. (2022). A machine learning framework to predict the next month's daily milking frequency for cows in robotic dairy farm. *Biosystems Engineering*, *216*, 186–197. doi:10.1016/j.biosystemseng.2022.02.013

Jiménez-Picón, N., Romero-Martín, M., Ponce-Blandón, J. A., Ramirez-Baena, L., Palomo-Lara, J. C., & Gómez-Salgado, J. (2021). The Relationship between Mindfulness and Emotional Intelligence as a Protective Factor for Healthcare Professionals: Systematic Review. *International Journal of Environmental Research and Public Health*, *18*(10), 5491. doi:10.3390/ijerph18105491 PMID:34065519

Johnson, J. (2003). Children, robotics, and education. *Artificial Life and Robotics*, *7*(1-2), 16–21. doi:10.1007/BF02480880

Jones, P. (2020). *The arts therapies: A revolution in healthcare*. Routledge. doi:10.4324/9781315536989

Jothimani, S., & Premalatha, K. (2022). MFF-SAug: Multi-feature fusion with spectrogram augmentation of speech emotion recognition using convolution neural network. *Chaos, Solitons, and Fractals*, *162*, 112512. doi:10.1016/j.chaos.2022.112512

Jung, S., & Won, E. (2018). Systematic Review of Research Trends in Robotics Education for Young Children. *Sustainability (Basel)*, *10*(4), 905. doi:10.3390u10040905

Kaddoura, S., & Al Husseiny, F. (2023). The rising trend of Metaverse in education: Challenges, opportunities, and ethical considerations. *PeerJ. Computer Science*, *9*, e1252. doi:10.7717/peerj-cs.1252 PMID:37346578

Kafetsios, K., & Hess, U. (2023). Reconceptualizing Emotion Recognition Ability. *Journal of Intelligence, 11*(6), 123. . doi:10.3390/jintelligence11060123

Katirai, A. (2023). Ethical considerations in emotion recognition technologies: A review of the literature. *AI and Ethics*. Advance online publication. doi:10.100743681-023-00307-3

Katz, R. (2018). *Capital humano para la transformación digital en América Latina* [Human capital for digital transformation in Latin America]. CEPAL. https://www.cepal.org/es/publicaciones/43529-capital-humano-la-transformacion-digital-america-latina

Kellner, D. (1998). Virilio on Vision Machines: On Paul Virilio, Open Sky. *Film-Philosophy*, *2*(1), 1–15. doi:10.3366/film.1998.0030

Kemper, T. D. (1987). How many emotions are there? Wedding the social and the autonomic components. *American Journal of Sociology*, *93*(2), 263–289. doi:10.1086/228745

Kenyon, K., Kinakh, V., & Harrison, J. (2023). Social virtual reality helps to reduce feelings of loneliness and social anxiety during the Covid-19 pandemic. *Scientific Reports*, *13*(1), 19282. Advance online publication. doi:10.103841598-023-46494-1 PMID:37935718

Kim, H. (2022). Keeping up with influencers: Exploring the impact of social presence and parasocial interactions on Instagram. *International Journal of Advertising*, *41*(3), 414–434. doi:10.1080/02650487.2021.1886477

Kirkwood, K. (2018). Integrating digital media into everyday culinary practices. *Communication Research and Practice*, *4*(3), 277–290. doi:10.1080/22041451.2018.1451210

Kitchenham, B. (2004). *Procedures for performing systematic reviews.* Keele University Technical Report 33.

Klein, H. K., & Myers, M. D. (1999). A set of principles for conducting and evaluating interpretive field studies in information systems. *Management Information Systems Quarterly*, *23*(1), 67–93. doi:10.2307/249410

Klos, M., Escoredo, M., Joerin, A., Lemos, V., Rauws, M., & Bunge, E. (2021). Artificial intelligence-based chatbot for anxiety and depression in university students: Pilot randomised controlled trial. *JMIR Formative Research, 12*(8). doi:10.2196/20678

Koch, C., & Tononi, G. (2008). Can Machines be Conscious? *IEEE Spectrum*, *45*(6), 55–59. doi:10.1109/MSPEC.2008.4531463

Kohn, L., Christiaens, W., Detraux, J., De Lepeleire, J., De Hert, M., Gillain, B., Delaunoit, B., Savoye, I., Mistiaen, P., & Jespers, V. (2022). Barriers to somatic health care for persons with severe mental illness in Belgium: A qualitative study of patients' and healthcare professionals' perspectives. *Frontiers in Psychiatry*, *12*, 798530. doi:10.3389/fpsyt.2021.798530 PMID:35153863

Korsmeyer, C. (2005). Seeing, Believing, Touching, Truth. In The Matrix and Philosophy: welcome to the desert of the real. Open Court.

Korstanje, M. E. (2022). Terrorism, Automated Hosts, and COVID-19: Critical Film Review of the HBO Saga Westworld. In Global Risk and Contingency Management Research in Times of Crisis (pp. 295-308). IGI Global.

Koury, M. (2017). Cultura emotiva e sentimentos de medo na cidade [Emotive culture and sentiments of fear in the city]. *Documentos de Trabajo del CIES*, (8). http://estudiosociologicos.org/portal/wp-content/uploads/2017/09/Documento-de-Trabajo-8-JULIO-2017.pdf

Kuhn, T. S. (1970). *The Structure of Scientific Revolutions. 2*. The University of Chicago Press.

Kuhn, T. S. (1998). *A Estrutura das Revoluções Científicas. 5*. Editora Perspectiva.

Kusal, S., Patil, S., Choudrie, J., Kotecha, K., Vora, D., & Pappas, I. (2023). A systematic review of applications of natural language processing and future challenges with special emphasis on text-based emotion detection. *Artificial Intelligence Review*, *56*(12), 1–87. doi:10.100710462-023-10509-0

Kye, B., Han, N., Kim, E., Park, Y., & Jo, S. (2021). Educational applications of metaverse: Possibilities and limitations. In *Journal of Educational Evaluation for Health Professions* (Vol. 18). Korea Health Personnel Licensing Examination Institute. doi:10.3352/jeehp.2021.18.32

LaGrandeur, K. (2015). Emotion, artificial Intelligence, and ethics. In Topics in intelligent engineering and informatics (pp. 97–109). doi:10.1007/978-3-319-09668-1_7

LaGrandeur, K. (2015). Androids and the Posthuman in Television and Film. In M. Hauskeller, T. D. Philbeck, & C. D. Carbonell (Eds.), *The Palgrave Handbook of Posthumanism in Film and Television* (pp. 111–119). Palgrave Macmillan. doi:10.1057/9781137430328_12

Lai Poh Emily Toh, A., Causo, A., Tzuo, P.-W., Chen, I.-M., & Yeo, S. H. (2016). A Review on the Use of Robots in Education and Young Children. *Journal of Educational Technology & Society*, *19*(2), 148–163.

Lan, L., Sikov, J., Lejeune, J., Ji, C., Brown, H., Bullock, K., & Spencer, A. E. (2023). A Systematic Review of using Virtual and Augmented Reality for the Diagnosis and Treatment of Psychotic Disorders. In Current Treatment Options in Psychiatry (Vol. 10, Issue 2, pp. 87–107). Springer Science and Business Media Deutschland GmbH. doi:10.100740501-023-00287-5

Lara, F., & Rueda, J. (2021). Virtual Reality Not for "Being Someone" but for "Being in Someone Else's Shoes": Avoiding Misconceptions in Empathy Enhancement. *Frontiers in Psychology*, *12*, 741516. Advance online publication. doi:10.3389/fpsyg.2021.741516 PMID:34504468

Lasaponara, S., Marson, F., Doricchi, F., & Cavallo, M. (2021). A scoping review of cognitive training in neurodegenerative diseases via computerized and virtual reality tools: What we know so far. In Brain Sciences (Vol. 11, Issue 5). MDPI AG. doi:10.3390/brainsci11050528

Lavelle, S. (2020). The Machine with a Human Face:From Artificial Intelligence to Artificial Sentience. In S. Dupuy-Chessa & H. Proper (Eds.), *Advanced Information Systems Engineering Workshops. CAiSE 2020. Lecture Notes in Business Information Processing* (Vol. 382). Springer.

Lavis, A. (2017). Food porn, pro-anorexia and the viscerality of virtual affect: Exploring eating in cyberspace. *Geoforum*, *84*, 198–205. doi:10.1016/j.geoforum.2015.05.014

Le Breton, D. (2012). Por una antropología de las emociones [For an anthropology of emotions]. *Revista Latinoamericana de Estudios sobre Cuerpos, Emociones y Sociedad – RELACES, 10*, 69-79. http://www.relaces.com.ar/index.php/relaces/article/view/239

Lee, J. A., Kim, J. G., & Kweon, H. (2023). A Study on Rehabilitation Specialists' Perception of Experience with a Virtual Reality Program. *Healthcare (Basel)*, *11*(6), 814. Advance online publication. doi:10.3390/healthcare11060814 PMID:36981471

Lee, K. (2023). Counseling Psychological Understanding and Considerations of the Metaverse: A Theoretical Review. *Health Care*, *11*(18), 2490. doi:10.3390/healthcare11182490 PMID:37761687

Lee, K. S., & Tao, C. W. (2021). Secretless pastry chefs on Instagram: The disclosure of culinary secrets on social media. *International Journal of Contemporary Hospitality Management*, *33*(2), 650–669. doi:10.1108/IJCHM-08-2020-0895

Lee, T. W., Mitchell, T. R., & Sablynski, C. J. (1999). Qualitative research in organizational and vocational psychology, 1979–1999. *Journal of Vocational Behavior*, *55*(2), 161–187. doi:10.1006/jvbe.1999.1707

Leidl, K. D., Bers, M. U., & Mihm, C. (2017). Programming with ScratchJr: A review of the first year of user analytics. In S. C. Kong, J. Sheldon, & K. Y. Li (Eds.), *Conference Proceedings of International Conference on Computational Thinking Education 2017* (pp. 116–121). The Education University of Hong Kong.

Leveau, P.-H. (2022). *The role of proprioception and gamification in virtual reality experiences on consumer embodiment and behavior*. Academic Press.

Leveau, P. H., & Camus, S. (2023). Embodiment, immersion, and enjoyment in virtual reality marketing experiences. *Psychology and Marketing*, *40*(7), 1329–1343. doi:10.1002/mar.21822

Ley, M., & Rambukkana, N. (2021). Touching at a Distance: Digital Intimacies, Haptic Platforms, and the Ethics of Consent. *Science and Engineering Ethics*, *27*(63), 1–17. doi:10.100711948-021-00338-1 PMID:34546467

Lieberman, A., & Schroeder, J. (2020). Two social lives: How differences between online and offline interaction influence social outcomes. In *Current Opinion in Psychology* (Vol. 31, pp. 16–21). Elsevier B.V., doi:10.1016/j.copsyc.2019.06.022

Lim, A., & Okuno, H. G. (2015). Developing Robot Emotions through Interaction with Caregivers. In *Handbook of Research on Synthesizing Human Emotion in Intelligent Systems and Robotics* (pp. 316–337). IGI Global. doi:10.4018/978-1-4666-7278-9.ch015

Lin, Y. H., Chang, L., Lee, Y. H., Tseng, H. W., Kuo, T. B., & Chen, S. (2014). Development and Validation of the Smartphone Addiction Inventory (SPAI). *PLoS One*, *9*(6), e98312. doi:10.1371/journal.pone.0098312 PMID:24896252

Lisdero, P. (2017). Conflicto social y sensibilidades. Un análisis a partir de las imágenes/observaciones de los saqueos de diciembre de 2013 en la ciudad de Córdoba (Argentina). (Social Conflict and Sensibiilties). In *Geometrías Sociales*. Estudios Sociológicos Editora.

Liu, S., Peng, C., & Srivastava, G. (2023). What Influences Computational Thinking? A Theoretical and Empirical Study Based on the Influence of Learning Engagement on Computational Thinking in Higher Education. *Computer Applications in Engineering Education*, *31*(6), 1690–1704. Advance online publication. doi:10.1002/cae.22669

Lofgren, J. M. (2013). *Changing tastes in food media: a study of recipe sharing traditions in the food blogging community* [Master's thesis]. Queensland University of Technology.

López-Ojeda, W., & Hurley, R. A. (2023). The Medical Metaverse, Part 1: Introduction, Definitions, and New Horizons for Neuropsychiatry. *The Journal of Neuropsychiatry and Clinical Neurosciences*, *35*(1), 1. doi:10.1176/appi.neuropsych.20220187 PMID:36633472

Lopez-Rodriguez, M. M., Fernández-Millan, A., Ruiz-Fernández, M. D., Dobarrio-Sanz, I., & Fernández-Medina, I. M. (2020). New technologies to improve pain, anxiety and depression in children and adolescents with cancer: A systematic review. In International Journal of Environmental Research and Public Health (Vol. 17, Issue 10). doi:10.3390/ijerph17103563

Lo, S. Y., & Lai, C. Y. (2023). Investigating how immersive virtual reality and active navigation mediate the experience of virtual concerts. *Scientific Reports*, *13*(1), 8507. Advance online publication. doi:10.103841598-023-35369-0 PMID:37231095

Love, E. G., Lim, J., & Bednar, M. K. (2017). The face of the firm: The influence of CEOs on corporate reputation. *Academy of Management Journal*, *60*(4), 1462–1481. doi:10.5465/amj.2014.0862

Loveless, A. M. (2002). *Literature Review in Creativity, New Technologies and Learning*. A NESTA Futurelab Research - report 4. https://citeseerx.ist.psu.edu/document?repid=rep1&type=pdf&doi=564bad6c5319dd1443e249af1d95001d7094360c

Luger, G., & Stubblefield, W. (1993). *AI: Structures and strategies for complex problem solving*. Academic Press.

Luhmann, N. (1986). *Love as Passion The Codzfication of Intimacy*. Harvard University Press.

Luhmann, N. (1998). Sistemas Sociales. Lineamientos para una teoría General [Social Systems: Guidelines for a general theory]. *Anthropos.*

Luna Zamora, R. (2007). Emociones y subjetividades. Continuidades y discontinuidades en los modelos culturales [Emotions and subjectivities. Continuities and discontinuities in cultural models]. In R. Luna, & A. Scribano (Comp.), Contigo Aprendí...Estudios Sociales de las Emociones, (pp. 233-247). CEA-CONICET-National University of Córdoba–CUSCH- University of Guadalajara.

Lupton, D. (2017). Digital media and body weight, shape, and size: An introduction and review. *Fat Studies*, *6*(2), 119–134. doi:10.1080/21604851.2017.1243392

Lupton, D. (2021). Afterword: Future methods for digital food studies. In J. Leer & S. G. Strøm Krogager (Eds.), *Research methods in digital food studies*. Routledge.

Lupton, D., & Feldman, Z. (2020). *Digital food cultures*. Routledge. doi:10.4324/9780429402135

Magrabi, F., Habli, I., Sujan, M., Wong, D., Thimbleby, H., Baker, M., & Coiera, E. (2019). Why is it so difficult to govern mobile apps in healthcare? *BMJ Health & Care Informatics*, *26*(1), e100006. doi:10.1136/bmjhci-2019-100006 PMID:31744843

Maldamé, J. M. (2013) Les Défis Éthiques des Nouvelles Technologies à la Lumière de la Doctrine Sociale de L'Église. *RCatT, 38*(1), 261-281. https://www.raco.cat/index.php/RevistaTeologia/article/download/267002/363061/

Management Association. (Ed.). (2022). Research Anthology on Computational Thinking, Programming, and Robotics in the Classroom (2 Volumes). IGI Global. doi:10.4018/978-1-6684-2411-7

Mantello, P., & Ho, T. M. (2023). Emotional AI and the future of well-being in the post-pandemic workplace. *AI & Society*. Advance online publication. doi:10.100700146-023-01639-8 PMID:36776535

Manyika, J., Chui, M., Miremadi, M., Bughin, J., George, K., Willmott, P., & Dewhurst, M. (2017). *A future that works: Automation, employment, and productivity*. McKinsey Global Institute.

Martínez-Miranda, J., & Aldea, A. (2005). Emotions in human and artificial intelligence. *Computers in Human Behavior, 21*(2), 323–341. doi:10.1016/j.chb.2004.02.010

Massetti, M., & Chiariello, G. A. (2023). The metaverse in medicine. *European Heart Journal Supplements, 25*(Supplement_B), B104–B107. doi:10.1093/eurheartjsuppuad083 PMID:37091647

Matamala-Gomez, M., Maselli, A., Malighetti, C., Realdon, O., Mantovani, F., & Riva, G. (2021). Virtual body ownership illusions for mental health: A narrative review. In Journal of Clinical Medicine (Vol. 10, Issue 1). doi:10.3390/jcm10010139

McLuhan, M. (1963). *The Gutenberg Galaxy*. University of Toronto Press.

McStay, A. (2020). Emotional AI, soft biometrics and the surveillance of emotional life: An unusual consensus on privacy. *Big Data & Society, 7*(1), 205395172090438. doi:10.1177/2053951720904386

McSweeney, T., & Joy, S. (2019). Introduction: Read that Back to Yourself and Ask If You Live in a Sane Society. In T. McSweeney & S. Joy (Eds.), *Through the black mirror: deconstructing the side effects of the digital age*. Palgrave Macmillan. doi:10.1007/978-3-030-19458-1_1

Medina, L. (2010). El tercer sector. Imaginación y sensibilidad ante 'La cuestión social' [The third sector. Imagination and sensibility to 'The social question']. *Razón y palabra,* (71).

Medvedev, O. N., & Krägeloh, C. U. (2023). Harnessing Artificial Intelligence for Mindfulness Research and Dissemination: Guidelines for Authors. *Mindfulness, 14*(5), 1019–1020. doi:10.100712671-023-02155-y

Mehmood, A., Bu, T., Zhao, E., Zelenina, V., Alexander, N., Wang, W., Siddiqi, S. M., Qiu, X., Yang, X., Qiao, Z., Zhou, J., & Yang, Y. (2021). Exploration of the psychological mechanism of smartphone addiction among international students of China by selecting the framework of the I-PACE model. Frontiers in Psychology, 12. doi:10.3389/fpsyg.2021.758610

Meissner, G. (2020). Artificial Intelligence: Consciousness and Conscience. *AI & Society, 35*(1), 225–235. doi:10.100700146-019-00880-4

Mengalli, N. M., de Carvalho, A. A., & Galvão, S. M. (2023). Metaverse Ecosystem and Consumer Society 5.0: Consumer Experience and Influencer Marketing in Phygital Transformation. In R. Bansal, S. A. Qalati, & A. Chakir (Eds.), *Influencer Marketing Applications Within the Metaverse* (pp. 33–56). IGI Global. doi:10.4018/978-1-6684-8898-0.ch003

Mijwel, M. (2015). History of Artificial Intelligence. *Computer Science, 1*(1), 1–6.

Miles, M. B., & Huberman, A. M. (1984). *Qualitative Data Analysis.* Sage Publications.

Miller, E., & Polson, D. (2019). Apps, Avatars and Robots: The Future of Mental Healthcare, mindfulness meditation for psychological distress and adjustment to college in incoming university students: A pragmatic, randomised, waitlist-controlled trial. *Psychology & Health, 35*(9), 1049–1074.

Minsky, M. (2007). *The emotion machine: Commonsense thinking, artificial intelligence, and the future of the human mind.* Simon and Schuster.

Miralles, I., Granell, C., Díaz-Sanahuja, L., Van Woensel, W., Bretón-López, J., Mira, A., Castilla, D., & Casteleyn, S. (2020). Smartphone apps for the treatment of mental disorders: Systematic review. *JMIR mHealth and uHealth, 8*(4), e14897. doi:10.2196/14897 PMID:32238332

Mirenayat, S. A., Bahar, I. B., Talif, R., & Mani, M. (2017). Science Fiction and Future Human: Cyborg, Transhuman and Posthuman. *Research Result: Theoretical and Applied Linguistics, 3*(1), 76–81. doi:10.18413/2313-8912-2017-3-1-76-81

Mitra, S., & Rana, M. (2022). A Comparison Study between Nature and Artificial Intelligence in Kazuo Ishiguro's Klara and the Sun. *European Chemical Bulletin, 12*(5), 582–589.

Moos, M., & McLuhan, M. (2014). *Media research: Technology, art and communication.* Routledge.

Morais, F., & Jaques, P. A. (2023). The dynamics of Brazilian students' emotions in digital learning systems. *International Journal of Artificial Intelligence in Education.* Advance online publication. doi:10.100740593-023-00339-0

Moreno Padilla, R. (2019). La llegada de la inteligencia artificial a la educación [The arrival of artificial intelligence in education]. *Revista de Investigación en Tecnologías de la información, 7*(14), 260–270. doi:10.36825/RITI.07.14.022

Moreno-Ligero, M. (2023). *mHealth intervention for improving patients with chronic pain.* Academic Press.

Morin, E. (1956). *Le Cinéma ou L'homme Imaginaire: Essai d'Anthropologie Sociologique.* Les Éditions de Minuit.

Morrow, E., Zidaru, T., Ross, F., Mason, C., Patel, K. D., Ream, M., & Stockley, R. (2023). Artificial intelligence technologies and compassion in healthcare: A systematic scoping review. *Frontiers in Psychology, 13*, 971044. https://www.frontiersin.org/articles/10.3389/fpsyg.2022.971044/full

Mubin, O., Stevens, C. J., Shahid, S., Al Mahmud, A., & Dong, J. (2013). A review of the applicability of robots in education. *Technology for Education and Learning*, *1*(1), 1–7. doi:10.2316/Journal.209.2013.1.209-0015

Mukhiddinov, M., Djuraev, O., Akhmedov, F., Mukhamadiyev, A., & Cho, J. (2023). Masked Face Emotion Recognition Based on Facial Landmarks and Deep Learning Approaches for Visually Impaired People. *Sensors (Basel)*, *23*(3), 1080. doi:10.339023031080 PMID:36772117

Mulligan, K., & Scherer, K. R. (2012). Toward a working definition of emotion. *Emotion Review*, *4*(4), 345–357. doi:10.1177/1754073912445818

Nagao Menezes, D. F. (2020). Las perspectivas del trabajo en la sociedad 4.0. *Revista Nacional de Administración*, *11*(1), 11–19. doi:10.22458/rna.v11i1.3011

Naisbitt, J. (1994). Global paradox: The bigger the world economy, the more powerful its smallest players. *Journal of Leisure Research*, *26*(4), 406–420. doi:10.1080/00222216.1994.11969972

Naremore, J. (2005) Love and death in A.I. Artificial Intelligence. *Michigan Quarterly Review*, *44*(2). http://hdl.handle.net/2027/spo.act2080.0044.210

Nash, C., & Gorman-Murray, A. (Eds.). (2019). *The Geographies of Digital Sexuality*. Palgrave Macmillan Singapore., doi:10.1007/978-981-13-6876-9

NayarP. K. (2014). *Posthumanism*. Polity.

Neary, M., & Schueller, S. M. (2018). State of the field of mental health apps. *Cognitive and Behavioral Practice*, *25*(4), 531–537. doi:10.1016/j.cbpra.2018.01.002 PMID:33100810

Neffen, G. (2016). *An app for managing dairy farms from your mobile*. Clarín. https://www.clarin.com/rural/aplicacion-gestionar-tambo-celu
lar_0_r1gC45QWx.html

Nester, M. S., Hawkins, S. L., & Brand, B. L. (2022). Barriers to accessing and continuing mental health treatment among individuals with dissociative symptoms. *European Journal of Psychotraumatology*, *13*(1), 2031594. doi:10.1080/20008198.2022.2031594 PMID:35186217

Ng, G. W., & Leung, W. C. (2020). Strong Artificial Intelligence and Consciousness. *Journal of Artificial Intelligence and Consciousness*, *7*(1), 63–72. doi:10.1142/S2705078520300042

Nietzsche, F. (1974). The gay science (W. Kaufmann, Trans.). Vintage.

Nixon, M. D. (2005). The Matrix possibility. In W. Irwin (Ed.), *The Matrix and Philosophy: welcome to the desert of the real* (pp. 16–27). Open Court.

Ocaña-Fernández, Y., Valenzuela-Fernández, L., & Garro-Aburto, L. (2019). Inteligencia artificial y sus implicaciones en la educación superior [Artificial intelligence and its implications in higher education]. *Propósitos y Representaciones*, *7*(2), 536–568. doi:10.20511/pyr2019.v7n2.274

Oducado, R., Parreño-Lachica, G. & Rabacal, J. (2021). Estrés percibido debido a la pandemia de COVID-19 entre los profesores profesionales empleados [Perceived stress due to the COVID-19 pandemic among employed professional teachers]. *IJERI: Revista internacional de investigación e innovación educativas, 15*, 305-316. doi:10.46661/ijeri.5284

OECD. (2018). *Future of Education and Skills 2030: Conceptual Learning Framework.* Education and AI: preparing for the future & AI, Attitudes and Values. 8th Informal Working Group (IWG) Meeting (29-31 October 2018), OECD Conference Centre, Paris, France. https://www.oecd.org/education/2030/Education-and-AI-preparing-for-the-future-AI-Attitudes-and-Values.pdf

OECD. (2022). *Framework for the classification of AI systems. OECD Digital economy papers, number 323.* OECD Publishing.

Omboni, S., Padwal, R. S., Alessa, T., Benczúr, B., Green, B. B., Hubbard, I., Kario, K., Khan, N. A., Konradi, A., Logan, A. G., Lu, Y., Mars, M., McManus, R. J., Melville, S., Neumann, C. L., Parati, G., Renna, N. F., Ryvlin, P., Saner, H., ... Wang, J. (2022). The worldwide impact of telemedicine during COVID-19: Current evidence and recommendations for the future. *Connected Health.* Advance online publication. doi:10.20517/ch.2021.03 PMID:35233563

Otzen, T., & Manterola, C. (2017). Técnicas de Muestreo sobre una Población a Estudio. *International Journal of Morphology, 35*(1), 227–232. doi:10.4067/S0717-95022017000100037

Page, M. J., McKenzie, J. E., Bossuyt, P. M., Boutron, I., Hoffmann, T., & Mulrow, C. (2021). The PRISMA 2020 statement: An updated guideline for reporting systematic reviews. *British Medical Journal, 372*(71). https://doi.org/. n71 doi:10.1136/bmj

Palermo, H., Radetich, N., Reygadas, L. (2020). Work mediated by digital technologies: meanings of work, new forms of control, and cyborg workers. *Latin American Journal of Labor Anthropology, 7.*

Pallone, S. (2008). Minority Report: A Nova Lei. *ComCiência*, 104. http://comciencia.scielo.br/pdf/cci/n104/a12n104.pdf

Papadakis, S., & Kalogiannakis, M. (Eds.). (2021). *Handbook of Research on Using Educational Robotics to Facilitate Student Learning.* IGI Global., doi:10.4018/978-1-7998-6717-3

Papert, S. A. (1993). *Mindstorms: Children, Computers, and Powerful Ideas.* Basic Books.

Park, S. M., & Kim, Y. G. (2022). A Metaverse: Taxonomy, Components, Applications, and Open Challenges. *IEEE Access : Practical Innovations, Open Solutions, 10*, 4209–4251. doi:10.1109/ACCESS.2021.3140175

Patiño-Vanegas, J., Mardones-Espinosa, R., Garcés-Giraldo, L., Valencia-Arias, A., & Rango-Botero, D. (2023). Tendencias investigativas frente al uso de Inteligencia Artificial en contextos universitarios [Research trends regarding the use of Artificial Intelligence in university context]. *Revista Ibérica de Sistemas e Tecnologias de Informação, 59*, 245–260.

Paul, G. (2004, April 23). *Artificial Intelligence and Consciousness.* 2nd Human-E-Tech Conference, SUNY Albany.

Pauly, T., Nicol, A., Lay, J. C., Ashe, M. C., Gerstorf, D., Graf, P., Linden, W., Madden, K. M., Mahmood, A., Murphy, R. A., & Hoppmann, C. A. (2023). Everyday Pain in Middle and Later Life: Associations with Daily and Momentary Present-Moment Awareness as One Key Facet of Mindfulness. *Canadian Journal on Aging*, *42*(4), 1–10. doi:10.1017/S0714980823000326 PMID:37565431

Perdigón Llanes, R., & González Benítez, N. (2021). Comparison and selection of artificial intelligence techniques for forecasting bovine milk production. *Cuban Journal of Computer Science*, *15*(2), 24–43.

Pérez, T. H. P. (2013). Aproximaciones al estado de la cuestión de la investigación en educación y derechos humanos [Approaches to the state of the art of research in education and human rights]. *Revista Interamericana de Investigación. Educación y Pedagogía, RIIEP*, *6*(1). Advance online publication. doi:10.153321657-107X.2013.0001.05

Petrigna, L., & Musumeci, G. (2022). The Metaverse: A New Challenge for the Healthcare System: A Scoping Review. In Journal of Functional Morphology and Kinesiology (Vol. 7, Issue 3). MDPI. doi:10.3390/jfmk7030063

Piedrahíta-Carvajal, P., Rodríguez-Marín, D., Terraza-Arciniegas, M., Amaya-Gómez, L., Duque-Muñoz, J., & Martínez-Vargas, D. (2021). Aplicación web para el análisis de emociones y atención de estudiantes. *TecnoLógicas*, *24*(51), e1821. doi:10.22430/22565337.1821

Pivetti, M., Di Battista, S., Agatolio, F., Simaku, B., Moro, M., & Menegatti, E. (2020). Educational Robotics for Children with Neurodevelopmental Disorders: A Systematic Review. *Heliyon*, *6*(10), e05160. doi:10.1016/j.heliyon.2020.e05160 PMID:33072917

Ponce de Leon, C., Mano, L., Fernandes, D., Paula, R., & Ribeiro, L. (2023). Artificial intelligence in the analysis of emotions of nursing students undergoing clinical simulation. *Revista Brasileira de Enfermagem*, *76*(4, suppl 4), e20210909. doi:10.1590/0034-7167-2021-0909 PMID:37075358

Popova, A., Evans, D., Breeding, M., & Arancibia, V. (2018). Teacher Professional Development around the World: The Gap between Evidence and Practice. *IDEAS Working Paper Series from RePEc*.

Powell, K., Wilcox, J., Clonan, A., Bissell, P., Preston, L., Peacock, M., & Holdworth, M. (2015). The role of social networks in the development of overweight and obesity among adults: A scoping review. *BMC Public Health*, *15*(1), 996. doi:10.118612889-015-2314-0 PMID:26423051

Priyadarshini, I., & Cotton, C. (2022). Ai cannot understand memes: Experiments with ocr and facial emotions. *Computers, Materials & Continua*, *70*(1), 781–800. doi:10.32604/cmc.2022.019284

Quaranta, G. (2000). Production restructuring and functional flexibility of agricultural work in Argentina. *Latin American Journal of Labor Studies*, *6*(12), 45–70.

Ramírez-Montoya, M., Castillo-Martínez, I., Sanabria-Zepeda, J., & Miranda, J. (2022). Complex thinking in the framework of education 4.0 and open innovation. A systematic literature review. *Journal of Open Innovation*, *8*(4), 4. Advance online publication. doi:10.3390/joitmc8010004

Ravenswood, K. (2011). Eisenhardt's impact on theory in case study research. *Journal of Business Research*, *64*(7), 680–686. doi:10.1016/j.jbusres.2010.08.014

Rawtaer, I., Mahendran, R., Yu, J., Fam, J., Feng, L., & Kua, E. H. (2015). Psychosocial interventions with art, music, T ai Chi and mindfulness for subsyndromal depression and anxiety in older adults: A naturalistic study in Singapore. *Asia-Pacific Psychiatry*, *7*(3), 240–250. doi:10.1111/appy.12201 PMID:26178378

Raymond, E. S. (1999). *The Cathedral & the Bazaar: Musings on Linux and Open Source by an Accidental Revolutionary*. O'Reilly Media. doi:10.100712130-999-1026-0

ReportM. (2002). https://www.youtube.com/watch?v=Dv6jgzcMu0Y

Rheingold, H. (1985). *Tools for thought*. MIT Press. http://www.rheingold.com/texts/tft/

Riva, G., & Gaggioli, A. (2019). Realtà virtuali: aspetti psicologici delle esperienze simulative ed il loro impatto sull'esperienza umana. Giunti Editore.

Riva, G., & Serino, S. (2020). Virtual reality in the assessment, understanding and treatment of mental health disorders. In Journal of Clinical Medicine (Vol. 9, Issue 11, pp. 1–9). MDPI. doi:10.3390/jcm9113434

Riva, G., Malighetti, C., & Serino, S. (2021). Virtual reality in the treatment of eating disorders. *Clinical Psychology & Psychotherapy*, *28*(3), 477–488. doi:10.1002/cpp.2622 PMID:34048622

Riva, G., Wiederhold, B. K., & Mantovani, F. (2019). Neuroscience of Virtual Reality: From Virtual Exposure to Embodied Medicine. *Cyberpsychology, Behavior, and Social Networking*, *22*(1), 82–96. doi:10.1089/cyber.2017.29099.gri PMID:30183347

Rodrigues, C. (2022). *25 años de TED ENTRAMAR. Nuestra trayectoria docente para docentes Programa de Tecnología Educativa Digital* [25 years of TED ENTRAMAR. Our teaching career for teachers. Digital Educational Technology Program]. Secretaria de Educación y Empleo, Municipalidad de Vicente López.

Rodríguez, A., Rey, B., Clemente, M., Wrzesien, M., & Alcañiz, M. (2015). Assessing brain activations associated with emotional regulation during virtual reality mood induction procedures. *Expert Systems with Applications*, *42*(3), 1699–1709. doi:10.1016/j.eswa.2014.10.006

Rotz, S., Duncan, E., Small, M., Botschner, J., Dara, R., Mosby, I., Reed, M., & Fraser, E. (2019). The Politics of Digital Agricultural Technologies: A Preliminary Review. *Sociologia Ruralis*, *59*(2), 203–229. doi:10.1111oru.12233

Rouhiainen, L. (2018). *Artificial Intelligence*. Alienta Editorial.

RunnerB. (1982). https://www.warnerbros.com/movies/blade-runner

Sáez, J. M., & Cózar, R. (2017). Pensamiento computacional y programación visual por bloques en el aula de Primaria [Computational thinking and visual block programming in the Primary classroom]. *Educar*, *53*(1), 129–146. doi:10.5565/rev/educar.841

Sahu, O. P., & Karmakar, M. (2022). Disposable culture, posthuman affect, and artificial human in Kazuo Ishiguro's Klara and the Sun (2021). *AI & Society*. Advance online publication. doi:10.100700146-022-01600-1 PMID:36465191

Salas-Pilco, S., & Yang, Y. (2022). Artificial intelligence applications in Latin American higher education: A systematic review. *International Journal of Educational Technology in Higher Education, 19*(21), 21. Advance online publication. doi:10.118641239-022-00326-w

Salmons, J. (2016). *Choosing methodologies and methods for online studies*. SAGE Publications. doi:10.4135/9781473921955.n2

Sarah, F., & Maricel, O. (2013). *Age and Ageing in Contemporary Speculative and Science Fiction*. Bloomsbury.

Saunders, R. (2019). Computer-generated pornography and convergence: Animation and algorithms as new digital desire. *Convergence (London), 25*(2), 241–259. doi:10.1177/1354856519833591

Saurí, J. (1984). *The phobias*. New Vision.

Sautu, R. (2005). *Manual de metodología: construcción del marco teórico, formulación de los objetivos y elección de la metodología*. Consejo Latinoamericano de Ciencias Sociales, CLACSO.

Schalkoff, R. J. (1990). *Artificial intelligence engine*. McGraw-Hill, Inc.

Schicktanz, S., Welsch, J., Schweda, M., Hein, A., Rieger, J. W., & Kirste, T. (2023). AI-assisted ethics? Considerations of AI simulation for the ethical assessment and design of assistive technologies. *Frontiers in Genetics, 14*, 1039839. Advance online publication. doi:10.3389/fgene.2023.1039839 PMID:37434952

Schneider, T., & Eli, K. (2021). Fieldwork in online foodscapes: How to bring an ethnographic approach to studies of digital food and digital eating. In J. Leer & S. G. Strøm Krogager (Eds.), *Research methods in digital food studies* (pp. 71–85). Routledge.

Schopp, A. (2019). Making Room for Our Personal Posthuman Prisons: Black Mirror's "Be Right Back". In T. McSweeney & S. Joy (Eds.), *Through the black mirror: deconstructing the side effects of the digital age*. Palgrave Macmillan. doi:10.1007/978-3-030-19458-1_5

Scribano, A. & Mairano, V. (2021) Narratives, emotions and artificial intelligence: a reading of artificial intelligence from emotions. *Springer Nature Switzerland*. doi:10.1007/s43545-021-00237-z

Scribano, A. (2012). Sociología de los cuerpos/emociones [Sociology of bodies/Emotions]. In *Revista Latinoamericana de Estudios sobre Cuerpos, Emociones y Sociedad - RELACES*. http://www.relaces.com.ar/index.php/relaces/article/view/224

Scribano, A. (2012). Sociología de los cuerpos/emociones [Sociology of bodies/emotions]. *RELACES, 10*, 93-113. https://dialnet.unirioja.es/servlet/articulo?codigo=6981013

Scribano, A. (2013). Una aproximación conceptual a la moral del disfrute: normalización, consumo y espectáculo. *RBSE – Revista Brasileira de Sociologia da Emoção*, *12*(36), 738-750.

Scribano, A. (2015). Sociabilidades, vivencialidades y sensibilidades: aproximar, alejar, suprimir [Socialibity, experiences and sensibilities]. Revista Cuerpos, emociones y sociedad, 7(17).

Scribano, A. (2023). *Emotions in a digital world: Social Research 4.0.* Routledge.

Scribano, A., & Lisdero, P. (2019) Digital gaze and visual experience. In Digital Labour, Society and the Politics of Sensibilities. Palgrave-Macmillan. doi:10.1007/978-3-030-12306-2_2

Scribano, A. (2012). Sociología de los cuerpos/emociones. *Revista Latinoamericana de Estudios sobre Cuerpos, Emociones y Sociedad, 10*(4), 91–111.

Scribano, A. (2012). Sociology of Bodies/Emotions. *Latin American Journal of Studies on Bodies, Emotions, and Society*, *4*(10), 91–111.

Scribano, A. (2013). Expressive creative encounters: A strategy for sociological research of expressiveness. *Global Journal of Human Social Science*, *13*(5), 33–38. doi:10.4324/9781003319771-7

Scribano, A. (2017). Instaimagen: Mirar tocando para sentir. *RBSE Revista Brasileira de Sociologia da Emoção*, *16*(47), 45–55.

Scribano, A. (2017). *Normalization, enjoyment and bodies/emotions: Argentine sensibilities.* Nova Science Publishers.

Scribano, A. (2017). *Normalization, Enjoyment and Bodies/Emotions: Argentines Sensibilities.* Nova Science Publications.

Scribano, A. (2019). Confianza en la sociedad 4.0. (The social trust in Society 4.0). In *Confianza y políticas de las sensibilidades* (pp. 147–168). Estudios Sociológicos Editora.

Scribano, A. (2019). Introduction: Politics of Sensibilities, Society 4.0 and Digital Labour. In A. Scribano & P. Lisdero (Eds.), *Digital labor, Society and Politics of Sensibilities* (pp. 1–18). Palgrave Macmillan. doi:10.1007/978-3-030-12306-2_1

Scribano, A. (2020). *Love as a collective action. Latin America, Emotions and Interstitial Practices*. Routledge.

Scribano, A. (2020). *Love as a Collective Action*. Routledge.

Scribano, A. (2021). ¡¡¡Sabor a bit!!!: Algunas conclusiones (adelantadas) sobre el impacto sociológico de la Food Tech. *Aposta, Revista de Ciencias Sociales. Núm.*, *90*, 12–31.

Scribano, A. (2022). Digital Creative Experiences. In A. Scribano, M. E. Korstanje, & A. Rafele (Eds.), *Global Emotion Communications* (pp. 223–242). Nova Science Publications.

Scribano, A. (2022). *Emotions in a digital world. Social Research 4.0.* Routledge. doi:10.4324/9781003319771

Scribano, A. (2023). *Emotions in a digital world: social research 4.0*. Routledge.

Scribano, A. O. (2007). *El proceso de investigación social cualitativo*. Ed. Prometeo.

Scribano, A., & Boragnio, A. (2021). Presentación del monográfico: El comer del siglo XXI: sensibilidades y prácticas alimentarias. *Aposta, Revista de Ciencias Sociales*, *90*, 8–11.

Scribano, A., & Duperré, J. (2021). Die Alone in Argentina: A View from Sensibilities in Times of the Pandemic. In K. Maximiliano & A. Scribano (Eds.), *Emotionality of COVID-19. Now and After: The War Against a Virus*. Nova Science Publishers.

Scribano, A., & Lisdero, P. (2019). *Digital Labour, society and the politics of sensibilities*. Palgrave Macmillan. doi:10.1007/978-3-030-12306-2

Scribano, A., & Mairano, M. V. (2021). *Narratives, Emotions and Artificial Intelligence. A reading of Artificial Intelligence from emotions. SN Social Sciences*. Springer.

Selvarajan, S., Srivastava, G., Khadidos, A. O., Khadidos, A. O., Baza, M., Alshehri, A., & Lin, J. C. W. (2023). An artificial intelligence lightweight blockchain security model for security and privacy in IIoT systems. *Journal of Cloud Computing (Heidelberg, Germany)*, *12*(1), 38. doi:10.118613677-023-00412-y PMID:36937654

Semensato, C. S. D. S. (2022). *The use of robotics in dairy cattle management in the Taquari Valley*. Academic Press.

Senneseth, M., Pollak, C., Urheim, R., Logan, C., & Palmstierna, T. (2022). Personal recovery and its challenges in forensic mental health: Systematic review and thematic synthesis of the qualitative literature. *BJPsych Open*, *8*(1), e17. doi:10.1192/bjo.2021.1068 PMID:34915963

Sestino, A., & D'Angelo, A. (2023). My doctor is an avatar! The effect of anthropomorphism and emotional receptivity on individuals' intention to use digital-based healthcare services. *Technological Forecasting and Social Change*, *191*, 122505. doi:10.1016/j.techfore.2023.122505

Shaw-Garlock, G. (2010). *Loving Machines: Theorizing Human and Sociable-Technology Interaction. International Conference on Human-Robot Personal Relationship*, Berlin, Germany.

Shelke, N., Chaudhury, S., Chakrabarti, S., Bangalore, S. L., Yogapriya, G., & Pandey, P. (2022). An efficient way of text-based emotion analysis from social media using LRA-DNN. *Neuroscience Informatics (Online)*, *2*(3), 100048. doi:10.1016/j.neuri.2022.100048

Shikhar, D., & Ray, K. S. (2022). Role Of 'Artificial' Hope At The Failure Of Medical Science: A Study Of Kazuo Ishiguro's Klara And The Sun. *Journal of Pharmaceutical Negative Results*, *13*(8), 1012–1015. https://doi.org/ doi:10.47750/pnr.2022.13.S08.126

Sibilia, P. (2008). *La intimidad como espectáculo*. Fondo de Cultura Económica.

Sibilia, P. (2013). El artista como espectáculo: Autenticidad y performance en la sociedad mediática. *Dixit*, (18), 4–19. doi:10.22235/d.v0i18.360

Siggelkow, N. (2007). Persuasion with case studies. *Academy of Management Journal*, *50*(1), 20–24. doi:10.5465/amj.2007.24160882

Simon, B. (2003). Introduction: Toward a Critique of Posthuman Futures. *Cultural Critique*, *53*(1), 1–9. doi:10.1353/cul.2003.0028

Sims, C. A. (2013). *Tech Anxiety: Artificial Intelligence and Ontological Awakening in Four Science Fiction Novels*. McFarland & Company, Inc.

Sim, W.-C. (2005). Kazuo Ishiguro. *Review of Contemporary Fiction*, *25*(1), 80–115.

Singh, A. D. (2023, October 16). *Anthropomorphism and Social Robotics in Kazuo Ishiguro's Klara and the Sun (2021). IEEE Humanitarian Technology Conference*, Rajkot.

Singler, B. (2020). Artificial Intelligence and the Parent–Child Narrative. In S. Cave, K. Dihal, & S. Dillon (Eds.), *AI Narratives A History of Imaginative Thinking about Intelligent Machines* (pp. 260–283). Oxford University Press. doi:10.1093/oso/9780198846666.003.0012

Slater, M. (2018). Immersion and the illusion of presence in virtual reality. In British Journal of Psychology (Vol. 109, Issue 3, pp. 431–433). John Wiley and Sons Ltd. doi:10.1111/bjop.12305

Slutsker, B., Konichezky, A., & Gothelf, D. (2010). Breaking the cycle: Cognitive behavioural therapy and biofeedback training in a case of cyclic vomiting syndrome. *Psychology Health and Medicine*, *15*(6), 625–631. doi:10.1080/13548506.2010.498893 PMID:21154016

Šmahel, D., Macháčková, H., Šmahelová, M., Čevelíček, M., Almenara, C. A., & Holubčíková, J. (2018). Digital technology, eating behaviors, and eating disorders. In *Digital Technology*. Eating Behaviors, and Eating Disorders. doi:10.1007/978-3-319-93221-7

Smith, M. J. (2018). Getting value from artificial intelligence in agriculture. *Animal Production Science*, *60*(1), 46–54. doi:10.1071/AN18522

Sorensen, G. (1995). Global Paradox. *Bulletin of the Atomic Scientists*, *51*(4), 69–73.

Sossa Azuela, J. H. (2020). *El papel de la Inteligencia Artificial en la industria 4.0* [The Role of AI in the industry 4.0]. Universidad Nacional Autónoma de México. Disponible en: https://ru.iibi.unam.mx/jspui/bitstream/IIBI_UNAM/89/1/01_inteligencia_artificial_juan_sossa.pdf

Srnicek, N. (2017). *Platform Capitalism*. Polity Press.

Stam, K. R., & Stanton, J. M. (2010). Events, emotions, and technology: Examining acceptance of workplace technology changes. *Information Technology & People*, *23*(1), 23–53. doi:10.1108/09593841011022537

Statement, P. R. I. S. M. A. (2021). *PRISMA endorsers*. http://www.prisma-statement.org/?AspxAutoDetectCookieSupport=1

Steinhoff, J. (2022). Toward a political economy of synthetic data: A data-intensive capitalism that is not a surveillance capitalism? *New Media & Society*, *0*(0), 1–17. doi:10.1177/14614448221099217

Strauss, A., & Corbin, J. (1998). *Basics of Qualitative Research: Techniques and Procedures for Developing Grounded Theory*. Sage Publications.

Strawhacker, A., & Bers, M. U. (2015). "I want my robot to look for food": Comparing Kindergartner's programming comprehension using tangible, graphic, and hybrid user interfaces. *International Journal of Technology and Design Education*, *25*(3), 293–319. doi:10.100710798-014-9287-7

Sullivan, A., & Bers, M. U. (2016). Robotics in the early childhood classroom: Learning outcomes from an 8-week robotics curriculum in pre-kindergarten through second grade. *International Journal of Technology and Design Education*, *26*(1), 3–20. doi:10.100710798-015-9304-5

Sullivan, A., Strawhacker, A., & Bers, M. U. (2017). Dancing, Drawing, and Dramatic Robots: Integrating Robotics and the Arts to Teach Foundational STEAM Concepts to Young Children. In M. S. Khine (Ed.), *Robotics in STEM Education: Redesigning the Learning Experience* (pp. 231–260). Springer International Publishing. doi:10.1007/978-3-319-57786-9_10

Sunkel, G. (2006). Las tecnologías de la información y de la comunicación (TIC) en la educación en América Latina. Una exploración de indicadores [Information and communication technologies (ICT) in education in Latin America. An exploration of indicators]. CEPAL.

Tang, X., Yin, Y., Lin, Q., Hadad, R., & Zhai, X. (2020). Assessing Computational Thinking: A Systematic Review of Empirical Studies. *Computers & Education*, *148*(April), 103798. doi:10.1016/j.compedu.2019.103798

Tariq, S., Iftikhar, A., Chaudhary, P., & Khurshid, K. (2022). Examining Some Serious Challenges and Possibility of AI Emulating Human Emotions, Consciousness, Understanding and 'Self'. *Journal of NeuroPhilosophy*, *1*(1), 55–75.

Taylor, S. J., Bogdan, R., & DeVault, M. L. (2016). Introduction to Qualitative Research Methods: A Guidebook and Resource. Wiley. Technology's Generational Moment with Generative AI: A CIO and CTO Guide. *McKinsey Digital*. https://www.mckinsey.com/capabilities/mckinsey-digital/our-insights/technologys-generational-moment-with-generative-ai-a-cio-and-cto-guide#/

Telotte, J. (2016). *Robot ecology and the science fiction film*. Routledge. doi:10.4324/9781315625775

Thakur, R., Hsu, S. H. Y., & Fontenot, G. (2012). Innovation in healthcare: Issues and future trends. *Journal of Business Research*, *65*(4), 562–569. doi:10.1016/j.jbusres.2011.02.022

The Matrix. (1999). Dir. The Wachowskis. English, 136 minutes. Warner Bros.

The Matrix. (1999). https://www.warnerbros.com/movies/matrix

The Terminator. (1984) https://www.primevideo.com/detail/The-Terminator/0L8IKW4SVSHPR66WSIZOEEAFYX/ref=atv_nb_lcl_pt_BR?ie=UTF8&language=pt_BR

The Terminator. (1984). *Dir James Cameron. English, 107 minutes*. Hemdale & Pacific Western Productions.

Tian, F., Hua, M., Zhang, W., Li, Y., & Yang, X. (2021). Emotional arousal in 2D versus 3D virtual reality environments. *PLoS ONE, 16*(9). doi:10.1371/journal.pone.0256211

Tilmes, N. (2022). Disability, fairness, and algorithmic bias in AI recruitment. *Ethics and Information Technology*, *24*(2), 21. doi:10.100710676-022-09633-2

Todo Lechería. (2022). *By the end of 2023, there will be around 300 milking robots in Argentina*. https://www.todolecheria.com.ar/a-fines-de-2023-habra-unos-300-robots-ordenando-en-argentina/

Todo Lechería. (2023). *Artificial intelligence applied to detect lame cows*. https://www.todolecheria.com.ar/aplican-inteligencia-artificial-para-detectar-vacas-rengas/

Trnka, R. (2023). Emotional Creativity: Emotional Experience as Creative Product. In *The Cambridge Handbook of Creativity and Emotions* (pp. 321-339). Cambridge University Press. https://ssrn.com/abstract=4578762

Tsamitros, N., Beck, A., Sebold, M., Schouler-Ocak, M., Bermpohl, F., & Gutwinski, S. (2023). The application of virtual reality in the treatment of mental disorders. *Der Nervenarzt*, *94*(1), 27–33. Advance online publication. doi:10.100700115-022-01378-z PMID:36053303

Turing, A. (1950). Computing Machinery and Intelligence. *Mind*, *59*(236), 433–460. doi:10.1093/mind/LIX.236.433

Turkle, S. (1984). *The Second Self: Computers and the Human Spirit*. Simon and Schuster.

Turner, J. H., & Stets, J. E. (2006). Sociological Theories of Human Emotions. *Annual Review of Sociology*, *32*(1), 25–52. doi:10.1146/annurev.soc.32.061604.123130

Twenge, J. M., Spitzberg, B. H., & Campbell, W. K. (2019). Less in-person social interaction with peers among U.S. adolescents in the 21st century and links to loneliness. *Journal of Social and Personal Relationships*, *36*(6), 1892–1913. doi:10.1177/0265407519836170

UNESCO. (2019). *El aporte de la inteligencia artificial y las TIC avanzadas a las sociedades del conocimiento: una perspectiva de derechos, apertura, acceso y múltiples actores* [Contribution of artificial intelligence and advanced ICT to knowledge societies: a perspective of rights, openness, access and multiple actors]. UNESCO.

Usmani, S. S., Sharath, M., & Mehendale, M. (2022). Future of mental health in the metaverse. *General Psychiatry*, *35*(4), e100825. doi:10.1136/gpsych-2022-100825 PMID:36189180

Van Dijk, J. A. (1999). The one-dimensional network society of Manuel Castells. *New Media & Society*, *1*(1), 127–138. doi:10.1177/1461444899001001015

Vergara, G., Fraire, V., Manavella, A., & Salessi, S. (2021). Prácticas, percepciones y emociones de docentes de Argentina en tiempos de pandemia Covid-19 [Practices, perceptions and emotions of teachers in Argentina in times of the Covid-19 pandemic]. *International Journal of Educational Research and Innovation*, *15*(15), 568–584. doi:10.46661/ijeri.5903

Vesci, M., Feola, R., Parente, R., & Radjou, N. (2021). How to save the world during a pandemic event. A case study of frugal innovation. *R & D Management*, *51*(4), 352–363. doi:10.1111/radm.12459

Villani, D., Grassi, A., & Riva, G. (2011). *Tecnologie emotive. nuovi media per migliorare la qualita' della vita e ridurre lo stress*. LED.

Vint, S. (2007). *Bodies of Tomorrow: Technology, Subjectivity, Science Fiction*. University of Toronto Press.

Virgen, D. (2015, October 14). *An explorative study on Instagram and food from the cook's perspective*. PALIM Food Heritage and Culinary Practices, Paris, France.

Virilio, P. (1995). Speed and information: cyberspace alarm! *Ctheory, 18*(3), 8-27.

Virilio, P., & Wilson, L. (1994). Cyberwar, god and television: Interview with Paul Virilio. *Ctheory, 21-31.*

Virilio, P. (2004). *The Paul Virilio Reader*. Columbia University Press.

Virtual Robot Curriculum. (2023). *Carnegie Mellon Robotics Academy*. Carnegie Mellon University. https://www.cmu.edu/roboticsacademy/roboticscurriculum/virtual_curriculum/index.html?gclid=CjwKCAjw6p-oBhAYEiwAgg2PgkINQEfNtqDEcnGTAkWBOUPgrgVn8i6xJrfI78ieS7uf1S09wU010hoCZ_gQAvD_BwE

Wallace, J. (2010). Literature and Posthumanism. *Literature Compass*, *7*(8), 692–701. doi:10.1111/j.1741-4113.2010.00723.x

Walsh, E., & Oakley, D. A. (2022). Editing reality in the brain. In Neuroscience of Consciousness (Vol. 2022, Issue 1). Oxford University Press. doi:10.1093/nc/niac009

Waltz, D. (1999). Perspectivas de la construcción de máquinas verdaderamente inteligentes. (The assemblage of machine in motion). In *The Artificial Intelligence debate: False Starts, Real Foundations* (pp. 218–242). Gedisa.

Wamba-Taguimdje, S. L., Fosso Wamba, S., Kala Kamdjoug, J. R., & Tchatchouang Wanko, C. E. (2020). Influence of artificial intelligence (AI) on firm performance: The business value of AI-based transformation projects. *Business Process Management Journal*, *26*(7), 1893–1924. doi:10.1108/BPMJ-10-2019-0411

Wang, E. F., & Jotwani, R. (2023). Virtual reality therapy for myofascial pain: Evolving towards an evidence-based non-pharmacologic adjuvant intervention. *Interventional Pain Medicine*, *2*(1), 100181. Advance online publication. doi:10.1016/j.inpm.2023.100181

Westworld. (1973). https://www.primevideo.com/detail/Westworld/0LY2YLBLMHJPEIZ6JDEXESBUW3

Westworld. (2016). Dir. Michael Crichton. English, 4 seasons, HBO TV.

Westworld. (2016). https://www.hbo.com/westworld

Why Some People Are More Likely to Become Lonely | Psychology Today. (n.d.). Retrieved January 22, 2022, from https://www.psychologytoday.com/us/blog/finding-new-home/202112/why-some-people-are-more-likely-become-lonely

Williams, S. (2021) Artificial Intelligence in the new era. *Int J Innov Sci Res Technol, 6*(4).

Williams, T. A., Gruber, D. A., Sutcliffe, K. M., Shepherd, D. A., & Zhao, E. Y. (2017). Organizational response to adversity: Fusing crisis management and resilience research streams. *The Academy of Management Annals, 11*(2), 733–769. doi:10.5465/annals.2015.0134

Wing, J. M. (2006). Computational Thinking. *Communications of the ACM, 49*(3), 33–35. doi:10.1145/1118178.1118215

Wong, K. P., Tse, M. M. Y., & Qin, J. (2022). Effectiveness of Virtual Reality-Based Interventions for Managing Chronic Pain on Pain Reduction, Anxiety, Depression and Mood: A Systematic Review. In Healthcare (Switzerland) (Vol. 10, Issue 10). MDPI. doi:10.3390/healthcare10102047

Wong, P. (2019). Democratizing algorithmic fairness. *Philosophy & Technology, 33*(2), 225–244. doi:10.100713347-019-00355-w

World Economic Forum. (2015). *New Vision for Education: Fostering social and Emotional Learning through Technology*. https://www.weforum.org/reports/new-vision-for-education-fosteringsocial-and-emotional-learning-through-technology

World Health Organization. (2021). *Guidance on community mental health services: Promoting person-centred and rights-based approaches*. Author.

Wu, Y.-J. A., Lan, Y.-J., Huang, S.-B. P., & Lin, Y.-T. R. (2019). Enhancing Medical Students' Communicative Skills in a 3D Virtual World. *Journal of Educational Technology & Society, 22*(4), 18–32.

Xiao, Y., & Watson, M. (2019). Guidance on conducting a systematic literature review. *Journal of Planning Education and Research, 39*(1), 93–112. doi:10.1177/0739456X17723971

Xiong, J., Hsiang, E. L., He, Z., Zhan, T., & Wu, S. T. (2021). Augmented reality and virtual reality displays: emerging technologies and future perspectives. In Light: Science and Applications (Vol. 10, Issue 1). Springer Nature. doi:10.103841377-021-00658-8

Xu, G., Xue, M., & Zhao, J. (2023). The Association between Artificial Intelligence Awareness and Employee Depression: The Mediating Role of Emotional Exhaustion and the Moderating Role of Perceived Organizational Support. *International Journal of Environmental Research and Public Health, 20*(6), 5147. doi:10.3390/ijerph20065147 PMID:36982055

Yin, R. K. (2014). Case Study Research: Design and Methods. Sage Publications.

Zallio, M., & Clarkson, P. J. (2022). Designing the metaverse: A study on inclusion, diversity, equity, accessibility and safety for digital immersive environments. *Telematics and Informatics, 75*, 101909. Advance online publication. doi:10.1016/j.tele.2022.101909

Zambelli, E., Speranza, T., & Cusimano, F. (2023). Metaverso: l'universo umano in formato digitale. Alpes.

Zanatta Crestani, T. G., & Colognese, S. A. (2021). Encruzilhadas metodológicas. Revisitando as etapas de um estudo etnográfico realizado num terreiro de umbanda [Methodological crossroads. Revisiting the stages of an ethnographic study carried out in an Umbanda terreiro]. *Revista Latinoamericana de Metodología de la Investigación Social – ReLMIS, 25*(13), 19-33.

Zawacki-Richter, O., Marín, V. I., Bond, M., & Gouverneur, F. (2019). Systematic review of research on artificial intelligence applications in higher education. Where are the educators? *International Journal of Educational Technology in Higher Education, 16*(1), 1–27. doi:10.118641239-019-0171-0

Zhang, D., Maslej, N., Brynjolfsson, E., & Etchemendy, J. (2022. The AI Index 2022 Annual Report. AI Index Steering Committee, Stanford Institute for Human-Centered AI. Stanford University.

Zhang, G., Cao, J., Liu, D., & Qi, J. (2022). Popularity of the metaverse: Embodied social presence theory perspective. *Frontiers in Psychology, 13*, 997751. Advance online publication. doi:10.3389/fpsyg.2022.997751 PMID:36248483

Zhang, X., Chen, Y., Hu, L., & Wang, Y. (2022). The metaverse in education: Definition, framework, features, potential applications, challenges, and future research topics. In *Frontiers in Psychology* (Vol. 13). Frontiers Media S.A. doi:10.3389/fpsyg.2022.1016300

Zhang, Z., Fort, J. M., & Giménez Mateu, L. (2023). Facial expression recognition in virtual reality environments: Challenges and opportunities. *Frontiers in Psychology, 14*, 1280136. Advance online publication. doi:10.3389/fpsyg.2023.1280136 PMID:37885738

Zhou, Z., Asghar, M. A., Nazir, D., Siddique, K., Shorfuzzaman, M., & Mehmood, R. M. (2023). An AI-empowered affect recognition model for healthcare and emotional well-being using physiological signals. *Cluster Computing, 26*(2), 1253–1266. doi:10.100710586-022-03705-0 PMID:36349064

Zilahy, D., & Mester, G. (2023). Managing Negative Emotions Caused by Self-Driving. *Interdisciplinary Description of Complex Systems, 21*(4), 351–355. doi:10.7906/indecs.21.4.4

Zukerfeld, M. (2020). Bits, plataformas y autómatas. Las tendencias del trabajo en el capitalismo informacional. *Revista Latinoamericana de Antropología del Trabajo*, (7).

About the Contributors

Adrian Scribano is a Ph.D. in Philosophy, University of Buenos Aires. MA (Master of Arts) in Developmental Science, ILADES, Santiago, Chile. BA in Political Science, Catholic University of Córdoba. Diploma in Human Rights from the Human Rights Institute at Complutense University in Madrid, Spain. Principal Researcher at CONICET Director of the Centre for Research and Sociological Studies (CIES), Argentina (estudiosociologicos.com.ar). Director of the Latinamerican Journal of Studies on Bodies, Emotions and Society (relaces.com.ar) Director of the Study Group on Sociology of Emotions and Bodies, in the Gino Germani Investigation Institute, Faculty of Social Sciences, University of Buenos Aires. Director of the "Research Program on Collective Action and Social Conflict" (accioncolectiva.com.ar).

Maximiliano E. Korstanje is editor in chief of International Journal of Safety and Security in Tourism (UP Argentina) and Editor in Chief Emeritus of International Journal of Cyber Warfare and Terrorism (IGI-Global US). Korstanje is Senior Researchers in the Department of Economics at University of Palermo, Argentina. In 2015 he was awarded as Visiting Research Fellow at School of Sociology and Social Policy, University of Leeds, UK and the University of La Habana Cuba. In 2017 is elected as Foreign Faculty Member of AMIT, Mexican Academy in the study of Tourism, which is the most prominent institutions dedicated to tourism research in Mexico. He had a vast experience in editorial projects working as advisory member of Elsevier, Routledge, Springer, IGI global and Cambridge Scholar publishing. Korstanje had visited and given seminars in many important universities worldwide. He has also recently been selected to take part of the 2018 Albert Nelson Marquis Lifetime Achievement Award. a great distinction given by Marquis Who´s Who in the world.

* * *

Florencia Chahbenderian has a degree in Economics (Faculty of Economic Sciences, University of Buenos Aires - UBA) and PhD in Social Sciences (Faculty of Social Sciences, UBA). CONICET Postdoctoral Fellow at the CIS, Universidad

Nacional de La Matanza (UNLaM). Deputy Researcher of the project "Consumption, emotions, social policies and education for consumption" directed by Angélica De Sena, Faculty of Education and Social Communication Sciences, University of El Salvador (USAL). Member of the Group of Studies on Sociology of Emotions and Bodies (IIGG-UBA, CIES), directed by PhD Adrián Scribano, and of the Study Group on Social Policies and Emotions (IIGG-UBA, CIES), directed by PhD Angelica De Sena. Collaborator in the Latin American Journal of Social Research Methodology (ReLMIS) and First Assistant in "Sociology of Organizations" (Faculty of Economic Sciences, UBA).

Laura De Clara, MD, psychologist, and psychotherapist, distinguishes herself as the co-founder of Metacare Srl, an innovative company at the forefront of mental health services utilizing emerging technologies such as virtual reality and the metaverse. Her extensive experience in psychotherapy and mental health treatment has guided the development of innovative approaches in the treatment and support of mental well-being, establishing a connection between advanced technology and psychological wellness.

Leandro Tomas del Corro is a Full Professor at the National University of Villa Maria, Cordoba. He is an experienced researcher in the field of sociology of emotions, mobilities and migration. Over the recent years, he has specialized and has written extensively on the complexity of labour division and migration.

Jorge Duperre is a teacher and researcher, holding a Bachelor's degree in Social Communication and a Specialist degree in Research in Social and Human Sciences (both awarded by the National University of San Luis, Argentina). Currently, he is completing his Doctorate in Social Studies of Latin America at the National University of Córdoba, Argentina. His studies primarily focus on how death is managed in contemporary societies, from a sociological perspective.

Giulio Ferrigno is a Senior Assistant Professor at Sant'Anna School of Advanced Studies of Pisa. He has held visiting positions at the University of Cambridge, Tilburg University, and the University of Umea. His main research themes include strategic alliances, big data, Industry 4.0, and innovation management. His works have been published in Small Business Economics, Technological Forecasting and Social Change, International Journal of Management Reviews, R&D Management, Technology Analysis & Strategic Management, Review of Managerial Science, International Journal of Entrepreneurial Behavior & Research, Journal of Business and Industrial Marketing. He is an Associate Editor of Technology Analysis & Strategic Management.

Pedro Lisdero, Ph.D., is a researcher affiliated with CONICET, CIES, and UNVM in Argentina (pedrolisdero@gmail.com). He holds a Bachelor's degree in Sociology from U. Siglo XXI, Córdoba, Argentina, and a Doctorate in Social Studies of Latin America from the Center for Advanced Studies at the National University of Córdoba. Dr. Lisdero serves as a researcher at the National Council of Science and Technology of Argentina (CONICET) and co-director of the Program of Studies on Collective Action and Social Conflict at the Center for Research and Studies on Cultures and Societies. Additionally, he is an Assistant Professor at the National University of Villa María, overseeing the "General Sociology" chair. Furthermore, Dr. Lisdero is the Director of Sociological Studies Editora (ESEditora - CIES) and a member of the editorial teams of RELACES, RELMIS, and Onteaiken

Maria Victoria Mairano has a degree in Sociology (University of Buenos Aires) PHD Doctoral fellowship. Studying for a master's degree in Social Science Research (University of Buenos Aires) and a specialization in Social Research Methodologies. Member of the Study Group on the Sociology of Emotions and Bodies (IIGG-UBA).

Joaquin Ignacio Mendiburu, PhD student in Latin American Social Studies (UNC-CEA). Degree in Local-Regional Development (UNVM), Certificate in Social, Urban and Territorial Conflict. Prevention, Management and Transformation (UNVM) and Diploma in Territorial Development (UNVM). Doctoral fellow CIT Villa María (CONICET y UNVM). His current research field deals with the restructuring processes of societies in the 21st century through the intersection of education and work.

Neli Mengalli is a senior professional who has been working for over twenty years in the educational area, interfacing with the areas of knowledge management, monitoring and measuring social media, society 5.0, phygital transformation, and disruptive technologies. She has worked both in the private sector and in public management. Her postgraduate [master's and doctorate] was carried out at the Pontifical Catholic University of São Paulo with an emphasis on new technologies. A highlight of the works produced is in communities of practice, in the management of online contexts, in disruptive technologies and in transform(active) methodologies. She participated in research groups with the theme of technology at the Pontifical Catholic University of São Paulo and in workshops that associated the language, education, and technology at FASB - Faculdade São Bernardo do Campo. In the professional trajectory are basic education, higher education, course evaluation and advisory in public policies. She was an interlocutor in the implementation of public policies in the educational area.

Ignacio Pellón Ferreyra. PhD student in Social Sciences (UBA), Master in Social Work with mention in Social Intervention (UNC), Certificate in Local, Territorial and Social Economy Development (FLACSO, Argentina) and Bachelor in International Trade (Universidad Siglo 21). Doctoral fellow at CIT Rafaela (CONICET and UNRaf). His field of research is based on the intersection of collective action and social conflict studies, with interest in the relationships between identity-work-consumption and in the sensitivities associated with waste, social-popular economy, environmental sustainability and animal protectionism.

Solana Salessi is an Assistant Researcher Conicet CIT-UNRaf. Associate Professor UNRaf. Adjunct Professor UNL. Director of the Research Institute, Faculty of Psychology, Catholic University of Santa Fe. Ph.D. in Psychology, UNLP. University teaching at UNCuyo. Degree in Psychology from UCSF Area of interest: organizational behavior and positive organizational psychology.

Angelica De Sena Sena de is a PhD in Social Sciences from the University of Buenos Aires. She specialized in the study of Social Policies and Emotions and Social Research Methodology. She is currently a researcher at CONICET-Universidad Nacional de La Matanza (UNLaM) and the Gino Germani Research Institute (FCS-UBA). She coordinates the Group of Studies on Social Policies and Emotions. She teaches undergraduate and postgraduate courses. She is the director of the Latin American Journal of Social Research. ORCID iD:

Aman Deep Singh joined Nirma University in February 2022 as an assistant professor (English) in the Department of Humanities and Social Sciences. Before joining Nirma University, Dr Aman Deep Singh worked as assistant professor at Indian Institute of Information Technology (IIIT) Vadodara for two and half years and taught subjects like English communication, Technical Writing, and Science Fiction.He did his Doctorate from the Central University of Rajasthan, post-graduation in English from Pondicherry University, and a Bachelorette in English Honors from the University of Delhi. His area of specialism includes Science Fiction Studies, Creative Writing, ELT, Literary theory and Criticism.

Ranjit Singha is a Doctorate Research Fellow at Christ (Deemed to be University) and holds the prestigious American Psychological Association (APA) membership. With a strong background in Research and Development, he has significantly contributed to various fields such as Mindfulness, Addiction Psychology, Women Empowerment, UN Sustainable Development Goals, and Data Science. With over 15 years of experience in Administration, Teaching, and Research, both in Industry and Higher Education Institutions (HEI), Mr Ranjit has established himself as a seasoned professional. Mr Ranjit is dedicatedly involved in research and teaching endeavours, primarily focusing on mindfulness and compassion-based interventions. His work in these areas aims to promote well-being and foster positive change in individuals and communities.

Gabriela Vergara is a sociologist (UNVM). Master's Degree in Social Sciences (ETS-UNC). PhD in Social Sciences (UBA). Researcher in The National Scientific and Technical Research Council (Cconfines-CONICET). Researcher in the Center for Sociological Studies and Research (CIES). Co-coordinator of Studies Social Group of Subjectivities and Conflic (GESSYCO). Regular Associate Professor in the National University of Rafaela. She is currently investigating about women, work, sensibilities and structuration process.

Index

E

F

G

H

I

K

L

M

Ensure Quality Research is Introduced to the Academic Community

Become an Evaluator for IGI Global Authored Book Projects

The overall success of an authored book project is dependent on quality and timely manuscript evaluations.

Applications and Inquiries may be sent to:
development@igi-global.com

Applicants must have a doctorate (or equivalent degree) as well as publishing, research, and reviewing experience. Authored Book Evaluators are appointed for one-year terms and are expected to complete at least three evaluations per term. Upon successful completion of this term, evaluators can be considered for an additional term.

If you have a colleague that may be interested in this opportunity, we encourage you to share this information with them.

www.ingramcontent.com/pod-product-compliance
Lightning Source LLC
LaVergne TN
LVHW080639011026
849160LV00014B/1265
* 9 7 9 8 3 6 9 3 4 4 6 4 4 *